The allocation of responsibility

Edited by Max Gluckman

The allocation of responsibility

Manchester University Press

Published by the University of Manchester at
THE UNIVERSITY PRESS
316–324 Oxford Road, Manchester M13 9NR

ISBN 0 7190 0491 8

Distributed in the USA by
HUMANITIES PRESS INC
303 Park Avenue South, New York, N.Y. 10010

Printed in Great Britain by Butler
& Tanner Ltd, Frome and London

Contents

Introduction page ix
by Max Gluckman *Research Professor in Social Anthropology in the University of Manchester and holder of a special Senior Fellowship from the Nuffield Foundation*

1
Moral crises: magical and secular solutions 1
Max Gluckman

2
Legal liability and evolutionary interpretation: some aspects of strict liability, self-help and collective responsibility 51
Sally F. Moore *Professor of Anthropology in the University of Southern California*

3
Aspects of the control of moral ambiguities: a comparative analysis of two culturally disparate modes of social control 109
E. Lloyd Peters *Professor of Social Anthropology in the University of Manchester*

4
Absence makes the heart grow fonder: some suggestions why witchcraft accusations are rare among East African pastoralists 163
P. T. W. Baxter *Senior Lecturer in Social Anthropology in the University of Manchester*

5
When witches are not named 193
Basil Sansom *Lecturer in Social Anthropology in the University of Manchester*

6
Sin, blame and ritual mediation 227
Richard P. Werbner *Lecturer in Social Anthropology in the University of Manchester*

7
Taking the blame and passing the buck, or, The carpet of Agamemnon: an essay on the problems of responsibility, legitimation and triviality 257
Ronald J. Frankenberg *Professor of Sociology in the University of North Staffordshire, sometime Reader in Sociology in the University of Manchester*

8
Some social contexts of personal violence 281
Emanuel Marx *Senior Lecturer in Social Anthropology in Tel-Aviv University, sometime Senior Simon Fellow and Senior Research Fellow in the University of Manchester*

Index 323

To Sir Edward Evan Evans-Pritchard
D. Litt. Honoris Causa (Manchester)
Emeritus Professor of Social Anthropology
in the University of Oxford
and Fellow of All Souls College

Introduction

Max Gluckman

1. *Professor Edward Evan Evans-Pritchard*

Evans-Pritchard's writings and teachings have stimulated many pieces of research, some developing his seminal ideas, others written to amend or reject them. Most of the essays in this book have been stimulated by his classic study *Witchcraft, Oracles and Magic among the Azande,* which was published in 1937, but whose first analyses appeared as long ago as 1926–30. The essays in this book have also drawn on the problems he raised in his later books, particularly his trilogy on the Nuer (*The Nuer*, 1940—first articles published in 1934; *Kinship and Marriage among the Nuer*, 1951—main argument published in 1938; *Nuer Religion*, 1956) and his *The Sanusi of Cyrenaica* (1949). From these books the present authors have concentrated on a general problem which has fascinated Evans-Pritchard throughout many of his analyses: *viz.* how in various types of groups individuals are held responsible for the injuries and misfortunes which befall the group and its members. Hence we have tried to deal in various situations with *The Allocation of Responsibility*, a general title which stresses that we are treating a problem of crucial importance in human society everywhere.

I state this at the outset in order to emphasize that though Evans-Pritchard has done his research in, and written about, relatively small-scale, and for us exotic, societies, equipped with *comparatively* simple technologies, his genius has enabled him to illuminate general problems in our understanding of the interaction of every population of human beings, each living in an ecological situation where they operate with tools within a cultural heritage of law and morals. Human interdependence in society has been the setting of his analyses, whether of beliefs in witchcraft oracles and magic, or of politics or domestic life, or of religion and law. These analyses start firmly rooted in superb research among particular peoples: they produce general propositions about the structure of social systems, propositions which can be applied independently of specific place and specific period.

The contributors to this book, save one, have all worked together for some years at Manchester. Dr P. T. W. Baxter, Professor E. L. Peters and I were all pupils of Evans-Pritchard's, and I also was a member of his staff at Oxford from 1947 to 1949. Professor R. J. Frankenberg, Dr E. Marx, Dr B. L. Sansom and Dr R. P. Werbner were pupils and colleagues of Peters and myself at Manchester. Hence the book is a tribute to Evans-Pritchard from the Manchester Department of Social Anthropology, whose indebtedness for its achievements to him was acknowledged by our University when in 1969 it conferred on him the degree of Doctor of Letters Honoris Causa.

The one contributor who—alas!—has not been a member of our Department is Professor Sally F. Moore. She and I have frequently discussed together problems arising in the study of tribal law, a study for which we both (with training in Western law) feel it to be important to draw on the wealth of jurisprudential analysis and wisdom. During one of these discussions she told me that she disagreed with certain of my views on the development of conceptions of responsibility in the history of law, and in comparisons of tribal law with modern Western law. At Manchester we had already planned this book on *The Allocation of Responsibility*, and I at once besought her to contribute an essay setting out her views on this theme, an essay whose argument she presented at a seminar in our Department.

All social anthropologists owe at least an indirect intellectual debt to Evans-Pritchard: ours at Manchester is a very direct one. Shortly after I was appointed in 1949 as the first holder of a Chair of Social Anthropology at Manchester, and when I was still teaching at Oxford, we were visited by a Dutch colleague. When I was introduced to him as shortly leaving for Manchester, he commented, 'Ah, in the same way as X has left the department at —— to go to ——.' Evans-Pritchard remarked: 'No, not in the same way. X is a refugee; Gluckman is a colonist.'

Evans-Pritchard was right: we have in many ways been a colony of his (though I hope we have established our independence). For it was with the general problems that he set out in his *Witchcraft,*

Oracles and Magic among the Azande that I, as the first social anthropologist at Manchester (saving the presence at one time in the Department of Anatomy of Sir Grafton Elliott-Smith and Dr W. Perry), impressed, with our technology, my Manchester colleagues in other disciplines. In a memorial to our then colleague in the Faculty of Economic and Social Studies, the late Ely Devons, Professor of Economic Statistics, my friend Professor W. J. M. Mackenzie, who left our Chair of Government to go to Glasgow, has kindly spoken of the catalytic influence which my coming had in the Faculty.[1] I ascribe the catalysis, if it was connected with me, to the first public lecture I gave. Manchester does not require its new professors to give inaugural lectures: for some of us there was instead a lecture to the Manchester Literary and Philosophical Society, a long-established institution which numbers among its important events (if I may move from the humble to the sublime) John Dalton's announcement of his atomic theory. I chose as my subject 'Social beliefs and individual thinking among primitive people',[2] for this, I felt, would enable me to exhibit the strength of social anthropology, which I held—and still hold—to lie in the complications of monographic analysis, illuminated by a number of general perceptions about human society in general. The monograph on which I rested for the above subject was Evans-Pritchard's *Witchcraft, Oracles and Magic among the Azande*, though I hope I was able to add my own portion of data from my own field research, and some of my own emphases.

The strength of Evans-Pritchard's insight into the specific logic of Azande beliefs in witchcraft and magic, and into the relation between this logic and both empirical reality and social morality, made an immediate impression on all my colleagues. It led Professors Ely Devons, Dorothy Emmet (Philosophy), Bill Mackenzie, and Michael Polanyi (Social Studies) to read his great book, to extend their reading in the subject, and to attend seminars in our subject, as we attended seminars in theirs. And they proceeded to use what they learnt in their own researches and writings. Evans-Pritchard has thus influenced scholars from other disciplines throughout the world: for example, Dr E. Friedson recently used his report on

1 Mackenzie in Cairncross's 'Ely Devons: a memoir' in *Papers on Planning and Economic Management by Ely Devons* (1970), pp. 11–12.

2 *Memoirs and Proceedings of the Manchester Literary and Philosophical Society*, vol. 91 (1949–50), pp. 1–26.

Azande witch-doctors as a counterpoint to illustrate what constitutes the *Profession of Medicine* (1970).[3] But I may perhaps be forgiven if I illustrate his influence by examples taken from the work of my Manchester colleagues. I shall do so with two specific examples where the influence is concentrated: that influence is marked on every page of Professor Emmet's two books, *Function, Purpose and Powers* (1958) and *Rules, Roles and Relations* (1966), and on Professor Mackenzie's *Politics and Social Science* (1967), as well as in their other writings. The examples of concentrated influence from the book with which we are mainly concerned here, the analysis of Azande social thought, are from the writings of Professors Ely Devons and Michael Polanyi.

I have in my own essay below summarized the crux of Evans-Pritchard's analysis. Two different types of causation are involved in the Azande's approach to misfortune and good fortune. He observes the empirical (as Evans-Pritchard calls it) cause of misfortune, whether it be an illness or a wild beast killing a man. But the Azande also asks why that victim should suffer that misfortune in that way at that time; and the answer provided by his beliefs is that a witch has caused him to be afflicted. This is a theory of dual causation. A witch is a person with an occult (Evans-Pritchard calls it 'mystical') power in his intestines which acts to cause the misfortune when its possessor feels envy, hatred, anger, spite, jealousy or other uncharitable motive against the victim. Here there is a theory of morality. Hence misfortune is ascribed to the ill-feeling of one's enemies against one. Good fortune is enjoyed when there is an absence of witchcraft. When a Zande suffers a misfortune, he divines to find out who is the witch who caused it: this is divination into the alignment of maleficent occult forces in the past and the present. But he also divines to assess whether a future course of action is likely to be successful—whether success will or will not attend hunting today in a certain direction, marrying his daughter to a particular suitor, building his homestead in one of a number of likely spots, undertaking a piece of business and the like. If the oracles indicate that he will not be successful, he abandons the proposed action for the time being. But he may later consult the oracles again, and even again, till they foretell success. Evans-Pritchard points out that these consultations embody a view

3 I owe this reference to Mrs Dianne Sansom.

of time different from ours: the future is not fixed, but is conditionally there in the present; for the present includes an alignment of occult powers (among the Azande, usually of witchcraft) which may threaten the future. This alignment of occult powers may change, over even a short period, so that the future, in the present, becomes prosperous instead of ominous, or *vice versa*. Hence even an oracle prophesying a beneficent future may be accurate at the time of consultation, yet prove inaccurate in the event, because of a shift in the alignment of occult powers.

Professor Ely Devons, both in his study of economics and out of his experience in business, government administration and university administration, was always fascinated by the problems involved in taking decisions. He immediately saw that there were general lessons about the taking of decisions to be illustrated from these Azande mechanisms. I believe he somewhat offended his colleagues when he drew the parallel in one of his four Newmarch lectures given at University College, London, in February 1954.[4] He emphasized how difficult it is for the government or nationalized industries to plan sensibly. He went on to say that

> these authorities dare not admit, either to themselves or to the public, complete ignorance of rational criteria on which to base . . . decisions. What more tempting facade of rationality than . . . some statistics which seem to point to policy in one direction rather than another?
>
> No Chancellor of the Exchequer could introduce his proposals for monetary and fiscal policy in the House of Commons by saying, 'I have looked at all the forecasts, and some go one way, some another; so I decided to toss a coin and assume inflationary tendencies if it came down heads and deflationary if it came down tails.'

This would not command public confidence, and no modern government could take decisions thus. Statisticians provide straws to clutch at, and people are readily taken in by exaggerated confidence in statistics.

Devons went on to suggest that there were striking similarities between the role of economic statistics in our society and some of the functions which magic and divination play in tribal society.

> Magic in primitive society makes it possible for decisions on important issues to be taken where there is apparently no rational basis of decision, given the knowledge and technique of the society. Magical oracles decide

4 Reprinted in Devons, *Essays in Economics* (1961), pp. 160*f*.

whether to hunt in one direction or another, or which husband to choose for your daughter.

Argument which was only ostensibly rational could proceed endlessly (as we all know), and the important thing is to take *some* decision. Given the issues to be settled, '. . . what more efficient and sensible system than to settle the issue by magic?

'We would not think of examining the entrails of a chicken, or consulting an oracle, or asking a diviner to find out whether the recession in the United States [this was in 1954] is going to get worse or not.' But there are a very large number of statisticians to settle, supposedly, issues like this; and

like tribal magicians, they can never be proved wrong. For as a failure in divination shows that the practitioner was unskilled, broke a taboo, used the wrong material—or that mystical forces have changed, so incorrect forecasts by statistics show that the statistician was mistaken, used a bad model, or had inadequate figures—or economic forces have changed.

When Devons mocks himself and his colleagues, he mocks at exaggerated faith. For he does not argue that use of statistics is foolish, only that they should be warily used, in looking at the immediate past, the present and the future. They remain scientific, even if sometimes used irrationally. They deal largely—though not entirely—with problems which are morally neutral, though they have moral implications. At least it is not believed that the problems are produced by the occult ill-will of enemies; while divination tries to solve problems which are in these terms of occult belief morally, as well as technically, critical. This is something which I discuss below in my own essay.

In my citation from Devons I quoted him as giving some of the secondary elaborations of belief which Evans-Pritchard reported to be used by Azande in defending their system of beliefs in *Witchcraft, Oracles and Magic* from apparently contradicting evidence, or against doubts put by the researcher himself. At the time when I lectured to the Manchester Literary and Philosophic Society, Michael Polanyi had recently moved from his Chair of Inorganic Chemistry to a Chair of Social Studies, and was preparing his 1951–2 Gifford Lectures on *Personal Knowledge: towards a Post-critical Philosophy* (published in 1958). He too seized on Evans-Pritchard's analysis of how a system of beliefs is maintained to illustrate the operation of all systems of 'implicit beliefs' and to illuminate 'The stability of scientific beliefs'.

He began by drawing attention to the derivation of Evans-Pritchard's view of the complete interdependence of Azande beliefs from Lévy-Bruhl, a debt which Evans-Pritchard has acknowledged. But Polanyi considered that Evans-Pritchard had 'given further prevision to . . . the intellectual force' shown by Africans in upholding his beliefs against 'evidence which to the European seems flagrantly to refute them'. For example, if the oracle-substance acts haphazardly it is assumed that the wrong variety had been gathered, or a breach of taboo committed, or that the owners of the forest had been angered and had avenged themselves by spoiling the substance. Again, Polanyi cites Azande resistance to experiment with the oracle outside the divinatory situation: when asked what would happen if they administered the oracle to a fowl [the standard method of divining] without posing a question to it, or gave a further dose to a fowl which had recovered from the first dose, their answer is that they would consider it a useless waste of the oracle-substance. Polanyi then quotes Evans-Pritchard's affirmation that Azande reason excellently 'in the idiom of their beliefs, but they cannot reason outside, or against, their beliefs because they have no other idiom in which to express their thoughts'. Hence, said Evans-Pritchard, scepticism itself must be expressed within the idiom of the system.

The stability of the system of such beliefs is maintained because 'the contradiction between experience and one mystical notion is explained by reference to other mystical notions'. Similarly, Polanyi argues, a particular system of scientific beliefs (and he gives examples) is maintained because objections are met one by one; because the circularity of a conceptual system tends to reinforce itself by every contact with a fresh topic; because the system itself is self-expanding and readily supplies elaborations which will cover almost any conceivable eventuality—it is epicyclical; and because the system prevents the germination of any alternative concepts based on doubts arising from any adverse piece of evidence. And in both types of system, magico-oracular and scientific—but particularly the latter—observations which do not fit the theory may be regarded as 'anomalies'.

The comparison of the logic involved in these very different systems was illuminating for Polanyi. But only in some respects—as is shown in his conclusion:

The process of selecting facts for our attention is indeed the same in science as among the Azande; but I believe that science is often right in its application of it, while Azande are quite wrong when using it to protect their superstitions.

I conclude that what earlier philosophers have alluded to by speaking of coherence as the criterion of truth is only a criterion of *stability* . . . [pp. 286–94]

I consider that here it is only fair to the Azande to insist, as Evans-Pritchard did in a critique and appreciation of Lévy-Bruhl, that Polanyi, in the final citation I have made, is comparing a Zande reasoning about witchcraft, oracles and magic with a European reasoning about science, and is aware of this. The Zande, though equally trapped, would appear to be less 'wrong' when defending his system of technological ideas, connected with agriculture and so forth. Moreover—as essays below bring out, following Evans-Pritchard—reasoning in terms of witchcraft and magic and oracles is a way of reasoning about social relationships; and presumably some of the most advanced and open-minded of scientists within their laboratories may well be less 'right' when considering the form of social relationships within which they are involved.

I cannot resist concluding this section by quoting, for those who do not know it, an alleged conversation reported by David Livingstone between himself and a rain doctor among the Bakwain, who had suffered four years of drought. It brings out better than anything I know how difficult it is for the proponents of diverse systems of thought to meet in argument; and I have therefore read it year after year to my first-year students, to, at least, my own continuing edification and insight:[5]

The natives, finding it irksome to sit and wait helplessly until God gives them rain from heaven, entertain the more comfortable idea that they can help themselves by a variety of preparations, such as charcoal made of burned bats, inspissated renal deposit of the mountain cony—*Hyrax*

5 Livingstone, *Missionary Travels and Researches in South Africa* (1857), pp. 22–8. This conversation is very connected, but in *Livingstone's Missionary Correspondence, 1841–1856* (edited by Schapera, 1961) various points in it appear scattered through various letters, at pp. 63–4, 102–3, and 120–1.

capensis—(which, by the way, is used, in the form of pills, as a good antispasmodic under the name of 'stone-sweat'), the internal parts of different animals—as jackals' livers, baboons' and lions' hearts, and hairy calculi from the bowels of old cows—serpents' skins and vertebrae, and every kind of tuber, bulb, root, and plant to be found in the country. Although you disbelieve their efficacy in charming the clouds to pour out their refreshing treasures, yet, conscious that civility is useful everywhere, you kindly state that you think they are mistaken as to their power; the rain doctor selects a particular bulbous root, pounds it, and administers a cold infusion to a sheep, which five minutes afterwards expires in convulsions. Part of the same bulb is converted into smoke, and ascends toward the sky; rain follows in a day or two. The inference is obvious. Were we as much harassed by droughts, the logic would be irresistible in England in 1857.

As the Bakwains believed there must be some connection between the presence of 'God's Word' in their town and these successive and distressing droughts, they looked with no good will at the church bell, but still they invariably treated us with kindness and respect. I am not aware of ever having an enemy in the tribe. The only avowed cause of dislike was expressed by a very influential and sensible man, the uncle of Sechele. 'We like you as well as if you had been born among us; you are the only white man we can become familiar with [*thoaëla*]; but we wish you to give up that everlasting preaching and praying; we cannot become familiar with that at all. You see, we never get rain, while those tribes who never pray as we do obtain abundance.' This was a fact; and we often saw it raining on the hills ten miles off, while it would not look at us 'even with one eye'. If the Prince of the power of the air had no hand in scorching us up, I fear I often gave him the credit of doing so.

As for the rain-makers, they carried the sympathies of the people along with them, and not without reason. With the following arguments they were all acquainted, and in order to understand their force, we must place ourselves in their position, and believe, as they do, that all medicines act by a mysterious charm. The term for cure may be translated 'charm' (*alaha*).

Medical Doctor. Hail, friend! How very many medicines you have about you this morning! Why, you have every medicine in the country here.

Rain Doctor. Very true, my friend; and I ought; for the whole country needs the rain which I am making.

M.D. So you really believe that you can command the clouds? I think that can be done by God alone.

R.D. We both believe the very same thing. It is God that makes the rain, but I pray to him by means of these medicines, and, the rain coming, of course it is then mine. It was I who made it for the Bakwains for many years, when they were at Shokuane; through my wisdom, too, their women become fat and shining. Ask them; they will tell you the same as I do.

M.D. But we are distinctly told in the parting words of our Saviour that we can pray to God acceptably in His name alone, and not by means of medicines.

R.D. Truly! but God told *us* differently. He made black men first, and did not love us as he did the white men. He made you beautiful, and gave you clothing, and guns, and gunpowder, and horses, and waggons, and many other things about which we know nothing. But towards us he had no heart. He gave us nothing except the assegai, and cattle, and rain-making; and he did not give us hearts like yours. We never love each other. Other tribes place medicines about our country to prevent the rain, so that we may be dispersed by hunger, and go to them, and augment their power. We must dissolve their charms by our medicines. God has given us one little thing which you know nothing of. He has given us the knowledge of certain medicines by which we can make rain. We do not despise those things which you possess, though we are ignorant of them. *We* don't understand your book, yet we don't despise it. *You* ought not to despise our little knowledge, though you are ignorant of it.

M.D. I don't despise what I am ignorant of; I only think you are mistaken in saying that you have medicines which can influence the rain at all.

R.D. That's just the way people speak when they talk on a subject of which they have no knowledge. When we first opened our eyes, we found our forefathers making rain, and we follow in their footsteps. You, who send to Kuruman for corn, and irrigate your garden, may do without rain; *we* cannot manage in that way. If we had not rain, the cattle would have no pasture, the cows give no milk, our children become lean and die, our wives run away to other tribes who do make rain and have corn, and the whole tribe become dispersed and lost; our fire would go out.

M.D. I quite agree with you as to the value of the rain; but you cannot charm the clouds by medicines. You wait till you see the clouds come, then you use your medicines, and take the credit which belongs to God only.

R.D. I use my medicines, and you employ yours; we are both doctors, and doctors are not deceivers. You give a patient medicine. Sometimes God is pleased to heal him by means of your medicine; sometimes not —he dies. When he is cured, you take the credit of what God does. I do the same. Sometimes God grants us rain, sometimes not. When he does, we take the credit of the charm. When a patient dies, you don't give up trust in your medicine, neither do I when rain fails. If you wish me to leave off my medicines, why continue your own?

M.D. I give medicine to living creatures within my reach, and can see the effects, though no cure follows; you pretend to charm the clouds, which are so far above us that your medicines never reach them. The clouds usually lie in one direction, and your smoke goes in another. God alone can command the clouds. Only try and wait patiently; God will give us rain without your medicines.

R.D. Mahala-ma-kapa-a-a!! Well, I always thought white men were wise till this morning. Who ever thought of making trial of starvation? Is death pleasant, then?

M.D. Could you make it rain on one spot and not on another?

R.D. I wouldn't think of trying. I like to see the whole country green, and all the people glad; the women clapping their hands, and giving me their ornaments for thankfulness, and lullilooing for joy.

M.D. I think you deceive both them and yourself.

R.D. Well, then, there is a pair of us (meaning both are rogues).

The above is only a specimen of their way of reasoning, in which, when the language is well understood, they are perceived to be remarkably acute. These arguments are generally known, and I never succeeded in convincing a single individual of their fallacy, though I tried to do so in every way I could think of. Their faith in medicines as charms is unbounded. The general effect of argument is to produce the impression that you are not anxious for rain at all; and it is very undesirable to allow the idea to spread that you do not take a generous interest in their welfare. An angry opponent of rain-making in a tribe would be looked upon as were some Greek merchants in England during the Russian war.

2. *The Essays*

The idea of this book dedicated to Evans-Pritchard arose out of my own essay, which consists of two lectures in memoriam Richard Ranulph Marett at Exeter College, Oxford. I took the opportunity to pay tribute also to Evans-Pritchard. The lectures provoked or inspired some of my colleagues at Manchester to offer other contributions on the problems I raised, to be dedicated to Evans-Pritchard. They cover one central theme, how responsibility is allocated among persons within a social system, but their contexts of analysis vary greatly. These contexts are traditional tribal organizations and these organizations as affected by their absorption in colonial systems; the law of pre-industrial and industrial societies; groups of 'young men' in a Welsh rural parish; committees in a Welsh village; the committee of the British chiefs of staff; industrial firms and British law courts. But in all the essays the problem set is how far rules hold that individuals are responsible towards others of different categories, and how far these are responsible towards those individuals; and how among such a set of persons decisions, and what types of decisions, are taken when there is either seemingly straightforward moral breach or some apparent breach in the tenor of life, where such breach arises from the conflict of rules, or purposes, both of which are legitimate.

The essays speak for themselves, but I draw attention to what seems to be a general mode of approaching problems in the essays of my colleagues. They are generally concerned to examine the 'public' or the 'audience' within which persons have to claim their rights, exercise moral coercion, levy overtly or covertly a charge of ill action through manipulation of occult forces, or draw attention to their plight. Persons are seen as operating with rules; but the rules are numerous, and they can be manipulated in several ways. Or sometimes, apparently, knowledge is manipulated to serve certain purposes by convincing a public. But the particular public to be convinced has to be mobilized for a particular occasion: this leads to a study of methods of dissemination of information, and to occasions of confrontation in which particular groups or sets of people are called together. The mobilization in some situations is regular and recurrent, even when the issues change; in others the main protagonist or protagonists may have a choice of venue and struggle to control who attends.

This mode of treatment leads both to understanding why particular types of societies operate particular types of rules and beliefs, and to understanding how individuals or groups select between the procedures open to them. For example, Baxter analyses why, although African pastoral tribes have beliefs in witchcraft akin to those of tribes practising agricultural and mixed economies, direct accusations of witchcraft are rarely made among them. He argues that pastoralists are frequently changing those with whom they associate to meet the needs of their stock; hence where they run into difficulties with their fellows they can freely change residence and associates, and do not need to invoke occult disturbances to alter their social fellows. Moreover, since they associate with a variable lot of fellows, it is difficult for them to mobilize support for an accusation, and similarly they run the risk, if they attack someone, that they will become involved with the unknown fellows of their enemy through such a charge. Sansom asks the same question of a South African tribe whose traditional organization, in which charges of sorcery were made, has been radically altered in modern times. Again, he finds that it is impossible to mobilize any public which would be sufficiently coherent socially to enable such a ceremony, involving total social degradation (after Garfinkel), as is involved in an accusation of sorcery to take place. Among these Pedi the stage in which extended families, with an agnatic line as core, have organized themselves to cope with the problems of dispersed work when many men go to white towns to work[6] has passed. Sets of men with what Sansom calls a 'high tempo of sociation' (like Baxter's pastoralists, they change fellows rapidly) now organize about ephemeral leaders to run affairs at home and to work together in towns: they do not constitute an audience which would support an allegation of sorcery.

Moore, in her essay, criticizes certain evolutionary theories of law which see a progression from private to public law, or from feud through strict composition with collective responsibility to individual responsibility. All law, she contends, has to be seen in a socio-political context, and all disputes have to be examined as they are waged in some 'public'. The public may be constituted by some corporate group, whether it be a developed State or the sections of a segmentary polity. Actions in both 'primitive' and developed legal systems may be initiated by individuals, but they lead to the mobilization of specific social relationships, personages, groups or sets. In a system marked by so-called self-help of the 'feuding' kind, the group or set of which the claimant or the alleged offender is a member must decide whether it will aid its member and share responsibility with him. It has a choice between fighting or conciliation or mediation; and it will take the decision what to do in terms of its long-term interests, which may not coincide with the short-term interests of the individual concerned. Where an individual's actions clash with its long-term interests the group may surrender him, or ultimately expel him from membership. In addition, while in a public battlefield or forum, consisting of two groups at some kind of structural odds, the responsibility of the two groups towards each other may be collective, within each group a man may

6 I have myself put Sansom's account of the Pedi (studied by him in the 1960's) into this particular historical perspective rather more than he does in his own essay.

be held to be individually responsible to his fellows for what they must do to aid him. Approached in this way, she argues, some legal problems are seen to be universal.

Werbner is more concerned with the choice of ritual or magical procedures open to the Kalanga of Botswana when they feel they have suffered some misfortune. To understand how the choice is made, each allegation of witchcraft or sorcery, or sacrifice to the ancestral shades, or performance of a ritual by a woman possessed by a demon of the bush, which fixes moral responsibility for misfortune, has to be analysed in terms of who is mobilized for the occasion: for example, a sufferer can try to get a divination that a particular woman possessed by a demon should perform the ritual. Fixing on a particular woman also determines the constitution of the congregation for the ritual, who will be there and who will be excluded. Since misfortunes are ascribed to particular faults in the relationships of closely involved kinsfolk, at a seance other faults can be brought to public attention. By selecting the venue the sufferer prevents others who may have complaints against her from bringing these to public attention. And allegations of sorcery can be made in a variety of ways and to a variety of persons: very different social effects flow from baiting another as a sorcerer in private; making an insinuation of sorcery in gossip; making a public denunciation, which may constitute slander actionable in law. This choice between procedures, ritual and secular, is open to closely related persons who are intensively inter-connected in a web of property relationships, economic obligations, and debts. The choice not only determines responsibility in a particular crisis; it also enables the sufferer to re-define his or her relationships: in the selected public '. . . kin can advance their interests through the leverage of sorcery accusations and rituals of affliction, sloughing away demands, or promoting them, dutifully'.

Marx's study of acts of personal violence in an Israeli development town deals with minor assaults, or threats of assaults, on officials on whom immigrants are very dependent; with wilful destruction of property in public; with assaults by spouses on each other or on a child; and with assaults on themselves by ostensible would-be suicides. He uses these acts of violence to present a general theory about the connection between certain types of violence and certain kinds of social relationship. Since an act of violence has thus to be related to a matrix of social ties, each act must be seen as performed to a certain public. Though the acts appear to be 'irrational', Marx argues that they are in fact rational efforts, in some social relationships, at coercing aid from specific parties, and in other social relationships they are rational attempts at appealing to closely related persons to take over some responsibility for the assailant's difficulties. Hence the attempts at coercion or appeal have to be examined in terms of the public before which they are performed. These types of violence are aimed at mobilizing help, with public support; but, he shows, not everyone dare attempt such a mobilization. One must oneself have sufficient resources, either in economic goods or in social relationships, if one is to hope to be successful.

The idea of the varying public of ritual procedures is developed in Peters' essay on the role of youth groups in a Welsh rural parish —re-analysed from Alwyn Rees' classic study of *Life in a Welsh Countryside* (1951). Peters starts with the series of different oracles used by the Azande, as reported by Evans-Pritchard. There is first the rubbing-board oracle, which a man uses in the privacy of his hut: he rubs one board on another while putting the names of persons he believes may be the witch responsible for his misfortune. The top board sticks at the name of a potential witch. Then he can pile a small heap of sticks in the open overnight and see how it has collapsed in the morning; or put two different kinds of twigs into a termites' nest and see which is the more eaten: he does so after asking the oracle to answer 'yes' or 'no' to a question whether X is or is not the responsible witch. He may summon witch doctors to a large public dance to attack unnamed or named persons as witches. He can carry out his test by giving oracle-substance to chickens and asking the oracle to kill or spare the chicken according as a named person is or is not the witch responsible. And here too he moves into the open, for though he consults the oracle in the privacy of the bush he can send through an intermediary a wing of a chicken which he states has died to a man's name as the alleged witch, in the form of an accusation.[7] Or he may climb a tree in the evening and shout that he has identified the witch, and that witch had better withdraw his maleficent ill-power. Ultimately, to fix an accusation, the test must be made by the chief's oracle. While Evans-Pritchard graded the oracles in terms of the extent to which they

7 In my essay I give a slightly fuller summary of the use of the chicken oracle.

were under control of the operator, Peters emphasizes more than Evans-Pritchard did that various degrees of publicity attend each type of oracle; in other words, in using any kind of oracle, a man is either acting in private, because he is uncertain of the support he will get, or is appealing to a public of varying size. And, Peters argues, he will appeal to a wide audience only if he feels he can carry the audience with him (though of course he may not work this out in full, conscious detail).

It is with this approach to the varying publicity given to actions to enforce from others the observance of rectitude and moral obligations that Peters analyses the behaviour of youth groups in the Welsh rural parish described by Rees. He sets out, in effect, to explain the paradox present in Rees' account, but not so described: seemingly irresponsible 'youths' (the term covers all the unmarried males from sixteen to thirty-five years old) are in some contexts guardians of public morality. These youths sit in the vicinity of the hamlet's shop drinking mineral water and eating sweets and tinned fruit, smoking, 'bantering and remarking on passers-by' (Rees). The remarks are embarrassing and often take the form of lewdness. But they also behave destructively. And they take action against some individuals. All their actions have a touch of the comic: for example, a middle-aged widow had been enjoying the seduction of a young lad, much her junior, until the youth group visited her home and took to stopping up the chimney with straw and throwing dead vermin and 'other obnoxious objects' through the doors and windows in an endeavour to break up the association. The group also punished with its japes an adulterer and a seducer. It harassed men from other areas coming to court girls. Peters argues that their punishing actions are all concerned with the sexual code, with offences not punishable in law. And the way they can punish or try to control can be set in the context of their routine 'boyish' comic behaviour, as a group, with no individual identified. But his main contention is that the youths are not in fact irresponsible on their own: on the contrary, their opinions on who should be punished are formed in their home and work situations, where they associate with adults. The flow of gossip helps form an adult opinion throughout the community, and this is applied by the youths against offenders against the moral code. The adult community backs up the youthful 'pranks'. Hence the youths are responsible, and not irresponsible. Moreover, since they are drawn from so many families and farms, they will act only against offenders against the general community, and not pursue private enmities. He argues further that the youth group plays this role because the community is egalitarian, and there is no superior to take action, while the people are so divided in their religious adherence that no minister can act as moral censor. The youths *are* the community in that they are the only group which represents all its sections; yet they *seem* to be outside its adult ranks.

In the sense that these youths are in some ways outside the ranks of the adults, yet apply moral judgments formed by adults, they may be seen as structurally equivalent to such outside agencies in social control as the leopard-skin chiefs ('the men of the earth', in the vernacular) of the Nuer, as described by Evans-Pritchard, and even of the diviner or oracle. It is this comparison which informs Frankenberg's essay. He had made the comparison explicitly in his study of the running of the committees of a Welsh village, where he found that when groups or categories or sets of the villagers were divided about the running of village activities, 'there were odd men out who were in some ways different from the rest and in one sense therefore protected from the informal pressures which restrained the majority from taking actions which would make divisions in the group overt'. In the absence of any possibility of appeal to higher authority, among equals these 'strangers behaved inconsistently, pushed hither and thither by the manipulation of first one and then another section of public opinion. Village unity was maintained even if . . . marginal men and women were thereby made uncomfortable.' The crux was that, however divided the village was into sectional interests, all the sections were agreed on certain village aims. Strangers were thus made responsible for decisions which might offend one or other section.

Frankenberg argues that similar procedures can be observed to be at work in many other contexts, culturally dissimilar but exhibiting the same consensus despite disagreements about methods, particularly among persons who are equal and particularly where there is a lack of technical knowledge to settle issues definitely. He illustrates this apparent shelving and pinning of responsibility by a detailed examination of the role of scientific experts in the controversy between Admiralty and Air Force over the diversion of aircraft to the strategic bombing of Germany or to the battle against enemy raiding ships, and by examining the roles of expert industrial consultant and of rate-fixers in two firms. Finally, he comments on the role of psychiatrists, and juries, in criminal trials in Britain.

I have summarized, without any justice to the complexity of their detailed arguments, some of the themes covered by my colleagues in their essays on the allocating of responsibility in a varied series of social situations. I have emphasized what appears to be one theme in most of the essays: that to understand the operation of any set of procedures or rules, one has to examine the public arenas within which individuals seek to operate the rules. This is a common theme in much of recent social science. Yet I think it is fair to say that all of them insist that if there is manipulation it is manipulation of rules, and that both individuals and publics do not act unrestrainedly. Their choices and their manipulation of those choices are set within certain limits, controlled by established rules and procedures. The manipulation is, however, predominantly affected by whether the organization is hierarchical, and by some kind of consensus created by the fact that there are also hierarchies of rules. There are, too, hierarchies of interests, which may vary for the individual and for the public to which he appeals; and, as Moore shows, some interests are longer-term than others. The problem of the general allocation of responsibility as against fixing responsibility in particular situations is the one which we have all sought to illuminate; and here, like all our colleagues, we are most deeply indebted to the riches of Evans-Pritchard's work.

I have had some trouble in deciding in what order to place our essays, and have felt tempted to settle it by the toss of a coin or drawing lots or dragging in a 'stranger'. After some hesitation I have put my own essay first because I begin it with the gist of the contribution of Evans-Pritchard's analysis of how and in what contexts Azande take decisions. Hence my essay will make plain to readers who are not professional anthropologists, and therefore do not know this contribution, what it is, and therefore how it has inspired my colleagues. I must emphasize that my essay consists of lectures to a general audience, and was aimed at acquainting them with recent work in social anthropology. Some parts of the argument are therefore also known to my fellow anthropologists where they have been covered in my own earlier publications. Anthropologists may therefore feel that they can skip parts. But I have tried to emphasize certain points more strongly, and to bring out their implications for comparison of ostensibly very different situations, on the lines followed by some of my colleagues.

Since I contrast, as two polar types (in the wake of many scholars), tribal with modern industrial social organizations, I have followed my essay with Moore's, which is critical of at least unsophisticated analyses of this kind.

I have placed Peters' essay third, partly because it too starts explicitly from Evans-Pritchard's work, and partly because historically his argument, as discussed in seminars and as partly presented in a review-article, has greatly influenced several of us.

I have then followed it with the three essays (Baxter, Sansom, Werbner) on the levying or not of accusations of witchcraft in terms of their acceptability to particular publics.

Finally come the essays by Frankenberg and Marx, which take up different problems from Evans-Pritchard's contribution on responsibility in his several books. Marx's essay on patterns of violence in an Israeli town indeed begins by analysing Evans-Pritchard's report on violence among the Nuer.

3. *Acknowledgments*

I am grateful to all my colleagues at Manchester who commented on my own lectures, and to those who were moved to contribute to the book. Some of them have waited patiently, after sending me their essays some time ago, for others to complete their contributions; and to them I give my apologies and thanks. I have marked the date at which each essay finally reached me. My own essay was in fact the longest delayed, since it was written first. Part of the delay was caused by my editorial inertia, due to the fact that the years 1968–70 were for me years of three severe illnesses. It is pertinent to my own analysis that though some of my social relationships through those years contained disagreements, sometimes serious, it never occurred to me to ascribe my misfortunes to the occult ill-will of others resulting from those strains: had I done so, I would have been consigned to a mental hospital instead of a general hospital.

Secondly, I want to express my deep thanks to the Fellows of Exeter College, Oxford, who invited me to deliver the Marett Lecture in 1963. Since Marett had started as a classical scholar, I thought it would be appropriate to try and apply recent anthropological findings to classical data; I selected Greek and Roman oracles and divination, as this would enable me to pay tribute at once to Marett and to Evans-Pritchard in Evans-Pritchard's presence at Oxford, in the Hall of Exeter College, of which we were both members. I buried myself as deeply as I could in accounts of Rome and Greece; but my work was interrupted by a severe attack of malaria, following a visit to Africa, and I had to ask leave to postpone delivering the lecture into the academic year 1964–65. The Fellows of Exeter generously responded to my ill-fortune by inviting me also to give the Marett Lecture due in 1965. But I found that it was, at any rate for me, impossible to build up that understanding of social relationships in which classical acts of divination would have to be set if I were to follow the modes of analysis initiated by Evans-Pritchard. There was plenty of information on classical means of divination: I learnt many of them, until my dreams were haunted by eagles flying on my left hand and vultures on my right, and so forth. But I found no accounts of actual divinations, save for the well known legendary political oracles at Delphi. In the end, I had to shift the bulk of my lectures to another problem; and I here apologize to the Fellows for my failure to carry out my projected undertaking. I did derive enough from the classical material to ask myself why divination of occult forces, and their future alignment, should be so important in both tribal societies and classical societies, and why it should not be resorted to in modern commercial and industrial societies. Current theories in social anthropology about divination, and the forces such as witchcraft which it brought to light, showed how accusations of witchcraft were related to social tensions or strains, hostilities and their underlying conflicts and struggles. Similar processes occur in an industrial society—but we do not relate them through beliefs in the occult to the occurrence of misfortune or good fortune. My citation from Devons above shows that we do not use divination to assess the alignment of forces in crisis. This led me to a comparison of an African village of kin, treated as a firm, with an industrial firm.

In my lectures I did in this context comment on classical oracles and divinations, *en passant*. But Mr Dacre Balsdon of Exeter College and Professor Moses Finley of Cambridge made clear to me that I must do much work on the problem. However, Professor Finley suggested that we organize a seminar on the problem of changing conceptions of responsibility; and we were lucky enough to get the funds to do so, at Jesus College, Cambridge, from the Faculty of Economic and Social Studies at Manchester and from the Faculty of Classics at Cambridge. Our deep thanks go to both. As this book has grown, I have not been able to put into it all that I learnt from that seminar; but I hope to do so one day. Meanwhile the thanks of Frankenberg and myself are due to the other scholars who attended that seminar: Professor Finley, Professor Charles L. Black, Jr, Professor Dorothy Emmet, Professor M. Fortes, Mr J. Kirk, Mr Simon Pembroke, Dr Gordon Rose, and Professors J.-P. Vernant and P. Vidal-Naquet of the Sorbonne.

Bibliography

Devons, E., *Essays in Economics*, London: Allen & Unwin (1961).

—*Papers on Planning and Economic Management*, ed. A. Cairncross, Manchester: Manchester University Press (1970).

Emmet, D., *Function, Purpose and Powers*, London: Macmillan (1958).

—*Rules, Roles and Relations*, London: Macmillan (1966).

Evans-Pritchard, E. E., *Witchcraft, Oracles and Magic among the Azande*, Oxford: Clarendon Press (1937).

—*The Nuer*, Oxford: Clarendon Press (1940).

—*The Sanusi of Cyrenaica*, Oxford: Clarendon Press (1949).

—*Kinship and Marriage among the Nuer*, Oxford: Clarendon Press (1951).

—*Nuer Religion*, Oxford: Clarendon Press (1956).

Gluckman, M., 'Social beliefs and individual thinking in primitive society', *Memoirs and Proceedings of the Manchester Literary and Philosophical Society*, 91 (1950), pp. 1–26, reprinted in, e.g. R. O. Manners and D. Kaplan, *Theory in Anthropology*, Chicago: Aldine (1968), pp. 453–65.

Livingstone, D., *Missionary Travels and Researches in Southern Africa*, London: Murray (1857).

Mackenzie, W. J. M., *Politics and Social Science*, Harmondsworth: Penguin (1967).

Peters, E. L., 'No time for the supernatural', *New Society*, 19 December, 1963.

Polanyi, M., *Personal Knowledge: towards a Post-critical Philosophy*, London: Routledge & Kegan Paul (1958).

Schapera, I., *Livingstone's Missionary Correspondence, 1841–56*, London: Chatto & Windus (1961).

1

Moral crises: magical and secular solutions

The Marett lectures, 1964 and 1965[1]

Max Gluckman

1. *Introduction*

It is a double honour for me to be invited to deliver lectures in honour of Richard Ranulph Marett in this Hall. Such an invitation must honour any anthropologist; and in addition I think I am correct in asserting that I was the last of his pupils to become a professional social anthropologist. In this Hall, too, I partook of that commensality which, even over meals we grumbled at, made me feel so deeply I was a member of your Society.

I have selected for the theme of my lectures two subjects on which Marett wrote at length: morals, and magical activity. Indeed, he first moved from the study of classics into social anthropology when he was awarded the Oxford University Green Moral Philosophy Prize for an essay on the ethics of tribal peoples (1893). His later, best-known work, *The Threshold of Religion* (1900), examined those forms of activity, such as magic and sorcery, which he held to precede religion. Marett, like most of his contemporaries, considered that one of the main functions of social anthropology was to set out the evolutionary series through which the institutions of human society have developed. I too am an evolutionist in that I consider that when we assess and try to understand the significance of institutions it is essential to examine them against the background of what has undoubtedly been a major trend in the history of human society as a whole—the increasing complexity of technology, and with it of economic organization. I believe that when we work out the forms of social organization and of social beliefs and ideas associated with different ranges of technology, we illuminate them all. This is now an unpopular line among social anthropologists, and has been for a long time, save for the school under Professor Leslie White at the University of Michigan. Of recent years the stress has been on what is common in the institutions of all human societies; and indeed there is much that is common to them all. Yet within this marked common area, it is possible to trace differences which acquire significance from their common matrix in social life.

A further theme that I shall discuss is that of the effect of customs, the standardized practices of a particular population of people, on behaviour; and the relation of various forms of custom to the general techno-economic background. This again is a theme which Marett used frequently to stress; hence the volume of essays presented to him by his pupils and admirers on his seventieth birthday was entitled *Custom is King* (1936: edited Buxton). And here too I take a line that is, at least among most younger British social anthropologists, a relatively unpopular one: for many of them have moved from the emphasis laid by their elders on social relationships to study human action apart from the constraining effect of custom, which Marett considered so to dominate in controlling human behaviour.

My problem may be briefly posed. Individuals in all societies run into moral crises. The crises with which I am concerned in these lectures are the crises that arise in situations where a person is moved by different social rules and values to opposed courses of action, so that no clear solution is available. I shall argue that in such situations tribal custom provides resolutions which are in some form or other magico[2]-religious, or ritual, depending on beliefs in occult forces, and I shall demonstrate this through an examination of a number of African societies. Durkheim and many other scholars have asked why there should be such customs, and this is the problem to which I shall address myself. I shall then report and analyse one similar crisis in an industrial society, and show how it is handled in terms of secular beliefs. From this comparison I shall suggest that there may be certain consistent contrasting approaches in the sets of beliefs of tribal societies and those of at least many members of a modern industrial society.

I must emphasize here initially one point to which I shall have to refer on other occasions. Recent work on the incidence of accusations of witchcraft and sorcery, or divinations of ancestral wrath, to explain the one cause of misfortune has related these to areas of tension in social life. For example, the set of beliefs I shall particularly examine are those in witchcraft, sorcery and divination. I have selected these because they enable me, in delivering a lecture to honour Marett, at the same time to honour his successor, Professor

E. E. Evans-Pritchard, at present Professor of Social Anthropology in the University of Oxford and, like myself, a member of this College by origin, though he holds his Chair in All Souls. His study, which initiated the line of research I shall follow, largely through my own work and the work of other of his pupils, is well known to social anthropologists and has influenced other disciplines. Furthermore, I shall in presenting the work that flowed from Evans-Pritchard's be setting out some analyses I have published before, though I hope that I succeed in emphasizing their major points more adequately and in developing further their implications. I fear it is inevitable in the Marett lectures, delivered to an audience composed largely of people who are not professional anthropologists, that I must go over some grounds known to my colleagues. But the function of tributary lectures of this sort is to acquaint 'outsiders' with developments in one's own subject. Moreover, because of my stress, following Marett, on the constraining effect of custom, as I have said I shall again draw attention to points of analysis which I consider have been overlooked by my colleagues in their recent concentration on human behaviour itself and in the dropping of evolutionary approaches.

I shall be talking about beliefs in witchcraft and sorcery and divination, and I must insist that they constitute only part of the set of beliefs and ideas of the peoples concerned. All of them have technologies which are highly developed relatively to an absence of tools, though they appear simple in comparison with modern industrial technology. Without an efficient technology they could not have survived. All of them also have codes of law: and I for one have presented in detail records of trials in one African society, the Barotse, in which I have demonstrated that their modes of judicial reasoning are in many respects akin to those of our own judges.[3] Africans insist in trials that man is distinguished from animals by his possession of 'reason' and 'sense', and this includes 'respect' for custom.[4] We shall see that they equally exhibit 'reason' in their beliefs in occult forces; and it is to a consideration of these that I now proceed.

It appears to me that one of the essential elements in a set of beliefs that ascribe a person's misfortunes to the witchcraft or sorcery of another is that individuals are made responsible, or at least can be held liable, for the welfare of their fellows in situations where, in other societies lacking such beliefs, there is no such responsible interdependence. Societies holding such beliefs have relatively under-developed technologies. Hence they have much less knowledge of the empirical causes of misfortune and good fortune, present and past. They also have less surety about the future. When they resort to divination to obtain further knowledge it may be, as Forde stressed in his Frazer lecture, because of the limits of their technical knowledge.[5] But we have still to explain why this uncertainty and ignorance are interpreted so strongly in moral terms. That accusations of witchcraft or sorcery, allegations of ancestral wrath, and rituals occur in situations of social tension and areas of social strain in itself is an inadequate explanation. Our own society is full of social strain and tension, but anyone who related his misfortunes to them through accusations of witchcraft or the like would be regarded as mentally ill.[6] We have to try and explain why some societies have such beliefs and others do not.

The beliefs argue by implication that if the moral situation of the individual in relationship with his fellows were satisfactory, all would go well. If he suffers misfortune, it is because he himself has committed some wrong; or because he has been wronged, possibly by occult means, by one of his fellows; or because—in major, widespread disasters—there is something wrong in the moral state of the society as a whole. As Durkheim showed for early society, there is less differentiation between the natural, the social and the moral orders. The same situation is inherent in divination about the future course of events. Evans-Pritchard showed for the Azande that there is involved in divination into the future a particular conception of time, where the future is there in the present. The divination foretells the future by bringing into the open the present alignment of occult forces—which depend on moral alignments—that will influence the course of events. Thereafter one must either wait for that alignment of occult (moral) forces to alter, or else strive to protect oneself, or alter the alignment, by magic.

These ideas are implicit in customary beliefs. One thing which they do, therefore, from our point of view as outside observers, is to exaggerate the dependence of people on one another. As we shall see, it is believed that if a man feels anger or envy against a fellow the latter may suffer some external misfortune: the effects of feelings are thus exaggerated. Direct moral interdependence is made greater by these beliefs than it would be without them. They thus reflect a characteristic of tribal societies, which is well expressed in a Barotse song:

> He who kills me, who will it be but my kinsman?
> He who succours me, who will it be but my kinsman?[7]

This song describes pithily the extent to which close relatives co-operate with and depend on one another, and the extent to which they yet compete with one another. The competition goes on within a highly valued solidarity which stresses mutuality and sharing, and which is very different from that organic solidarity which Durkheim ascribed to the increasing division of labour that finally results in modern industrial situations; here, he argued, the individual is more dependent on the specialized organs of society, yet he is more isolated and alone. Durkheim argued incorrectly that this was accompanied by a shift from repressive law to restitutive law:[8] I shall try to show that it is accompanied by a varying emphasis, in occult beliefs, in the placing of responsibility towards one's fellows, though there are common ideas about responsibility in all societies in judicial or proto-judicial situations. Examination of this varying emphasis leads to an attempt to determine in what situations occult and legal responsibility respectively will be fixed.

I consider that it should be possible to bring out a comparison of shifting emphasis if we looked at units of production in traditional African societies in contrast with units of production in an industrial society. An African village can be regarded as a family firm, with resources and jobs, a number of possible workers who are at the same time shareholders, and a limited number of executive positions. What happens when the number of worker–shareholders and of competitors for executive positions increases beyond the capacity of the firm? Set in this way, we can compare events in an African village with what happens when a similar situation arises in a family firm in industrial England; and we are fortunate in that Dr C. Sofer has provided us with an excellent study of such a situation.[9] In Africa the response is to call in a witch-detective, or a diviner; and I shall argue that what he does, in terms of his occult beliefs, is to exaggerate the wickedness of individuals and, as we see it, to hold them responsible for crises arising from struggles rooted in the conflicts in social structure itself. In Sofer's study an industrial consultant is called in, and he seems to do the opposite to the diviner: he seeks to diminish resort to explanations in terms of individual wickedness or weakness, and to relate difficulties objectively to the exposure of the conflicts within the social system (conflicts of role, etc). Similar procedures are used in investigations of non-family firms. Thus the tendency is to diminish, rather than to exaggerate, the responsibility of persons for group and individual misfortunes, and not to exaggerate it. Finally I ask whether one can relate this difference to changing views on criminal responsibility.

2. *Evans-Pritchard's study of witchcraft beliefs*

From 1926 onwards Evans-Pritchard published a series of essays on beliefs in witchcraft and mystical beings, on divination and on magical practices which completely altered our understanding of these phenomena. In 1937 he pulled his analyses together in a book which is still studied by both students and research workers: *Witchcraft, Oracles and Magic among the Azande* of the Anglo-Egyptian Sudan.

First, he examined beliefs in witchcraft as a theory of causation. Briefly, the Azande ask about every unfortunate happening, How did it happen? and Why did it happen? For example, if an elephant tramples on and crushes a hunter, the Azande see how he was killed in terms of the might and weight of the elephant which crushes a man. But they also ask, Why did this elephant, and not another elephant, kill this hunter, and not another hunter, on this occasion, and not another occasion? Again, men seek shade in the heat of a tropical day by sitting under their granaries, which are built above the ground on poles. Termites eat these supports, and the weight of the granary brings it down, perhaps to crush the people sitting in its shade. Azande see that it is the termites that destroy the supports and cause the fall of the granary, whose weight crushes a man as the weight of an elephant does. But they ask again, Why did the granary fall at the particular moment when these particular people were sitting under it? Azande answer these 'whys' by saying that a witch caused that elephant to kill that hunter on that occasion, or that granary to fall just at the moment when those people were sitting in its shade.

I have stated that in many technical and social situations Africans —including the Azande—argue in the same terms as we do about events and responsibility. An Azande cannot, for example, plead that witchcraft made him commit adultery, theft or treason. Azande also observe clearly and generalize certain aspects of the empirical 'hows' of misfortunes: a heavy weight crushes a man; wild beasts attack hunters. But they also try to explain what can be called the 'particularity' of misfortunes—why particular persons suffer them. Here beliefs in witchcraft enter. Similarly, beliefs in witchcraft explain why one man's crops fail and not another's, why a man falls ill when he has previously been well and his fellows are still well, why a small wound festers instead of healing, and so forth. Among the Azande the belief is also used to explain why particular warriors, and not others, are killed by particular enemies in battle. Clearly those slain were killed by enemy spears: but an internal enemy, the witch, has caused this particular death. And this witch is held responsible, and may be liable to pay compensation or suffer punishment in internal tribal relationships.

Thus when an Azande suffers a misfortune his society's beliefs offer him an agent, in the form of a witch, who can be held liable. He seeks the particular witch responsible for his immediate misfortunes by consulting oracles or a diviner or witch-detective (a better term than witch-doctor). These modes of seeking for the witch bring out that beliefs in witchcraft are a theory of morality as well as a theory of particular causation. When the sufferer consults an oracle he thinks of people who have cause to wish him harm and puts their names to one of the oracles. The most important oracle consists in giving a vegetable substance, collected and prepared with many taboos, to chickens while asking questions, such as whether a particular person is the witch you are seeking. The chicken dies or vomits the substance to answer 'yes' or 'no' to the question. The substance, used widely in Africa, is probably a strychnine which is 'haphazard' in its effect, since the operator cannot determine what quantity of the substance will be lethal or will be vomited. Since the consultant puts the name of several personal enemies to the oracle, in the end a man he believes wishes him ill will be indicated as the witch.

Early observers had noted that a man almost always accused a personal enemy of bewitching him. They therefore concluded that the whole business was fraudulent. Evans-Pritchard demonstrated that this alleged fraudulence was essential to the reasonableness and credibility of the system of beliefs. And it is essential to note that the misfortune is suffered first, and this crystallizes belief in witchcraft: accusation of witchcraft follows on misfortune.

An Azande witch is a person with a certain black substance in his intestines, which can be seen after an autopsy. (It is probably a passing state of digestion.) A man may not be aware that he possesses this substance, which is the power of witchcraft. Even if he has this power it will remain 'cool' inside him unless he entertains vicious feelings against a fellow. But if he hates another, feels anger against him, or is envious of him, grudging him good fortune and resenting his success, the witchcraft becomes 'hot'. Its 'soul' will leave the witch's body to consume the 'soul' of the internal organs of the other to make him ill, or it will cause him some other misfortune. The power of witchcraft is believed by Azande to be inherited in the patrilineal line, so a man is not himself responsible for possessing this power. But if he is a good man it will harm no one. Vicious feelings set witchcraft to work. This is why a sufferer seeks among his personal enemies for the witch who has caused his misfortune. Zande beliefs in witchcraft are a theory of morality, and they condemn the same vicious feelings that we regard as sinful.

Witchcraft beliefs condemn these vicious feelings even more severely than we do. For in witchcraft beliefs these vicious feelings are endowed with an occult power, by virtue of which they can, without the knowledge or will of their bearer, cause misfortune to others. Hence they embody a belief that persons bear high responsibility to their fellows.

The morality which is implicit in witchcraft beliefs is shown even more clearly if we look at Azande beliefs in 'sorcery', which Evans-Pritchard distinguishes from 'witchcraft'. A witch's ill feelings are endowed with power to harm others by the substance in his stomach. But a man may wish another harm without possessing this substance. Then he can only harm his enemy either directly and openly, or by resorting to sorcery, which involves the deliberate decision to use noxious magic. Sorcery is used by Azande to account for sudden illnesses and deaths. Witchcraft takes longer to achieve its object. Evans-Pritchard further made a full analysis of how beliefs in witchcraft, oracles and magic accommodate and absorb experiences that appear to show them to be invalid. He shows, for example, how experiences of this kind are explained as due to breach of taboo in preparing the oracle-substance which makes a false detection. Each apparent failure is thus rationalized in terms of other mystical beliefs. Thus the whole system is bolstered by apparently contradicting evidence.

Among the Azande, if a sufferer's oracles say that a particular man, X, is causing him harm, he sends an intermediary to X with the wing of the chicken that died to X's name. X is then constrained by good manners to blow water over the wing while he states that he was ignorant of causing harm and, if he has been doing so, he hereby 'cools' his witchcraft. The accused acts thus even if he does not accept the charge as valid. In the past, if a death was in question, the verdict of the dead person's kin's oracles had to be confirmed by the chief's oracles: the accused used to pay damages. After the Anglo-Egyptian government forbade accusations the deceased's kin made vengeance-magic to punish the witch, and as people died in the neighbourhood the oracle was asked if each was the guilty witch, till an affirmative answer was obtained.

This set of beliefs, therefore, in certain situations obviously condemns vicious feelings which are condemned throughout human society. Furthermore, men and women are constrained to control the exhibition of these feelings, for those who show anger, envy or hatred towards others in their social relationships are likely to have their names put to the oracles.

But witchcraft beliefs do not operate in all social relationships. Among the Azande accusations are excluded from among the patrilineally related kinsmen who have to avenge one another's deaths. Nor does a commoner accuse a prince, not only because he is afraid to but also because their behaviour to one another is determined by notions of status. Men do not accuse women. Witchcraft is believed to operate only over short distances, and men accuse their neighbours. Evans-Pritchard sums up thus: Azande 'are most likely to quarrel with those with whom they come into closest contact, when this contact is not softened by sentiments of kinship or is not buffered by distinctions of age, sex and class'.

Subsequent research in Africa has confirmed Evans-Pritchard's analysis of the logic of witchcraft, oracles and magic, and this research has developed his preliminary analysis of the social relationships within which accusations are made or from which they are excluded by cultural norms. It is clear that accusations of witchcraft are not only a straightforward reflection of animosities—otherwise Azande would accuse their patrilineal kin, with whom they must surely at times quarrel. Indeed, it is with these kin that quarrels may be most frequent. Later research on other tribes shows that it is not sufficient to say, as Evans-Pritchard does, that the softening of contact by sentiments of kinship excludes accusations. We know that quarrels often become most bitter where relationships are closest. We can see that the belief in patrilineal inheritance of witchcraft is consistent with the exclusion of accusations against patrilineal kinsmen. By contrast, in the patrilineal societies of southern Africa it is believed that the unrelated women who marry into the group of patrilineally related kinsmen bring witchcraft into their midst. And witchcraft in one of these tribes is believed to be inherited, as in fact haemophilia is among us: women pass it to their children but, while their sons suffer from the taint, they cannot pass it on. Daughters marry out of the group and transmit the taint to their husbands' children.

We shall not be able to explain this difference in beliefs, or in the levying of accusations, until we have a full analysis of the structure and development of patrilineal groups among the Azande. For, in sharp contrast, in most other African societies, both patrilineal and matrilineal, accusations of witchcraft are often made against closely related kin, within the effective corporate group whose members hold property together and should support one another. These accusations are the outcome of profound moral crises in relationships within the group.

According to Evans-Pritchard's analysis, a Zande accuses another of witchcraft against him in a social relationship which is confined to their mutual dealings with each other, and which is not set in a wider context of interaction in a group. Such accusations, among the Azande and other peoples, arise out of patent causes of hostility, which may well arise in turn from relatively chance encounters: jealousy over a woman, or skill at dancing, a quarrel over land, and so forth. Other accusations may be made in standardized situations of competition, between seekers after political office or, nowadays, between the employees within a single industrial enterprise. One such standardized situation is that of the fellow wives of a common husband: on the surface this appears to be straightforward jealousy arising from competition for the husband's favours. Indeed, in many African languages one word for 'jealousy' also describes 'polygyny'. I shall argue that the jealousy of fellow wives, in so far as it appears in accusations of witchcraft, is not due simply to sexual rivalry but reflects, in some tribes at least, conflicts deep within the social structure. An analysis of this situation will lead us to examine the context within which people of most African tribes often accuse their nearest kin of attacking them with sorcery or witchcraft—that is, they accuse those persons whose equivalents among the Azande are immune from such charges.

3. *Conflicts of value in the South-eastern Bantu agnatic systems*[10]

The tribes of south-eastern Africa (such as the Zulu, Swazi, Mpondo and Xhosa) are organized in patrilineal lineages. In this system, men who are related to one another by common descent through males from a single ancestor some four to five generations back live together in a group of neighbouring homesteads. They are what the Romans called 'agnates'. Each homestead contains a number of males closely related in this way; and it is linked to its neighbours by more distant patrilineal ties.

The homestead is not a mere centre of residence, from which men and women go out to diverse ways of earning their living, and to which they return to consume goods as separate families. The members of a homestead assist one another in various productive activities: it is a family firm. Nowadays they even try to operate a rota under which men take turns to stay at home to care for gardens, cattle, women and children, and then to go out to work in European enterprises for money for the whole group.[11] Because when individuals acquire goods they share them with their fellows, and all the men tend to eat together, separately from the women and small children.

The men in each homestead have claims on one another's property in land, in cattle and in marriage payments for women of their families, as well as claims to succeed to one another's social positions. These claims extend in an elaborate pattern into the other homesteads of the patrilineal group, should all the men of the first homestead die. The claims of men within this system are fixed in orders of priority, partly by the nearness of their relationship through male progenitors, and partly by the respective status of their mothers—the wives of these progenitors. These wives must be married from outside the group. Indeed, they must be virtually unrelated to the group. For a number of these patrilineal groups are held to have common descent, through males, from a long-dead ancestor. This constitutes the Zulu clan. A man may not marry a woman of his clan. Nor may he marry a woman who is a member of his mother's clan.

Ideally, a Zulu marries several wives. Each wife has an established position and is ranked in relation to her fellow-wives. The ranking of wives is determined partly by the order in which they are married, partly by their husband's dispositions and affections, and partly by the status of each wife's father.[12] Though the idea of ranking should eliminate uncertainty about the status of each wife and the claims of her sons, these varied rules produce uncertainty and potentially breed disputes between the women. Straightforward competition between fellow wives for their husband's favours is aggravated by competition in the interests of their respective sons begotten by him. It is even held that a good wife and mother should look to the interests of her husband and children, though this may set her against the interests of other wives and their children and against the interests of the group of male agnates as a whole. Polygyny thus produces quarrels inside the patrilineal group, and these quarrels centre on the strangers—the wives who have married into the group.

These quarrels, centred on the wives of the group, penetrate even more deeply. Most men in fact marry only one wife. She remains liable to be accused of witchcraft by her mother-in-law or her sister-in-law or her brother-in-law. Ideally, the group of males linked by patrilineal descent should remain united and bound together in shared loyalty to one another. With this unity, a premium is placed on each male having many sons both to perpetuate and to strengthen the group. A man can achieve this goal only if his wife bears sons for him. This is therefore regarded as the highest duty of a wife: she suffers severely if she is barren or bears only daughters. But in the very process of fulfilling her duty by producing sons to strengthen the group the wife weakens the group: for her sons will have to compete with their cousins— their father's brothers' sons—for the positions and the patrimony of the group. Moreover, though every man is by one set of values closely identified with his brothers, with half-brothers by his father's other wives, and beyond them with his patrilineal cousins, by another set of values he fulfils himself as an individual through marriage and the begetting of his own sons. He is entitled to look to the welfare of his own wife and her children, and to see in them the nucleus of a following which will establish him independently of his patrilineal kinsmen. The wife, in the very process of fulfilling her creative duty to bear children to strengthen her husband's lineage, sows the seeds of dissension and break-up in the group.

Zulu themselves see the woman who marries into the patrilineal group as a mischief-maker who starts quarrels between her husband and his brothers or patrilineal cousins. And the Zulu are not the only patriarchal people who hold this stereotype about the wickedness of daughters-in-law and sisters-in-law. It is a stereotype which is held strongly in the Chinese and Indian joint families. The daughter-in-law is soon at odds with her husband's mother, because she is under the older woman's domination. Explanations in these terms explain the cause of tension; they do not explain why the tension should be reflected in occult beliefs. For example, Freedman, in a fine study of the South-eastern Chinese lineage, refers to my work on the Zulu without drawing attention to the attempted explanation of the occult beliefs.[13] This very real source of quarrelling between them is, I have suggested, underlain by a deeper conflict of values: the mother-in-law represents the unity of all her sons, while in contrast each of her sons' wives represents the independence of her particular husband from the other sons.

It is this deeper conflict which, I suggest, is represented in this type of society in a whole series of beliefs about the inherent evil of femininity—an evil which is endowed with occult power that can harm others. Since the conflict arises out of the reproductive powers of the woman, logically it is associated with her intense sexual desires. Many agnatic societies have analogous ideas. Chinese believe that contact with women who are *yin*—like the moon and cold and winter—compromise male vigour—*yang*, which is like the sun and heat and summer. Hindus believe that in sexual intercourse the male yields part of his life and virtue. The South-eastern Bantu—and many others—believe in the mystically polluting and harmful effects of the blood of birth and menstrual blood, which they may yet consider is built up into the flesh of the strongly desired children.[14] Additionally, the Zulu fear that a woman's desires will attract to her sexual familiars—both sprites and animals—who will then demand from her the lives of her husband's kin.

Wives are thus believed by the Zulu to be full of inherent evil power—a power they carry into the heavens, where dangerous forked lightning is female, while harmless sheet lightning is male. Only female ancestral spirits afflict their former husband's living kin capriciously with misfortune: male ancestral spirits are believed to remedy misfortunes they have sent when proper sacrifice is made to them; female spirits may not respond thus reasonably. And among the living a man's ill-wishes or nature do not of themselves inflict misfortune. A man must deliberately make the choice to attack another, either openly by force or secretly by practising the evil magic of a sorcerer. Women are witches, with inherent evil power. But women's powers are ambivalent: in addition to threatening evil power, women also contain ritual power for good, power which can be directed to fertility or to the detection of occult evils.

Because of the strong suspicion with which the Zulu viewed all whites, I found it difficult when I was studying them to collect detailed records of divining sessions where the causes of misfortunes were sought—an activity which was illegal under South African law. The cases I did collect bear out what Zulu say, and what was recorded by earlier students of the Zulu—namely, that most witches detected were women. Detection followed the line of customary belief because the principal form of Zulu divining is controlled by the consultants, and not by the witch-detective. The consulting party come to the witch-detective, who, after preparing himself, asks a series of questions, such as 'Something is lost?' 'Cattle are ill?' 'A person is ill?' while the afflicted clap their hands steadily and chant, 'We agree, we agree, we agree. . . .' When the diviner hits on the misfortune concerned, they clap and chant more rapidly and loudly. Then, if someone is ill, the diviner seeks similarly for the occult cause of that illness: someone has broken a taboo, an ancestral spirit has sent the illness, a witch is responsible. Louder and faster clapping and chanting indicate when he has stated the present fears of his clients. He then specifies, say, ancestral spirit or witch or sorcerer by sex, age and kinship or other relationship to the victim.

The clients are clearly in control of this method of detecting which occult agent is held responsible for a misfortune. In the 1860's Bishop Callaway recorded a text from some young men in Natal who said that, realizing this, they decided to maintain a steady tempo and tone in their responses. The diviner told them to go away and send to consult him some elders who knew how to divine.

Other Zulu diviners work by methods which are less under the control of those who have come to consult. Least under control is the diviner who goes into a trance, during which his (or, more commonly, her) ancestral spirits speak in whistling whispers from the rafters of the hut. Presumably such a diviner works on the basis of local knowledge. Other diviners cast collections of bones and other objects, representing various persons and elements in Zulu life; and these are read according to the patterns in which they fall—patterns which are known to the public. These bones are, as one early ethnographer described them, 'a résumé of their whole social order',[15] so they cover all possible social contingencies.

Immediately I must confess that when I was studying the Zulu I was not alert to the importance of trying to investigate in detail whether afflicted Zulu consult various types of diviners according to the internal situation within their social relationships. I suspect now that when relationships within a patrilineal group have developed to a point where break-up is imminent, and misfortune befalls those who wish to assert independence, they are likely to consult by the clapping of hands so that they will get the answer they desire. Their reasoning would not, of course, take this form: they will reason that the case is, in an American phrase, more or less open and shut, so an ordinary diviner will suffice. But at more peaceable phases of a group's development it is likely that open-ended methods of divination are used, with the diviner or his apparatus selecting from several possibilities.[16] After all, the clients above all want to know accurately what occult power has caused their troubles in order to end it: it is not in their interests, as they see these, to 'cheat'.

These guesses I am making now, all too many years after I finished my research in Zululand, are guesses inspired by the recent work of younger anthropologists,[17] who have concentrated on the details of developments within particular homesteads or villages as their members mature, marry and produce children, who in turn mature and marry. These recent analyses emphasize that a struggle to control the divinatory decision may proceed between different contestants for superior positions in a village, or between the head of a village and the leader of a section within it who is attempting to establish independence. The struggle to control the divinatory decision is hidden from the protagonists themselves, since—I repeat—they are all motivated by the wish to discover what occult agent is responsible for the misfortune at issue in order that remedial measures may be taken. They are, of course, aware of the issues that lie between them; but they believe that the divination gives an unbiased answer—and indeed some methods of divination operate more or less mechanically. But if the decision does not favour one protagonist he may go to another diviner, and yet another, or seek some practitioner who uses different methods, to get the answer he wishes. This kind of jockeying for position at the divinatory seance appears to occur when the course of the group's cycle of development has reached a crisis.

I shall later return to these analyses, after I have emphasized some points which have already emerged. The first is that since such high value is placed by the society on kin remaining united and continuing to reside together, a threat to the well-being of some members of the group, a threat which is ascribed to witchcraft or sorcery on the part of another, often seems to be required to justify separation. Either the evil-doer and his close dependants are driven out, or the sufferer and his dependants move away. In South-east Africa, Monica Wilson has reported this process from the Mpondo and Xhosa, and I have noted it among the Zulu. Several anthropologists have described the process in other parts of Africa. I emphasize that this 'excuse' is not always necessary: Professor I. Schapera tells me that sorcery was the ostensible cause of Tswana wards splitting in well under half of such divisions on which he has adequate information. Elsewhere the proportion of divisions related to witchcraft is higher. We can say that, in many African cultures, before a man can act against the high value set on maintaining unity he himself often has to feel, and demonstrate publicly, that though he desires unity he and his have suffered or are threatened by disaster caused by maleficent occult agents, and they must separate.

This statement immediately raises the question: why should this rationalization to justify separation be required? Why cannot those who wish to do so simply move away? We know that in some cases—as Schapera again tells me about the Tswana—where there is palpable shortage of land for cultivation or congestion in living quarters people agree amicably to move off: but sometimes even in this kind of situation a misfortune attributed to occult causes is held to justify the separation.

Our problem is, then, why in some societies the total process of development in a group of kinsfolk is conceived to be permeated by occult forces operating either advantageously or maleficently—forces which must be specified through divination. I suggest that one reason may be that the people cannot know the full implications of their own social rules. The Zulu and Mpondo, for instance, see women as mischief-makers, but they cannot recognize that the duty they impose on their women to be fruitful of children, especially sons, must ultimately, if fulfilled, produce effects opposite from those they desire. Were they to do so, they could no longer set such high value at the same time both on the persistence of agnatic unity and on the female fecundity which must destroy that unity.

The ideology and values of the Zulu, the Mpondo and similarly organized tribes are those of stationary societies. They do not accept the idea of radical changes in social pattern—which have indeed occurred. Furthermore, even changes that are within the established cultural pattern (i.e. changes in the personnel of actual groups and in the incumbents of particular established social positions) tend to be handled with ritual precautions. These ritual precautions render safe an implicit interference with the occult forces that are believed to preserve the well-being of a society. For every change in life—whether it be the birth of a child, a boy's or maiden's growing to maturity, or a transfer of land—tends to be treated as a disturbance and becomes the focus of a ritual in which related persons participate by performing actions which symbolize their interest in the central parties or object. These rituals have a strong moral element in them: they state the moral character of the relationships between the persons concerned.[18] This moral element is highly emphasized in the approach to misfortune. For a misfortune is regarded as a break in the orderly course of events, a break which results from a disturbance in the moral relationships between the sufferer and his fellows. The breach may be by either the victim; or someone connected with him, or by an alleged wrongdoer.[19] The moral disturbance either prompts a fellow to harm with witchcraft or sorcery, or provokes ancestral spirits or other occult beings to send ill fortune. Looked at from outside, we see that in these ostensibly stationary societies the natural order, the social order with its moral code, and the occult order permeate one another. Hence there is continual resort to divination, either to detect the occult cause which is connected with present misfortune, or to measure the pressures of occult forces which will influence good and ill fortune in the future.

But these beliefs in the moral aspect of occult causes and forces do not apply most strongly to patent breaches of morality. Patent breaches of morality can be dealt with in a straightforward, rational, secular manner, for example by discussion or by arbitration or by judicial consideration. It seems that occult beliefs are most significant when some major ambiguity is present in social life. My suggestion is that Zulu belief in the inherent evil of femininity can be referred to the major conflict resulting from the effects of female fecundity on the structure of Zulu agnatic groups. In short, a belief of this kind has to be referred to a deep-seated conflict of social rules, or principles of organization, or processes of development, and not to superficial quarrels arising out of divergent interests between men and women. The essence of these situations is that the people concerned are not aware of these conflicts. As I have said of the Zulu, were they aware of the conflict they could no longer operate the system. The occult belief, which is phrased to stress what are apparently common, realizable norms and values, and which indeed stresses the observance of morality, conceals the conflict and the disharmony it in fact produces. Divination selects some alleged slip from morality—be it in feeling only, or an allegation that a woman has a highly sexed sprite as a familiar—as the alleged cause of misfortune which is related to observed social difficulties, even though these arise from the structure of society itself.

We may note that these beliefs predicate that in some situations an illness or death is due to the evil motives of some related person who competes with one for land or cattle. In a sense, therefore, there is an element of psychological truth in them. For at the level of subsistence, when resources become scarce, possession of cattle or land may make the difference between hunger and satisfaction, between illness and good health, between life and death. He who covets the cattle and land to which I aspire, by implication wishes me to be hungry, to be ill, even to die. Yet nevertheless, viewed objectively, the beliefs 'exaggerate', so to speak, the responsibility of a pre-selected individual for the harm suffered by another.

4. *Conflicts of moral principle*

We owe our insight into the relation between conflict of social principles and the occurrence of occult beliefs and rituals to Professor M. Fortes (now of Cambridge, but formerly a member of this College) and Evans-Pritchard in a joint Introduction to a series of essays on *African Political Systems* (1940). Most of these essays emphasized the occult attributes of political offices, and the ritual responsibilities of chiefs and other leaders. Fortes and Evans-Pritchard pointed out that political rituals aim to achieve prosperity for a political unit as a whole: rain and sunshine at appropriate seasons to produce good crops and pasture, fertility of both people and cattle, success in hunting and war, freedom from disease, and so forth. These are communal goods, and they derive from weather, land, people and beasts. But individual men (taking the men's point of view) get their good crops from weather which may benefit a small area, affecting only individual plots of land, and they get their calves from individual cows and their children from individual women. Men may compete and struggle with others over these plots of land, these cows and these women. Communal good—the general prosperity of the country as a whole and the fertility of all women and beasts—thus arises out of individual prosperity based on individual plots of land, individual women and individual beasts, over all of which there may be dispute. There is in one sense a deep conflict between general prosperity and individual prosperity. The political system as a whole provides the moral order in which men may hope to hold and work their land, herd their cattle, and marry wives and raise children: so it becomes invested with occult values which hide the potential conflict between communal well-being and well-being for all individuals. These values are expressed in beliefs and rituals.

Since this idea was advanced, several anthropologists have followed its lead. Nadel found among the Nupe of northern Nigeria beliefs similar to those of the Zulu. In Nupe the evil witches who kill are women, while male witches defend their fellows against the female witches. Only female witches are believed to kill, but since this evil deed requires that male defenders default from duty, in effect the female requires the assistance of a male. Nevertheless, the evil again resides in femininity. Women are considered to be sexually insatiable. Nadel seeks to answer why. He finds a striking conflict between the roles which, ideally, women ought to play and what many women in fact do. Ideally, a Nupe woman should be a good wife, subservient to her husband, bearing him many children and staying at home to care for them and their father. In reality a great deal of trade is in the hands of the women. They absent themselves to trade, and some become richer than their husbands. Instead of the husband supporting his wife, she may help him; and she, and not her husband, may help their sons find the marriage payments for their brides. On top of this, those women who prosper at trading often travel to distant markets, where they add to their earnings by prostituting themselves. Some of them are alleged to practise abortion to avoid having children who would interfere with their trading activities. Yet women who work hard at trading to acquire wealth, and then help their menfolk, are also approved. Out of this insoluble conflict between two ideals and hard reality, says Nadel, emerges the ascription by men of witchcraft power to women. A Nupe woman aiming at independent trading faces problems similar to those of a modern Englishwoman pursuing a career; the latter escapes being suspected of witchcraft.

I would add that the Nupe have the same sort of patrilineal lineage structure as the Zulu; and, with all respect, I suggest that the position of the relatively few women traders exacerbates a conflict over female fertility, a conflict which is represented in Nupe beliefs about women's sexual voracity.[21]

M. Wilson[22] stresses in the same way conflicts between social principles in an attempt to explain why, in two tribes which she studied, witches are believed to be motivated in one by sexual lust, and in the other by greed for meat and milk. The first tribe, the Mpondo of South Africa, are organized in the main on the same lines as the Zulu. Men of agnatic lineages reside close together, and have claims on one another's land, cattle and social positions. They eat together. They are forbidden to have sexual relationships with any woman of their agnatic clan and with a large number of women related to them in other ways. Hence many women in a district are sexually taboo to a man. On top of this, they are now part of South African society, with its strict colour bar and its strong, legally punishable condemnation of sexual relationships between persons of different colour. Wilson suggests that this situation leads to the belief that both male and female witches are moved by extreme sexual desires and acquire familiars which then demand the lives of their kin or relatives-in-law.

The other tribe that Wilson studied was the Nyakyusa of Tanganyika. Their organization also contains agnatic lineages whose men have rights in one another's cattle. But the men of these lineages do not reside together. It is forbidden here for a man to be near his daughter-in-law. Hence, as boys of a neighbourhood mature they move out of their fathers' villages and build a separate new village. Each village is inhabited, therefore, by men of the same age. Here they bring their wives, but they eat as a group of men, not each man with his wife and children. Great value is placed in these Nyakyusa villages of age-mates on hospitality and good companionship: yet the prized foods, meat and milk, are derived from cattle which are 'owned' jointly not by fellow villagers but by agnatic lineages some of whose men are dispersed over several age-villages which own the land of the village. Cattle are sacrificed to lineage spirits, and consumed at gatherings of lineage mates. There is a conflict between obligations of hospitality to fellow age-mates in one's village, and the obligations to one's lineage fellows with whom one holds cattle. Wilson argues that therefore, although the Nyakusa are better off as regards food supplies than the Mpondo, they believe that witches are moved by greed for food. The belief arises from conflict between membership of agnatic lineage and membership of age-village.

All these societies have in many respects their own well developed technologies. Yet in comparison with us their control over the hazards of life is relatively slight. Drought, floods, crop pests and cattle epidemics threaten their communal well-being; if famine comes they have no way to obtain food. Their medical lore is inefficient. Infantile and maternal mortality rates are extremely high, and diseases kill many of those who have survived beyond infancy. It is not surprising that in this situation they believe that they are subject to the influences of occult powers, which affect their good and ill fortune. Furthermore, since these powers work outside sensory observations, it is also not surprising that these peoples should seek, through divination, operating also by occult means, to assess what these powers have done in the immediate past or portend in the future. But what we have to examine is the fact that divination is not concerned merely to unravel a technical problem; beyond this, the problem set for the diviner is a moral problem. And what the studies I have cited suggest is that often it is an insoluble moral problem, since it arises from discrepancies and conflicts in the structure of society itself. The Nyakyusa cannot abolish either his cattle-owning agnatic lineage or his residential age-village. He is caught permanently between the two. My analysis and Wilson's theory that the Mpondo believe witches are motivated by sexual lust because so many persons around them are sexually taboo to them supplement each other. Between them they explain a further point. Wilson is inclined to think that Mpondo beliefs in witchcraft are less concerned with morality than are Nyakyusa beliefs. Yet sex is a subject on which moral codes have at least as much to say as they have about food. Certainly this is so among the Mpondo and their cognate tribes. I suggest that Nyakyusa beliefs deal patently with individual moral lapses because the conflict between membership of age-village and membership of agnatic lineage, though inescapable, is clear even to the people themselves. On the other hand, if I am right the Mpondo conflict is beyond their view, since it resides in the ambivalent effects of women's fertility. Hence the belief in witchcraft does not appear to be so directly connected with individual morality: it deals with inescapable, but unseen, conflicts in social morality.

Clearly, if it is disturbances due to inescapable conflicts in social structure itself that produce the strains and pose insoluble choices for people, no rational assessment of them is possible. The human mind, enmeshed in the culture of a particular society of this type, cannot withdraw to consider, so to speak, judicially what is at fault. Divination provides, in various degrees, an external, seemingly unbiased, means of deciding where the moral fault lies.

But why must there be a moral fault to explain a misfortune? To answer this question we may pursue the beliefs of the Nyakyusa. They believe that the power of witchcraft comes from several black pythons in the stomach—pythons which can be seen on autopsy. These pythons lust for meat, and witches fly on them at night and throttle the hated victim or eat his flesh so that he dies. The pythons of witchcraft are fought by defenders of the village—senior men who possess power to destroy witchcraft and witches. This defending power comes from possession of a single python in the stomach (which is not visible on autopsy). If a man is ill, various people may interpret the cause of his illness differently: he may think he is being attacked by the pythons of witches, others may say he is a witch who is being punished by the python of a defender.

This belief (and below I shall quote similar beliefs from other tribes) indicates that there is in a sense a similarity between the powers of witchcraft and the powers of anti-witchcraft. I have already cited how Nupe female witches attack, while male witches defend. In many religions, similarly, the line between the powers of good and evil spiritual beings is a fine one. Here, I think, we are looking at the possible opposite effects of a man's use of his talents, or a woman's use of her talents. These talents are potentially of value to society: equally, they may harm the possessor's fellows. In a stationary society, and one in which men cannot easily separate from those with whom they compete or quarrel, this ambivalence of use of talent is most marked. It is excess that is condemned. Many tribes believe that a man succeeds to political office by killing his rivals with sorcery or witchcraft. Yet a man, to be a man, should not be spiritless. What is the golden mean of legitimate striving between spiritlessness and overweening ambition? What is the golden mean which makes a woman a good wife and mother, between the vice of barrenness[23] and the vice of overbreeding?—the latter especially if other women are barren. Richards records of the Bemba of Zambia that to find one beehive in the woods is luck, to find two is very good luck, to find three is witchcraft. There is a mean of industriousness, somewhere between under-working and over-working, since it is believed that if a man's crops are too fruitful he has used sorcery to steal the crops of his neighbours.[24] In Britain, among university students there is a mean between slacking and swotting, and among industrial workers between being a rate-buster and a chiseller; but he who exceeds the mean, or does not attain it, is not accused of witchcraft.

Under these African beliefs those who are lucky or unduly productive both fear that they will be the target of sorcery or witchcraft from their envious neighbours and in practice are likely to be accused of sorcery or witchcraft by the less lucky or productive. The beliefs are appropriate to societies which are basically egalitarian, which have simple tools and no great variation in productiveness of their members, and which produce simple consumers' goods so that there is little variation in standards of living. Given, too, that they have few types of occupation and categories of elites in which related men may fulfil their ambitions without competing with one another, the universal ethical problem of achieving balance, a golden mean, takes an acute form. A man rises in status at the expense of those closely related to him: a woman breeds many children at the expense of other women closely linked to her but who are barren. Prosperity is achieved possibly at the cost of one's near kin. So that every talent and achievement is highly ambivalent.

5. *Beliefs in witchcraft and ancestral wrath*

I have so far described (in what was my first lecture) how in some tribal societies misfortunes are seen as resulting from breakdowns in the moral relations between members of groups of kinsfolk. The occurrence of misfortune is referred to the evil activity of a witch or sorcerer. In tribal belief it is predicated that the evil-doer is likely to stand in a particular kind of social relationship to the sufferer.

Accusations of witchcraft or sorcery fall in certain patterns in different tribes and occult evil-doers are believed to be animated by motives inappropriate to their social relationships. An accusation that a particular person is guilty has to be levied or validated by some divinatory or oracular apparatus. Ostensibly, this apparatus works out of the control of the accusers: it is external and appears to be unbiased, although those accused may allege that it has not been properly used.

I described further how in some agnatically organized societies—that is, societies where property and position pass in the male line—people believe that it is women who possess the inherent evil propensity of witchcraft, and indeed other forms of occult evil. I tried to relate this belief to the ambivalent effects of women's fertility. A duty is laid on women married from outside into a group of agnates that they bear sons to perpetuate and strengthen their husbands' groups. But the effect of the birth of sons is to produce competitors for the limited land, cattle, important positions and privileges of each group. Their competition produces dissension because of the very increase which first strengthens the numbers of the group's membership. This dissension, and the breaking off of relationships to which it may lead, enable a man to achieve the independence to which he is entitled. But he achieves this goal only in conflict with the highly valued goal that he should remain united with his agnates. The goals aimed at are thus mutually exclusive; and it seems that in order to separate into independence a man must frequently get a divinatory declaration that he and his dependants have suffered a misfortune which shows that they are being attacked by occult evil. Misfortune comes first; divination of occult causes follows after. This alone legitimates his flouting the value of unity. I argued further that since the conflict in pursuit of goals arises from the birth of sons, it means that wives both strengthen and weaken the group when they discharge their duty to be fertile. This conflict arising from the duty laid on women is concealed by the belief that they are witches moved by insatiable sexual desires.

Many problems can be extracted both from these beliefs and from their social setting. I have concentrated my analysis on the moral crisis created for a group which sets a high value on unity as its own development leads to a proliferation of conflicting interests within it. The interests of members of the group may conflict because of increasing pressure on land, or difficulties in sharing out cattle, or desires for independence and positions of prestige. A situation is created in which persons are moved by different but equally highly regarded social rules and values to opposed courses of action: this I have called a 'moral crisis'. The situation is well illustrated in Middleton's study of the Lugbara of Uganda, but here it is the wrath of ancestral spirits against junior kinsmen who do not respect their seniors that threatens to bring illness—rather more than witchcraft and sorcery.

As long ago as 1934 Schapera[25] analysed a Bechuana belief under which if a senior relative was indignant against a junior relative, the pair's ancestral spirits would cause misfortune to the junior. The senior did nothing: his indignation set the spirits to work. The wronged senior was not in these circumstances guilty of sorcery; and he had to take a lead in the ritual treatment necessary for the sufferer to be cured. A similar Lugbara belief has been set by Middleton in the full context of an agnatic group's development.[26]

The Lugbara are organized in small, agnatic lineages, with ritual seniority passing down the generations through the eldest sons of senior wives of successive progenitors within each lineage. Seniority is marked by control over certain shrines, at which offerings must be made to cure those who have fallen ill. Illness is commonly believed to result from the legitimate indignation of a senior kinsman against his junior. The ghosts of dead ancestors become aware of this indignation and, without being explicitly invoked, send illness to the wrong-doing junior. The senior is not aware of what is happening until illness strikes. The cause of illness is determined through divination. Therefore if a junior falls ill, it is a validation of the senior's authority if the divination indicates that it is his indignation which has moved the ghosts to punish the junior who has failed to conform to the norms of morality.

When a group has grown in numbers, and becomes differentiated internally in several different lines of descent, a senior man in a junior line may try to assert that it is he whose indignation is causing the ghosts to send illness to his own subordinates. He attempts thus to argue that the sick person's illness no longer arises from the indignation of the elder who had previously been divined as unconsciously moving the ghosts to punish the patient. If this is confirmed by the oracles and by recovery of the patient after offering has been made, the leader of the junior line is becoming successful in asserting his independence. When the junior elder is invited to go as representative of his own following to sacrifices by other segments of the lineage and is allowed to make ritual addresses, he is recognized as independent. During the crisis which leads to this phase, and after it is reached, the new leader will essay to amend the genealogy of the lineage so that his line appears to be equal, if not superior, to that of the erstwhile common leader.

I have had to summarize and over-simplify very complex processes; but I hope I have made clear that here again a misfortune —illness—is referred to a moral crisis in a group, and occult forces are believed to be working through that crisis. To obtain independence the aspiring leader has to claim that dead ancestors are acting on his behalf. The former leader will resist this declaration of independent status and its validation by the divination which detects on whose behalf the ghosts have acted. Each competitor strains to get accepted the divination of the oracle-operator to whom he went; and each man frames the questions answered in his consultation.

In these tense situations of competition men have to go for confirmatory divinations to diviners not related to the group, rather than to the several oracular apparatuses they themselves own, in order to determine who is responsible for the illness of a junior. When the client puts questions to the diviner he frames them in terms of the current crises in the group. Lugbara are aware that social 'considerations enter into the consultation of the oracles'; but since they believe that sickness is due to occult causes, they concentrate attention on these causes (p. 187). Even an elder aspiring to independence accepted the oracles' verdict that the leader of the group with whom he was competing had brought sickness on him: 'he was very worried by [his] sickness, and thought that perhaps [the leader's] mystical powers of eldership were behind it' (p. 175).

The situation is very complicated, because several occult agencies are at work. Only God is responsible for deaths, and at times the extant leader may have God divined as the cause of a misfortune. This supports his position, because God is outside and above lineage sectional interests, though concerned in readjustments of authority and status. God's support through the oracle is very weighty.

Here, then, with similar processes at work to those described for the Zulu, we have elders competing for the right to be named as responsible for sickness. It may seem strange that people should wish to be declared responsible for the ills of those in their care, but they should do this only to maintain lineage authority and its moral code. And the anthropologist was told by one Lugbara, who was divined to have been afflicted by his mother's people, 'Yes, it is right that sickness has come from [them] . . . Do they not love me as their child? They watch over me. They are my people there . . .' (p. 191).

Sickness of this sort should punish only breaches against the moral code. Here a difficult dilemma arises for elders. As a lineage approaches the point where it will divide, competing elders try to be declared responsible as often as possible to validate their authority. Yet if an elder is held to be responsible too often, he becomes unpopular, and his juniors may allege that he is practising witchcraft. Witches are believed to attack only their agnates, and if one is acting illegitimately one uses witchcraft instead of invoking the ghosts. Middleton writes that 'there is a very slight difference only between . . . being regarded as an ideal elder, exercising his authority for the well-being of his lineage, and . . . being accused of being a witch, abusing his mystical powers for his own selfish ends' (pp. 200–1). A man should claim to be responsible for illness sent by ghosts only if he is insulted in his position as elder; it is witchcraft if he reacts to an insult against him as an individual. Even the same word describes moving the ghosts to action and using witchcraft. Again, the line between rightful and wrongful use of one's talent and authority is difficult to draw, and it may be drawn differently by various parties involved in the situation.

The setting of this dilemma is the same conflict of values. It is proper for men to be ambitious and to want authority. Not to be ambitious is to be 'immature'. And on the other hand, 'some men try to acquire authority which they should not possess and . . . others abuse it when they have acquired it'. As the Lugbara (in Middleton's words) 'usually . . . see the total structure of their society . . . as something static' (p. 216), competition for authority involving breach of the highly valued duty of unity is immoral, even though a man is entitled also to independence. And since division in the lineage often happens after the funerals of key elders, it is significant that men at dances staged at these funerals may have 'incestuous' relationships with their clanswomen and are liable to fight with their agnates (pp. 203–4), thus breaking the two most stringent rules in the moral code of the agnatic lineage—those rules that mark its unity.

One may well ask why, if the Lugbara have agnatic lineages like the south-eastern African tribes, they do not similarly relate the occult causes of their misfortune to the witchcraft of their wives married into these lineages. And the Azande also have groups of patrilineally related kinsmen, who are indeed required to avenge all deaths: they too do not blame their wives for witchcraft, but unrelated neighbours. This may have been a new pattern of accusations, since when Evans-Pritchard studied the Azande their old pattern of settlement had been disrupted. The Sudan government, in trying to move the Azande out of sleeping-sickness areas, had settled them in lines of homesteads along the roads running on the watersheds. We do not yet know how to explain fully these varied patterns of belief. But the explanation may lie in patterns of inheritance of property and position. As I have described, in south-eastern African tribes, including the Zulu, each wife becomes the centre of a separate estate within the total of her husband's estate. She is allotted cattle and land to which her own sons are heirs as against their half-brothers by their father's other wives. Among the Lugbara[26] and the Azande, and other tribes dwelling in the same cultural region, instead of each wife being the focus of a separate estate, it seems that the whole of a man's estate passes first to his brothers and even cousins before dropping a generation. The heir then administers the property for all the agnates. In a comparative analysis of *Witchcraft and Sorcery in East Africa* (1963, at pp. 15–16) Middleton and Winter conclude that, in tribes who ascribe misfortunes to witchcraft, it is where each wife is the centre of a separate estate within her husband's property that women are accused of this inherent evil. It seems indeed plausible that, where one man is responsible for administering a whole estate in his and all his kinsmen's interests, occult fears are more likely to focus directly on relationships between the males rather than indirectly *via* wives and mothers onto those relationships between men. Occult fears focus on women where property interests centre on women.

Middleton's study of the Lugbara culminates in an analysis of the thirty-three occasions of divination during a period of fifteen months in the history of a single lineage nearing segmentation. At the end of this period, which was full of struggle between leaders competing to be divined as responsible for illness, the accredited senior leader died and the lineage split into segments. Earlier studies of these types of situation had set out general principles, and illustrated those principles by examples which were apt at any point in the analysis. This method tended to focus attention only upon the relationship between two apparently isolated persons, the pair of accuser and alleged witch/sorcerer, or between the pair of offended senior, who was supported by the ghosts, and the offending junior. A new generation of anthropologists has analysed divinations and accusations in their full context of social relationships, as Middleton did. They have seen that the divination of a particular occult agent as the cause of misfortune cannot always be handled in isolation. Each divination may have to be related to earlier divinations; and all have to be set in the total context of a group's development. This method enabled them to penetrate more deeply both into divinations and into the complexity of social relationships. The new method was first applied by Mitchell to the Yao of Malawi.[27]

6. *Conflicts of value in matrilineal systems*

Among the Yao social position and authority are obtained and inherited in the matrilineal, and not the agnatic, line. In agnatic systems, growth of the group leads to difficulties which focus on wives, who are the source of increase in numbers and the points at which divisions occur. In matrilineally organized societies, women are also the points of growth and of incipient division, but here it is women in their role as sisters, and not in their role as wives. For under matriliny a woman's children are attached for purposes of group organization to her brothers and her mother's brothers, and not to her husband who is their father. Uterine brothers and sisters by one mother form a closely mutually identified group, with the eldest brother entitled to be in charge of all. But the brothers also compete with one another to secure the support of their sisters, for it is largely through this support that each brother can obtain the following which will enable him to win prestige. The elder brother prevents his younger brother from doing this, unless the younger brother can persuade his sisters that the elder is incapable of looking after them, including protecting them and their children from sorcery, or is himself a sorcerer attacking the sisters and their children. 'Hence,' says Mitchell, '. . . accusations of sorcery are frequent among brothers: it is a rationalization of a hostility arising from the structural position of uterine brothers, which, in view of the commonly accepted strong sentiments uniting brothers, may not be otherwise expressed.' In short, here again there is a conflict between the legitimate aspiration for authority, which drives men to independence, and the high value set on unity of kinsfolk and the unity of a big village.

The competition is even more acute between a man and his sister's sons as the latter strive to win their sisters from their common uncle's care. And accusations of sorcery are frequently made by nephews against uncles, though not by uncles against nephews (see below). Mitchell states that 'conflicts between sister's sons and mother's brothers are frequent' as 'a facet of the general political process in which groups are for ever trying at once to demonstrate their autonomy by setting up new villages, and their unity by remaining in large integrated villages' (p. 179). The nephew aims to demonstrate that the mother's brother is himself a sorcerer or neglects to protect the younger man's sisters and their children against sorcery. And the sisters may in this process accuse one another, or a brother, or mother's brother, of sorcery. Accusations of sorcery are also made between the men of segments within a larger matrilineage, residing in a single village.

Mitchell traced the variety of accusations that arose from seemingly chance quarrels and illnesses in a single village through seven years (the earlier ones were told him by informants and he observed the later processes). People aligned themselves in varied ways, but constant throughout was the opposition of two younger men, each of whom represented the interests of two segments descended from women who shared a common grandmother. Mitchell summarized the history of quarrelling thus:

> Consistently in the accounts of the divinations each reject[ed] the diviner's finding if it accuse[d] a member of his lineage segment . . . the divination seance itself [became] a field in which the opposition of the segments [was] expressed. [One man] continued consulting diviners until finally he got the answer he wanted. His opponents rejected these findings and eventually even discounted [the most important,] the chicken ordeal. The diviners' findings, and the results of the poison ordeals, therefore, [were] bandied about between the opposed groups, and though the whole procedure of divination and accusations of sorcery [was] directed towards the extirpation of discordant elements in the community, in fact, it [was] only a facet of the underlying cause of the tension—the opposition of segments in an ever-segmenting lineage. [p. 174]

In a study of the nearby Chewa, who have an organization similar to that of the Yao, Marwick[28] analysed how all the quarrels and misfortunes he recorded in his field work were handled. He found that accusations of sorcery are most frequent within matrilineal groups:

> . . . the issue, either between sorcerer and victim or between accuser and sorcerer, seems to be an outcome of their competing for a strongly desired object in a situation in which there is an irreconcilable conflict in the rights, principles and claims that apply. [Further,] there is some form of impediment—usually because of the irreconcilable nature of the conflict—to the settlement of the dispute by judicial or other rational forms of arbitration.

Hatred continues to smoulder. Finally, either sorcerer or victim has committed a recent breach of moral rules (p. 151; see also p. 212). Chewa themselves point out that the matrilineal lineage is 'the natural arena for quarrels about succession to office and the ownership of property'. Here are present, says Marwick,

> the strong motives [that are] often found as ingredients in tensions expressed in terms of sorcery . . . [T]hese motives are given relatively free play . . . [because] of conflict between the principles governing competitive interaction.

In the matrilineal lineage, relationships are highly personal and charged with emotion, and cannot 'be quietly dismantled' (as conjugal relationships can be, in a society with easy divorce and a high rate of divorce) (p. 294). Though the people said co-wives and spouses frequently bewitched each other, Marwick collected no cases between co-wives and only two between spouses. Between different matrilineages judicial proceedings can operate. Marwick states, therefore, that while there is a chance of a lineage remaining united, the struggle in terms of accusations of sorcery is to control it: but when its break-up is apparent, accusations of sorcery accelerate and justify the incipient division (p. 147; also p. 220).

In a review of Marwick's book Douglas[29] criticized Marwick for following too closely, in his study of the Chewa, Mitchell's analysis of the role of accusations of witchcraft in the processes of lineage segmentation among the Yao. In a most stimulating, if compressed, analysis she argues that when Mitchell observed the Yao they had an unstable system of lineages in small villages, as the fruits of their long contact with the Arabs and commerce, and later of the imposition of British rule, which cut their trade at the source and liberated their slaves. She points out that among the Yao accusations are in fact made by junior men against their seniors and that this is compatible with a rapidly segmenting system. On the other hand, in practice most accusations within Chewa matrilineages are made by seniors against juniors. This seems to be compatible with the fact that Chewa villages are larger than Yao villages, and this in turn suggests that lineages do not segment so rapidly; charges of witchcraft thus buttress and protect the positions of seniors among the Chewa. She suggests that they have been less influenced by forces which have affected the Yao. Douglas's essay was published well after I had worked out my argument, which it does not touch in itself. One must note, however, that Mitchell described two types of Yao village—large, persisting villages, hiving off sections, and smaller, segmenting villages. But since Douglas proceeds to argue in a wider comparative study that accusations of this kind occur in 'the range of small-scale, ambiguously defined, strictly local relations', and not within major large-scale political relationships, I feel that the tenor of her comparative analysis stresses the main point from which I start.

The analysis of divinations through a series of moral crises and ruptures in the history of single groups thus enables us to compare the kinds of situation where different types of solution, magical and secular, can be applied. Turner (who followed Mitchell and influenced Middleton), in a study of the Ndembu of Zambia,[30] traced the course of a whole series of disputes in one village for a period of twenty years, partly as described to him, partly as he observed them. He found that where the parties are disputing about their rights in terms of a single legal rule, or under rules that can be arranged in a hierarchy, judicial arbitration can be applied. But judicial action cannot be employed when disputes arise as a result of appeals by the parties to different social rules which are discrepant or even in conflict. The rules cannot be affirmed clearly to constrain both parties. In such a situation one party, suffering a misfortune, will accuse the other of sorcery or witchcraft, or allege that ancestral spirits have been offended by the other. Divination—an ostensibly external, unbiased mechanism—selects the occult cause, and appropriate steps can be taken. Often ritual is performed. Ritual may even be employed after a judicial decision appears to have settled rights and wrongs, when in fact the cause of dispute is beyond settlement. And finally, when all attempts to preserve existing relationships have failed, final breaches, often provoked by witchcraft charges, are confirmed by rituals which re-state the norms as consistent and enduring, even though new relationships have been established. 'Those who disputed bitterly for headmanship within a village may become helpful relatives when they reside in two different villages when each appears to conform to the Ndembu ideal' (pp. 123*f*). In addition, judicial remedies can apply when the living quarrel. But if it is natural misfortune, such as death or sickness, that is the breach of regularity to be redressed, and misfortune is ascribed to occult agents, only detection through divination of the one responsible can clarify issues for adjustment (p. 127). And there is dispute and struggle to control the divinatory apparatus, within the limits set by its mechanism.

All these studies stress that a natural misfortune, like a quarrel, inside one of these intimately involved groups, where men and women seek to satisfy manifold interests, provokes a severe moral crisis. The crisis is not always created by individuals or sections nakedly pursuing their selfish interests. It arises from the very process of development of the group, a development which results in conflict between values as well as quarrels between people. The conflict of values seems to give rise to occult fears, and divination focuses these fears onto a specific occult agent. Redress is sought either in ritual or by the breaking of highly valued ties.

7. *The golden mean of morality*

I stressed earlier that (in these relatively stationary societies) a man or woman has to conform to a golden mean in behaviour. Failure to attain the mean is a moral fault and is despised; it inspires envy, which leads to witchcraft or sorcery. Excess, in performance or ambition or exercise of authority, is believed also to be a moral fault, and it may be ascribed to evil occult power. I must now return to this point in order to make a further step in my analysis.

The situation is manifest in the beliefs of the Tiv of Nigeria, as reported on by Professor and Mrs Bohannan.[31] A Tiv elder, skilled in handling social affairs and in settling disputes, 'must have' what the Tiv call '*tsav*, that is talent, ability, and a certain witchcraft potential. The possession of *tsav*,' say the Bohannans, 'grants power to bewitch and to prevent bewitching; in both aspects it is the most powerful means of discipline in the hands of the elders and, in practice, the force by which their decisions are upheld.' There could not, surely, be a belief which states more clearly the ambivalent potential of men's talents in society. I quote further from the Bohannans: '*Tsav* can be either good or bad.' '*Tsav* . . . gives power over other people, and, in a furiously egalitarian society . . . such power sets a man apart; it is distrusted, for Tiv believe firmly that no one can rise above his fellows except at their expense.' But a man must will to use his *tsav* against others, and these victims can only be members of his agnatic lineage. On the other hand, elders with *tsav* need human lives to obtain prosperity for their social group—the fertility of farms, crops and women, success in hunting, good health. These human lives, sacrificed so to speak in the group's interests, the elders without their own knowledge take from among their agnatic kin. It is very significant that kin who may compete can be killed for good or for evil.

Tsav grows on the hearts of human beings and varies in shape and colour as it is good or bad. This can be seen on autopsy. And *tsav* develops slowly, as a 'man's personality develops', though its growth may be accelerated by a diet of human flesh—consumed in occult form. The Bohannans read this belief at one level as referring 'to people of small talent who get ahead by misuse of the substance of others . . .'

During certain crises the Tiv agnatic group holds divinatory seances. Bohannan, in his book *Justice and Judgment among the Tiv* (1957), gives a number of graphic accounts of the solemn and ritually controlled jockeying which occurs at these Tiv seances. They are always concerned with disturbances among relatively closely related persons. In a severe crisis each party, including the dead, is represented by either his local age-mates or his maternal kin, who are related to him as an individual but who are not members of the disturbed agnatic group. And each party or his representatives consults a diviner in advance and brings to the seance the diviner's selection of possible causes of occult disturbance, as possibly associated with misfortunes and quarrels in the group. Death and illnesses provoke seances; or brothers may be quarrelling over their rights to control the marriages of women, or to inherit wives of dead members.

As the elders investigate these problems they may light on the omission of a ritual to a fetish, or witchcraft, as the cause of difficulty, or perhaps as the future outcome of some dispute among the close kin. In the course of the proceedings they endeavour to set aright secular disorder, but the proceedings always end with a ritual. The characteristic of these proceedings, says Bohannan, is that they

> settle disputes between persons in relationships that can never be broken or ignored. The function of a [seance] is only incidentally the settlement of particular grievances; its main function is to make it possible for people who must live together to do so harmoniously. Marriage ties can be broken; marriage disputes can be heard in court. But ties of agnation are unchangeable, and are the basis of all citizenship rights of adult males. One must either get along with one's agnates or become an expatriate . . . Tiv recognize that [seances] do settle disputes. But they also insist that the real purpose of the [seance] is not to settle the dispute itself but to allay the mystical factors which are behind it, which caused it, or which it caused.

Hence every seance ends with a ritual, either to allay or to be prophylactic against these occult factors.

The elders who control the discussion are themselves interested in the internal politics of the group. They have also been involved in quarrels and alliances with the protagonists and with dead men and women who belonged to the group. They may have claims on the property and women discussed. Hence there is struggle for position, and not only 'judicial' assessment of facts in the light of law though this is present. In an impasse nothing may be done; and in the end, divination decides the issue.

The decisive role of occult factors emerges clearly in a seance which followed on a certain man's death. The deceased's full sister had died three or four months earlier, and the divination said she had been killed by *tsav* (either witchcraft or the elders' power used for community ends). Nobody asked the divining apparatus whose 'witchcraft power' it was. When an autopsy was performed on her she had no *tsav* (black substance) on her heart. It was clear that she did not die because she had *tsav* of witchcraft and had been punished, and therefore she must have died either because an evil witch in the group had killed her or because the elders needed a life for the community's fertility and prosperity. Loud and bitter accusations were made by her close male kinsmen, and a special pot 'of ashes and [magical substances], which is the symbol of right and justice' was used to seek out the unnamed wrongdoer. He or she was 'cursed' upon the pot. When the woman's death was followed by her brother's illness and death, it was necessary to determine whether he was killed by the righteous medicine punishing his own evil witchcraft, or as a sacrifice by his agnatic kin, or by the witchcraft of one of them. Only autopsy on his corpse could settle the matter. His kinsmen opposed the autopsy. They protested that they knew he was innocent, and it was unnecessary. His age-set, composed of age-mates from outside the village, insisted on the autopsy. They protested that they knew he was innocent and demanded that his innocence be proved.

The autopsy was performed by the leader of the dead man's age-set. It disclosed two 'sacks' of blood on the heart, one dull blue, the other bright red. The leader of the age-set pointed these out to the anthropologist as bewitching *tsav*, and added, 'But *tsav* need not be evil. But this *tsav* is evil. It is large and of two colours.' Slowly it was agreed that the man had been killed by the righteous medicines of justice which punished his witchcraft. The deceased's age-set, after argument with the agnates, took under its protection his younger brother and widows. The 'justice-seeking' medicine was then again invoked against anyone who had 'done evil deeds in this matter'.

Bohannan brings out the process of dispute arising from self-interest and from assertion of various rights in terms of complex relationships between the parties reaching back into the past. These are seen in terms of moral rules. He discusses the full duality of *tsav*, whose potential power for good and evil is itself symbolic of the ambivalence inherent in social life—in which it may kill kinsfolk for the good or the ill of the group. But he does not, in my opinion, sufficiently stress the profound moral crisis which faces an agnatic group with these beliefs whenever misfortune occurs. Nor does he draw attention to the manner in which those most deeply involved insist that confidence in the innocence of their brother makes an autopsy unnecessary. In a way they may have feared that he would be found innocent, for that would have left the rankling problem that another of them was guilty. The related outsiders,[32] starting from the same premise that the dead man was innocent, force action and temporary resolution of the moral crisis. The outsiders seem to act to clarify moral relationships within the group. Where the divination is observation of an organic condition, it is not the apparatus which is external, unbiased and compelling, but compulsion comes from persons not involved in the crisis. Something complex may lie behind Evans-Pritchard's statement that among the

Zande in the past a blood brother used to carry out the autopsy on an alleged witch.[33]

In the first part of this essay I tried to relate the forms of a belief in occult causes of evil to conflicts of social values in some African tribes; in the latter part I have examined how divinations of ancestral indignation or of witchcraft, as against judicial arbitration, are set in struggles within proliferating groups, both agnatic and matrilineal. There are African societies where the relation of ritual practice to this kind of process is not so evident, particularly those where the beliefs focus on spiritual beings which can be better described as gods or, to use Lienhardt's term, divinities.[34] In his essay in this book Baxter considers these cultural situations.

8. *Situations of moral crisis in Britain*

Moral decisions arising from conflicting principles are clearly involved in dealing with events and developments within the smaller groups of our society. In discussing Bohannan's account of a Tiv seance to determine the occult causes of deaths within an agnatic lineage I stressed the incapacity of the lineage itself to tackle its moral crisis, and how related outsiders forced the autopsy which decided whether the most recently deceased member was or was not the killing witch in its ranks. In most societies, even when occult fears are not aroused, persons who are outside the group involved but related to at least some of its members are called in to deal with certain moral disturbances. This process may be operated consciously or unconsciously. The witch-detective, or witch-doctor, is a professional outsider. In Britain we have many professional outsiders whom we can consult in moral crises: priests, lawyers and other consultants or conciliators, or arbitrators, doctors, marriage guidance counsellors and other social welfare workers, and the like. I can look only at the role of one kind of such person, the industrial consultant, who advises on problems of reorganizing a social subsystem. I have selected this in order to make my comparison with the situation in Africa of the extended family unit running a productive enterprise.

When a family owning a firm expands in numbers, unless the firm's business increases very rapidly a situation is likely to arise when it becomes difficult to fit in the members of new generations, and competition between the members of the family for the limited number of leading positions in the organization may become acute. Here, as in Africa, a group's sentiments of kinship emphasizing unity and the rights of all members of the family come into conflict with the limitations of resources and the principles of efficient running of the business.

We have practically no scientific accounts of how a crisis of this sort is handled, though there are plenty of novels on the theme. Fortunately Dr Cyril Sofer, then a sociological consultant with the Tavistock Institute, has published a study of one family firm.[35] His organization was called in to advise the firm on how to deal with a crisis which had arisen over the accountant, who had married a great-granddaughter of the firm's founder. The firm was proposing to introduce mechanized accounting, which this relative-in-law of the rest of the senior managers could not operate. They offered to give him training but still felt that, since 60 per cent of the firm's shares were held by the general public, they should really look for an unrelated man already skilled. The accountant had asked as an alternative that he be sent as assistant manager to the firm's branch in Australia, but had been turned down for this job; later it turned out that one of his brothers-in-law was interested in the position. The accountant was bitter because he said his father-in-law had promised he would eventually become a member of the board of directors, while his present relatives-in-law said the board was not committed to this—these relatives-in-law being, as far as I can work out, an uncle, two cousins and two brothers of his wife. The consultant discussed these problems with the directors and contestants separately and in a group, and brought out fears that had long been suppressed, such as the fear of younger members of the family that they were getting on in the firm because they were of the family, and not on merit—and for some decades now our civilization has laid stress on merit. Eventually he got the matter temporarily adjusted: the accountant was interviewed in open competition for the job of mechanical accounting and for the Australian post, and given the latter. A new post was created for his wife's brother. And the firm agreed that the consulting organization provide a vocational counselling service for the fourth generation of the family, to see if there were not professions and posts outside the firm for which they were better suited, training for which would be financed by the whole family. In short, the consultant made clear to the family that they lived in modern times where opportunities are relatively unrestricted as compared with the more limited opportunities of even Victorian society.

All this advice was eminently sensible; but the consultant's account does not seem to me to weigh sufficiently that the firm's crisis was a crisis of moral choices. He does not give a genealogy; but the pseudonyms he has given to the directors indicate that in the first or second generation from the founder, sons of daughters as well as sons of sons were well provided for. Maybe daughters' husbands had previously been taken into the firm. In the next generation the critical problem was a choice between the men related by blood into the family and the men related by marriage. It is not easy to sack your kinswoman's husband, even when he is competing with you, the blood kinsmen, and it seems to me that the introduction of mechanical accounting may have been used unconsciously, to force the relative-in-law out of the firm. We are not told whether it was an economic necessity. And looming over all was the problem of the next generation. In these circumstances only an outsider—and here it was a highly skilled outsider—was able to clarify the issues, and to disentangle technical from sentimental problems, so that at least the technical problems could be dealt with. The firm became less dominated by family interests. The rationale of a scientific civilization was brought into a moral crisis, for an apparently objective secular solution; and this was possible because there are opportunities in our society for achievement which is not at the cost of one's near kin.

I believe that some of the same issues arise even in firms which do not belong to one family. Someone has said that 'a critical survey has now established that the clients who approach a business consultant do so with one of two motives. On the one hand they may want scapegoats for the reorganization upon which they have already decided. On the other they may want to prevent reorganization taking place.' I consider this statement to be too cynical. In practice the problem may be to put over a solution which seems objectively sensible but which if proposed by an insider would be judged by others as an attempt to advance his own interests. And even where the proposal seems against his interests the others may suspect some deeply concealed plot. But (as it is put in the north of England) 'there's nowt so queer as folk', and the queerest thing about folk is that they are not moved entirely by self-interest but are influenced also by moral considerations. Every firm is a closely linked network of personal and sectional interests, but these are affected by the moral principles of our whole civilization and of the overall purposes of the firm itself. They are also influenced by loyalties to other individuals as well as by personal animosities. Not all men easily engage in naked power politics with those who have worked with them in the moral comity of common purpose. Hence even apparently straightforward technical adjustments in a firm may cause a moral crisis, insoluble perhaps because of the conflict between the value of loyalty to colleagues and the value of efficiency.

Those involved cannot solve the crisis. They call in, if they are wise, a trained outsider; besides using technical skills, he can act as a moral catalyst to help produce an at least temporarily satisfactory solution. The industrial consultant is not a witch-detective: he achieves a secular solution which, in the opposite manner to the occult solution, focuses attention onto structural difficulties. He studies jobs and roles, brings conflicts centred on a role into the open, tries to get the firm to reorganize itself so that one person does not fill conflicting roles. He points out that it is the firm's arrangements, not the shortcomings of individuals, that are causing difficulties. He can do this, I argue, not only because of developments in social science but also because there are other opportunities in our society available to those adversely affected by reorganization in the firm. In short, the industrial consultant tries to distract the attention of people away from the alleged shortcomings, weaknesses and wrongdoing of their associates.

We may well say that our increasing understanding of the working of the natural world, with the development of the sciences investigating it, has expanded the area within which we can use theories of empirical causation to explain the occurrence of good and ill fortune. But Evans-Pritchard's analysis of beliefs in witchcraft brought out that Africans have similar insight into empirical causation; what the belief in witchcraft explains is why a particular individual suffers a misfortune or enjoys good fortune. Increase in technical knowledge alone does not deal with this problem. This is graphically brought out in a story reported by Wilson from Mpondoland. A Mpondo teacher told her that his child, who had died of typhus, had been bewitched. When Wilson protested that the child died of typhus because an infected louse had bitten it, the teacher replied that he knew that that was why his child got typhus, but why had the louse gone to his child, and not to one of the other children with whom he was playing? We too suffer ill-fortune which cannot be accounted for wholly by theories of empirical causation: the standard scientific explanation why some people suffer car accidents is to say that it is to some extent statistical chance—which does not really explain the particularity of the misfortune. And there are major disasters, such as economic recessions, whose causes are little understood, or which result from the concatenation of variables that are too complex for us to measure (as, for example, is shown in my citation from Devons in the Introduction to this book). Yet we do not ascribe these individual or community disasters to witchcraft, or to some other occult agent. Even a so-called 'witch hunt' for Communists, or capitalists, or the like, in some society or the other, as responsible for social ills, is phrased in secular terms. Hence I believe that it is not sufficient to explain changes in attitudes about the responsibility we bear for what happens to our fellow citizens, or the responsibility of individuals for breakdowns or wrongdoing in the tenor of life, only by ascribing these changes to the expanding growth of our technical knowledge, including that in the social and behavioural sciences.

I suggest that we may at least partly ascribe these attitudes which reduce mutual responsibility to the steadily increasing extent to which we no longer depend, in order to make our living, on those with whom we are intimately and sentimentally connected by kinship or in-lawship. This removes an intensifying element in the ambivalence in key relationships, since we do not have to compete as well as collaborate in those relationships. Instead, our dealings, including competition, are increasingly with unrelated persons in differentiated social ties, even when we also co-operate with some of those with whom we compete.

The ambivalence in the close personal relationships which dominate in a tribal society leads to an exaggerated emphasis on the importance of others, as part of their responsibility to their fellows, feeling towards these fellows the correct sentiments. Since any defection in duty between close relatives may affect not only their personal relationships but also the working of productive and political units, and so forth, a premium is set on all such people feeling correctly, as well as acting correctly, towards one another. Conversely, feelings of anger and envy and hatred are believed to set in train by occult means disasters which may strike the object of the animus. In practice, when there is a disaster, some misfortune, it is interpreted to be the result of such animus. As I have repeatedly stressed, in fact these alleged harmful feelings are often ascribed to struggles which arise out of conflicts between highly approved social principles whose clash precipitates moral crises. It is here, far more than in simple clashes of interest under single principles, that occult beliefs operate. Hence, I argue, as the individual becomes increasingly less dependent on his close relatives, so it is possible to envisage his taking advantage of the opportunities to move freely in the greater society, away from his relatives. He becomes isolable as a moral person from his relatives.[36] This line or argument fits in with Durkheim's (and others') general thesis that there is a reduction in ritualization as the division of labour increases, but it fills in details in a sphere with which he did not deal.

I would argue further that it is this general situation, and not only developments in biology, psychology and social science, that has led some members of our own society to focus more and more on the criminal as an individual whose capacity for responsibility for his wrongdoing is severely restricted by the organic, emotional and social circumstances that have shaped him. In an essay in this book Professor S. F. Moore states that it is incorrect to contrast too sharply, as I tended to do in an earlier publication,[37] the ideas of strict liability which I took to be implicit in the law of feuding societies, and generally in the occult beliefs of tribal societies, with the ideas on liability and responsibility which I took to be characteristic of the law of a modern Western industrial society. Her comments and those of other colleagues convince me that I then went too far. I perhaps under-stated the extent to which, in many tribal situations (including some I reported from Barotse trials), enquiry is made into the alleged actual state of mind of a party before the court, where motives are inferred as the only reasonable interpretation of the evidence. I should too have taken account of what I have cited above from Evans-Pritchard: *viz.* that a Zande cannot plead that witchcraft made him commit adultery, theft or treason. Let me say that, in my argument about a movement from strict liability to increasing enquiry into individual motivation, I did not assert that either system of law had the one without the other. I stated that there was a movement, not a complete achievement. And for that statement I quoted authorities in jurisprudence who had seen a general movement away from strict liability as marking the development of law. I have not space, even were I competent, to set out here all the complications involved. Yet I venture to assert that those authorities' opinions still stand, though there are a number of offences in modern Anglo-American law where strict liability, even without culpability, prevails. And H. L. A. Hart in his recent collection of essays on *Punishment and Responsibility* (1968) still emphasizes such a development. He says that strict liability has '. . . acquired such odium among Anglo-American lawyers' (p. 136), and that it '. . . appears as a sacrifice of a valued principle . . .' (p. 152; see also *passim*). The principle was little questioned in early European, or in tribal, law. Hence I consider I am justified in continuing to regard concentration on the circumstances of the individual criminal as a strengthening trend in legal philosophy, and criminology, and perhaps even in the law.

This trend has culminated in a paradoxical form, propagated by some of the most liberal of criminologists, such as Professor Lady Wootton. They argue that strict liability should be determined for all offences as a first stage in trial, where a man may be found to have committed some wrongful action, but that the fixing of responsibility or culpability should be eliminated at this stage. If it be found that the accused has committed the action complained of, then there should follow an enquiry into him as an individual and into the specific circumstances of his case, to lead to a determination of whether and how he should be punished or treated. This doctrine seems to me to present an extreme view, a view in which the social concomitants of a crime are radically separated from the individual found to have committed the crime (here one cannot speak of him as being found 'guilty' of the crime).

But I am here dealing with trends in disputation about the nature of criminal responsibility, and about the form and function of retributive and deterrent punishment as against remedial treatment. As Hart says, ours '. . . is morally a plural society . . .' (p. 171): different people hold different views on these problems. I can only suggest, as a problem for research, that it might be fruitful to try to work out how far the holders of the so-called more liberal views are the most socially mobile members of society and hence those least enmeshed in networks of close relationships with a limited number of others (the opposite situation from that of members of tribal society). I have not been able to trace work on this point, though we know that where people are involved in close-knit networks they tend to have similar views on offences, as against those whose networks are less closely knit.

At least I may say, in raising this problem, that theories which argue towards a 'diminished responsibility' for the criminal, and regard him as a sick product of society and of his own personal and social circumstances, stand sharply distinct from the kind of beliefs about the responsibility of people towards their fellows which are implicit in beliefs of witchcraft and ancestral indignation. Under these beliefs, ill-feeling alone is endowed with power to do harm. These new theories may be *one* potential logical end—which will never be attained—of a separation of the individual from complete dependence on his kin, a dependence which produces high moral evaluation of all his actions and all his feelings. The modern tendency contrasts sharply with the situation in Africa from which I started. In Africa you break with your own kin only with difficulty and at high cost. There restriction of opportunities keeps you in competition as well as co-operation with your kin; and hence, I suggest, a high ambivalence in all social relationships invests these relationships with occult fears as well as hopes.

I suggest too that the Greek concept of *moira*, a man's fate, may be understood in this light. In his Frazer lecture on *Oedipus and Job in West African Religion* (1959), Professor Fortes considered West African beliefs in the Pre-natal Destiny which an individual is held to select before birth and which determines his fate. Among the Tallensi of Ghana this Pre-natal Destiny may be evil, preventing a woman from having children and a man from becoming a true man. Fortes says the belief is used to explain why an individual fails 'to fulfil the roles and achieve the performance regarded as normal for his status in the social structure'. The failure is irremediable if ritual redressive action has failed to alter his or her circumstances, and hence destiny. Fortes argues that a Pre-natal Destiny 'could best be described as an innate disposition that can be realized for good or ill'. The victim of an evil Destiny is held to have rejected society itself: '. . . this is not a conscious or deliberate rejection, since the sufferer is not aware of his predisposition until he learns it through divination . . . The fault lies in his inescapable, inborn wishes' (pp. 68–9), expressed when he selected his Destiny before he was born. Fortes compares this belief with the fate or lot of Oedipus, a moral man condemned from birth to two heinous crimes. Under such beliefs an individual is morally responsible for the occult determination of his own fate, and its moral crisis, even if he does his best to evade that fate. This occult exaggeration of moral responsibility stands at the opposite extreme from arguments to exculpate the individual by diminishing his moral responsibility for the crisis he has caused, and instead focusing blame on personal circumstance and conflicts within society.

[1965]

Notes

1 Delivered at Exeter College, Oxford, on 18 and 25 February, 1965. The text has been left in lecture form.
2 I use 'occult' following Turner and Fortes, rather than 'mystical' as I did in earlier work, following Evans-Pritchard, because 'mystical' has other meanings. 'Occult' emphasizes that hidden forces are at work.
3 *The Judicial Process among the Barotse* (1955, 1967).
4 Epstein, 'Injury and liability in African customary law in Zambia' (1969), and Introduction to book in which that essay was published.
5 *The Context of Belief* (1957).
6 It seems to me that this point is overlooked by Horton ('Ritual man in Africa', 1964) in his approach to theories which take this into account, but taken up in his later 'African traditional thought and Western science' (1967).
7 In his general study of *Kinship and the Social Order* (1969), at p. 238*n*, Fortes cites, from my *Judicial Process among the Barotse* (1955, p. 154), this song in reference to the deep conflicts within kinship amity, and their connections with suspicions and accusations of witchcraft and sorcery.
8 Durkheim's contention in *De la Division du travail social* (1893) is examined in Moore's essay in this book.
9 *The Organization from Within* (1961), pp. 3–40.
10 For material on the Zulu I depend partly on my own field research in 1936–8, partly on a working through of a mass of literary records in my doctoral thesis on 'The realm of the supernatural among the South-eastern Bantu' (Oxford, 1936). There I also covered literature on Mpondo, Xhosa and Tsonga (Thonga): see especially Junod, *The Life of a South African Tribe* (1927), on Tsonga; for later work on Mpondo, Hunter, *Reaction to Conquest* (1936), and on the Xhosa, Wilson *et al.*, *Keiskammahoek Rural Survey* (1952). On *Swazi*, Kuper has written a most illuminating play, *A witch in my heart* (1970), with the background of her *An African Aristocracy* (1947).
11 I have written this account of the Zulu in the analytic present; but by

'nowadays' in the above sentence I referred to the period when I worked in Zululand (1936–8). This kind of reaction by the extended family to the conditions of labour migration was widely reported from many tribes of South and Central, and indeed other parts of, Africa. Sansom discusses the situation in a South African tribe where the extended family has lost this role (see his essay in this book). I continue my analysis of the indigenous system in the analytic present.

12 In 1950 I named this well known system 'the house–property complex' in my 'Kinship and marriage among the Zulu of Natal and the Lozi of Northern Rhodesia'. There is a fine account in Kuper, *An African Aristocracy* (1947).

13 *Lineage Organization in South-eastern China* (1958), pp. 134–5.

14 Cf. Leach, *Rethinking Anthropology* (1961), chapter 1, on the complex variations in beliefs about maternal and paternal contributions to the child.

15 Junod, *Life of a South African Tribe* (1927), ii, pp. 541*f*.

16 See Peters' essay in this book, and his 'No time for the supernatural' (1963).

17 See discussion of the work of Mitchell, Turner and Middleton below, and also Van Velsen, *The Politics of Kinship* (1964).

18 See Gluckman, 'Les Rites de passage' (1962) and, for other elaborations and background, *Custom and Conflict in Africa* (1955) and *Law, Politics and Ritual in Tribal Society* (1965).

19 The situation of the members of this triad is well discussed in Marwick, *Sorcery in its Social Setting* (1965), *passim*. Any one of them may have broken a rule.

20 I have discussed the way in which customs 'exaggerate' biological and other differences among men and women, and between them, in the works cited in note 18.

21 Nadel, *Nupe Religion* (1954), pp. 180–1. Nadel also refers the beliefs to psycho-sexual processes, in a manner discussed by Devons and Gluckman in the Conclusion to *Closed Systems and Open Minds* (1964), pp. 251*f*.

22 'Witch beliefs and social structure' (1951). For background see her *Reaction to Conquest* (1936) and *Good Company* (1951).

23 Kuper's play *A witch in my heart* (1970) deals with the plight of a barren woman among the Swazi.

24 Well described in Richards, *Land, Labour and Diet in Northern Rhodesia* (1940).

25 'Oral sorcery among the natives of Bechuanaland' (1934).

26 *Lugbara Religion* (1960); page references in parentheses in the text are to this work. For a more general account see his *The Lugbara of Uganda* (1965).

27 *The Yao Village* (1956); subsequent page references in parentheses in

the text are to this work. The development of the new mode of analysis is discussed in my 'Ethnographic data in British social anthropology' (1961) and in Epstein (ed.), *The Craft of Social Anthropology* (1967).

28 *Sorcery in its Social Setting* (1965): subsequent page references in parentheses in the text are to this work.

29 'Witch beliefs in Central Africa' (1967).

30 *Schism and Continuity in an African Society* (1957).

31 The case material below is cited from P. J. Bohannan, *Justice and Judgment among the Tiv* (1951), and most of the accounts of *tsav* from P. J. and L. Bohannan, *The Tiv of Central Nigeria* (1953), pp. 34, 82, 84–6.

32 On this general point see Frankenberg's essay in this book and his *Village on the Border* (1957).

33 *Witchcraft, Oracles and Magic* . . . (1937), at p. 43: Dr Elaine Baldwin drew my attention to this point, which I had overlooked, like most commentators on the book.

34 *Divinity and Experience* (1961).

35 *The Organization from Within* (1961). The other studies of non-family organizations in the book also illustrate the argument I make.

36 Bott, *Family and Social Network* (1957), discusses the coincidence of moral norms held by, and normal judgments made by, persons with what she termed a 'close-knit' network', i.e. with kin closely resident together. I have considered the illumination which her analysis throws on to the beliefs of tribal society in my Preface to the second edition of her book (1967).

37 *The Ideas in Barotse Jurisprudence* (1967), chapter VII.

Bibliography

Bohannan, P. J., *Justice and Judgment among the Tiv*, London: Oxford University Press for the International African Institute (1957).

Bohannan, P. J. and L., 'The Tiv of central Nigeria', *Ethnographic Survey of Africa*, ed. C. D. Forde, *Western Africa*, Part VIII, London: International African Institute (1953).

Bott, E., *Family and Social Network*, London: Tavistock (1957, 1971).

Buxton, L. H. D. (ed.), *Custom is King: Essays presented to Richard Ranulph Marett*, London: Hutchinson (1936).

Devons, E., and Gluckman, M., 'Conclusion' to *Closed Systems and Open Minds*, ed. M. Gluckman, Edinburgh: Oliver & Boyd; Chicago: Aldine Press (1964).

Douglas, M., 'Witch beliefs in Central Africa', *Africa*, XXXVII (1967), pp. 72–80.

Durkheim, E., *De la Division du travail social*, Paris: Alcan (1893). Translated by G. Simpson as *The Division of Labour*, Glencoe, Ill.: Free Press (1933).

Epstein, A. L., 'Injury and liability in African customary law in Zambia' in *Ideas and Procedures in African Customary Law*, ed. M. Gluckman London: International African Institute (1969).

Epstein, A. L. (ed.), *The Craft of Social Anthropology*, London: Tavistock (1967).

Evans-Pritchard, E. E., *Witchcraft, Oracles and Magic among the Azande*, Oxford: Clarendon Press (1937).

Fauconnet, P., *La Responsabilité*, Paris: Alcan (1928).

Forde, C. D., *The Context of Belief: a Consideration of Fetishism among the Yako*, Liverpool: Liverpool University Press (1957).

Fortes, M., *Oedipus and Job in West African Religion*, Cambridge: Cambridge University Press (1959).

—'Religious premises and logical techniques in divinatory ritual', *Philosophical Transactions of the Royal Society of London* (1966), pp. 409–22.

—*Kinship and the Social Order: the Legacy of Lewis Henry Morgan*, Chicago: Aldine (1969).

Fortes, M., and Evans-Pritchard, E. E. (ed.), *African Political Systems*, London: Oxford University Press for the International African Institute (1940).

Frankenberg, R. J., *Village on the Border*, London: Cohen & West (1957).

Freedman, M., *Lineage Organization in South-eastern China*, L.S.E. *Monographs on Social Anthropology* No. 18, London: Athlone Press (1958).

Gluckman, M., 'Zulu women in hoe culture ritual', *Bantu Studies*, IX (1935).

—'The realm of the supernatural among the south eastern Bantu, D.Phil. thesis, Oxford University, 1936.

—'Analysis of a social situation in modern Zululand', *Bantu Studies* (1940) and 'Some processes of social change illustrated with Zululand data', *African Studies*, 1942, republished as *Analysis of a Social Situation in Modern Zululand*, Rhodes-Livingstone Paper No. 28, Manchester: Manchester University Press for the Rhodes-Livingstone Institute (1958).

—'Kinship and marriage among the Zulu of Natal and the Lozi of Northern Rhodesia' in *African Systems of Kinship and Marriage*, ed. A. R. Radcliffe-Brown and C. D. Forde, London: Oxford University Press for the International African Institute (last section reprinted and *Postscript* on recent work in *Reader on Marriage*, ed. J. Goody, Harmondsworth, Penguin Books (1971).

—*Custom and Conflict in Africa*, Oxford: Blackwell (1955).
—*The Judicial Process among the Barotse of Northern Rhodesia*, Manchester: Manchester University Press for the Rhodes-Livingstone Institute (1955; second, enlarged edition 1967).
—'Ethnographic data in British social anthropology', *Sociological Review*, n.s. vol. 9, No. 1 (1961).
—'Les Rites de passage' in *Essays on the Rituals of Social Relations*, ed. M. Gluckman, Manchester: Manchester University Press (1962).
—*The ideas in Barotse jurisprudence*, New Haven: Yale University Press (1965, second edition Manchester University Press, 1971).
—*Politics, Law and Ritual in Tribal Society*, Oxford: Blackwell; Chicago: Aldine Press; New York: Mentor Books (1965).
Hart, H. L. A. *Punishment and Responsibility*, Oxford: Clarendon Press (1968).
Horton, R. 'African traditional thought and Western science', *Africa*, XXVII (1967), pp. 50–72.
—'Ritual man in Africa', *Africa*, XXXIV (1964), pp. 85–104.
Hunter, M. *Reaction to Conquest*, London: Oxford University Press for the International African Institute (1936).
Junod, H. A. *The Life of a South African Tribe*, London: Macmillan (1927).
Kuper, A. *An African Aristocracy: Rank among the Swazi of the Protectorate*, London: Oxford University Press for the International African Institute (1947).
—*A witch in my heart: a play about the Swazi people*, Oxford University Press for the International African Institute (1970).
Leach, E. R., *Rethinking Anthropology*, L.S.E. *Monographs in Social Anthropology*, No. 22, London: Athlone Press (1961).
Lienhardt, G., *Divinity and Experience: the Religion of the Dinka*, Oxford: Clarendon Press (1961).
Marett, R. R., *The Threshold of Religion*, London: Methuen (1900).
Marwick, M. G., *Sorcery in its Social Setting: a Study of the Northern Rhodesian Cewa*, Manchester: Manchester University Press (1965).
Middleton, J., *Lugbara Religion: Ritual and Authority among an East African People*, London: Oxford University Press for the International African Institute (1960).
—*The Lugbara of Uganda*, New York: Holt, Rinehart & Winston (1965).
Middleton, J., and Winter, E. (ed.), *Witchcraft and Sorcery in East Africa*, London: Routledge & Kegan Paul (1960).
Mitchell, J. C., *The Yao Village*, Manchester: Manchester University Press for the Rhodes-Livingstone Institute (1956).
Nadel, S. F., *Nupe Religion*, London: Routledge & Kegan Paul (1954).
Peters, E. L., 'No time for the supernatural', *New Society*, 19 December 1963.

Richards, A. I., *Land, Labour and Diet in Northern Rhodesia*, London: Oxford University Press for the International African Institute (1940).

Schapera, I., 'Oral sorcery among the natives of Bechuanaland' in *Essays presented to C. G. Seligman*, ed. E. E. Evans-Pritchard, R. Firth, B. Malinowski and I. Schapera, London: Routledge (1934), pp. 293–305.

Sofer, C., *The Organization from Within: a Comparative Study of Social Institutions based on a Socio-therapeutic Approach*, London: Tavistock (1961).

Turner, V. W., *Schism and Continuity in an African Society*, Manchester: Manchester University Press for the Rhodes-Livingstone Institute (1957).

Van Velsen, J., *The Politics of Kinship: a Study in Social Manipulation among the Lakeside Tonga of Nyasaland*, Manchester: Manchester University Press for the Rhodes-Livingtone Institute (1964).

Wilson, G. and M., *The Analysis of Social Change*, Cambridge: Cambridge University Press (1945).

Wilson, M., *Good Company*, London: Oxford University Press for the International African Institute (1951), quoted from US edition, Boston: Beacon Press (1963).

—'Witch beliefs and social structure', *American Journal of Sociology*, 56 (1951), pp. 307–13.

Wilson, M., Kaplan, S., Maki, T., and Walton, E. M., *Keiskammahoek Rural Survey*, vol. III: *Social structure*, Pietermaritzburg: Shuter & Shooter (1952).

2
Legal liability and evolutionary interpretation: some aspects of strict liability, self-help and collective responsibility

Sally F. Moore

1. *Introduction: some sherds of the theoretical pot*

When Evans-Pritchard described the Nuer 'tribe' as 'the largest group within which legal obligation is acknowledged', he was using as one of his principal criteria for the definition of a political unit the potential resolution of disputes within it.[1] The implications of this formulation, that law is to be understood in a socio-political framework, go far beyond the operation of acephalous societies. This paper will have a look at some evolutionary conceptions of the trend of legal development in the light of this idea. There are significant differences in the social and political role of legal disputes in different types of societies, though one would never know it from the content of most legal evolutionary schemes. I shall suggest some of these differences.

The issues are apparent when one examines such modes of allocating and enforcing legal responsibility as strict liability, self-help, and collective responsibility. Self-help, particularly when it involves the mobilization of others in one's cause, and collective responsibility, which by definition involves a social aggregate, are particularly clear illustrations of the social and political context in which legal obligations may be set and enforced. Strict liability, usually dealt with by jurists in terms of a presumed primitive legal disregard of motive and intention, is also, as Gluckman has argued, more comprehensible if analysed in terms of its social setting.[2] All three —strict liability, self-help, and collective responsibility—are often thought of as especially characteristic of 'primitive' legal systems. Yet some instances and forms of all three appear in the legal systems of complex societies, and all three appear in quite varied forms in pre-industrial societies.

It is useful to review some of the scholarly contexts in which these ways of dealing with responsibility have been treated as 'primitive'.

An inspection of these contexts makes one aware of those assumptions of various prominent writers about the nature of modern law which cause them to paint its antecedents in appropriate colours. If modern law is conceived as essentially comprised of a set of principles, quite separable from any particular social environment, then legal evolution is treated as the sequential and cumulative development of those principles. As is so often the case in other fields, in law the supposedly primitive is frequently alluded to and used to support certain conceptions of contemporary institutions rather than to explain the institutions of pre-industrial societies. A case in point is Roscoe Pound's *The Spirit of the Common Law* (1921).

There is much that is interesting about the rhetoric of the Anglo-American law, particularly as spoken by its saints. Pound approaches the common law tradition as a genealogy of ideas, and, as in most genealogies, this one is adjustable and is presented as a single unbroken tradition which has succeeded in incorporating innumerable alien ideas 'without disturbing its essential unity . . .'[3] Pound described the stages of legal evolution as four in number. Each was characterized by a different basis for the allocation of liability. Since he put it that 'the staple institutions of primitive society are reprisals, private war and the blood feud', the first stage of legal evolution was that which developed 'composition for the desire to be avenged'.[4] In the second stage the State superseded self-help in all but exceptional cases and the law was characterized as, 'the strict law'.[5] By this Pound meant a highly formal, inelastic and inflexible formal system of rules in which 'the chief end sought is certainty . . . The strict law is indifferent to the moral aspects of conduct or of transactions that satisfy its letters . . . But the strict law gives us as permanent contributions the ideas of certainty and uniformity and of rule and form as means thereto'.[6] The third stage is the stage of equity, or natural law. The watchwords of this period were morality, equity and good conscience. At this stage law is identified with morals, and moral duties become legal duties. Liability is allocated only where there is moral fault. Reason rather than strict adherence to the letter of the rules is relied on to administer justice. 'Aside from liberalization of the law, the permanent contributions of this stage are the conception of good faith and moral conduct to be attained through reason, ethical solution of controversies and enforcement of duties.'[7] The fourth state is a happy marriage of stages three and four with certainty and equity married, 'the watchwords are equality and security'.[8]

Pound also described the modern Anglo-American legal tradition as characterized by 'an extreme individualism' tempered only by 'a tendency . . . to look to relations rather than to legal transactions as the basis of legal consequences'.[9] The individualism is on the equity side of the fourth stage (above); 'relations' are the certainty part. What he meant by individualism was 'unlimited valuation of individual liberty and respect for individual property'.[10] What he meant by 'relations' were such categorical role-pairs as employer–employee, landlord–tenant, debtor–creditor, and so on. These he understood to be statuses. When Pound said that Maine was quite wrong about the shift from status to contract, Pound meant that the rules pertaining to these relationships (or, as he considered them, statuses) fixed duties and liabilities independently of the will of those bound. He does not seem to have realized that Maine explicitly reserved status for familial status, or, better, status in a kinship group. Pound thought in 1921 that the law was about to enter a new, fifth stage of development, a stage of 'socialization of law' in which the interest and protection of the general public rather than the individual would be paramount.[11]

The terms of this evolutionary sequence were and are cliches, categories in general circulation in Anglo-American law. They have strongly affected the theoretical approach of E. A. Hoebel, doyen of American legal anthropologists, whose training was in this tradition. Doctrines which Pound put in evolutionary sequence and saw as accumulating to form the compound of modern law are commonly found in Anglo-American cases as paired opposites. Strict rules yield certainty but are sometimes unfair. Equity gives attention to fairness and morality, but at the expense of legal certainty. The individual must be free to act, but he must also be bound by law, the rules governing social relations. While individual freedom must be preserved and protected, it must not encroach on the public good. The general march of civilization is from the extremes of selfish individual or kin group self-interest (self-help, feud, war) in the direction of taming and curbing such private self-interest in favour of the general public good. This last, as we shall see, is one of the dominant concepts in Hoebel's approach.

That legal systems are not to be understood exclusively in terms of the value-laden principles they invoke, and that adequate description can scarcely be condensed into one principle at a time, anyone would grant today. The tenets which Pound used to characterize stages of legal evolution, and which are frequently cited as the bases of case decisions, are more illuminating, not when taken literally, but rather when studied as a system of categories and legitimating classes, or as ideological aphorisms. Yet the attitudes which this kind of material represents have inevitably affected the choice of problem to which some anthropologists have addressed themselves. If one wants to generalize about the law of pre-industrial society in contrast with our own, there is no escaping the fact that Maine and Durkheim and Pound and Malinowski have already had something to say on the subject, and that they have thought of it in terms of the traditional rationalizations of Western law.

The three modes of allocating responsibility with which this paper will deal—strict liability, self-help and collective responsibility—all fit neatly into Pound's evolutionary sequence. Strict liability fits into Pound's stage of 'strict law', self-help into the prior stage of 'composition for the desire to be avenged', and collective responsibility is by implication assigned a primitive place when Pound cites the Anglo-American emphasis on 'extreme individualism'. I am not arguing that Pound's scheme itself specifically has affected the work of anthropologists, but rather that it is a good representation of certain ideas in the Western legal tradition which have affected anthropology.

For some of the legal evolutionists, self-help epitomizes the dominance of private interests instead of impartial public justice; strict liability suggests insufficient regard for the question of moral fault, hence it too leads to 'injustice', and collective responsibility shows inadequate regard for individual culpability, identifying the guilty with the innocent. In this framework historical changes in legal systems can be perceived as some sort of progress toward 'justice'. And a warm air of self-congratulation suffuses the evolutionary sequence.

Two things are wrong with this traditional jurisprudential way of looking at these problems: first, the social-structural setting of the practices is not given sufficient attention, hence the meaning attributed to them is out of context; second, the practices are taken to epitomize legal principles which are assumed not to exist, or to be of no importance, in complex societies. It is one thing to acknowledge that certain practices have changed. It is another to explain what this means. One anthropologist has gone so far as to say that there are two entirely different types of legal systems, and only two basic ones; those which include collective responsibility as well as individual responsibility, and those in which there is individual responsibility only—liability for one's own acts and one's own acts alone. He then develops a culture and personality explanation of collective liability, and describes the child-rearing practices on which the emotional identification supposedly necessary to collective liability are founded.[12] This is not the place to amplify some of the critical comments I have made on this study previously; its very existence is sufficient to show a way in which evolutionary jurisprudential ideas have found their way into anthropology.[13]

There is a distorted self-image of Western law to which the legal systems of pre-industrial societies frequently are contrasted, blurring the analysis of both. This paper is offered as an attempt towards clarification. It will not turn the evolutionary schemes upside down nor inside out, but will try to re-define the problems involved in the analysis of strict liability, self-help and collective responsibility in such a way as to show the inadequacies of some of the criteria on which these schemes are founded. The phenomena of which they take cognizance exist, but the meanings which they are given are in terms of a traditional conception of our own legal arrangements and their 'opposites' in pre-industrial systems. It is to those meanings that I am addressing myself.

The contention is often made that strict liability for injury and damage characterizes pre-industrial legal systems and that these give little or no attention to the motive behind a damaging act. Elias, and more recently Gluckman, have sought to explain strict liability and modify assumptions about disregard of intention.[14] Gluckman has reinterpreted strict liability in a social context. One of the purposes of this paper is to review some of Gluckman's ideas on this subject. He has sought to expose the logic of strict liability in terms of the way he interprets the structure of those societies he characterizes as 'tribal', and has done so very ingeniously, but in my opinion he has generalized too broadly, and I differ with him on some aspects of his explanation.

Gluckman deals with absolute and strict liability in terms of a time-honoured issue in jurisprudence: the relationship between intention and responsibility. Carrying this theme further, I shall explore a form of liability in which intention is not germane to responsibility—namely collective responsibility. Like strict liability, collective responsibility has figured prominently in evolutionary thinking about law. The two ideas are in fact connected, since attention to individual moral fault and motive, the antithesis of strict liability, is often associated in evolutionary thinking with the supposed modern importance of the individual.

Maine and Durkheim, for example, though their lines of argument were different and their preoccupations various, had in common the extremely important nineteenth century theme that the general movement of legal–historical change was from an emphasis on legal community and collectivity to an emphasis on legal individuality. Maine conceived of primitive society as an 'aggregation of families' modern society as 'a collection of individuals'.[15] In primitive society 'The moral elevation and moral debasement of the individual appear to be confounded with . . . the merits and offences of the group to which the individual belongs.'[16] Durkheim's formulation saw legal development as reflecting a movement of society from a period of cohesion based on uniformity (mechanical solidarity) to a period of cohesion based on differentiation (organic solidarity). In Durkheim's scheme criminal law was antecedent in development to civil law. Any rule-breaking challenged the very basis of cohesion in mechanically solid societies because such societies were founded on likeness and uniformity. Hence, in Durkheim's scheme, public law developed before private law. Civil, or private, law, the restitutive claims of one *individual* against another, were a later development, characteristic of societies whose cohesion was founded on a highly diversified and specialized division of labour. Law was the visible symbol of different kinds of solidarity, the index of social evolution. The shift from social sameness to social individuality epitomized this development.[17]

These ideas have permeated subsequent general discussions of law in anthropology. Whether they are being cited, refuted or amended, they have shaped the direction of many of the generalizations which subsequent generations have made. In *Crime and Custom in Savage Society* (1926) Malinowski tried to turn the Durkheimian evolutionary sequence upside down, and to destroy what he saw as the exaggerated myth of collectivity. The reciprocity of mutual obligations was to serve as a demonstration of the importance of civil obligations in primitive society; the great diversity of individual rights and duties was to show the non-existence of collective ownership. The individuation which Maine and Durkheim saw as the culmination of the legal evolutionary sequence, Malinowski thought he found in the Trobriands.

More recently Hoebel has echoed Malinowski's reversal of the evolutionary sequence. He casts it in terms of 'public' and 'private' law rather than civil and criminal, which latter pair he finds to be merely different degrees of the same thing.[18]

Private law precedes public law in Hoebel's formulation. He describes legal development through the ages as a process in which the special private interests of individuals and their kin groups are gradually subordinated to the interests of society as a whole.[19] This view of the whole movement of legal development must be understood in terms of Pound's heralding of a fifth stage of legal evolution, the 'socialization of law', the progressive broadening of the public interest. Pound had said this in 1921, but by the 1930's and '40's it was not a matter for the future. Emphasis on the public interest was a much invoked legal principle in America in this period and it fitted with the political climate. Hoebel was trained in this general tradition at Columbia Law School, and it appears to have affected strongly his conception of the developmental trend of the law.

For Hoebel law is a matter of culturally determined, enforceable rules, and physical enforcement is the key concept in sorting legal from other norms. Consequently Hoebel sees shifts in the locus of the power to apply force as one of the most significant elements in legal evolution. It moves out of private hands into public hands. Hoebel makes fun of Malinowski for being too tender-hearted to give enough place to force. But in other respects Hoebel follows closely along the lines of Malinowski's reversal of Durkheim. While Durkheim had used 'public law' to mean action on behalf of the collectivity against individual law-breakers, Hoebel uses the term specifically to refer to the development of public officials and formal legal institutions. Part of Hoebel's apparent reversal of Durkheim is due to this difference of definition. Hoebel sees the whole trend of the law as 'one in which the tendency is to shift the privilege rights of prosecution and imposition of legal sanctions from the individual and his kinship group over to clearly defined public officials representing the society as such'.[20] The shift from self-help to official action thus occupies the central position in his conception of legal development, and it is this which he characterizes as the shift from private to public law. In the third and fourth sections of this paper I shall deal with self-help and its relation to collective responsibility, and with the concepts 'public' and 'private' law. There are a number of assumptions worth re-examining in Hoebel's sanguine assertion that 'Private law dominates on the primitive scene'.[21]

If one is going to talk about public and private law, it is useful to define what constitutes a public. In a sociological view of the law, norms are seen as applicable to particular social relationships. They exist in, and are enforceable in terms of, a framework of defined groups, categories, networks and the like. Procedure reflects structure. Hoebel looks at law in terms of cultural norms and certain procedures of enforcement. In his legal postulates he touches only indirectly and peripherally on the systems of social relationship which are the context of the norms and procedures.

M. G. Smith has provided what seems to me for certain problems a very serviceable definition of a public. He makes a 'public' equivalent to a 'corporate group'. Smith's model for comparative politics presumes as the basis of social structure a multiplicity of durable, internally organized social units. These 'corporate groups' or 'publics' he defines as 'enduring, presumably perpetual groups with determinate boundaries and membership, having an internal organization and a unitary set of external relations, an exclusive body of common affairs, and autonomy and procedures adequate to regulate them'.[22] In some societies corporations are all discrete units, in others they overlap or some contain others. The corporations within a society may be structural replicas of one another, or they may have varied rules of internal organization and external relations. Smith asserts that '. . . corporations provide the frameworks of law and authoritative regulation for the societies that they constitute'.[23]

Very much in the same vein as this, much of Smith's corporate model is the formulation of Pospisil, who holds that law is to be understood not as a single system but as a whole series of systems, each pertinent to a particular group, the groups varying in inclusiveness. Thus any individual may be a member of a number of groups and sub-groups and may be simultaneously subject to the legal systems of each.[24]

Using Smith's corporate definition of a public, it is not only possible but necessary for public law to exist in all societies in which there are corporate groups, and one is supplied with a formal framework within which some illuminating comparisons become possible. But as we shall see, it is not a framework adapted to all situations. Since Hoebel defines law in terms of cultural norms rather than in terms of groups, his 'society' knows cultural rather than corporate borders. When he speaks of evolutionary development towards systems having 'public officials representing the society as such', he seems to be thinking of the development of political centralization, and of centralized political entities as equivalent to cultural units. A corporate definition of 'public' permits one to consider the distinction between public and private legal matters in everything from a village in an acephalous society to a sophisticated nation State. What is public in the context of one group may be a private matter in the context of a larger unit which encompasses it. Public law in this definition may exist in the absence of centralization. The limitations of the Smith–Pospisil model emerge only when one deals with certain non-corporate aspects of law.

In contrast to Smith, Pospisil and Gluckman, Hoebel does not focus on groups or their organization. Hoebel's view of law is very much a mixture of three elements: a cultural-pattern normative point of view, an emphasis on physical enforcement, and lastly a general conception of law as settling 'trouble cases', disputes between individuals, or between a rather vaguely conceived 'society' (sometimes in the form of public officials) and individuals. Outside the matter of centralization, politics is not part of it.

My general position is that one of the most important differences among legal systems is in the degree to which 'private' disputes between individuals have potential political or structural importance.[25] Far from agreeing with Hoebel that 'Private law dominates on the primitive scene', this paper will argue that many apparently 'private' disputes between individuals have a much wider range of potential structural importance in pre-industrial societies than do factually comparable disputes in complex societies. The interlocking of the public and private domains, and the relationship between the personal, and political dimensions of disputes, are dramatically demonstrable when one takes a look at self-help and at collective responsibility.[26]

2. *State of mind and strict liability*

Not only in Pound's evolutionary scheme but in many other writings there appears and reappears the notion that absolute or even strict liability for injury or damage is some sort of crude, undiscriminating, primitive legal notion, and that it is far more civilized to take motive into account when assessing liability. Elias (1956) quotes with disapproval a passage where Lowie had said, in 1920, 'after all qualifications are made, it remains true that the ethical motive of an act is more frequently regarded as irrelevant in the ruder cultures than in our own courts of justice'.[27] Elias seeks to redress the balance by showing that in many African law cases *mens rea*, motive and intention play a major part in the outcome.[28]

A comparative judgment of the sort Lowie made ought to be supported by comparative data if one is to pay attention to it. One need do no more than refer to the existence of a whole range of American cases arising from Workmen's Compensation to cases involving certain forms of negligence to show that attention to motive is by no means relevant to liability in Western law. In fact Seavey describes the Western legal tradition in terms of oscillations between, and balancings of, two contradictory principles:

The first concept requires that one who engages in an activity, employs others, or controls things should be liable for harm caused by his activities, agencies or things, even though he is without fault. The second requires that a person whose conduct is not wrongful should not be required to pay for the harm it causes.[29]

The first principle is said to protect the security of individuals, the second protects their freedom of action. Like many other writers, Seavey too says (p. 378), 'The primitive law stressed security.'

While Gluckman accepts the view that strict liability is characteristic of much of the African law of injury, he argues that the mental elements of an offence are nevertheless always taken into account, even when this is not explicit. Intention and motivation are 'presumed to be what a reasonable man in those social circumstances would have felt.'[30] I interpret his discussion to mean that it is not necessarily the actual thoughts and intentions of the individual that are significant but some legal measure of his motivation. This legal assessment of motive is founded on a reasonable interpretation of the event at issue and the surrounding circumstances.

These *may* include actual motive, but Gluckman argues that a far more important element in tribal societies is the relative social position of the protagonists.

Gluckman illustrates his argument about the fundamental relevance of social relationship to legal liability by citing the Nuer rules on homicide as given by Evans-Pritchard and Howell.[31] (See discussion in section 3 of this paper of Peters's revisionist view of the segmentary lineage model.) Gluckman examines the outcome in three different circumstances: where the killer and his victim belonged to two different 'tribes', where the two belonged to more closely related 'vengeance groups', and last, where both parties were members of the same 'vengeance group'. In the first instance, a killing between tribes, compensation was not paid, and the outcome was likely to be a retaliatory killing, since a chronic state of feud prevailed between tribes. Here Gluckman says intention is imputed to the slayer from the social situation itself. 'It is assumed,' he says, 'that if a man kills a member of a group with which his own group is at feud . . . that he must have done so deliberately . . . intention is presumed from action.'[32] In the second Nuer situation, in that range of inter-group relationships in which compensation is paid, liability is absolute. For any homicide, there must be a compensatory payment. But the intention of the killer is relevant to the *extent* of liability. In the third situation, in which a Nuer kills a kinsman, no compensation can be paid, because those who are legally obliged to pay are the same people who would receive the payment.[33] However, the killer must undergo ritual purification. Here it would seem that intention is quite irrelevant to the liability question. It is out of this Nuer material that Gluckman constructs his initial critical argument.

Far from dealing with explicit attention to actual motive as if it represented some kind of intellectual advance, Gluckman simply assumes that there must be a logic to strict liability in the social context in which it occurs, just as there must be a logic to attention to specific motive in the situations and societies in which this is the emphasis. He does not place any higher value on attention to actual motive than on disregard of it. Instead he is looking for the functional relationship between social structure and the rules by which liability is allocated. So far, so good. However, it is with Gluckman's ultimate, more general remarks that I disagree.

Gluckman contrasts the law of tribal societies, 'in which the law emphasized duty to others, with strict liability in transaction and injury', with the law of more technologically developed societies, which he sees as putting the 'onus on the plaintiff to prove that he had a right to expect a duty from the defendant'.[34] He sees this shift as part of the general change from societies dominated by a model of kinship relationships to a situation dominated by a model of ephemeral social relationships. He sees the complex interdependence of persons in small-scale societies as putting people in certain social relationships under a special burden to be careful in their dealings with one another, even in their thoughts about one another. Gluckman extends to the area of injury and responsibility the emphasis on obligation and good faith in transactions which he finds characteristic of societies dominated by kin relationships.[35] He speaks of the general position of African law as 'applying strict liability arising out of duty to avoid harming others'.[36]

In my opinion, on the complex society side Gluckman has not sufficiently taken into account the existence of strict liability in our own society, its various *raisons d'être*, and the many strict rules which govern what Pound described as 'relations' (landlord–tenant, debtor–creditor, employer–employee, etc), rules which apply in Western law irrespective of the will or motive or intentions of the parties to these 'relations'. This passing rapidly over the question of intention in Western law would not matter if it were not for the fact that a great deal of his speculative argument (as opposed to his direct analysis of the African data) is founded on a dramatic contrast between tribal and large-scale societies.

Second, the duty to avoid harming others from which at one point he says strict liability arises[36] seems to me to be a doctrine inferred by Gluckman rather than coming directly out of the material.

Another rationale might serve better. It seems to me that strict liability, in so far as it results from the general conditions of tribal life, can be more economically explained by interpreting it as a means of assuaging the resentment of those who have been injured or damaged in a social situation in which injurer and injured must go on in a continuing social relationship. A rule that the agency of misfortune pays for it does not necessarily imply special moral or legal duties which have not been fulfilled. But there is good reason why Gluckman finds 'the duty to avoid harming others' a more attractive explanation. It resolves a paradox.

The puzzle that Gluckman set himself grows out of the fact that initially he chose to discuss the problem of legal responsibility in terms of the time-honoured differentiation between an intentional wrong and an accidental or negligent wrong. He seeks the logic of a system which emphasizes state of mind to an extreme point in some contexts and apparently disregards it in others. He cites a number of instances of injury in tribal settings in which a man's intention is not investigated, and only his action is taken into account and liability is absolute.

He contrasts these with the treatment of witchcraft beliefs in which, at times, not action but mere thoughts or feelings may be culpable. How, he asks, is this paradox to be understood, that in the same society state of mind weighs so heavily in the one case, yet is quite passed over in the other? In the very same tribal systems in which absolute and strict liability appears as a significant feature, so does the belief in witchcraft, and not infrequently in witchcraft cases people are held legally responsible for state of mind, or mere intention alone. Gluckman resolves the paradox by inferring a legal doctrine that will embrace both kinds of case: the duty not to harm, either by deed or immoral feeling.[37] This duty rationalizes strict liability for harmful acts irrespective of intention, and at the same time rationalizes legal responsibility for mere intention. He has ingeniously reconciled seemingly disparate rules by constructing an inclusive, overriding doctrine.

But can one define in general terms a duty to avoid harming certain others that is special to kin-based societies? One might guess that some such vague general precept is socially universal, and yet that in every society it is also subject to some important exceptions. What evidence is there of a special obligation to avoid harming others in what Gluckman calls 'tribal' societies? How does this special obligation differ from the general condition that all social life requires some control of hostile and aggressive feelings? And if it exists, what is the relationship of this special obligation to strict liability?

In this matter Gluckman's reasoning is similar to that of a common law judge applying principles like those enunciated in Pound's third stage of legal evolution. Every liability is read back as incurred through some moral fault, through the breach of a matching moral duty. This *may* be the way some African societies reason out their rules, but I would contend that this cannot be inferred from the existence of the liability itself. One can rationalize liability for thoughts that harm and liability for unintentional harm by concluding simply that anyone who causes harm must pay for it, by whatever means it was caused. That does not mean that there is an especially extensive duty not to harm. It just means that there is a broad duty to pay.

When Gluckman speaks of strict liability as arising from 'the duty to avoid harming others in thought or deed'[38] he is by implication connecting strict liability with his idea that there is a general intensification of moral responsibility in tribal society, founded on the nature of multiplex social relationships. I would argue that at best the supposed duty not to harm is only one side of the picture, and that it is useful to consider the possible connections between strict liability and the habit of using force. For example, consider where the 'duty to avoid harming others' fits in with the following statements of Evans-Pritchard:

As Nuer are very prone to fighting, people are frequently killed. Indeed it is rare that one sees a senior man who does not show marks of club or spear . . . A Nuer will at once fight if he considers that he has been insulted, and they are very sensitive and easily take offence . . . From their earliest years children are encouraged by their elders to settle all disputes by fighting, and they grow up to regard skill in fighting the most necessary accomplishment and courage the highest virtue.[39]

One gathers from Howell that what the Nuer emphasize is not care lest they harm one another, but between killing in a fair fight (*nak*) and killing by stealth or ambush (*biem*).[40] Howell says,

self-help and retaliation are still common enough in Nuerland. There is still little restraint put on the actions of the young and hot-blooded by a body of public opinion consciously opposed to bloodshed as a moral wrong. Nuer will admit that homicide is wrong (*duer*) [a word which also means 'mistake'[41]] and that fighting is undesirable, but this is because they realise that these lead to a most uncomfortable state of insecurity. Nuer are always acutely conscious of the need for social cohesion. There is, however, very little expression of an unfavourable reaction to the taking of life in the abstract, and homicide is not considered a crime against society. On the other hand, what we call 'cold-blooded murder', which is extremely rare, offends Nuer ideas of morality because the victim has had no chance to defend himself. It is the Nuer code of honour which has been contravened. People are profoundly shocked in these circumstances, a feeling which extends well beyond those who by reason of their relationship to the deceased are expected to take a vindictive attitude towards the killer and his kinsmen.[42]

Nor are the Nuer alone in such truculent habits. Smith and Dale say of the Ila, 'Quarrels are of frequent occurrence in a village, specially when the men are heated by drinking much beer during a feast. Free fights take place with sticks and spears'.[43] They then describe the strict liability of one who kills another. Elsewhere (at p. 350) they speak of how men enlisted the aid of their most combative friends when a claim was to be pressed through self-help. Gulliver tells us of the Arusha, the agricultural Masai of northern Tanzania,

> . . . most homicide occurs as a result of fights arising out of quarrels, often drunken brawls, for men are prone in this society to resort to individual violence. *Murran* habitually carry swords and spears, and all men usually carry a heavy stick; and they are all inclined to use them readily. Although a fight may occur between men who have a long-standing and bitter quarrel, which is the root cause of it, I am not aware of an instance where a man has cold-bloodedly planned to kill his opponent; and in many instances the two men seem to have had little or no previous ill-will . . . Whether the act was premeditated, in self-defence, the result of accident or uncontrolled temper, etc, is irrelevant to the settlement processes, although people distinguish these cases from an ethical point of view.[44]

Unlike the Nuer, the Arusha did not at the time of observation practise self-help or vengeance in homicide cases. Even of the peaceable Tallensi, Fortes reports 'They are quick to resent a trespass on their rights and readily snatch up a weapon or a missile if they are provoked.'[45] He attributes much of the suppression of fighting to the presence of the British colonial administration.[46] Hence violent inclinations are not attributable simply to the simultaneous exigencies of self-help, though they may be historically related.

In every respect the Nuer and the Ila, the Arusha and the Tallensi meet Gluckman's definition of a tribal society, of the kind of close, small-scale, technologically simple, kin-based structure he has in mind. How does this material on aggressiveness and fighting fit in with Gluckman's contention that an especially strict duty to avoid harming others in certain social relationships is a necessary consequence of the conditions of life in a tribal society?

One would, it seems, also have to infer from the material on fighting an obligation to be extremely vigilant against any encroachment on one's honour or rights, and an accompanying readiness to protect these by force. The duty to be on the ready and the duty not to harm would seem to have quite conflicting effects—which does not, of course, mean that they could not exist together. Man is not over-given to consistency, particularly in matters of principle. But can one explain strict liability in terms of a duty not to harm without paying close attention to the concurrent attitude that exists in some societies that one must be ever on the alert and ready forcefully to protect one's interests?

Some instances of strict liability in tribal societies can perhaps be most simply explained by arguing, as I did earlier, that in certain social situations the resentment of the injured or damaged must be assuaged if social relations are to go on, whether or not the injurer was apparently at fault. Perhaps one should also think of strict liability in some cases as more like insurance than like punitive damages. Either of these possible explanations seem to me to be congruent with the conditions of life in tribal societies, and neither requires the postulation of any absolute duty not to harm to support it. They also apply as conveniently to social relations between groups as within them. Both these explanations fit particularly well in societies in which touchiness about insult or injury is part of every man's stance. There is a difference between being obliged to pay for any harm one causes and having an absolute duty not to harm.

The invariable pairing of duty and liability is a kind of common law reasoning which certainly occurs outside the Anglo-American tradition. But it is not universal, nor is it by any means the only basis for the allocation of legal liability, even in our own system. Moral fault is not the basis of all liability. By inferring a stringent duty not to harm, Gluckman is assuming a special moral element to explain a special liability. But absolute and strict liability may simply emphasise causality, not necessarily morality.

If one imagines a restraining duty not to harm at one end of the stick, the right to resort to retaliation and self-help would seem to be the other end, since this involves the condoned use of force by persons who perceive themselves as injured or damaged or insulted. It involves at least the risk, if not the intention, of doing harm.

Though I have indicated my reservations about Gluckman's idea that an especially stringent duty not to harm exists in certain social relationships in all tribal societies, and that it is closely connected with strict liability, I have no doubt that there is some form of restraining doctrine in all societies. Even in self-help systems there are clear limitations on sanctioned violence. One must not harm *except* to right a wrong, or even a score, and then only in prescribed ways and circumstances. There is no way to prove that there is a historical connection between self-help and strict liability, but it seems to me that there is a logical connection. In a system in which there is a good deal of freedom of action to use force in one's own interest, abuse of that freedom may be somewhat curtailed by the knowledge that everyone must pay for the consequences of his actions and that the plea of accident or good intention will not excuse one. Strict liability may be the counterpart of the right to use force (or the habit of using force) in some of the social contexts in which it appears. That strict liability has other forms and other reasons for existence in the same and other contexts is also undoubtedly true. I have no doubt that Gluckman is right about many situations in which strict liability is tied to on-going social relationships in tribal society. My reservations about his argument refer essentially to the notion that strict liability carries with it a special duty not to harm, and Gluckman has agreed that he would now speak only in terms of a strict duty to pay, not in terms of a strict duty not to harm.[47]

3. *Self-help and the principle of expanding disputes*

Self-help has at least three important qualities. The first, already indicated, is that it is undertaken in the *name of right*. It is not forceful action admittedly embarked upon solely for naked advantage. It is rationalized with an argument about the protection of rights, the collection of what is due, or the avenging of (or retaliation for) a wrong. A second quality is that self-help is the *intransigent side of conciliation*. Disputes in systems of self-help can be resolved if both parties are willing to do so. Furthermore they can usually find a structural rationale for doing so, not only moral and pragmatic reasons. In other words, societies in which self-help is a widely used form of enforcement normally have well-established conciliation procedures and well-established ideological frameworks which support both conciliation and fighting.

'Self-help' sounds too much as if it always meant enforcement action by a single individual on his own behalf. While the term covers this case, societies characterized as having systems of self-help usually permit the mobilization of a number of persons in an individual's cause, given suitable circumstances. A third, significant quality of systems of self-help thus lies in the consequent *expandability of certain disputes* and the *containment* of others. Some disputes remain disputes between individuals. Other disputes over exactly the same substantive matters expand into confrontations of groups. At that point self-help becomes entangled with collective liability. As we shall see, where the enforcement of rights and the avenging of wrongs has a collective aspect, so do responsibility and liability ordinarily have their collective aspects.

Limitations are frequently placed on the use of self-help in particular relationships. Fortes' scattered material on debt among the Tallensi is a good illustration of; (1) the corporate conceptual framework of a group-backed self-help; (2) the extension for particular purposes of inside-the-corporate-unit status to certain groups and individuals outside the corporate group, i.e. the disregard of corporate borders for certain purposes; and (3) the margin of flexibility and adjustment within the Tallensi theoretical framework.[48]

Fortes tells us that in pre-colonial times the Tallensi 'tolerated the use of violence as the proper ultimate means of asserting one's rights' and that 'This attitude still survives to some extent.'[49] However, group raiding as a mode of self-help against a debtor was not proper within the clan, between linked clans, or between persons in certain kinship relationships.[50] Hence clan-linking gave the equivalent of internal standing to external corporate groups in the matter of debt enforcement. Though raiding was not itself an act of war, it often led to war if men were killed. In short, raiding as a form of self-help was an approved method of redress only between groups and members of groups in general hostile opposition, irrespective of the facts of the case of the debt itself.

Inside a Tallensi nuclear lineage or an expanded family or between close cognates, borrowing did not give rise to 'debts'. Yet there was an implicit obligation to reciprocate and repay goods or services in some form later on, and if repayment were not forthcoming counter-'borrowing' by the 'creditor' might be used to collect the obligation.[51] Yet this counter-'borrowing', a very polite form of self-help, was in no way comparable to the violent kind of armed raiding by a group of kinsmen which might attend the collection of a debt outside the clan.[52]

It was also a Tallensi rule that mother's brother and sister's son, though they were supposed to be involved in a life-long exchange of gifts and services, could not contract debts toward each other.[53] Like the instance of linked clans, this is a case in which persons outside the corporate group were accorded internal status in regard to particular kinds of transactions. What was being granted was not membership in a corporation but quasi-status for certain defined purposes.

This kind of legal manipulation of corporate borders is very common in kin-based societies, and in the self-help context it is particularly interesting because it suggests that in self-help 'systems' alternative modes of social control are operative in those relationships in which armed, group-backed self-help is disapproved. Fortes tells us that, among other things, a defaulter in those relationships found it difficult to borrow again.[54] In the Tallensi case such group-backed self-help evidently was disapproved in those very relationships in which there were likely to be the greatest number of property transactions. In section 4 on collective responsibility, I shall have more to say about complementary systems of social control, about 'moral' obligations *versus* 'legal' obligations, and about the different modes of enforcing obligations and allocating responsibility which each implies. For the moment, I shall confine myself to the forced meeting of liabilities by means of self-help.

Despite the existence of theoretical rules about which Tallensi relationships do give rise to debts and which relationships do not, Fortes tells us that in fact 'what happens in practice varies from case to case and from lineage to lineage'.[55] Certain very close relationships seem to have unambiguously precluded 'debt', but beyond that immediate circle of close kinsmen there seems to have been some option about definition. The persons involved could consider either the transaction or the relationship as governing the definition of their dealings as a loan or debt, depending upon the way they chose to interpret the situation. Presumably the relationships between and among clans also shifted over time, and debt relationships could be re-defined in terms of changes in alignment or *vice versa*.

It would seem from Fortes' material itself that considerations other than simple theoretical rules about relative social positions governed the actual outcome of particular transactions. The fact that self-help in its more violent forms was suppressed by the colonial power leaves the details unknown for the Tallensi. But the general outlines seem clear enough. A theoretical framework of social alignments existed. Disputes between individuals could expand into fights between groups. Expanded disputes over debts took place between the same sets of allies who chronically made war on one another in other contexts as well. Within each aggregation of allies, disputes over obligations also took place but were not supposed to expand into confrontations of groups lest the alliances be severed. Inter-personal violence between kinsmen or allies was disapproved, though it existed.[56]

There is very definite information in other ethnographic sources on the containment of in-group disputes. For example, when a fight broke out between two men in a Nuer village, no third person was supposed to take sides.[57] In this way the fight was limited and not allowed to extend beyond the original participants. The alignment of partisans below a certain level could not be allowed vigorous or violent expression unless segmentation were imminent. This is true not only of the violent fights of the Nuer but also of partisanship in more peaceful confrontations in systems in which group-supported self-help is disapproved. Gulliver indicates that among the Arusha (who have a dispute-expanding process but among whom group self-help is forbidden) in a dispute between members of an inner lineage (offspring of one father) the concern of the other members is only in achieving a reconciliation. There is supposed to be no taking of sides. Gulliver explains this on the grounds that 'in practice the number of men in an inner lineage is too small to allow segmentation whilst yet retaining its unity'.[58] It would appear from the Nuer example that a group need not be nearly as small as an Arusha inner lineage to take measures to prevent internal segmentation.

The general conclusion which the Tallensi, Nuer and Arusha examples suggest is that the principle of the expandable dispute, so important in legal enforcement between members of different social units, is operative only above a certain minimal organizational level. That level varies from one society to another. This means, in other words, that the principle of expandable dispute need not be consistently applied throughout a social system, but may operate only at specified structural levels. The minimal level of segmentation may vary according to the issue. Sub-segmentation which may be allowed to be manifest in peaceful contexts may not be permitted expression in situations of dispute. Such would seem to be the implication of the Tallensi and Nuer data.

Wars, raids, fueds, fights, seizures and less violent measures all may be forms of self-help in particular cases. In the literature the distinctions among them are variously drawn. Sometimes the terms are distinguished according to the kind of structural unit involved, sometimes according to the style of conducting hostilities, and sometimes—but by no means always—there are differences in the subject matter of the disputes dealt with in these various ways.

Pospisil states vigorously that wars and feuds are extra-legal by their nature, that law is exclusively an intra-group phenomenon because law in his definition exists only where both parties to a dispute are subject to some common authority.[59] He conceives 'authority' very broadly. While Pospisil's definition properly distinguishes certain kinds of structural units from others, and certain modes of resolving disputes from others, it does not follow that dividing the material in this way is the best approach to all problems. Disputes over precisely the same substantive matters may arise between individuals whether they do or do not recognize a common authority. For example, in pre-colonial times among the Nyakyusa, adultery, bad debts, assault, injury and homicide were the subject of violent disputes between individuals of the same villages, between individuals of different villages of the same chiefdom, and between individuals of entirely different chiefdoms.[60] The common features in these disputes provide a good reason for looking at the social context of all the situations in which they occurred, irrespective of any limiting definition of law.

There is another standard distinction which seems far less absolute when one examines the Nyakyusa material. That is the distinction between 'systems' of self-help and 'systems' in which there is an official adjudicative and enforcing machinery to which an individual can have recourse. Monica Wilson's classic description of the Nyakyusa serves to illustrate the fact that self-help and official action ('recognition of a common authority') can operate within the same social structure. They need not be total alternatives.

In minor cases Nyakuyusa disputants would usually settle their differences through conciliation and arbitration. They would ask a respected friend or the village headman to resolve the controversy between them. This method was available not only within a single village but also in quarrels between persons residing in different villages as well. If the headman failed to settle matters, then they went to the senior headman of his side of the chiefdom, thence to the chief of that cluster of villages. Village headmen could not enforce their decisions, but the chief could do so. The cases settled by conciliation were 'mainly disputes over the ownership, destruction or sale of . . . minor property'. A small number of minor accusations of assault or insulting behaviour also were settled in this manner.[61]

Serious injuries to person or property brought more violent responses. A killing was principally the concern of the agnatic lineage of the victim. These kinsmen either killed the slayer or brought him before the chief, who imposed a fine which went to the relatives.[62] It is significant in evaluating the chief's judicial role and the nature of such disputes that the option lay with the victim's kin whether to retaliate or settle. Inter-village adultery cases sometimes blew up into inter-village wars, when the wronged husband and his supporters killed a co-villager of the adulterer in reprisal. Adultery was sometimes a cover for property disputes, as a man from whom something had been stolen or to whom a debt had not been repaid might go to the thief or debtor's village and seize the wife of any village-mate of the man who owed him property.[63]

In pre-European days there appear to have been chronic fights between villages and between chiefdoms.[64] These wars evidently took place in a setting in which there was no total shortage of land in relation to population.[65] Nevertheless, there were boundary disputes, and there was a continuous and regular process in which villages were moved and lands redistributed among them. This suggests that though there may have been no overall shortage of land, there were temporary shortages of socially valuable land, land in particular locations, which may have been the root of some of these inter-village hostilities, even those which were purportedly over debts, wife abductions, killings and the like.

The Nyakyusa situation presents a variety of possibilities for resolving disputes. Individuals could reach agreement with the help of neutral friends. They could have recourse to the mediating services of officials, village headmen, senior headmen, or chiefs.[66] Or they could instead, at least outside the village, choose the course of self-help and use force themselves. Wilson does not indicate whether self-help could ever be used inside the village. 'Most

Nyakyusa would hold that in the old days quarrelsomeness within the village was bad, that towards members of another village of the same chiefdom it was allowable, and towards members of another chiefdom it was good.'[67] Self-help outside the village usually required the mobilization of kinsmen to carry it off. Such action could spill over and involve whole villages in inter-village warfare.

Is it useful to think of the Tallensi and Nyakyusa kinds of expanded dispute as private law, as Hoebel seems to?[68] I think not. Such a view over-emphasizes the dispute between individuals which sparks off the larger confrontation, and it ignores the prior or nascent structural oppositions and competitions between groups which are served by enlarging the dispute.

It seems to me that the characterization of primitive law as private law by Hoebel and others has in part to do with certain prevalent ideas about partisanship and impartiality which have their source in an idealization of our own social structure and legal system. Justice and fairness are conceived as depending upon an impartial evaluation of the rights of disputant parties, or the culpability of wrongdoers, by neutral persons. These neutral persons are public officials who represent 'the law' conceived as the norms and interests of society at large. Self-help seems exactly the opposite of this conception of fairness and justice, since it is the purest partisanship. In these models private and partisan are equated. Moreover, public officials are associated with centralized government and the well-being of all, while private causes are associated with the personal advantage of individuals.[69]

There is an accompanying conception of Western law in which police and public prosecutors are conceived to move on their own against violations of law, like impersonal angels of justice, punishing wrongdoers on behalf of 'society'. In fact, in industrialized societies, even in criminal prosecutions, officials are frequently set in motion by citizens who have suffered some damage or injury and have complained. Thus Evans-Pritchard (citing Peristiany) goes too far when, in the Malinowski tradition, he says of the Kipsigis, 'almost all cases were civil in the old days, for even when a community punished a man, it was always at the instigation of some person he had offended'.[70] This is an equation of civil law with action *instigated* by an offended party. It is in keeping with the position Hoebel takes when he says that 'private law dominates on the primitive scene'.[71]

It is not solely on the instigation of process or the impartiality of proceedings that analysis should be focused if one is trying to decide whether a matter is one of private or public involvement. The question is what kinds of networks, groups or administrative structures are set in motion and what kinds of things they do. When a man invokes the help of others he is likely to avail himself of relationships and structures already existing in terms of other contexts of action. He may mobilize his lineage or his village. He may mobilize local political or religious leaders. His cause then also serves the purposes of others and will reinforce pre-existing groupings, relationships and political positions.

The sociological evaluation of what constitutes a private or a public legal matter depends on the extent of its social effect and its structural importance, not on whether it also serves private interests. Inevitably all public matters—matters connected with the common affairs of corporate units—involve action by individuals, and sometimes that action redounds to their private interest. On the other hand, not all individual action or private controversy has widespread effects. A large area of overlap exists between 'public' and 'private' disputes. Though one can easily identify the polar extremes of public and private matters, many disputes fall somewhere between and one is reduced to identifying their public and private *aspects* rather than allocating the dispute wholly to one realm or the other.

Consequently, I find it completely confusing to use the civil–criminal, private–public dichotomies as a way of characterizing whole systems, or the trend of 'legal evolution' as Durkheim and Hoebel and, by implication, Malinowski have done. There are functional analogues of certain aspects of Western civil and criminal, public and private law in all societies because some of the social problems with which these deal are universal. On cannot characterize whole systems by any of these terms.

In the small corporate groups of pre-industrial societies, and in their relationships with one another, disputes between individuals are far more likely to be disruptive to the social fabric than in impersonal, large-scale societies. In part, this is inherently so because of the small numbers, but it is the more so because of the way in which structurally determined partisan commitments spread the effects of what start as individual disputes. The ways in which that partisanship is determined and the way in which confrontations of partisan collectivities are conducted or prevented constitute a basic aspect of public law in pre-industrial societies.

The question whether a dispute between individuals will be contained between them or will be allowed to expand into a political confrontation depends not so much on the subject of the dispute as on the desirability of the confrontation from the point of view of the social units potentially involved, and on the question whether the rules apply according to which disputes may be expanded, i.e. whether the relative social positions of the parties lend themselves to opposing alignments.

As indicated by the materials cited earlier, the occasions for these confrontations are often personal wrongs against individuals, such as homicide, assault, adultery and unpaid debts. Since the classic work of Evans-Pritchard on the Nuer, the resolution of disputes arising from such wrongs has been said to depend upon the social distances between the disputing parties—in the Nuer case, on their places in the segmentary lineage system.

E. L. Peters has now proposed very convincingly that this conception of the matter requires revision. In a paper on the camel herding Bedouin of Cyrenaica Peters gives many examples of homicides in which the outcome does not fit with the segmentary lineage model. Peters shows how the 'irregularities' are rationalized away and the conceptual model preserved.[72] Like the Nuer, the Bedouin explain that disputes are resolved in terms of the segmentary lineage system, yet for both peoples the reality of behaviour is not always congruent with the segmentary lineage concept. Evans-Pritchard described these disparities as an ideal–real dichotomy.[73] Peters has gone much further and argues that the models of society which people use to explain and rationalize their system are not to be understood as a normative framework.

Peters has cast his material as a critique of over-literal uses of segmentary lineage models. I should like to carry a step further the suggestions in his discussion. Building on Gluckman's earlier work on conflicts[74] and enlarging on Peters' recent contribution, these expandable legal disputes between individuals may be seen *to be serving complex structural ends, and simultaneously to be rationalized in terms of simplified ideological frameworks.*

Instead of proceeding in the conventional way and asking, 'What are the consequences of homicide in X society?' or even going a step further and asking 'What are the legal consequences of a homicide if it involves persons of such and such social positions?' the whole question can be turned around, and one can proceed from a macrocosm to microcosm. If one looks at corporate groups first and asks instead, 'When and under what circumstances do they mobilize as units against each other? What kinds of events may be used (*or not*) as the occasion for confrontations? How are confrontations rationalized?' one is seeing certain incidents between individuals as opportunities for collective action, and one sees in this collective action an element of choice.

Groups are in competition with one another for power and resources, and individuals likewise compete with one another for valued social positions and goods. These competitions can be long-term or short-term, cool, smouldering or flaming. But they are always in the background. Peters says of feud:

> Ultimately, feud is a violent form of hostility between corporations which has its source in the competition for proprietory rights in land and water. Thus competition makes it necessary for groups to combine to prevent the encroachments of others in similar combinations and also to expand their resources whenever the opportunity arises.[75]

The group decision when it is opportune to expand, or the group decision that there has been an encroachment which must be resisted, is in some (not all) ways analogous to the decisions of individuals to advance themselves at the expense of others, or to react to the self-seeking of others. On both levels there are many choices. On both levels, when action is undertaken it is neatly rationalized, and perceived as justified and proper in the context of some overall conception of how society works.

Many considerations are involved in the question of timing, of when and where and against whom to turn a quiescent competitive position into active hostile competition. The most fundamental of these presumably have to do with the degree of underlying pressure on power and resources, and the degree of encroachment of one's competitors and the opportunities for bettering one's own position. Between counterpoised groups these basic pressures and positions tend to be long-term and the consequence of a cumulative series of events. The issues involved may be so fundamental that they are much more far-reaching than any particular event in the series. Yet active confrontation, if it is to occur, must happen at a particular time, place and occasion. The legal wrong, because of its specificity in time, place and circumstances, can provide the occasion for action. The legal wrong, moreover, makes it possible to have a show-down without necessarily acknowledging the deeper long-term motives or objectives which may accompany such action.

It can be put another way. Just as constitutional theories are condensed and simplified ways of thinking about the supposedly fixed relationships of social units, so certain events (in this case legal disputes) can serve as condensed and substitutive media in terms of which it is possible to conceive of, and play out, real social cleavages and structural competitions. Conventional conceptions of social structure serve to make apparently stable, simple order out of very complex, interwoven and continuously shifting relationships. Disputes between individuals belonging to different groups can serve to bring into active expression some of the conflicts inherent in the social structure itself. Yet these emerge in a disguised form. The open fights appear to be no more than a system of self-help, a part of an orderly method of keeping people to their legal responsibilities. Such a translation of issues provides terms in which not only fights, but also settlements and peaceful intervals, can be arranged. Legal disputes function in this context of groups jockeying for position in somewhat the same way that political issues may in other societies.

From this point of view the apparent inconsistencies Peters has so well analysed become altogether comprehensible. It also becomes clear that there are two fundamental conceptual frameworks to which conventional indigenous explanations of such confrontations have reference. A segmentary lineage system, for example, is an explanation in terms of relationships, groupings and alignments—what I have called elsewhere the 'constitutional theory' of a society. The other is an explanation in terms of a kind of value order that classifies acts as hostile or friendly. One explanatory frame of reference refers to categories of persons: 'They are allies/enemies.' The other refers to categories of acts: 'Such-and-such an act is friendly/hostile.' One supposedly describes the social placement of people, the other the social evaluation of events. Certain acts are appropriate to certain relationships. The orders of persons and acts are theoretically parallel.

Since the question of alliance or enmity often depends on the context of action between persons, and the amicability or hostility of an act often depends on the context of relationship of the actors, these are two interlocked frameworks of rationalization. I agree with Peters that segmentary lineage systems, like other constitutional theories, are neither sociological models nor norms for behaviour but ways of conceiving and explaining the social world. The 'value order' of acts is no more normative than the 'constitutional theory'. It is equally manipulable and sometimes invoked to justify 'righting' entirely fictitious or imputed, provoked, or even anticipated 'wrongs'. Both are ways of conceiving, depicting and rationalizing action in the social field.

Between groups which have regular encounters or dealings with each other acts which are or can be interpreted as hostile, as insults or wrongs, may be presumed to recur with a certain frequency. They recur irregularly, but presumably in some proportionate relationship to the total number of inter-group transactions.

Provocative occasions may even be conventionalized. The relationships of Bedouins which Peters calls feud 'are of a kind which requires at least a show of hostility whenever the parties happen to meet'. He then describes unexpected encounters in which pot-shots and blows were exchanged.[76] Less improvised and more formal shows of hostility are found in the mock battles of the Ngombe funeral or the Nuer dances, each of which could potentially erupt into real fighting.[77] In short, the raw materials for confrontation, the focusing events themselves, are probably not far to seek if a confrontation is desired.

One of the regularities in hostility and the re-statement of opposition is probably in the kind of event over which collective confrontations take place in particular societies. In the impersonal milieu of complex societies, particular wrongs against individuals or legal disputes between individuals are not usually the events which become the rationale for group confrontations. There have been some notable exceptions in the recent riots between blacks and whites in the United States, many of them touched off by just such incidents. Group confrontations within centralized States usually focus around the filling of office. But in societies having the principle of expanding dispute, legal quarrels between individuals may serve groups in their mutual antagonisms.

Deep economic or political reasons for the structural opposition of groups which may lie in the background of such controversies need never be directly acknowledged. The legal dispute between individuals of opposing groups can serve as a simpler, more concrete way of talking about and thinking about alignments based on those more profound problems which are less easily delineated and less easily resolved. Just as the segmentary lineage model serves to rationalize certain social systems, so certain legal disputes can be used to rationalize active structural conflict and bring it to a head at a particular moment. A legal dispute can be used as if it were a condensed replica of a wider and more complicated relationship. Surely one of the most important differences among legal systems must be in the varied ways that legal disputes between individuals can serve these structural purposes in different societies. The basic distinctions delineated here have been between self-help undertaken by individuals and self-help by corporate groups on behalf of individuals. A third possibility, to be taken up among others in the next section, is the case in which a man mobilizes a number of other men to support him in his 'self-help' but the supporters do not constitute a corporate group. In ethnographic fact, all three kinds of self-help may be available ways of proceeding in the same society, or one or another may exist alone, as the only possible or approved form.

4. *Collective responsibility and corporateness: collectivities inside and outside*

Collective responsibility is a term which usually means no more than that a number of persons are together answerable for certain of the obligations of one or more of them. Sometimes it is even extended to describe the obligations of an individual for a group he leads or represents, as where a man is legally responsible for the obligations incurred by all the members of his household, or a headman for the taxes of his village. In short, like 'totemism' and other nineteenth-century staples, it is a very general term. It covers a wide range of situations in which liability is incurred for the acts of another or others.

Since there are two elements in the term, each requires some amplification. One must ask, what kinds of collectivities may be involved, and to what kinds of responsibilities are they committed? Much of this section will be devoted to expanding on those two questions, using as a base the very loose definition that collective responsibility encompasses any situation in which a number of persons are together answerable for certain obligations incurred by one or more of their number, or their agents. This definition covers such a wide range of ethnographic variety that only a small part of it can be touched on here. Rather than make any attempt to cover the field, this essay will try to identify and analyse some of the variable elements in pre-industrial collective obligation and some of the combinations these elements may form. Distinctions emerge from such an analysis which are usually quite blurred or passed over in the literature. The further development of these distinctions may ultimately supply us with some legal criteria for classifying types of organization, and relationships between organizations.

There are two kinds of collective obligation in situations of self-help involving expanding dispute: the economic liability and the duty to give physical support. When precisely the same group of persons bears both obligations and is a corporate group, that is the simplest and neatest situation. It is neater still if one can say that the obligations are more or less equally and equitably distributed within the group as a whole, and they are mutual and common to all the members of the unit bearing collective responsibility. But such a tidy arrangement is by no means the only form possible.

The allies of a man exercising self-help, i.e. the persons he calls upon for aid in enforcing his rights, need not be a corporate group nor form any part of one. And reciprocally, the persons who are aggregately going to make good any debt or damage his opponent has done may not be a corporate group of any kind either. Gulliver gives us the example of the Jie and Turkana stock associates.[78] Stock associates are all those individuals with whom a man maintains reciprocal rights to claim gifts of domestic animals on the more important occasions of social life. A man's stock associates include his close agnates, close maternal kin, close affines and bond friends. Each man has his own assortment, though obviously brothers would overlap in the first two categories. Disputes are settled by payments of stock solicited from the stock associates who in turn expect a share of any payments received. Under the indigenous system of self-help, stock associates were expected to lend verbal, and if necessary physical, support in obtaining compensation.

In M. G. Smith's definition, this kind of non-corporate assemblage would not be a public, nor would the confrontation in a dispute of the opponents and their stock associates be a matter of 'public affairs'. This shows both the limitations and the usefulness of looking on legal processes in corporate terms. The 'stock associates' Gulliver has described are certainly a major element in the social structure and legal system of the Jie and Turkana. If one thinks of law as having to do with rights supported by the use of force, the stock associates were the major instrument of law in the indigenous system. But they are politically irrelevant. They are neither political units nor sub-parts of political units. Hence when the supporters of two disputants clash the fight is exclusively concerned with which individual shall prevail in a particular dispute and which group of followers will share in the proceeds. There are no long-term structural oppositions to be served in the confrontations.

What is useful about Smith's definitional model is that by so emphasizing political units it clearly distinguishes for us a major difference between situations of self-help which involve corporations and corporate affairs, and situations of self-help which do not. One could, in fact, easily define collective responsibility in such a way that it would exclude non-corporate aggregates sharing responsibility, and one would then not have to cope with the stock associates among the Jie and Turkana. However, I think the heuristic value of defined categories is lost if one designs them to exclude related but inconvenient phenomena. I think it important to recognize that from the point of view of the disputants there are some significant similarities between situations of self-help by stock associates and by corporate groups. In both cases there is a dispute between individuals which then expands to include other persons on each side. In both cases force is used (or threatened) in the name of right to settle a dispute. In both cases the brunt of the settlement is borne by a number of people, and, on the winning side, a number of people share in the proceeds.

But the similarities do not necessarily end there. The stock associates' responsibilities fall on them by virtue of their social relationship to one of the disputing parties, not by virtue of their relationship to one another. Something very similar can be true inside a corporate group. The assembling of fighting companions to help to press a claim may take place in terms of a set drawn from an individual's network of kinsmen, rather than necessarily involving the whole of a corporate group.[79]

Smith and Dale say of the Ila, 'When a man induces two or three stalwart friends to accompany him and assist in prosecuting his claim, the other party replies by summoning his clansmen to his aid.'[80] Such a fight might spread to involve two whole districts, but could be left to be sorted out between the personal supporters of each combatant if the whole of each clan did not see fit to take up the cudgels. 'In any case where a clan takes up a dispute, responsibility is collective and therefore vicarious . . . any member of the clan is liable to be punished. The dispute is against a rival clan, not against an individual; the initiative is taken by common consent, not by an individual, and as the result of due deliberation by the elders.'[81] One may thus distinguish enforcement procedures that involve an individual's networks and those that involve the whole of a corporate group. The one may, but need not, turn into the other.

On the economic side, the putting together of a collective payment may also take place in terms of a set drawn from an individual's network rather than involve the mobilization of the whole of the group to which he belongs. When a Kipsigis or a Lango had to assemble a blood payment to compensate another group of kin for a homicide he had committed, he had to make a major contribution himself, and then went from relative to relative begging for beasts.[82] These were given him, or refused him, as an individual. His claims for aid against his kinsmen are in this respect (though not in some others) like the claims of a Jie or Turkana against his stock associates.

In contrast to an economc obligation involving ego-centred sets, we find the corporate unity of the Suku. Kopytoff describes continuous sharing and circulation of property within the lineage among the Suku:[83] 'Obligations contracted by any member bind the lineage as a whole . . . self-help may be resorted to indiscriminately against any one of them by a wronged lineage.' The collective responsibility of the Suku extended to 'legal fines and compensations; bride-wealth collected or disbursed; tribute and, more recently, taxes—all these impinge on the lineage as a unit, every member contributing as much as he can convince others he can afford, collecting as much as he can demonstrate he needs. When a person dies, the inheritance reverts to the lineage as a whole.' The corporate (rather than network or set) payment of blood-wealth is also well exemplified by the Arusha Masai. Among the Arusha blood-wealth is always 'paid by contributions from all the sections of the moiety of the killer'.[84] The allocation of these contributions is made at a moiety assembly by the lineage counsellors of the moiety.

To what extent can one look upon the property of the members of an aggregate or group as a pool of assets where the members have the right to claim material help from one another in legal settlement and other times of need? The answer is not simply a matter of looking at an ambiguous situation which can be read either way. Many peoples have ideological terms in which assets are spoken of as the common resource of a particular social group—'cattle of the lineage', for example. However, the uniformity of such general expressions must not be mistaken for uniformity in the legal rights they subsume. These may be quite varied. There is a distinguishable range of degrees and kinds of property and manpower pooling inside corporate kinship units, and there are also varying types of networks of mutual aid.

Four variant forms of the economic responsibility to aid in meeting legal obligations exist even in the few ethnographic examples mentioned above. The first is that of the Jie and Turkana stock associates, which are not corporate groups and whose assets are in no sense a common pool.[85] The beasts of stock associates are a resource for an individual. Stock associates are ego-centred aggregates which function as action sets only on rare occasions at the behest of the ego who constitutes their common point of connection. A second type is that of the Lango and Kipsigis, in which, perceived from the outside, the group of kinsmen is a property-holding unit liable to bear collective responsibility, but, as seen from the inside, the payment obligations of members are not altogether corporate or collective. Here each individual is the centre of a set of concentric circles of kinsmen to whom he may appeal for help. The closer to the centre, the closer the relationship, and the more urgent his claims on them. The peripherally related persons in the outer circles are pressed to help only if the inner ones cannot.[86] The whole of the group need not be involved. The third type is the Suku, among whom the lineage is a corporate group with assets regarded as allocated to individuals but circulating freely and treated as a common resource for virtually all purposes, everyone chipping in to make payments whenever necessary.[87] The fourth is the Arusha, among whom the sub-sections of a widespread corporate group may occasionally be assessed for special obligations, but whose assets are otherwise quite separate.[88]

Throughout these examples there are variations in the social relationships of the persons bearing collective economic responsibility, and the degree to which, and the ways in which, the property involved functions as a common resource and pool for insurance. All the relationships are personal relationships, and most enjoin mutual aid in many contexts. All the property involved is, in fact, in the possession of individuals entwined in these relationships. The pooling aspect resides essentially in the strength, frequency and nature of the contingent claims to which the property is subject. By way of contrast, there is the collective liability of the business corporation of modern industrial society in which there is a pooling of certain assets by persons who do not necessarily have any other ties or other obligations of mutual aid to one another, and who do not hold specific pieces of corporate property but rather hold shares in the corporation.

By definition, in situations of 'collective responsbility' the property of a number of persons serves as a resource from which to pay legal claims. Yet in all of the situations mentioned, including the modern business corporation, the capital is primarily available for other purposes. I think it can safely be said that the settling of legal disputes is *always* peripheral to the main purpose for which the capital is available, and hence that legal obligations are not comprehensible outside their wider economic and social settings.

It may clarify matters to distinguish three questions and briefly to compare some aspects of the modern business corporation[89] with pre-industrial 'collective liability' on these three points: the question of limitations on liability, the question against whom claims may lie which may be paid out of collective assets, and the question what kinds of claims these may be. We tend to think of limited liability as a modern invention. The shareholder in a business corporation is not liable beyond the extent of his share. The ethnographic data suggest that certain limitations on liability also play a part in pre-industrial collective arrangements.

Let us consider the Jie and Turkana stock associates. Could any man expect or claim unlimited economic help from any particular stock associate? It does not seem so. He expects a *contribution* when he needs it, and presumably that contribution has a relation to at least the following factors: the nature of his past exchanges with that associate—what animals have been given and what received; the means of the associate; the extent of the need; and the prospects of ultimate reciprocation or 'repayment'. Among the Kipsigis and the Lango the blood debtor is in the position of a supplicant asking for help. He may expect contributions from kin, but surely these also are limited by all sorts of norms of standard payment and principles of reasonableness. Moreover, there is a system of priorities according to which contributions are solicited from closest kin first, the implication being that some kind of measure of their means determines how widely requests for beasts may be made. In the Suku case one understands that there is a general distribution of charges, but is there any question of the unlimited liability of any individual or of the group as a whole? I would doubt it. Among the Arusha bloodwealth is fixed at forty-nine cattle and collected from a wide group. Many equitable principles govern the setting of each contribution. Liability is clearly limited. In all these pre-industrial societies anyone rendered indigent by a legal payment became dependent on the same people who might help him with the payment.

Later I shall argue that the right to expel members is an extremely important element in units bearing collective responsibility in pre-industrial society. It seems to me that this, too, suggests a definite ceiling on liability. Except in the sense of vulnerability to attack in vengeful raiding, kinsmen and associates can limit their liability simply by refusing to support an individual who has imposed too much on their assets.

As for the second and third questions—against whom claims lie which may be paid out of collective assets, and what kind of claims these may be—here there is a most important distinction between aggregates or groups bearing collective liability in pre-industrial societies and certain modern business enterprises. In the pre-industrial situations mentioned here, any claim against any individual who is a member of the relevant corporate group (or has a network of supporting associates) may ultimately be paid out of the assets of other members of that group or network. There is an undifferentiated (but, as indicated earlier, not unlimited) general commitment to aid in times of need. In the industrial business corporation only a claim against the corporation acting through its agents in the conduct of its specialized affairs may be paid out of corporate assets. Corporate business is legally distinguishable from other affairs of shareholders and agents. Corporate assets are similiarly distinguishable. And the roles of shareholder, manager and agent are distinct and may be occupied by different individuals. In sum, I would argue that certain *quantitative* limitations on liability exist both in pre-industrial and certain industrial units bearing collective liability;

and that a much more important basis of distinction between the two is that there are many *qualitative* limitations on liability in industrial corporations which do not exist in comparatively undifferentiated societies.

Curiously, even in the pre-industrial world, collective obligations are not always and only to outsiders, though we tend to think of them that way. Even concerning blood payments, a collective obligation can exist internally in a collectivity. Gulliver has described the blood payments made by the whole moiety of the Arusha when homicides occurred within the moiety or maximal lineage.[90] Penwill reports something similar among the Kamba of Kenya: 'If a man kills a son or a near relative, the payment must still be made.'[91] He then goes on to describe the division of the payments.

Both the social relationships of those collectively responsible and the degree of pooling of property are matters of the *internal* organization of the unit of collective responsibility. But there is another variable of major importance, and that is the character of the *external* relationships of those collectively responsible. How is a corporate group committed to collective liability to outsiders? This may depend on its internal organization; on who is authorized to commit the group—every member or only particular ones; and what procedures commit the group in what instances. On the other hand, the commitment of the corporate group may depend not only upon such internal factors but also upon the whole character of its external relationships.

Collective vulnerability to violence is one aspect of collective liability in societies in which the expansion of dispute and self-help exist together. In its not uncommon fortuitousness, violence differs in a structurally significant way from negotiated indemnification, which is always systematically and socially allocated within the paying group. When warring or feuding villages raid one another, it can be a matter of chance who is killed, or what property is taken or destroyed, as when a city is bombed in a modern war. Violence is brought to bear by outsiders to whom the internal organization of the collectivity may (but need not) be a matter of indifference. Avenging, attacking outsiders can treat it as a homogeneous indivisible unit; they assault or plunder the most convenient victim rather than seek out the one against whom the immediate grievance lies.

A village treated as a unit from the outside by attackers may show its internal segmentations in later, peaceful settlements. As indicated earlier for the Nyakyusa, inter-village wars were one possible sequel to inter-village homicide in pre-colonial times. But in certain cases, where not war but some compensatory settlement was made between the villages, the offender found himself with heavy obligations. He not only had to pay the kin of the man he had killed in the other village, but he also had to compensate anyone in his own village who had been the victim of a retaliatory attack. He incurred this obligation on the ground that it was his original act which had provoked the retaliatory injury and brought trouble on his village, hence it was his responsibility to pay for it.[92] Elizabeth Colson reports a similar situation among the Plateau Tonga.[93] In both these cases the village was treated as a unit from the standpoint of the attackers, but from within the division between kinsmen and neighbours was decisive.

In making inter-village wars impossible the colonial powers removed one major context of Nyakyusa village collectivity. For the Nyakyusa one might say that there were two levels of collective obligation. The principal collective obligation was that of close agnates, these probably being identifiable as a set drawn out of the network of agnatic kinsmen. However, though villages were not made up of kinsmen, there were occasions when in confrontations, in fights, whole villages supported their members. Two kinds of group were thus involved in Nyakyusa self-help and collective obligation, and members of the two groups had essentially two kinds of obligation. Cattle circulated among kinsmen, and economic aid and physical support in legal dispute were always expected of kinsmen. But neighbours did not have the same stringent duties as kinsmen either in helping their co-villagers or in pooling property.[94] Co-residence, or contiguous residence, is often implied by collective vulnerability to violence. Such residential proximity is clearly not necessary to collective economic liability. The hit-or-miss quality of certain types of violence (because of the haste of the attackers, who want to minimize the risks to themselves) is itself a contributor to collectivity. Collective vulnerability to violence in some cases, like the Nyakyusa one, may be one of the most important contexts in which a particular social entity was dealt with as a unit bearing collective liability.

In many societies particular social groups may be freely treated as collectivities by outsiders, who may recover property equally well from any member of the collectivity, and in some cases, may wreak retaliation on any member.[95] However, there are other groups which, though they aid members in case of need, cannot be treated with impunity as collective responsibility units by outsiders.[96] And, as seen in the Nyakyusa case, in some societies outsiders may treat a social unit as a collectivity, yet insiders may deal with one another as if there were no collective liability.

Treating a corporate group as a unit bearing collective liability from the outside can be a very effective mode of social control irrespective of whether there is any collective liability from the point of views of insiders. The outsiders can leave it to the insiders to sort out the matter of individual responsibility and to bring culprits to heel. Among the Mbembe of Nigeria, who have a double unilineal system of calculating descent, the matrilineal group was economically collectively responsible to outsiders for any offence committed by a member. Villages tended to be endogamous and were composed of a number of patriclans, cross-cut by shallow, small matrilineages. Movable property was inherited within the matrilineage, land patrilineally. Certain village-wide associations had the responsibility for detecting particular offences and fining those who broke certain rules. The association 'normally imposed a "fine", seizing any animal . . . at random and eating it; and it then became the responsibility for [*sic*] the offender's matrilineage to compensate the owner'.[97] Punishing the wrongdoer was then left to 'the matrilineage, which normally had the right to punish individuals . . . and . . . which, in the last resort, might condemn a persistent offender to death. In such case the exasperated matrikinsmen might publicly refuse to pay any more fines on a rogue's behalf and the man would be forced to hang himself before all the people of the village.'[98]

Meek says of analogous examples of Ibo collective responsibility,

These regulations do not imply that there was any collective ownership of property, or that a person was held morally responsible for the sins of his relatives. They were an obvious method of obtaining redress through those who were in a position to bring pressure. And they were evidence of the strength of kinship and local group solidarity, which, indeed, they served to cement.[99]

Fortes makes a similar point about the Tallensi:

Thus in the old days a creditor could raid the livestock of any clansman of his debtor, but not those of a neighbour of his debtor who belonged to a different clan. In the latter case a reprisal raid was the penalty. In the former case the victim of the raid could demand restitution from his clansman, the original debtor; and I know of men who pawned a child or sold him into slavery in order to find the means of repaying a clansman who had been raided, rather than let the affair become a source of conflict in the clan. This is a good illustration, incidentally, of the statement previously made that collective responsibility is not a principle of Tale jural relations. It is not the clan but the debtor himself who is responsible for his debt. Self-help is a technique for putting pressure on a debtor through the mechanism of clan and lineage cohesion.[100]

Thus even in a society which stresses that ultimate liability is entirely individual it is possible for social collectivities to be vulnerable to seizures of property or other attacks by outsiders because a member has defaulted in his obligations. In many of the pre-industrial societies in which the principle of expanding dispute is allowed expression in self-help, a group bearing corporate liability may be committed to potential liability by any member, acting on his own, without authorization or sanction of the group for his particular acts. It is my hypothesis that *where every member of a corporate group has the power to commit it in this way to a collective liability, a corollary rule always exists whereby the corporation may discipline, expel or yield up to enemies members who abuse this power or whom the corporation does not choose to support in the situation in which he has placed them.*

When a member of one Lango patriclan killed a member of another, in another village, either his kinsmen would join to help him pay the blood money or they might throw him to his enemies. He would be driven away if they felt he had imposed on them too often, or if they felt that they were weak in fighting strength and were in danger of invasion by a strong village and could save themselves only by these means.[101] La Fontaine says that to forestall an avenging attack or save themselves from the payment of blood-wealth the Gisu formerly sometimes killed a member of their own lineage who had killed an outsider. When they thought the killer not worth supporting they did away with him themselves.[102] Bohannan tells us that among the Tiv war could be avoided if the murderer's lineage surrendered him to the victim's lineage, or if the murderer's lineage obliged the murderer to kill himself.[103] Evans-Pritchard says in his Introduction to Peristiany's book on the Kipsigis, '. . . public opinion might be expressed actively and collectively by the imposition on an habitual wrongdoer of the collective curse of the village, or by public outlawry of him by his kin which deprived him of their protection and enabled those whom he had offended to put him to death without fear of retaliation'.[104]

These instances support the hypothesis offered above, that a corollary of the power to commit a corporate group is the possibility of being expelled from it. *Expulsion is a qualifier of collective liability.* It also supports the proposition discussed earlier, that there is often an element of choice in the confrontation of groups, and that incidents around which such confrontations are organized may not inevitably cause a confrontation.

Giving expulsion its full importance commits one to consider another proposition: that expulsion may be one of the ultimate legal penalties for breaches of obligations normally thought of as subject to moral or 'social' sanctions only. For example, Gulliver has stated emphatically about the Jie and Turkana stock associates, and the inner lineage of the Arusha, that an individual appealing to these sources for help has no legal right to their aid.[105]

In keeping with standard usage, Gulliver by 'legal' means 'supported by the use of force'. He describes non-legal rights as maintained by reciprocity, i.e. by social sanctions rather than legal ones. This is not unlike Fortes' characterization of the obligations of kinship as essentially moral obligations.[106]

I would argue that in a number of pre-industrial societies the difference between certain moral obligations and legal obligations is that the application of physical force is the ultimate sanction for the former and a more immediate sanction for the latter. The absence of 'legal' sanctions inside mutual-aid aggregations may be more apparent than real if one gives full consideration to expulsion, selling into slavery, accusations of witchcraft, and other remedies available to such units.

A man who defaults in his obligations to his kinsmen or close neighbours or abuses his rights may not immediately experience anything more than social penalties, but legal sanctions may nevertheless be applied ultimately when his kinsmen are thoroughly fed up with him.[107] When 'social sanctions' imply physical force as a possible ultimate resort, must they not be considered to have a legal element? Penalties attaching to the breach of 'moral' obligations may be deferred, long-term results of the cumulative social record of the individual, not immediate measures undertaken to enforce specific performance of a particular duty, or repair of a particular wrong.

In contrast, 'legal' obligations are those in which such specific performance or repair may be immediately achieved through physical force. 'Moral' obligations are those in which the sanction of social pressure is used to obtain performance. The ultimate penalty for repeated or serious failures in meeting 'moral' obligations may involve force; but such action aims not at performance as its objective, but rather at ridding the social unit of an undesirable member, one who is not sufficiently vulnerable to mere social pressures. The existence of some functional parallels between expulsion and modern criminal penalties is clear. Imprisonment may be a form of internal expulsion. I am not suggesting that what have heretofore been called 'moral' obligations should henceforth be called 'legal' ones. I think the traditional distinction has much to commend it, since it marks differences in the quality of immediate sanctions on breaches of obligation, the difference between social penalties and physical force. What I wish to do is call attention to the existence of legal penalties for stubborn resistance to social penalties. Again and again in the literature, where expulsion is mentioned, or execution by one's own group, it is the gross violator or recidivist who is mentioned. This has a bearing on Durkheim's argument about the presence of criminal penalties in technologically simple societies, and the punishment of the criminal for assailing the basis of group cohesion, part of which is surely conformity without physical force. From the way Durkheim writes, it was not in terms of recidivism that he conceived of primitive criminal penalties, but rather as falling immediately on anyone who broke the rules. That he erred on this score does not matter. What is significant is that he was right about the larger picture, the existence of ultimate penalties for that source of group disruption, the trouble-maker, the individual who will not conform.

Expulsion is surely the ultimate withdrawal of reciprocity, of which there are undoubtedly many more subtle and less drastic forms. In fact, just as reciprocal ties may be established one by one (as between Jie and Turkana bond friends, or those established by trade or agistment in many societies), so presumably can these reciprocities be withdrawn one by one, and not necessarily all together. Sometimes one can distinguish clearly between corporate action in such a case and separate actions by individuals. However, where a corporate group is very small, and the withdrawal of reciprocity involves a number of members, it may be difficult to distinguish one from the other, nor is there any particular reason to do so. Where the aggregate involved is not a corporate group, presumably piecemeal support or withdrawal of support is all the more characteristic.

In citing ethnographies which mention expulsion, on the whole I have not included the very large number of instances of expulsion or other punishment for sorcery and witchcraft, because these are more ambiguous. But it is necessary to mention them, as a great many expulsions come under this heading, and some of them are doubtless also expulsions for faults of character, failure in obligations, or misfeasance, though, of course, other considerations entirely, such as structural competition, or conflict, or catastrophe, may also lead to accusations of witchcraft. Presumably, also, some offenders leave before they are expelled, since it is more graceful to resign than to be fired, less dangerous to retire or withdraw rather than be thrown out.

This raises another point which cannot be expanded on here, but which deserves mention: the question of how much of a penalty expulsion really is. The seriousness of the penalty of expulsion depends upon how easy it is to attach oneself to another community and to what extent one is a second-class citizen in that community. Does one become an 'outlaw', a refugee or a welcome immigrant? In some societies, such as the Nuer, it appears to be quite a simple matter to settle oneself in one community after another, and many people do so without any stigma attaching to such mobility. In other societies the status of attached aliens seems to be much more precarious than that of proper citizens. Yet on whatsoever basic rule membership in a community is founded, however exclusive it may be, there are ordinarily also other rules under which exceptions are made. Under these sub-rules persons who do not fit the normal definition for membership can nevertheless adhere to the social unit.

The degree of normal movement among communities varies very much from one society to another, and has also been very much affected by the inter-community peace established by colonial powers. Communal expulsion in one society is not always equivalent to expulsion in another. Moreover, expulsion may vary in its significance from one moment in political history to another. However, in a society in which it is necessary to belong to a unit bearing collective responsibility or exercising mutual aid, to be expelled from the unit in which one has one's firmest social footing is undoubtedly quite serious, unless one can easily become a member of another.

The penalty of expulsion forces one to consider that a collective obligation, while it may appear altogether collective when viewed from the outside or at a distance, is not so from the inside. Inside the collectivity the actions of members are weighed individually, and often, as indicated earlier, quite specific and varied individual obligations may exist with respect to debts of the collectivity. In the pre-industrial world, when an individual brings about a situation in which a corporate group to which he belongs is involved in heavy obligation, it may honour his claims wholly or in part, or it may turn him out. Certainly, even if he is given help he may be exhausting his potential claims and bringing himself closer to the point of refusal or expulsion. It becomes part of the history of his relationships with his fellows, a history which will bear on all his future dealings. Within the group he is in this way being held individually responsible for what he did, even though his kinsmen (and/or associates) may bail him and themselves out, and he may not 'pay' them for his act at once. The Kipsigis say a man may solicit help in making a blood payment only once; if he does so a second time he is disowned.[108] Whether there is usually as clear a measure as one chance for such collective help, or whether in other societies the rules are less precise, there is no doubt that within a group or aggregate bearing collective liability, in the long run individuals are held individually responsible for their actions. Collective responsibility does not exclude or substitute for individual responsibility. Both can and do operate simultaneously at different social levels.

5. *Conclusions*

The introduction of this paper reviewed some evolutionary or developmental ideas about law, and considered various theses of Pound, Durkheim, Maine, Malinowski, Gluckman, Hoebel and Smith. The recurrent themes—collectivity and individuality in the law, public and private law, civil and criminal law, and strict liability—crop up repeatedly in contrasts between the law of pre-industrial societies and that of industrial ones.

The body of the paper has examined some aspects of strict liability, self-help and collective responsibility. This examination was undertaken with the idea that by discussing the variety of phenomena to which these very general terms refer, and the variations in social context in which they occur, it could be shown that the evolutionary schemes in which such terms are prominent could do with some revision. I have addressed myself to examining some conceptions of what constitute the basic contrasts between the law of pre-industrial societies and our own. I conclude that some re-definitions and re-explanations are in order.

The evolutionary schemes considered here are all conceived with the notion that there are certain overriding legal principles according to which (and means by which) responsibility is allocated, and that these principles and means differ according to the degree of development of legal systems. Strict liability, 'private law' (self-help, civil law) and collective responsibility are often mentioned as primitive features. Moral fault as the basis of liability, 'public law' (criminal law, official enforcement) and individual legal responsibility are contrasted as developments of complex societies. There is some validity to these contrasts and some distortion as well. There is no doubt that in many pre-industrial systems certain kinds of personal injury are treated as cases of strict liability which are not so treated in Western law. There is no doubt that self-help is a prominent feature of many pre-industrial systems, while official enforcement characterizes centralized political systems. Certain obligations which are met collectively in pre-industrial societies are met by individuals in our own.

However, if one puts the problem slightly differently one gets different answers. What becomes apparent is that the questions which lead to these evolutionary answers may not be conceived in sufficiently broad terms. To be sure, the kind of collectivity which is collectively liable has changed very much from pre-industrial society to industrial society, but collective economic liability is an extremely important feature of Western law. For example, if one thinks of personal injury and homicide as exclusively cases for individual liability in Western law, has one not forgotten the importance of insurance companies, business and government corporations, Workmen's Compensation, and public health and welfare agencies? The standard lay answer which is usually made to such arguments is 'Oh, that's all very well as far as economic liability is concerned, but criminal liability is collective in tribal society, yet is entirely individual in our own.' A significant fallacy is involved in the comparisons usually made. Retaliatory vengeance killing between groups is not at all equivalent to criminal penalty. What is equivalent to criminal penalty is the kind of individual assessment of character inside corporate groups which can lead ultimately to expulsion or execution. This exists as much on an individual basis in pre-industrial society as in any complex one. One can get some very peculiar results if one does not compare comparables.

All this brings us back to M. G. Smith's definition of a corporate group as a 'public' and to Pospisil's conception that law must be seen in terms of the groups to which it is pertinent, and to Gluckman's insistence on the structural context of law. If groups are publics, then social control inside groups must be seen as public law, even if the pre-industrial equivalent involves small groups and modes of social control more suited to small groups than large ones. Though expulsion is often mentioned in ethnographies, too little attention has been given to the theoretical implications of expulsion as a legal measure in pre-industrial society. For example. A. R. Radcliffe-Brown mentions expulsion as a sanction but does not develop the point.[109] It is not unless one uses models of society that emphasize the degree of boundedness of groups, and consequently pays close attention to the significance of movement from one group to another, that the variant forms and consequences of expulsion can be given proper weight.

Expulsion may be an ultimate remedy, and in some cases may require provocation over a long period of time to be invoked. But it is there, in the background. Moreover, the issue of expulsion is not always expressed directly in the form which would make it most recognizable to Western eyes as an analogue of criminal penalty. Deaths which give rise to inquests and disasters which provoke witchcraft accusations provide occasions for expressing hostilities, some of which have their root in competition, but others, surely, are related to improper behaviour. These are subtle things; issues are mixed; the terms of discussion are mystical substitutes for direct confrontations of difficult questions. Individual dislikes and 'public opinion' are difficult to distinguish. In some cases it may be sensible to consider inquests and witchcraft accusations as quasi-judicial proceedings. They may be quite systematic in appealing for, and testing out, public support. Emrys Peters has made this point about

Evans-Pritchard's material on Azande witchcraft. He argues that the consultation of different oracles involves different degrees of publicity.[110] The social context of the consultation of the oracles may shift to ever larger audiences, with the consultation of more important ones. 'Public opinion' may thus be tested out, and public endorsement obtained.

It is the mixing of issues and the substitution of issues and the subtlety of personal relationships which make social control in small groups as difficult to study systematically as it is important to study them. But those who, like Hoebel, argue that criminal law and public law scarcely exist in pre-industrial society have never squarely faced the importance of the threat of expulsion or expulsion itself, or, for that matter, the positive importance of membership in good standing in the corporate groups of such societies.

Gluckman has stressed precisely this side of life in pre-industrial society when talking about strict liability. He has very emphatically taken social structure into account. But it is from his conception of the moral underpinning of that structure that he comes to some of his more speculative conclusions. He connects a strict duty not to harm in thought or deed with the fact of strict liability for injury or damage. If one is set on putting the matter into a rights–duties form, I think it simpler to postulate a general duty to make good, or make amends for, any injury or damage one causes in order that social relations may continue. It is not necessary to go so far as to postulate a pervasive strict duty not to harm. My view puts an emphasis on repair, while Gluckman's emphasizes a kind of moral attitude which he considers more stringent in 'tribal' societies than in complex ones. A basic theoretical problem raised by Gluckman's approach—a problem to which there is no easy answer—is the question how one decides what other aspects of social life are functionally related to particular characteristics of law. One methodological route towards such an objective is to try to distinguish separable aspects of the same phenomenon when this is possible.

In section 3 of this paper such a distinction was made between self-help by an individual and what I have called 'the principle of expanding dispute', in which an individual mobilizes many persons in his cause and confronts a like group or aggregation of persons. In some societies such a confrontation involves the use of force, and may appear as a form of self-help on an enlarged scale. However, the principle of expanding dispute can operate in systems which prohibit violent confrontations between groups, as shown by Gulliver's material on the Arusha.

One of the important qualities of expanding dispute is that the widening of dispute from the original individuals to the groups to which they belong, and to any networks on which they may call, is often a *potentiality* within certain social situations rather than an inevitable rule governed by the relative social positions of the parties, or the subject of their dispute. This bears on two matters. First, it shows, as Peters has so convincingly argued, that such models of organization as segmentary lineage systems must be understood as frameworks of explanation of the social order rather than as sociological norms. Second, I have argued that it shows how an event (in this case a legal dispute) may be used to epitomize or characterize complex, long-term relationships between groups (or categories) as condensed or simplified versions of those relationships. Thus there is a partly symbolic, partly effective connection between certain events and the social relationships they both *represent* and *involve*. This double connection between events and systems of relationship bridges one analytical gap between the conception of social process and that of social system. The dispute between individuals that expands provides both a specific *occasion* for confrontation and a set of concrete, self-justifying *terms* in which the confrontation can be thought of and discussed.

The structured symbolizing habits of societies have received a great deal of attention in their most positive and striking forms. The more arbitrary a symbol, or system of symbols, the more easily it is recognized as such. However, when, as in law, there is what appears to be a rational connection between the reasons given for social action and the action itself, it is sometimes more difficult to analyse the relationship among the rationalizations, the actions, and their setting.[111] Rationalized events can have some of the qualities of symbols. They may be partial or distorted representations of wider issues or structural situations. The relationship is something like that between symbols and referents, but it is more complex because, unlike symbols and referents, the outcome of the 'symbolic' event may in fact affect the social facts of which it is a kind of representation. The substitution of political issues for one another is a familiar form of this phenomenon. A focus of one issue may take out of immediate public discussion a whole series of others, yet in the process of its resolution may imply the bargaining over or settling of issues supposedly not being considered. In law there is the often observed paradox that in theory norms rule the outcome of cases, yet at the same time some cases define norms. So events in social life are conditioned by pre-existent social relationships, yet events may alter social relationships. Legal disputes can be key events of this kind.

When social structures are described it is in terms of the reiteration of certain relationships and processes. 'Structure' is a succinct way of describing a process of repetition. Social relationships are, however, not by any means always repetitive. Legal fights in societies having a principle of expanding dispute figure significantly in the continuous process of definition and re-definition of major structural relationships. Self-help and expanding dispute so conceived can scarcely be thought of as private law. As Gulliver has shown, a major difference between many pre-industrial systems and ours is in the kind of political role that certain legal disputes between individuals have in the former and not in the latter.[112]

The social units to which disputes between individuals expand are sometimes also units of collective responsibility. The material on collective responsibility reviewed in this paper has shown that collective responsibility can operate as a means of assembling capital, and/or manpower, and that it can be a device used by persons outside a collectivity to force the group that has ultimate face-to-face control of individuals to bring pressure on some particular individual. The outsider may be some other group, an individual, or an administrative superior.

Where there is an aggregation of persons who are collectively responsible, they may constitute a corporate group or they may not. In one society they may be answerable only to the member-individual who claims their aid. He in turn may be the only person who is directly answerable to outsiders. In another society the whole collectivity or any of its members may be answerable to outsiders for the obligations of any member. There are a variety of situations intermediate between these two.

Adequate comparisons are possible only if each situation of collective responsibility is examined from at least two points of view: from the standpoint of an outsider dealing with the parties joined in potential liability, and from the inside, from the point of view of the persons so joined. Collective responsibility is as varied as the structural situations in which it occurs. Therefore it is only with reference to a few matters that one can make inferences about the general nature of collectivities so obligated from the mere existence of collective responsibility. In the examples reviewed here, there were only a few striking and general circumstances. One was the universal fact that the collective responsibility for obligations incurred in legal dispute were always secondary and peripheral to the more regular or ordinary functions of the collectivity. The aspect of social aggregates or groups that has to do with legal liability is fully intelligible only if attention is given to the other functions.

Two other general propositions emerged from the material on collective responsibility, but these are more restricted in scope and refer to those instances in pre-industrial society in which the group bearing collective responsibility is corporate. The first is that while liability may be collective from the point of view of persons outside a collectivity, there is nevertheless individual legal responsibility for the same act from the perspective of the person inside the group. The second is that where there is collective liability towards outsiders for the act of a member of the collectivity, the group has the right to expel a member who repeatedly or unwarrantedly puts it in that position, or in a case in which the group does not want to undertake the risks or expenses which it would otherwise incur on his behalf. Both these phenomena are, of course, familiar ones in the on-going life of many enduring groups in industrial societies in which the issue is generally not legal liability but responsibility and answerability in a more informal sense.

The two circumstances described above—the simultaneity of collective and individual liability, and the corporate option of expulsion—both not only bear on an understanding of collective liability, but as we have seen, also pertain to a number of the issues raised in the introduction of this paper.

In a segmentary society of exclusive, collectively responsible corporate groups, individual responsibility exists essentially inside the corporation. Legal individuality on the whole seems to be a factor of the internal affairs of social corporations. Centralized political organization greatly increases the size of the largest corporate group in society, i.e. it concomitantly increases the size of the unit within which, and in relation to which, there may be individual responsibility. The fact that the milieu within which a person can be held individually responsible greatly increases in size gives an illusory impression of a great increase in emphasis on individual responsibility. In fact, individual responsibility always exists inside corporate groups. The smaller the maximal corporate groups in a society, the smaller the units within which legal individuality is significant.

Political centralization also has the implication that the use of self-help in combination with the principle of expanding dispute is ultimately suppressed for political reasons—to eliminate corporate competition with the superordinate corporation. This changes the character of legal dispute and contributes to the impression of the increasing importance of individuals, since it removes a dramatic function of the corporate group. However, units of *collective economic responsibility* go on being important, and are of as great importance in complex societies as in simple ones. Units of collective force which mobilize to confront other like units come to exist on the level of the maximal political unit only.

It is clear from the ethnographic material available today that what Pound conceived of as four basic stages of legal evolution—payment instead of vengeance, strict law, moral law, and a combination of equity and certainty—can all be found together in pre-industrial systems. These pieces of theoretical pottery, while arranged by Pound in apparently successive stratigraphic layers, can be found glued together to form a single pot. This is not to say that all legal systems are alike, but that the criteria Pound used for differentiating them are not the most useful distinguishing features. His evolutionary criteria are not useful because they are not founded on societal characteristics, and are principles that exist together, not only in that ultimate compound, our own supposedly remarkable society, but also in technologically simple societies. Less severe strictures apply to the legal–collectivity, legal–individuality discussions of Maine, Durkheim and Malinowski, because they never abstracted legal principles altogether from the social context in which they occurred. But the analytic fault in their evolutionary statements lies in their being over-focused on particular elements. In the case of Durkheim and Maine their vision of ever-increasing individuality in legal matters was legitimate as far as it concerned the particular problems to which they chose to address themselves. Malinowski looked at quite different materials and redressed the balance somewhat. But surely collectivity and individuality in legal matters are aspects of all systems, not alternative systems. To speak of the temporal precedence in legal development, of civil or criminal law, of public or private law, or of collectivity and individuality, does not make sociological sense. The generalizations couched in these terms use one aspect of a system to characterize the whole, which is a procedure of dubious worth.

[1968]

Notes

1 Evans-Pritchard, *The Nuer* (1940), p. 279.
2 Gluckman, *The Ideas in Barotse Jurisprudence* (1965), pp. 204–41.
3 Pound, *The Spirit of the Common Law* (1921); 1963 edition, p. 5.
4 *Ibid*., pp. 85, 139
5 *Ibid*., pp. 140–1.
6 *Ibid*.
7 *Ibid*., p. 141.
8 *Ibid*., p. 142.
9 *Ibid*., pp. 13–14.
10 *Ibid*., p. 13.
11 *Ibid*., p. 195.
12 Cohen, *The Transition from Childhood to Adolescence* (1964), pp. 130–3.
13 Moore, 'Comment on Cohen' (1965), pp. 748–51.
14 Elias, *The Nature of African Customary Law* (1956), p. 135; Gluckman, *The Ideas in Barotse Jurisprudence* (1965), ch. 7.
15 Maine, *Ancient Law* (1861); 1894 edition, p. 126.
16 *Ibid*., p. 127.
17 Durkheim, *De la Division du travail social* (1893), trans. Simpson, 1964 edition, pp. 64, 130–1.
18 Hoebel, *The Law of Primitive Man* (1954), p. 28.
19 *Ibid*., p. 327.
20 *Ibid*.
21 *Ibid*., p. 28.
22 M. G. Smith, 'A structural approach to comparative politics' (1966), p. 166.
23 *Ibid*., p. 119.
24 Pospisil, *Kapauku Papuans and their Law* (1958) pp. 272–8.
25 See Gulliver, *Social Control in an African Society* (1963).
26 The ethnographic examples in this paper are all drawn from African materials for quite arbitrary reasons of convenience. It will be evident from the content of the paper that my main purpose is to indicate what a wide variety of phenomena are subsumed under the terms 'self-help'

and 'collective responsibility'. I am sure I have not examined all the variations. I *know* of some I have not discussed. There must be others as well.

27 Elias, *The Nature of African Customary Law* (1956), p. 135; Lowie, *Primitive Society* (1920), pp. 401–2.
28 Elias, *The Nature of African Customary Law* (1956), pp. 135*ff*.
29 Seavey, 'Principles of Torts' (1963), p. 379.
30 Gluckman, *The Ideas in Barotse Jurisprudence* (1965), p. 213.
31 Evans-Pritchard, *The Nuer* (1940); Howell, *A Manual of Nuer Law* (1954). See discussion in section 3 of this paper of Peters' revisionist view of the segmentary lineage model.
32 Gluckman, *The Ideas in Barotse Jurisprudence* (1965), p. 207.
33 *Howell, A Manual of Nuer Law* (1954), p. 62.
34 Gluckman, *The Ideas in Barotse Jurisprudence* (1965), p. 235.
35 *Ibid.*, p. 203.
36 *Ibid.*, p. 234.
37 Gluckman, *The Ideas in Barotse Jurisprudence* (1965), pp. 237–8.
38 *Ibid.*, p. 234.
39 *The Nuer* (1940), p. 151.
40 *A Manual of Nuer Law* (1954), p. 42.
41 *Ibid.*, p. 244.
42 *Ibid.*, pp. 39–40.
43 *The Ila-speaking Peoples of Northern Rhodesia* (1920), vol. 1, p. 417.
44 *Social Control in an African Society* (1963), p. 128.
45 Fortes, *The Dynamics of Clanship among the Tallensi* (1945), p. 234.
46 *Ibid.*, p. 236.
47 Correspondence, 1968.
48 Fortes, *The Dynamics of Clanship among the Tallensi* (1945) and *The Web of Kinship among the Tallensi* (1949).
49 Fortes, *The Dynamics of Clanship among the Tallensi* (1945), p. 236.
50 *Ibid.*, pp. 236, 250.
51 Fortes, *The Web of Kinship among the Tallensi* (1949), p. 215.
52 Fortes, *The Dynamics of Clanship among the Tallensi* (1945), p. 236.
53 Fortes, *The Web of Kinship among the Tallensi* (1949), pp. 305–306.
54 *Ibid.*, p. 214.
55 *Ibid.*, p. 215.
56 Fortes, *The Dynamics of Clanship among the Tallensi* (1945), p. 177.
57 Evans-Pritchard, *The Nuer* (1940), p. 151.
58 Gulliver, *Social Control in an African Society* (1963), pp. 76, 135.
59 *Kapauku Papuans and their Law* (1958).
60 Wilson, *Good Company* (1951); 1963 edition, pp. 136*ff*.

61 *Ibid.*, pp. 137, 140–1.
62 *Ibid.*, p. 149.
63 *Ibid.*, p. 150.
64 *Ibid.*, pp. 25, 150–1, 173.
65. *Ibid.*, pp. 45–173; Gulliver, *Land Tenure and Social Change among the Nyakyusa* (1958), pp. 3–10.
66 To a similar effect, describing the simultaneous existence of chiefs' courts and self-help formerly in Busoga, see Fallers, 'Homicide and suicide in Busoga' (1960), p. 69.
67 Wilson, *Good Company* (1951); 1963 edition, p. 80.
68 Hoebel, *The Law of Primitive Man* (1954), pp. 28, 322.
69 *Ibid.*, p. 327.
70. Peristiany, *The Social Institutions of the Kipsigis* (1939), pp. xxv, 185.
71 Hoebel, *The Law of Primitive Man* (1954), p. 28.
72 'Some structural aspects of the feud among the camel-herding Bedouin of Cyrenaica' (1967), pp. 261, 282.
73 *The Nuer* (1940), p. 138.
74 Gluckman, *Custom and Conflict in Africa* (1955).
75 'Some structural aspects of the feud . . .' (1967), p. 279.
76 *Ibid.*, pp. 268–9.
77 Wolfe, 'The dynamics of the Ngombe segmentary system' (1959), p. 172; Evans-Pritchard, *The Nuer* (1940). See, for example, Lévi-Strauss, *Tristes Tropiques* (1955); 1967 edition, p. 297, and for Nyakyusa funeral dances Wilson, *Good Company* (1951); 1963 edition p. 80; also Fortes on Tallensi wars in *The Dynamics of Clanship among the Tallensi* (1945), p. 242.
78 Gulliver, *The Family Herds* (1955), pp. 196–200.
79 See A. C. Mayer, for a discussion of set in 'Quasi-groups in the study of complex societies' (1966), pp. 98–102.
80 *The Ila-speaking Peoples of Northern Rhodesia* (1920), vol. 1, p. 350.
81 *Loc. cit.*
82 Peristiany, *The Social Institutions of the Kipsigis* (1939), p. 195; Driberg, *The Lango* (1923), pp. 208–10; see also Roscoe, *The Baganda* (1911), p. 267, and Mair, *An African People in the Twentieth Century* (1934), pp. 188–9.
83 Kopytoff, 'Family and lineage among the Suku of the Congo' (1964), pp. 92–4.
84 Gulliver, *Social Control in an African Society* (1963), p. 128.
85 Gulliver, *The Family Herds* (1955), pp. 196–200.
86 Peristiany, *The Social Institutions of the Kipsigis* (1939), p. 195; Driberg, *The Lango* (1923), pp. 208–11.
87 Kopytoff, 'Family and lineage among the Suku of the Congo' (1964), pp. 92–4.

88 Gulliver, *Social Control in an African Society* (1963), p. 128.
89 The choice of the Anglo-American business corporation for comparison with pre-industrial collective responsibility units was made largely because it is a form of organization familiar in its outlines to persons not technically informed about legal matters. However, partnerships and other kinds of organizational form should also be considered if the comparisons are to be really comprehensive. Specializations and differentiations of function in complex societies are accompanied by specialization and differentiation of legal obligation. A great variety of industrial institutional forms have to be inspected if one is looking for either functional or organizational equivalence with pre-industrial forms.
90 *Social Control in an African Society* (1963), p. 138.
91 *Kamba Customary Law* (1951), p. 82.
92 Wilson, *Good Company* (1951); 1963 edition, p. 150.
93 'The Plateau Tonga of Northern Rhodesia' (1951), p. 121.
94 Wilson, *Good Company* (1951); 1963 edition, pp. 44–60.
95 For example Harris, *The Political Organization of the Mbembe, Nigeria* (1965) p. 44; Lawrence, *The Iteso* (1957) pp. 257–8; Meek, *Law and Authority in a Nigerian Tribe* (1937), pp. 126–7; Kopytoff, 'Family and Lineage among the Suku of the Congo' (1964), p. 91; La Fontaine, 'Homicide and Suicide among the Gisu' (1960) pp. 96–9; Fortes, *The Dynamics of Clanship among the Tallensi* (1945), pp. 236–45; Nadel, *The Nuba* (1947), p. 461; Southwold, 'The Ganda of Uganda' (1965), p. 98; Peristiany, *The Social Institutions of the Kipsigis* (1939), p. 121.
96 Gulliver, *Social Control in an African Society* (1963), p. 84; Mair, *An African People in the Twentieth Century* (1934), p. 189.
97 Harris, *The Political Organization of the Mbembe* (1965), p. 44.
98 *Ibid.*, p. 26.
99 Meek, *Law and Authority in a Nigerian Tribe* (1937), p. 127.
100 Fortes, *The Dynamics of Clanship among the Tallensi* (1945), p. 245.
101 Driberg, *The Lango* (1923), pp. 208–9.
102 La Fontaine, 'Homicide and suicide among the Gisu' (1960) p. 99.
103 Bohannan, *Justice and Judgment Among the Tiv* (1957), p. 148.
104 Peristiany, *The Social Institutions of the Kipsigis* (1939), p. xxv. For other mentions of expulsion see Gulliver, *Social Control in an African Society* (1963), p. 107; Rattray, *Ashanti Law and Constitution* (1929), p. 289; Mangin, *Les Mossi* (1921); H.R.A.F. translation, p. 31; Pacques, *Les Bambara* (1954); H.R.A.F. translation, p. 626; Meek, *Law and Authority in a Nigerian Tribe* (1937), p. 208; Kopytoff, 'Family and Lineage among the Suku of the Congo' (1964), p. 91; Cory, *Sukuma Law and Custom* (1953), pp. 113–14; Gutmann, *Das*

Recht der Dschagga (1926); H.R.A.F. translation, p. 209; Wilson, *Good Company* (1951); 1963 edition, p. 152; Leakey, *Mau Mau and the Kikuyu* (1952), p. 78.

105 *The Family Herds* (1955), p. 203; *Social Control in an African Society* (1963), p. 85.

106 Fortes, *The Web of Kinship among the Tallensi* (1949), p. 346.

107 Gluckman, *The Ideas in Barotse Jurisprudence* (1965), p. 162.

108 Peristiany, *The Social Institutions of the Kipsigis* (1939), p. 199.

109 *Structure and Function in Primitive Society* (1952; original article 1933), pp. 208, 218.

110 Peters, 'No time for the supernatural' (1963).

111 See Gluckman's discussion of the 'extended case' method and of the work of Mitchell and Turner in which disputes are examined as part of on-going social processes, in *Politics, Law and Ritual in Tribal Society* (1965), p. 235.

112 *Social Control in an African Society* (1963).

Bibliography

Bohannan, P. J., *Justice and Judgment among the Tiv*, London: Oxford University Press for the International African Institute (1951).

Cohen, Y. A., *The Transition from Childhood to Adolescence*, Chicago: Aldine Press (1964).

Colson, E., 'The Plateau Tonga of Northern Rhodesia' in *Seven Tribes of British Central Africa*, ed. E. Colson and M. Gluckman, Manchester: Manchester University Press (1951).

Cory, H., *Sukuma Law and Custom*, London: Oxford University Press for the International African Institute (1953).

Driberg, J. H., *The Lango*, London: Unwin (1953).

Durkheim, E., *De la Division du travail social*, Paris: Alcan (1893), trans. as *The Division of Labour in Society* by G. Simpson, Glencoe, Ill.: Free Press (1964).

Elias, T. O., *The Nature of African Customary Law*, Manchester: Manchester University Press (1956).

Evans-Pritchard, E. E., *The Nuer*, Oxford: Clarendon Press (1940).

Fortes, M., *The Dynamics of Clanship among the Tallensi*, London: Oxford University Press for the International African Institute (1945).

— *The Web of Kinship among the Tallensi*, London: Oxford University Press, for the International African Institute (1949).

Gluckman, M., *Custom and Conflict in Africa*, Oxford: Blackwell (1955).

— *The Ideas in Barotse Jurisprudence*, New Haven: Yale University Press (1965; second edition Manchester University Press, 1971).

Gluckman, M., *Politics, Law and Ritual in Tribal Society*, Oxford: Blackwell (1965).

Gulliver, P. H., *The Family Herds*, London Routledge & Kegan Paul (1955).

— *Land Tenure and Social Change among the Nyakyusa*, Kampala, Uganda: East African Institute of Social Research (1958).

— *Social Control in an African Society*, London: Routledge & Kegan Paul (1963).

Gutmann, B., *Das Recht der Dschagga*, Munich: Beck, quoted from translation, Human Relations Area Files (1926).

Harris, R., *The Political Organisation of the Mbembe, Nigeria*, Ministry of Overseas Development, Overseas Research Publication No. 10, London: HMSO (1965).

Hoebel, E. A., *The Law of Primitive Man*, Cambridge, Mass.: Harvard University Press (1954).

Howell, P. P., *A Manual of Nuer Law*, London: Oxford University Press for the International African Institute (1954).

Kopytoff, I., 'Family and lineage among the Suku of the Congo' in *The Family Estate in Africa*, ed. R. B. Gray and P. H. Gulliver, London: Routledge & Kegan Paul (1964).

La Fontaine, J., 'Homicide and suicide among the Gisu' in *African homicide and suicide*, ed. P. J. Bohannan, Princeton: Princeton University Press (1960).

Lawrence, J. C. D., *The Iteso*, London: Oxford University Press (1957).

Leakey, L. S. B., *Mau Mau and the Kikuyu*, London: Methuen (1952).

Lévi-Strauss, C., *Tristes Tropiques*, Paris: Plon (1955); trans. John Russell, New York: Atheneum (1967).

Lowie, R. H., *Primitive Society*, New York: Boni & Liveright (1920).

Maine, H. S., *Ancient Law*, London: Murray (1861).

Mair, L. P., *An African People in the Twentieth Century*, London: Routledge (1934).

Malinowski, B., *Crime and Custom in Savage Society*, London: Kegan Paul (1926).

Mangin, E., *Les Mossi*, Paris: Augustin Challamel (1921), quoted from Human Relations Area Files translation.

Mayer, A. C., 'The significance of quasi-groups in the study of complex societies' in *A.S.A. Monographs, No. 4, The Social Anthropology of Complex Societies*, ed. M. Banton, London: Tavistock Publications (1966).

Meek, C. K., *Law and Authority in a Nigerian Tribe*, London: Oxford University Press (1937).

Moore, S. F., 'Comment on Cohen', *American Anthropologist*, 67 (June 1965), pp. 748–51.

Nadel, S. F., *The Nuba*, London: Oxford University Press (1947).
Pacques, V., *Les Bambara*, Paris: Presses Universitaires de France (1954), quoted from Human Relations Area Files translation.
Penwill, D. J., *Kamba Customary Law*, London: Macmillan (1951).
Peristiany, J. G., *The Social Institutions of the Kipsigis*, London: Routledge (1939).
Peters, E. L., 'Some structural aspects of the feud among the camel-herding Bedouin of Cyrenaica', *Africa*, 37, 2 (July 1967), pp. 261–82.
Pospisil, L., *Kapauku Papuans and their Law*, *Yale Publications in Anthropology*, No. 54, New Haven: Yale University Press (1958).
Pound, R., *The Spirit of the Common Law*, Boston, Mass. (1921), quoted from reprint, Boston: Beacon Press (1963).
Radcliffe-Brown, A. R., 'Social sanctions' in *Structure and Function in Primitive Society*, London: Cohen & West (1952) (original publication of article, 1933).
Rattray, R. S., *Ashanti Law and Constitution*, Oxford: Clarendon Press (1929).
Roscoe, J., *The Baganda*, London: Macmillan (1911).
Seavey, W. A., 'Principles of torts', 56 *Harvard Law Review* 72 (1942), reprinted in *Landmarks of Law*, ed. R. D. Henson, Boston, Mass: Beacon Press (1963).
Smith, E. W., and Dale, A. M., *The Ila-speaking Peoples of Northern Rhodesia*, London: Macmillan (1920).
Smith, M. G., 'A structural approach to comparative politics' in *Varieties of Political Theory*, ed. D. Easton, Engelwood Cliffs, N.J.: Prentice-Hall (1966).
Southwold, M. 'The Ganda of Uganda' in *Peoples of Africa*, ed. J. Gibbs, New York: Holt, Rinehart & Winston (1965).
Wilson, M., *Good Company*, London: Oxford University Press for the International African Institute (1951), quoted from reprint, Boston, Mass.: Beacon Press (1963).
Wolfe, A., 'The dynamics of the Ngombe segmentary system' in *Continuity and Change in African Cultures*, ed W. R. Bascom and M. J. Herskovits, Chicago: Chicago University Press (1959), Phoenix edition, 1962, sixth impression (1965).

3
Aspects of the control of moral ambiguities[1]
A comparative analysis of two culturally disparate modes of social control

E. Lloyd Peters

Groups of youths meet nightly at numerous places in the Welsh countryside and behave in a way which appears bizarre to anyone unfamiliar with the area, causing reactions among the local inhabitants ranging from delighted amusement to embarrassment or even outrage. Details of this behaviour are given in that ethnographic classic *Life in a Welsh Countryside*, by Alwyn D. Rees,[2] and my analysis of the behaviour will be based largely on his data; but I was, at one time, well familiar with the antics of Welsh youths in the countryside—albeit not as a member of a group—and I propose to use some information drawn from this experience also. At the outset, in this article, my concern is to show how certain forms of morality are controlled by the adult community acting through its unmarried sons, and to derive from their behaviour the characteristics of this mode of control. Next, witchcraft accusations among the Azande of the southern Sudan—a pattern of behaviour wholly different to that of the Welsh youth groups and in its apparent forms equally bizarre—are used to show how generalities derived from them provided the clues to the behaviour of Welsh youths. Finally the two patterns are compared in an attempt to draw generalities about the patterns themselves and the situations in which these culturally disparate but social anthropologically similar forms of control appear.

The area in Wales which is described in Mr Rees' monograph is to be found in Montgomeryshire, in the parish of Llanfihangel yng Ngwynfa. Place names prefixed by Llan- occur abundantly in Wales, the word Llan meaning a church with its glebe land; following the author, I abbreviate the name of the parish to the ubiquity of Llan, which also happens to be the name of the hamlet located roughly at its centre. This hamlet is the meeting place of a youth group. There are two other meeting places for youth groups in hamlets located almost exactly on the parish border, to the west and south of the Llan hamlet (pp. 82, 102). While it is clear that the latter group draws most of its recruits from within the parish, the catchment areas for the other two groups are undefinable, even in a general manner. For the present argument this is of little consequence, since the latter two groups are mentioned in Rees' account only because they happen to fall within the periphery of the parish, and social linkages, whether of religious, kinship, marital or other kinds, are not co-terminus with the administrative boundary.

The youth group which meets in the Llan hamlet, like such groups elsewhere in the countryside, is composed of unmarried males between the ages of sixteen and thirty-five years (p. 82). Entry to the group and exit from it are only roughly determined by age; a youth is accepted into the group when he is considered to be sufficiently mature, and drops out of it, inconspicuously, when he reaches the age of about thirty-five years and it seems that he has accepted becoming a confirmed bachelor. 'Youth group', then, is an inaccurate designation as far as physical age is concerned, because it includes men who are fully adult and some of whom are on the verge of middle age. In terms of social status, however, the designation is appropriate, for they are all capable of undertaking most farm tasks, any one of them can entertain ideas of marriage and an independent home, but none has yet broken away from the parental farm to rise to the status of farm manager or proprietor. They are known collectively as *y bechgyn*, or *y llanciau*, 'the boys' or 'the lads', and while this translation will suffice for the present, the sentiments which these words evoke will assume importance at a later stage in the argument.

Most evenings the youth group gathers in numbers varying from about fifteen to forty near a shop in the hamlet. Although the hamlet is always small, often consisting of no more than a shop, a smithy, a few widows' cottages and perhaps a church and schoolroom, it gives a focus for gathering, and draws youths from surrounding farms, scattered here and there each among its own fields, from distances of up to about three miles away. Assembled at the shop, the youths often begin the evening with a game of quoits, but after the preliminaries of meeting are over they crowd into the passageway of the shop or, if the weather permits, they sit outside.

Boxes are brought out of the shop to serve as seats, and there they will remain until almost midnight, drinking mineral water, eating tinned food, smoking, chatting, bantering and remarking on passers by. And as night draws on they will sing hymns, ballads and popular songs [p. 82].

Most nights this kind of behaviour is routine. Since it will be of consequence later in the argument, three points relating to this part of the youths' behaviour need to be noted now: (*a*) its triviality—indeed, so persistently trivial as to appear contrived, (*b*) the expenditure of small sums of money on trifles, as a matter of routine—the sweets, tinned fruit and so on are consumed with an air of solemn deliberation, and to watch the youths eating these things gives the impression that they are doing so under compulsion; (*c*) the remarks made about passers-by always contain an element of ridicule, sometimes ridicule with biting effect, and sometimes lewd or obscene; but while the casual passer-by might be subjected to indignity, there is little that is planned about this, and since it is largely (although not entirely) a matter of chance whether any particular person passes the shop area, or whether the youths will be able to assemble outside the shop, the remarks they make will be relatively spontaneous. Spontaneity does not, however, blunt the cutting edge of a remark, and the victims are not restricted to adults either, for I have heard the youths make sexually suggestive remarks to boys and girls in their early 'teens. Inconsequential as this behaviour appears to be, it is of critical significance to the argument, for its persistent form and regular performance provide the group with the kind of characterization which enables it to take planned action in other specific situations.

One segment of the behaviour of the youth group is the banter and ribaldry it foists onto people indiscriminately. The other segment of its behaviour is concerned with premeditated actions taken against selected individuals. These actions are sometimes only derisive, but sometimes they take the form of harsh penalties, occasionally with destructive effect. Whatever the exact details of the actions, however, there is always a touch of comedy about them, as a summary of Rees' information shows. A middle-aged widow had been enjoying her seduction of a young lad, until the youth group decided to wreck the association. Each time the two were known to be together the youth group stuffed the chimney with straw, and threw dead vermin and, Rees adds darkly, 'other obnoxious objects' in through the doors and windows. In another case a married man who had been associating with another woman was met one night as he was returning from his nocturnal adventures. He was plastered with cow dung and dragged through a river.

The youth group, moreover, is hostile to youths of other communities who impinge on its domain when attempting to court girls belonging to its community. The youths attempt to quell the ardour of an intruding suitor by following him to his rendezvous, passing insulting remarks about him, teasing and tripping him, throwing turf at him, hiding his bicycle or pony, and if he threatens retaliation he is set upon by the whole group. Clearly, since the total population of the entire parish is only 500, marriages with people outside the community must occur, for this population universe is much too small to be self-sufficient for marriage purposes.[3] Nevertheless, the actions the youth group take in this context have the effect of limiting advances to serious suitors, and of accepting strangers as prospective candidates for their adult community.

Members of the adult community—to give a final case of youth-group action from Rees' data—who antagonize the youths can expect retaliatory penalties, because they particularly resent interference or any suggestion of control by their adult community. Penal actions, such as the removal of gates, irregular shapes cut in cornfields, chimneys stuffed with straw, or a hen thrust down the chimney while jam-making is in progress around the open hearth, would be inflicted on someone who persisted in being obstructive or pressed criticisms publicly.[4]

I wish to add to these cases of youth-group action two more, which, although they refer to a group functioning elsewhere in the countryside, are illustrative of the kinds of social relationship with which Welsh youth groups deal wherever they appear. The first concerns a man who was the son of one of the larger, more prosperous farms. He was alleged to have impregnated an unmarried young lady, but he denied paternity. One night the youths removed the babe from its mother's care, took it to the farm of the mother's alleged lover and placed it in bed with him. The return of the child had to be made publicly, thereby forcing the man to acknowledge that his denial of paternity was not accepted by the majority of opinion in the community. He continued to reject the responsibility of paternity, but for many years thereafter he privately provided for the mother and her child.

The second case concerns a woman who was known for her intolerable uppishness, who not only indulged in all the irritating foibles which accompany this blemish of character, but was strongly self-willed as well, with a tendency to assert herself even when obviously in error—such as singing loudly, in church, slightly out of time compared with the precentor and the rest of the congregation. The youths seized with alacrity any opportunity to belittle her. I need recount only one event by way of illustration. During a Sunday night service in church, when the woman had arrived dressed in her finery, the youths tied a ticket to the point of her umbrella on which they had inscribed 'Sale price *6d*'. After the service this woman, with her umbrella held aloft, busied herself in conversation with people gathered outside the church, and then strutted off along the road like a peacock. The youths followed behind, within earshot, giggled and audibly speculated whether her clothes had also been bought cheaply on the sales. Suggestions of wry smiles on the faces of adults and the furtive glances in the direction of the top of her umbrella finally led her to the painful realization of what had happened. Red with rage, and that look of strange surprise in the eyes usually associated with unexpected death, she summarily left her companions, and, too hysterical to mutter anything other than gibberish, she hurried away at an undignified pace. At the time, the event was uproariously funny and the youths enjoyed their success, but for the forsaken woman the anguish of being left defenceless—indeed, with no known enemy to strike—must have been deeply wounding. The sanction of ridicule sears the soul.

Before attempting an analysis of the various aspects of youth-group behaviour, a few further points contained in Rees' work need to be mentioned. The youths form well defined groups, as can be seen from the mock hostility in which they indulge towards groups of other localities, which sometimes takes the form of creating rowdiness in another community when some kind of social event is in progress (pp. 83–4). Again, at fairs, jealousy over girls sometimes leads to fights, after dark, between youths of different districts (p. 135). Youth groups are very closely knit, and the youths in them are kept solidly together by acting collectively—implication in acts which, if performed by an individual, would have serious consequences for him not only disperses the guilt and responsibility when undertaken by a group, but is a sure way of securing the loyalty of all its members. Actions taken under cover of darkness make concealment easier. But if the youths never give one another away, it is equally important that the adult population does not hunt the culprit. It is enough for the adults to know that 'the youths did it'. Rees, commenting on the behaviour of youth groups, offers the opinion that it is not as anti-social as it may seem, because he considers that the majority of the community secretly approve of the actions taken by the group. The youths' acts of verbal or physical rebuke he speaks of as teaching people a lesson, and, when discussing their role in courtships, he sees them as custodians of community customs. Yet, since their acts take the form of pranks, he is tempted to follow Radcliffe-Brown in viewing their behaviour as an example of consociation, 'a device whereby an ambivalence of feelings is given expression in mock hostility, excessive familiarity and joking' (p. 84).

In order to clarify the position thus far, prior to attempting to probe the relationship of the youth group to its adult community further, it is necessary to indicate roughly the main points in its pattern of behaviour. These are four in number, as follows:

1. Routine behaviour at frequent intervals from a known meeting place, not premeditatedly directed at anyone, but coincidentally liable to affect everyone. The effect of this varies from an exchange of jocularities or mild embarrassment for a passer-by, to serious embarrassment or insult. But since this behaviour is seemingly wholly spontaneous and subject to the chance of people passing by, it is not regarded as a serious rebuke to the victims.

2. Chance plays a much smaller part in the youths' interference with courtships than in their routine behaviour. The latter requires agreement among them to join together to challenge a particular person's right to pursue a particular girl, a challenge which, moreover, could lead to a brawl. Although the action is specifically directed, its consequences need not appear to be serious because it may amount to nothing more than mild teasing, the suitor may continue to pursue his girl-friend, the action may peter out altogether, or the youths may befriend the suitor. Superficially, such behaviour can be readily dismissed as a convention of courtship.

3. Premeditated action against an individual is planned, unlike interference with courtship, which, although specifically directed, is in the nature of an *ad hoc* decision. The issues involved are

usually serious breaches of norms, and the consequences sufficiently damaging to leave scars.

4. The youth group jealously guards its own integrity, whether against criticisms locally, or in its relations with like groups. This kind of action evokes strong loyalties from the youths, and, in a sense, is emblematic of the unity of the community from which they are drawn.

A cardinal feature of the youth group is that most of its members are not youths in terms of physical age. The majority of them are likely to be of the twenty to twenty-nine-years age group, some of them over thirty years of age.[5] Regardless of age, however, they are referred as *y llanciau* ('youths' or 'lads'), and this term itself, in people's sentiments, is weighted with affection. It also carries with it a suggestion of innocence, and of the mischievousness which so often accompanies the innocence of the young. This kind of mischievousness has the flavour of irresponsibility about it, and this is appropriate in as much as the youths constitute a category of irresponsible persons. They are irresponsible in the general sense that they are not subject to the same constraints on behaviour as adults. More particularly, they are irresponsible in that they have yet to mature to the status of full social adulthood. They are dependent on their fathers, who do not pay them wages but instead provide them only with their keep. Their fathers assume responsibility for them in that they speak for them whenever necessary. They are treated as juniors on the farms and they have little say in the management of farm affairs. Their independence is further limited by the fact that, even when attending fairs, they are given only very small amounts of pocket money (p. 63). As lads they cannot be trusted with the burdensome responsibilities of farm management and money matters—and the evidence of the recklessness with which they fritter away small sums on mineral waters and sweets is ample corroboration of this.

It will be argued that the youths can function successfully only if they have the backing of the adult population. The fact that men of the youth group are referred to as lads by socially mature adults enables them to pass off their behaviour as boyish pranks, and therefore it does not merit serious consideration, much less retributive penalty. Their actions are not publicly and critically discussed by adults, for, after all, they are only 'lads'. Moreover, the form their behaviour takes always contains an element of comedy, and this further assists the adults in excusing it. If a catalogue of their acts is taken uncritically there is a danger of misconstruing the significance of the youth group; for most of these acts relate to whimsical or trivial behaviour—the sort of bantering teasing and horseplay in which they engage virtually every night. The planned actions against specific persons referred to earlier, would, in a catalogue of their doings, be overwhelmingly outnumbered by their silly pranks and practical jokes.

Nevertheless, the latter behaviour is critical to the relationship of the youth group and its community of social adults, because it is this which enables the adults to fob off any and all of their actions as falling into a general pattern of joking. It is the persistent bantering, the quips, the satirical songs, the immaturely trivial practical jokes which create the image of the relationship, and permit the youths to perform their critical actions. It would be quite impossible for the youths to impose penal sanctions under the guise of joking if such actions were confined to situations of social stress, since then it would not be possible to pass off an act as one in a series of a general type; it would, indeed, be no joke at all because it would remain uncharacterized. For the image to emerge, the pattern of behaviour must be persistent and appear seemingly haphazardly in trivial and serious situations alike. Only if the image is retained in all circumstances can the youths proceed to exercise control, and the adult community to condone their behaviour with a nod and a wink.

Actions are ascribed to the group, not to any one of its individuals, and even a person who is embarrassed by the youths as he passes by their meeting place will, when recounting the incident in the privacy of his home, refer to 'the lads', not to an individual among them. Preservation of anonymity is essential for the success of the group, but it is not maintained merely by the youths congregating as a group, or by loyally refusing to yield the identity of those who actually committed offensive acts, or by accepting collective responsibility, or by taking action under cover of darkness. These are all important attributes of the youth group, but in fact anonymity is a fiction which is sustained by the community of adults. It would be an easy matter to identify the particular culprit if necessary, because the members of the group are sons of local farmers and it would be difficult for them to conceal their secrets if members of their household instituted enquiries about their activities. But the adults stultify the threat of separate identification and foster the fiction of collective responsibility by allotting blame to 'the lads', thus stultifying the possibility of counter-action. If any one of the several youths constituting the group were to be singled out as responsible, then the situation would be particularized in such a way that the parents of the culprit and the victim—social equals in the adult community—would be ranged against each other in an impasse of relations which would immediately threaten to rupture wider areas of relationships. In short, the youth group's success is a measure of the co-operation it receives from the whole community. The cover of anonymity afforded the group by adults is much more of an impenetrable veil than the cover of darkness.

Irresponsible in the sense that the form the youths' behaviour takes is usually somewhat ludicrous, the youths are highly responsible when they take specific action against a particular person. If adults are prepared to co-operate with the youth group with regard to its anonymity, this implies their tacit approval of the penalties the youths inflict on people. The youths, I will now argue, act in conformity with the consensus of public opinion in the community, and not capriciously, as the whim takes them, which the details of their doings seem to indicate. If this is so, it becomes necessary to show how a consensus is reached, and how the youths gain access to it.

The youths act on an intimate knowledge of other people's affairs, often intimately private affairs. While they gossip among themselves they would be severely restricted if the only information available to them for sifting was that derived from their own observations; but the prime interest of the group is that it is fed its information, and—more important—opinions about this information, by the responsible adults of the community. This comes about because each of the youths belongs to one of the farms of the locality. The process of gathering data for discussion at meetings of the youths does not end with what each of them hears within the narrow range of his own family at home. This is certainly an important source, especially since a group represents virtually all the farms in a community. Rees states that each group gathers together between fifteen and forty youths (p. 82). The total number of smallholdings he gives as 114 (p. 18), and the number of males in the whole of the parish area whose ages and bachelor status would qualify them for membership is about sixty.[6] There are, however, two youth groups other than that which meets in the Llan hamlet, and although it is likely that these draw some, if not their main, support from farms outside the parish, they certainly draw a small part of it from within the Llan parish boundary. On the other hand, the group which meets in the Llan hamlet is unlikely, because of its central position, to draw recruits from farms outside the parish boundary. Thus the total number of possible recruits available for this group, if, of the sixty youths of the parish, an estimated sixteen are counted as recruits for the two groups which meet in hamlets on the west and south borders of the parish, would be forty-four—a number consistent with the maximum attendance Rees reports.

The Llan youth group, therefore, has a maximum representation of the unmarried men between the ages of sixteen and thirty-five in its area of operation. The total number of smallholdings in the parish is 114, of which five are in the hands of bachelors, and five are held by unmarried siblings (p. 70). Since these farms could not contribute to the membership of the youth group anyway, they are excluded. Of the remaining 104 farms, the youths of twenty-seven of them[7] are likely to be recruited by the two border youth groups, leaving a total of seventy-seven farms as the largest possible catchment area for the Llan hamlet group. This number must be decreased still more (perhaps it is in fact substantially lower) to allow for what Rees calls 'anomalies'[8] in the composition of farm families. Bearing all these qualifications in mind, it is clear that the Llam hamlet youth group represents, not only the entire male population of the right age and status for recruitment, but also the maximum number of farmsteads in its community.

The group consequently has information made available to it from a wide span of the population it serves—but not merely in the form of unrelated snippets from some ninety farms. Bits and pieces of information do not constitute a consensus. For the youth group to act, a consensus of opinion must be available, otherwise the threat of fragmentation would soon disintegrate the group. Nor can it act on its own consensus alone, since that would deprive it of the backing of its adult community, without which, as we have seen, culprits would be identified, with the consequence of possible penal restitution to follow. Consensus must come from the community of adults in the first instance.

The process by which this is achieved is dispersed among the various chapters of Rees' work. At one point he writes about near neighbours exchanging informal visits regularly after the day's work is done, and of more formal visits among a different range of neighbours who are asked to call, particularly during the slack winter period (p. 97). Significantly, he adds that 'there is usually a remarkable agreement among neighbours as to the character of each individual' (p. 98). So that, among neighbours who are casual callers and the wider range of those called to visit, there is ample opportunity to discuss matters, especially 'the character' of people known to them. Kinship connections widen the range of those among whom there is regular and frequent consultation, and it is important to notice that these connections are by no means congruent, geographically, with neighbourhood nuclei—the only available farm for a son to occupy, after marriage, may be two or three miles away from the parent farm, so that—albeit within a limited geographic range—the kindred tend to be dispersed, non-kin occupying the interstices. A kinsman, on a visit, brings with him not only his own information but the news and views of his neighbourhood, and since more than one farm in any neighbourhood is likely to be connected with one or more other neighbourhoods through kinship, each neighbourhood has access to detailed information on the majority of people in the whole community.

Economic relations serve to proliferate groups. Farms with excess labour lend sons to other economically related farms.[9] Large farms have a circle of smaller farms dependent on them for borrowing the more expensive items of equipment, and there is reciprocal exchange of labour between them (p. 93). Certain agricultural tasks, such as threshing, sheep dipping and shearing, gathering in the corn harvest, necessitate that farms group together, and the co-operating groups differ for the different tasks (pp. 94, 95). Finally, groups of people meet in the context of religion, both for Sunday services and for various other functions which the churches and chapels promote. Save for casual calling on immediate neighbours, groups meet, whether in homes or elsewhere, for specific purposes; then, the business done, people invariably make time for a discussion of neighbourhood matters. In one form or another this is done throughout the year, with the effect that groups of different social span are meeting continuously at different farms.

In this way the opportunity always exists for a wide range of adults to arrive at an increasingly larger consensus about affairs in their community. The tendency to fractionize certain institutionalized sets of social relations is inherent in dispersed habitat, and it is his appreciation of this which, presumably, led Rees to refer to the area as 'the diffused society' (pp. 100, 101*ff*), but this does not mean that a sense of community, in relation to other sets of social relations,[10] is necessarily lacking. The facts already related give clear indication that bonds of the kind which the image of a community brings to mind are nurtured in Llan, and it will be argued later that these are definable. It is in relation to these other sets of social relations that the youths act. When they meet to discuss such matters among themselves they do so with a knowledge of the findings of all sections of the community at their disposal, for they are privy to the various clusterings of adults where opinions are formed and hardened into judgments. Thus not only is the information they use in their discussions accurate, but by the time they have sifted it through the sieve of their own gossip it comes to represent a sophisticated assessment of the opinion of all adults in the population.

The raw material and the views about it come from socially mature adults, yet the same adults delegate the responsibility of action to the youths, the social minors in the community. Paradoxically, the institutionalized strength of the community is vested in adults, but the strength appears to be of a kind which generates the weakness of frustration in dealing with the problems that arise within it. By deflecting responsibility onto an irresponsible group of youths the adult community is able to maintain its own integrity. Sometimes the information passed on to the youths amounts to little more than that a person is uppish, and he or she will suffer the deflation of embarrassment. Sometimes it is a serious issue of paternity, and heavy penal restitution is exacted. But whatever the fault against which they act, the origin of the criticism lies not in the youth group but in the adults of the community. The youths do not act on one report alone, but on many. They receive full cooperation from their adults. All adults are, in one way or another, involved in their activities. When, therefore, the youth group acts, it does so in strict conformity with the consensus of public opinion.

While stressing that the origin of their actions lies outside their youth group, among adult farmers and wives, and while acknowledging that action is delegated to them, the youths nevertheless take the decision to act, and determine the nature of the punishment. If one family or small group of farmsteads did not like an individual, and were to exaggerate his faults or foibles in the hope that the youths would inflict embarrassment or some other damage, it is unlikely that the hope would be fulfilled. Information from one family or neighbourhood is matched against information from others. Before an action is initiated a consensus must be reached among the youths themselves. After this, the severity of the penalty is a matter for them to decide. The control of certain social relationships, that is to say, is vested in the succeeding generation, not with that which has achieved full adult status. Judgments are made, and penalties inflicted, by those whose views about the social relationships they control may differ from those of the adults, even though the judgments and desire for penalty are common to both.

Where they differ, however, is in the details of their evaluation of people's behaviour and what they consider to be appropriate punishment. The youths have always been susceptible to new ideas, whether propagated through the modern media of radio and television or through their contacts with other people at fairs or neighbouring towns, or through visits from kinsmen who have migrated elsewhere to live. These kinds of influences shape their ideas about problems in their daily lives, and these changes of attitude to, say, pre-marital sex relations, or connubiality, can be transmitted by them through their judgments and penalties. They do not act merely to maintain the *status quo* of adult customary behaviour, but inject into it their changing conceptions. The youth group serves as the vehicle by which changes in conceptualizations of certain social relationships can be negotiated and carried forward with a minimal disturbance to existing institutions, and without shock to current cultural sentiments. Social change never means the abandonment of all cultural modes of behaviour; on the contrary, certain modes—particularly those associated with the diffusiveness of morality—possess that amorphous quality about them which enables them to persist in the face of flux while at the same time converting their content to the circumstances of changed contexts.

Externality is a characteristic of the youth group, but this should not be confused with the kind of externality reported from other societies, where a category of people, whether by birth, origin or status, remain permanently fixed in their externality in a variety of sets of relations.[11] Such strangers or outsiders do not progress through age or marital status or both to full social and jural adulthood in the communities where they reside, but are precluded from doing so by some status disability attached to them—non-membership of a lineage corporation, for example. It is a critical feature of the youths who constitute Welsh youth groups that they are not thus incapacitated. They are essentially a part of the community, not only in the general sense that they live their lives there and participate with adults in common activities most of the time, but also in the sense that the adult community is recruited from the group. This is obvious, but it is this simple fact which gives the group its continuity and is the source from which much of its strength derives. All male adults have experienced membership of the group, however brief, and they have all in their time participated in its actions. When an adult is critical of its behaviour his opposition can be effectively blunted by reminding him of his past, and if this is not effective the youth group bestows on him punishment of the kind he once helped mete out to others. The youth group is part of the community, therefore, in the significant sense that the male adult community is its status extension, fully conversant with its sentiments and its manner of arriving at decisions about them.

The precedence implied by this latter statement is deliberate, since this, it seems to me, is the analytically correct order, as is shown also by the fact that it is the youths who carry the responsibility of sifting information or making decisions, and of dispensing punishments; and as is shown, perhaps even more crucially, in the control over courtships. The horseplay in which they indulge towards suitors who are strangers can mislead one into passing this interference off as merely another instance of their general behaviour. Concealed in all this nonsense is the assertion, by the youths, of their right of priority to their own girls. I have known instances of stranger suitors surrendering to youth group pressure and discontinuing a courtship. In discriminately accepting or rejecting suitors, the youths are also expressing their preference for candidates wishing to join the community through wedlock; and it follows from this that they at least assist in determining the configuration of affinal linkages. A girl who flouts their wishes does so only by accepting a loss of status (p. 84); in this respect, the youths can be said to grant or withhold general feminine moral status. Once satisfied that a suitor is suitable, and the match an appropriate one, the youths indicate their approval by staging a spectacle during the nuptials—they build an arch of evergreens over the church gate 'if the couple is popular with the local lads', and during the evening of the nuptials they stage revelries outside the house until they are let in, the extent of their roistering marking the 'measure of popularity of the couple and their families' (p. 90).

This is not to deny the externality contained in their status *qua* youths, but it would be erroneous to include within this concept of externality the whole significance of youth groups. As joking partners of their social adults, they are in partnership with them for the purpose of moulding sets of social relationships which are the serious concern of both. Joking partners are never disinterested and detached intruders. A joking partnership does not arise merely so that a person or category of people can be called on to take action in a field of relationships where they have no interests. Youths are vitally interested in the relations they control; and the externality of their status, at best confined situationally, and biographically of short duration, is largely peripheral to the problem.

From the discussion of the types of commission the youths discharge it appears that they restrict or circumvent certain areas of social relationships. It now becomes necessary to enquire into the nature of these relationships, since what has hitherto been said of them has left them unspecified, or they have been given an implied characterization only. Also, the discussion has already suggested from the specific instances of behaviour cited—the co-operation of the adults, the representativeness of their information, the manner of its collection and sifting to clean it of the dross to reveal consensus—that the judgments the youth group makes concern values. Its actions, moreover, condemn pride of person, improper sex relations, attempts to renegue the social consequences of sex relations, inappropriate courtships, free association between local girls and male strangers. In short, the values it constrains to uphold lie in the general field of morality. The youths act in accordance with the consensus of opinion in relation to a community's conception of its moral order. They act in relation to those somewhat ambiguous, but ubiquitous, social relationships where the community wishes to express itself with regard to the general fairness or otherwise of an individual's conduct, where the consensus of opinion adjudicates the merit of the particular case, taking into account the peculiarities or the complexities involved.

The entire span of morality is not covered by the control the youth group exerts on behaviour. Morality is partly captured by law, and the case of disputed paternity quoted earlier impinged on its domain,[12] but since the illegitimacy rate (or pre-marital pregnancy rate) is so phenomenally high,[13] recourse to law is clearly the last, not the first step. Religion, in its institutional role, rather than as a reservoir of moral notions, claims a large part of the field of morality and has the power to exercise jurisdiction over it. The kinship of the household and of 'the family' claims its private morality, which remains secluded unless relations deteriorate to the point of becoming public. Each of these institutions, with the clarity of formality in the definition of the social relationships which fall within their purview, are all authoritarian and in the command of the fully adult population. Lacking the flexibility to deal with daily living, they are of a more universal character, and for this very reason fail to comprehend the details of doings in a particular locale. The youth group garners the harvest of social relations which the formal institutions fail to contain.

Yet because much of morality lies outside its competence, the area of morality, which has hitherto been referred to in a general sense, must now be restricted. In all the cases of premeditated action taken by the youth group the social relations to which the action referred were between the sexes, originating directly or indirectly from sexual relations. If the view that the youth group achieves its significance in the area of relations between the sexes is right—more data would be required to limit it more narrowly to sexual relationships—this still omits several types of its activities. The youths also act against overbearing pride, ostentatious pretension, bumptiousness, niggardliness (p. 95), and criticism of them from adults. While not wishing to detract from the significance of these latter activities, it is suggested that they are the attributes of the youth group image, and not the crux of the control the group commands.

Control of the morality which lies embedded in the relations between the sexes is always restricted in terms of its social and geographical universe, because such control is possible only if the detailed intimacies of people's private lives are known. Throughout the discussion it has been implicit that the social span of the youths' activities is defined by the domain of their community. The problem I now wish to enquire into is the nature and definition of this community. We must begin with the assumption that there is some sort of a community, since youths, recruited from a large number of farms, display a lively sense of group consciousness, expressed, for example, when they fight other youth groups or act against strangers. What they are in effect doing, in both cases, by this practice of inclusion and exclusion is setting social limits to their membership, and at the same time they are defining the range of some sort of community to which they and their activities refer. Close scrutiny of Rees' material for evidence of a community around which a boundary can be drawn (related to a youth group) leads to negation, but the pursuit reveals characteristics of considerable interest in this type of habitat, and in the frustration of definition an answer may be found. Several kinds of groupings other than youth groups occur within the parish.

1. I begin with what might be termed socio-religious groupings. A harvest festival is held in the church of Llan hamlet, and this has come to be non-denominational. A musical festival is also held there on the second Sunday of the new year (p. 126). Both events occur once annually only, the congregations which gather at them do not gather for any other purpose, and what Rees refers to are relatively large congregations, but not any systematic representation. Funerals are attended by large numbers of people, the exact number and the particular people depending on the personal bonds of an individual; attendances at funerals are evidence of the linkages in a person's network of relationships, but they do not serve to delimit a group (pp. 92, 93, 98).

2. Politically the area is divided, for although there was greater unanimity in the past when fairly general agreement expressed the hostility to Church (of England) tithes, church burial grounds, and alien landlords, this situation no longer obtains (pp. 153*ff*).

3. Economic co-operating groups assemble for a variety of purposes, but the number of farms in each group is very small. A network linking thirteen farms, shown in a diagram, includes 'the spheres of co-operation of four adjoining farms' (p. 94). Sheep shearing is alluded to as an important event of co-operation, but the assistants come from a maximum of only about twelve farms, and in other instances this number drops to half (p. 95). A farming co-operative society was formed in 1920, the headquarters of which are outside the parish, and its functions are commercial rather than social (p. 28).

4. Kinship could, possibly, provide a means of demarcation, and Rees' preliminary insistence on giving social relationships priority over consanguinity (p. 73), followed by the observation that all

classifications of kinship must needs be arbitrary (p. 74) in as much as social anthropologists tend to deal with terms rather than the nuances of meaning put into the terms, suggests that he aims to eschew the practice of weaving a web out of the strands of formal degrees of kinship in favour of a more purposeful analysis based on behaviour. Instead, the evidence presented relates to knowledge of genealogical connections, and the kinship map he provides (even though it includes only second degree relatives) is so dense a tangle of interconnecting lines that it is difficult to do more than agree with Rees' adoption of a local saying, that kinship ties 'are woven together "like a pig's entrails"' (p. 75); and the connections shown tell 'less than half the complete story' because if they were all included the 'network' would extend across the artificial boundary of the parish, linking up relatives 'in the wider neighbourhood' (p. 75), and, no doubt, even further afield for that matter. It is possible, however, to discern three denser patches on the map, and, within these, smaller clusters of connected kin. Moreover, in another part of the book there are references to kinship groups which 'vary considerably in their collective wealth and prestige' (p. 142), and to the crucial fact that 'of the wives of thirty-eight farmers with over fifty acres who were themselves farmers' sons, thirty-two were farmers' daughters, and only five were the daughters of wage-earners'—clearly evidence that 'a farmer's son is expected to marry the daughter of a farmer of comparable wealth' (p. 146). We are also told that there are kin groups known by their 'collective virtues and vices' (p. 78), and families regarded as *pobl gefnog* (people of means) (p. 30). Finally, somewhat surprisingly, twenty farms are not connected with any others within the parish, although since the kinship map does not show connections outside the parish, they may be linked to other places. Kinship throws a flimsy web over a very large area indeed, but underneath are many clusters where relationships are very intense. These relationships correspond to degree of kinship only roughly, but they are cast within the conceptual mould of kinship and subject to its constraints and privileges. With a different type of evidence it is possible that kinship could provide the kind of delimitations being sought, but the existing data, in which clusters of socially significant kin are obscured under the cloud of a vague 'belonging', suggest that kinship divides the population into small cells, interconnected in such a generalized way as to defy definition.

5. Religion is often a ready means of identifying communities, and in Llan it certainly does this. 'Before the Methodist revival the parish church at the Llan [hamlet] was the only place of worship. Nonconformity destroyed this unity' (p. 104). A measure of the disunity is that the population of 500 is served by twelve churches and chapels, representing four Nonconformist sects and the Episcopal Church (p. 104), allowing one church or chapel for every twelve to fifteen families (p. 50). There is a tendency to identify named neighbourhoods with chapels (p. 105), and Rees' map showing the distribution of chapels and churches in relation to these neighbourhoods indicates some consistency between the location of places of worship and the farms from which congregations are gathered, as might be expected; but there are ten of these.

Thus in the five major realms of social control examined, the result has been the same for each—marked divisive tendencies characterize them all. To this should be added that the topographical map (p. 12) shows six quite distinct divisions. Moreover, each of these realms—religious, economic, kinship, neighbourhood and territorial—follows a fairly consistent distribution pattern. This in turn means a type of fractionization displaying a multiplicity of mutually supporting linkages. Fractionization, inherent in dispersed habitat, has the general effect of knotting ties into small bundles, attached to small localities, and effecting the intensification of local interests at the expense of wide-span linkages. Since the span of the youth group is considerably wider than any of these small localities, the boundary of the youth group community cannot be envisaged in socio-geographical terms. While these terms can tell us much about the quantity and directions of social relationships, a mechanical treatment of them wholly fails to feel their texture.

Despite the divisions, everyone living in the parish is familiar with everyone else to a greater or lesser degree. In this sense it might be permissible to refer to the parish as a face-to-face community, but practically all residential districts anywhere compel people, by reason of propinquity, to indulge in face-to-face relationships of sorts. My experience in a recently occupied housing estate is that people get to know one another in a remarkably short time, and it takes only a little longer before they enter into frequent and regularized relationships. Left at the level of mere face-to-face relationships, the kind and intensity of social intercourse in Llan would remain indistinct from a general typification so nebulous that it could be applied to virtually all human communities but saying little about any of them. I begin, therefore by referring to some of the details of social relationships in the parish of Llan.

First, the population is remarkably stable. Of the total population, 85 per cent of the householders and housewives were born either there or in the surrounding parishes, as were 75 per cent of their parents. About half the heads of households were born in the parish itself, and the same was true of their fathers. Although there has been much movement between farms over the area as a whole (discounting the drift into the industrial areas after 1841, which reduced the population by half in a century), the contemporary population has deep historical roots there (p. 14). Not only are they people who know the details of one another's lives over the period of a lifetime, but each individual's characteristics are enriched by those which he inherits; and the latter are known by his neighbours. It is significant in attempting to typify social relationships in Llan that the mode of identification is not by name but by connections with others.[14] Identification is not a matter of an individual's status, but of his position in a web of relationships. (Such identification, while giving a context to each individual, also differentiates clusters of people sharing a closer identity among themselves than they do with others.) I have witnessed this mode of identification, and what is striking about it is that as one proceeds along the chain of people which links one individual to another, many of the characteristics of these intervening people are given, providing a density to social relationships quite alien to other situations where there may be considerable face-to-face relationships but from which inherited intimacies are excluded.

The absence of stratification further intensifies relationships, since, although there is a considerable range in the size of farms,[15] from a few acres to several hundred, this economic differentiation does not obstruct sociability; inhabitants enjoy the social freedom of people whose lives are not so different as to divert their relationships into the stratification of a class structure. Education is of the same kind for all. Religious gatherings, and the form chapel services often take—prayer meetings which approximate to a public confessionary—means that members are not merely a congregation of co-religionists but part of a group which reveals such delicate intimacies that social relationships in secular contexts which threatened a breach of this confidence could not be tolerated. Perhaps of greater importance than any of these indices of the nature of social relationships are the two facts that the population is small, and that the poverty of the environment saddles the farmers with debt (p. 31). Without the means to seek pleasures further afield, cut off from the diversionary pressures of external interests, and bereft of the instruments of modern mass media, every detail of social relationships comes to have a significance which would assume the irrelevance of trivia in a more sophisticated community. Inter-marriage[16] increases the knowledge of other people's affairs, but it also creates an involvement of interests. It is one thing to have an appetite for gossip, but quite another thing when the gossip is relevant to urgent and various interests.

These eight criteria—inherited social relationships and the historical depth of relationships implied by them, the positioning of individuals in a web of relationships, the sociability of a rank-free community, an evenness of education, the privacy of religious worship in small groups, the paucity of the economy, and a multiplicity of marital interconnections—are the kinds of index, it is suggested, which must be given priority in any attempt to give accuracy to the typification of these social relationships. Previously an attempt was made to narrow the area of morality which the youth group controlled. The behavioural indices which have now been suggested should facilitate the definition of the moral community in geographical and population terms. The information given by Rees is not, unfortunately, sufficiently specific[17] to set exact territorial boundaries to the territorial domain of the youth group of Llan hamlet, but if the data scattered throughout the book are considered alongside his three maps showing the physical features and the distribution of dwellings (p. 12, fig. 2), kinship (p. 76, fig. 28) and neighbourhoods and places of worship (p. 102, fig. 31), I estimate that it encompasses about eighty of the 114 farms in the parish, located mainly in the eastern half but including the north central area as well.[18]

In thus designating the population over which the group exerts controls, I am aware that the area is not congruent with any of the specific sets of relationships discussed in this paper. What this assumes in turn is that a moral community is not bounded by one thread of social relationships but is laced around by many. Hence the difficulty of giving it territorial definition. In practice it would be relatively easy to say where its periphery lay by noting the farms from which the youths are recruited and the people against whom they take action. Indeed, part of the prime importance of these youth groups in Wales derives from the fact that they serve the purpose of fencing off communities within which certain moral characteristics are definable; their significance in this context is thrown into relief by the fact that their domain, alone among various sets of social relationships, shows the knitting together of otherwise isolated nuclei, and it characterizes a domain of accepted morality to constitute a community. Against this view it may be argued that morality, in the Welsh countryside, does not begin and end in a particular locality. In a general sense this is obviously true; but the particulars of morality, and the specialization of sentiments which wraps it around, are localized, and they are bounded by the span of youth-group control with regard to both acts and actors.

Thus far in the argument attention has been focused on the moral community and its control by a youth group in order to delimit the type of behaviour on which constraints are set, and the general field of social relationships which circumscribe the community. It is now necessary to ask the question: in what kind of general social circumstances is this type of social control likely to occur? In suggesting an approach to an answer, I wish to refer briefly to conditions in a south Lebanese village which I have studied.[19] Here people live in a nucleated village, perched on a hill, clearly defined territorially and certain of its social relationships, if not completely bounded by its territorial limits, showing conspicuous consistency with these limits. An impressive range of crops are grown, providing a rich subsistence base for virtually all households. Moreover, there is a sufficient economic surplus to support rank. Roughly one fifth of the total population, owning about half the cultivated land, live a leisured life without the necessity of engaging in the manual labour of cultivation.

This leisured group—which I have referred to elsewhere as the 'learned families'—is vested with moral authority on account of either a claim to descent from the Prophet Muhammad or a claim to superior religious learning. This moral authority is exercised over a wide field of social relationships; it would be true to say that several forms of control are in the keeping of this group. When it exerts its moral authority, its actions include areas of moral relations similar to those controlled by the youth group in the Llan hamlet. Its members interfere in cases of adultery; they solemnize marriages;

they have the authority to break off betrothals; they are permitted to rebuke in public for sexual or other misdemeanours; they regulate marriage alliances between Muslims and Christians, since such marriages are invalid unless the non-Muslim has been accepted by them as a convert. Because they assume these controls on the grounds of their superior knowledge of Koranic laws and precepts they enjoy a wide manipulative latitude in their activities. Rank vested with religious authority, of the kind which is permanently present in a residential sense in a local community and spread over a category of people, thus making it an effective participant, so to speak, in the daily lives of people, is a significant factor; and the absence of this type of rank in Llan, by the same token, is critical to the existence of the youth group. The brief stipulations added to the term 'rank' are necessary because, unqualified, it loses its utility. Rank appears in various forms in Llan, and among the people with whom comparison will be made presently—the Azande—but in neither case is it so locally anchored in its interests that it becomes caught up in the minutiae of individual idiosyncratic behaviour.

In south Lebanon groups of men, usually of substantial number, are residents in villages, and they are equipped religiously to deal with matters of morality. Religion rests heavily on Llan also, if the number of churches and chapels is any indication. Prior to the advent of Nonconformity in Wales there was only one religious denomination in the countryside, the Church of England. It is possible that, with this unity, and the tendency to centralize, the Church was able to dominate fields of relationships now denied to it. Whatever its role might have been in the past, the present three Episcopal Churches of the parish, can now claim the allegiance of only about one third of all the families, and only one fifth belong to the parish church in the Llan hamlet (Rees, p. 104). The control of the rector of Llan hamlet is, therefore, closely circumscribed, even in a titular sense; and when he attempted to capture part of the youth group's activities—he opened the Old School room to them for table-tennis and other games—the reaction of the youths was contemptuous and destructive (p. 82). Nonconformity, from the outset, was never able to grip the whole population in a unity, or even an entire small segment of it, for when it came to Wales it came in disunity: in 1842 the Independents and Wesleyans were building chapels within two hundred yards of each other, there are twelve religious groups, one restricts its communion to members of its own sect, one has a creed but others do not (p. 114), and so on. Moreover, since the chapels are numerous and the congregations very small, not one of them is able to support its own resident minister (p. 123). The effect of Nonconformity, at least in the context of this argument, was to fractionize the community into very small groups and stamp them with the seal of religion. Organized Christianity has shown itself incapable of touching the sensitive areas of relationships, where Islam, without an elaborate bureaucratic apparatus, has been able to probe deeply into them.[20]

In another part of the Islamic world, however, morality is not in the keeping of a category of religious experts. Among the Bedouin of eastern Libya men who claim to be endowed with *Baraka* (divine goodness or blessing) function as teachers of the Koran, among other things, and to this extent impinge on the field of morality, but they do not intrude on moral relationships between individuals. Bedouin groups constitute corporations, and it is the corporation which asserts moral authority over its members. Adultery, for example, is a matter for the corporation, and so are other offences such as pre-marital pregnancy and certain husband–wife relationships. These kinds of relations are subject to corporate control because they are viewed as affecting the collectivity (which is defined as a corporation) and not as affecting individuals. It would be tempting to view a corporation as a moral community in the same way as the domain of the youth group can be viewed as one moral community, but a Bedouin corporation expands its field of activities to include many more, and distinctively disparate, sets of relationships, including important jural and political affairs. Moreover, these corporations exist where resources are both ephemerally and uncontrollably scarce, and are distributed in such a way that division into individual lots would be economically catastrophic. Resources in Wales, although on the margin of economic sufficiency, are stabler and richer than those of the Bedouin, and they can consequently be broken up into smaller parcels of possessions. The Bedouin case, therefore, comparatively promising superficially, serves only the purpose—albeit an important one—of excluding the possibility of corporations for the purpose of moral control in the Welsh countryside, and in doing so assists the task of specifying the circumstances in which moral control of the kind performed by youth groups appears.

A third study I have carried out in Islam was centred on an olive plantation of 184 farms in Tripolitania, in western Libya. Here habitat is dispersed, although more systematically than in Llan. Farms, in pairs or in groups of four, were built at intervals by the Italians in the late 1930's, with distances of about one to three kilometres between them. Except for a small number, these farms are now occupied by Arabs,[21] drawn from the tents, the towns and the surrounding villages. Like Llan, the population is divided religiously, for although the Arabs are all Sunni Muslims, the congregations which gather for prayers on feast day and for festivities in farm houses afterwards are roughly equal to the number of religious groups in Llan. The number of schools is of the same order as the number of religious groups. When I began my field work there were eight shack shops distributed throughout the plantation. Kinship connects little nuclei of people on the plantation and, from these, linkages spread out beyond the boundaries of the plantations in different directions; as in Llan, some of the farms are unconnected within the administrative boundaries.

Again, superficially this area appears to compare closely with Llan, but there is no suggestion of any instrument of moral control sociologically similar to the youth group. Each nucleus is its own moral authority, save where kinship connections outside the plantation (these are mainly to Bedouin areas farther south) are coincident with economic interests, and larger groups of people may become involved.

As an example of this fractionization of morality I cite the case of a man who accused another of philandering with women at a wedding. The accusation was made at a police station, and soon became a court case. The accuser met with rebuff, was sacked from his job as roadman, and shortly afterwards left the farm, in which he was a shareholder, to join his kinsfolk in the camps. The interest of the case—containing an accusation of a kind I have not before seen taken to law during any of my field work periods among Arabs—is that this somewhat nebulous matter of morality, which by its very nature could be only a matter of opinion, was taken directly to law, and was not adjudicated by a community. The matter is put in this way because it seems to be a case, *par excellence*, where the consensus of opinion should count; but this presumes a community. Here, when the small nucleus of two or four farms fails to deal with a moral problem, the recourse is to a court standing removed from the general area of plantation life altogether.

Now, one of the features of olive farming, at least when it is carried out systematically, is that there is little need for economic co-operation between farms. A man ploughs the ground between the lines of trees several times a year, taking two or three days each time, but one man can do the entire ploughing without difficulty. Picking requires more labour, but the people available on one farm, in most cases, and on two in a minority of cases, provide sufficient labour. Divided in terms of social relationships, economic necessity does not coerce co-operation, and in failing to do so exaggerates the isolation of each nucleus. Only three people resident on the plantation knew the inhabitants of all the farms: an Arab dispenser, an Italian who tended the water pumps and collected the water tax, and myself. When people do not know one another, they are not concerned with each other's affairs. Dispersed settlement *per se* does not give rise to youth groups or their sociological equivalent. Therefore, to the stress given earlier to the condition of dispersed habitat, as one factor related to youth groups, stress on the need to co-operate in production must now be added. Productive co-operation, however, is too unrefined. Two of its elements need to be noted: the groups which co-operate are not co-terminus with the other groupings which are present, and the co-operating groups vary in composition with the several tasks undertaken.

It can therefore be said that the kind of control of morality exercised by Welsh youth groups will not appear where rank is present, nor where resources are held by a jural collectivity, which we defined as a corporation, nor where dispersal of habitat leads to the fractionization of a population into nuclei unconnected by the strands of productive co-operation. The conditions conducive to their appearance are those where an intensity of relationships knots people into overlapping groups, but where formalized categories such as rank are absent. Of the many social anthropologically significant elements embedded in Welsh youth groups, one of these elements alone can never provide for their appearance, but taken together they constitute a marked density and diversity of relationships, and, in turn, these give people a sufficient identity of interests to invest their moral concerns in an institutionalized form of behaviour.[22] Unable to act themselves, adults delegate both decisions and actions to youths, jurally minors, and, in this limited sense only, external to the situations in which they operate. Perhaps the inexperience of youth, the freedom from involvement in the travail of jural social relationships, endows youths with the clarity to see essential issues obscured from adults by the tangle of considerations surrounding each problem, plaguing them with the doubt of indecision because they are so aware that each relationship percolates into many others. The ignorance of immaturity gives the youth group the irresponsible freedom to act; maturity traps adults into the measured responsibility of inaction.

My interest in the behaviour of Welsh youth groups had its origin in a quite different problem. It arose from a concern with the joking relationship between a man and his mother's brother among the Cyrenaican Bedouin. The joking between two such related people is so persistent that it is contrived. Whenever they meet, the sister's son indulges in some form of buffoonery with his mother's brother, whether it is horseplay, verbal teasing or talk about women and sexual relations. Behaviour towards patrilateral relatives of the ascending generation is in marked contrast to this. Women are never mentioned, teasing of any sort is excluded, and instead young men are expected to show respect and deference to senior agnates, corroborating what they say and acquiescing when contradicted. A man can demand his equal share, however, from agnates; his mother's brother, when he gives, offers as a grace. When in need, and unable to make a demand in terms of an agnatic relationship, a man can supplicate his mother's brother for assistance. This applies especially to marriage, since if a man cannot approach his father or senior agnates directly he has perforce to call on his mother's brother. It is not the purpose to expound the relationship fully here; these brief references are intended only as a characterization sufficient to indicate how I arrived at my present position.

This initial interest in a Bedouin joking relationship led me to Colson's work on Tonga joking relationships.[23] Among the Tonga, clans are paired for joking, and in this relationship people are permitted, among other things, to rebuke publicly the immorality of a joking partner. Like the Bedouin joking relationships, Tonga joking operates on an individual plane and relates partly to male–female affairs. Also, in both cases individuals can supplicate a joking partner. On a number of issues there appeared to be cultural comparability between the two, and, to strengthen this comparability I sought other instances of joking patterns in culturally disparate contexts. After roaming through some of the literature on superficially similar patterns of behaviour in Mediterranean countries, parts of Africa and some Pacific islands, I was left with a bewildering variety of types of joking relationships, some of which were between kin of the same generation only, some between kin of adjacent generations, some between non-kin, some associated with political office, and some between groups of people. This morass of similarity in the form of behaviour had come to mean little more than an accumulation of instances, until, largely by chance, I took up Rees' work.

Partly because of the intrinsic interest of the data, and partly because I was familiar with youth-group activities in Wales, Rees' work provided the stimulus to re-consider the whole problem of joking relationships. As a beginning to a theoretical reappraisal I re-read Radcliffe-Brown's two articles on joking relationships.[24] In these two articles all the forms of joking relationships he could uncover in the literature are included, and he treated this wide diversity of types with the aim of formulating a single theory about them, and of defining 'the kind of structural situation in which we may expect to find well marked joking relationships'.[25] In his view, joking relationships complement other forms of behaviour in a society; more than this, the behaviour complements antagonistically —it is a 'reversal' of 'the usual behaviour'.[26] As an example of this he offers the recurring pattern of privileged familiarity a man enjoys with his mother's brother in societies where descent in the patriline is of cardinal importance in a number of jural matters, like the definition of a person's status, his right to inheritance and so on. He contrasts the legal rights and duties, and the accompanying stresses and strains they contain, which accrue to a man by virtue of birth into a patrilineal clan or lineage, with his relation to his mother's lineage, to which he stands external, 'though one in whom they [members of his mother's lineage] have a very special and tender interest'.[27] The joking relationship with the mother's brother, he claimed, is derived from the mother's relationship with the child, characterized by tenderness, indulgence[28] and affectionate care,[27] and by extension the child grows up to expect the same assistance and indulgence from the mother's relatives. He contrasts this relationship to agnatic behaviour as its exact opposite, and the 'one basic determinant' of the opposition between joking and highly formal relationships 'is that the social structure separates them in such a way as to make many of their interests divergent, so that conflict or hostility might result'.[29] Finally, joking relationships with the wife's brothers and sisters 'can be regarded as the means of establishing and maintaining social equilibrium in a type of structural situation that results in many societies from marriage'.[30]

There are many objections to Radcliffe-Brown's views, but since I am not proposing a detailed criticism here I list briefly some of my objections.

1. The analysis proceeds on the assumption that the mother's brother/sister's son is always a one-to-one relationship, whereas in reality this is rare. My Cyrenaican Bedouin genealogies show a man who had twenty-three children, who were all maternal relatives to one man. These twenty-three children, moreover, were the children of several wives, and each group of half-siblings had relationships with different maternal relatives, although they all had various relationships with the kin of all their mothers. Complexities arising out of this kind of situation cannot be comprehended by Radcliffe-Brown's analysis, they can only be excluded. Or are some to be given preferential selection, and, if so, which of them? One instance of these complexities will suffice to illustrate the difficulty of following Radcliffe-Brown. A man had two sons by a freed slave woman. They inherited part of his wealth, but the chief beneficiary was his sister's son, whom he had had circumcised, to whom he gave what little religious education he had, and whom he provided with wealth for marriage. Anyone who performs these duties for a male junior becomes his *de facto* father. The mother's brother, in this case, behaved something like a father but was not the father in the fullest sense; yet he was not like a mother's brother either, because he had abrogated important duties of a father. He had also singled out one of three brothers to bestow his favours on, with the result that his relations with the other two were sour, and their relations with the favoured brother turned to hostility. Are details of this sort to be neglected in analysis?

2. It is a central point in Radcliffe-Brown's argument that the mother's brother is structurally external. He does not participate in the jural relationships of his sister's son's lineage, and largely because of this, instead of having to fulfil onerous duties, he accepts and gives privileged disrespect. Among the Bedouin of Cyrenaica parallel cousin marriage—sometimes first parallel cousin marriage—is practised, and consequently a mother's brother of the first degree can also be a paternal uncle of the second degree. Two complications of the relationships follow from this:

3. The hostilities built into the contractual relationship of agnation and the permissiveness of the joking relationship are coincident in one person.

4. Since this coincidence occurs in one person, the divergence of interests disappears. Radcliffe-Brown's analysis is inappropriate unless the two roles appear separately in two persons. Even in the situation where the mother's brother is located in a lineage other than that of his sister's son, I cannot accept that joking is a function of divergent interests.

5. The same indulgence and affection of women for their children appears in three other Arab areas in which I have worked. In all four, the kinship terms for father's brother (*ʿAmm*) and mother's brother (*Khāl*) are the same; indeed, as far as I know, there is universal consistency in the use of these two terms, applied to these two relatives, throughout the Arab world, while most of the other kinship terms show local variation. Yet among the Bedouin a marked joking relationship is found in association with the term *Khāl* but is absent in the other three. In any event, the general sentiment of the mother's loving care for her children is so common that it cannot possibly be considered as basic to a joking partnership.

6. My main objection to Radcliffe-Brown's analysis is the use he makes of the comparative method. For what he has done is to throw together fragments of evidence, from various areas, of types of joking relationship which are clearly quite unlike. He did this because he focused his analysis on the form of the behaviour while neglecting to ascertain the actual social acts which the form seemingly, in his case, obscured. A world-wide comparison of joking relationships is as futile a pursuit as a similar comparison of bride-wealth, or witchcraft, when all that the various manifestations of each have in common is the English term with which we have chosen to label them. Therefore a general theory of joking relationships is not feasible, and any suggestions of general worth which come from such a study are coincidental. While I do not wish to commend Griaule's[31] analysis of joking relationships, I accept his view, as given by Radcliffe-Brown, 'that to classify together the various examples of "joking relationships" and to look for a general explanation is like classifying together the ceremonies at which church bells are rung, such as funerals and weddings, calling them all *cérémonies à cloches*'.[32]

Although I did not set out in search of a general theory of joking relationships, I must admit that I first kept to joking relationships, but when I re-read Radcliffe-Brown I soon saw the folly of following the facile familiarity of the form of the behaviour. At about the same time I happened to be teaching the theory of Azande witchcraft to a class at Manchester, and those of its features related to the control of certain relationships seemed comparable to the control exercised by Welsh youth groups. Most of the analysis of these groups presented in this article stemmed directly from Evans-Pritchard's account of *Witchcraft, Oracles and Magic among the Azande*.[33] I wish now to show how this came about.

When Evans-Pritchard worked among the Azande, the people lived concentrated along roads or in large settlements, and the distance between them varied from one to several miles (Evans-Pritchard, p. 15). During the rainy season the tall savannah grass cuts off communities of people and restricts movement to well trodden paths. When drought comes, the bush is fired and the countryside is seen to be intersected by innumerable small streams (p. 17). The relative isolation of these small communities is reinforced by the general isolation in which Azande find themselves (pp. 16, 17).

The population is divided into kingdoms, ruled over by kings, and separated from one another by uninhabited bush (p. 15). Kings, princes, nobles and commoners present a hierarchical order of stratification which suggests a basic difference between the Azande and the communities of Welshmen in Llan, but when differentiation was examined in the latter the emphasis was not on the total absence of ranked differences, but on the inability of rank to control areas of morality. In the case of the Azande, Evans-Pritchard makes it clear that, since it is the social situation which indicates the 'cause' of witchcraft, neither the Vongara (the clan from which kings are recruited) aristocracy nor its nobles participate in what might be called the witchcraft communities of commoners, since they are not caught up in their social affairs. Indeed, Evans-Pritchard speaks of a social cleavage between the Vongara and commoner classes (p. 15), and elsewhere in the book he claims that princes do 'not wish to be troubled with every little' accusation of witchcraft among commoners (p. 94), that however jealous princes may be of each other they do not allow commoners to bring them into contempt with accusations of witchcraft (p. 173), and that they are contemptuous of their subjects (p. 13). Throughout the book the analysis is concerned with the social affairs of commoners, and although an accusation of witchcraft may be taken to the prince's poison oracle for validation, it is the infallability of the oracle which is decisive, rather than the prince in person interfering in matters about which he knows little, if anything. Therefore, following both the specific and general directives in Evans-Pritchard's analysis, I exclude the ranked differences among the Azande as significant controls of the social relationships subsumed under witchcraft.[34]

In using the phrase 'witchcraft communities' earlier, the implication was that there are communities of people within which accusations of witchcraft occur, but that accusations are not made from one community to another. This limitation of the socio-geographic area within which accusations are made is set effectively by the beliefs of witchcraft themselves. Witchcraft, if it is to strike a person successfully, must speed directly to its target, for witchcraft which fails to find its victim is likely to return to the person from whom it emanates, and such witchcraft is highly dangerous. Witchcraft, also, speeds its way to its victim at night, and consequently, for it to hit its mark, the exact location of the victim must always be known. Since these conditions cannot be satisfied with regard to persons of other settlements or villages, accusations are confined to co-residents (pp. 33–7). Other references make it clear that accusations are localized in this way. Thus when discussing a Zande's interest in 'witchcraft only as an agent on definite occasions', the question Evans-Pritchard states a Zande asks is 'Who among his neighbours have grudges against him?' (p. 26). Also, in a passage on witches, the statement is made that 'it is generally only those who make themselves disliked by many of their neighbours who are often accused of witchcraft' (p. 114); and, in reference to the manner of dealing with witchcraft, 'the injured man and his kinsmen are angry at . . . an attack on their welfare by a neighbour' (p. 85). Moreover, they are neighbours who share both an intimacy and a history of personal relationships, as Evans-Pritchard's comments on the significance of oracular consultations make clear, for enmities among people develop over time (pp. 102, 103) and a newcomer to a neighbourhood is thus immune from accusations (p. 172). Again, the success of witch-doctors in identifying witches rests largely on their information 'about local enmities and squabbles' (p. 170). Finally, there is the explicit assertion: 'Witchcraft does not strike a man at a great distance, but only injures people in the vicinity'

(p. 36). Apart from these specific references to the limitation of witchcraft activity imposed 'by conditions of space' (p. 36), much of the argument in the book is slanted towards the connection between certain intense social relationships (to be examined later) and accusations of witchcraft; these relations are mainly of a kind which obtain among people who, if not necessarily close neighbours in a spatial sense, are intimately involved in each others' affairs. Intimacy of social relationships is the breeding ground of accusations, and while relationships between communities may be regular, frequent and important in certain respects, they are excluded from the realm of relationships controlled by witchcraft.

'Being part of the body, witchcraft-substance grows as the body grows' (p. 30). But since it is not in fact a part of the body, witchcraft has nothing to do with physical age. The growth of witchcraft in a person is a growth in social maturity and the progressive involvement in the complexities of social relationships which accompanies it. Boys are excluded, not because they fall between the ages of twelve to sixteen, but because they do not yet carry the social responsibilities which inevitably surround older persons with suspicion; for this reason it is the young, in their innocence, who act as operators at an oracular consultation, when the poison oracle is used (p. 323). If boys are not usually accused of witchcraft it is not because it is not present in them. Most Azande, at one time or another, are accused, and since witchcraft is inherited from father to son and from mother to daughter, it resides in most people, regardless of age. On the same basis, an accusation is against the clan of the accused, since he has inherited witchcraft with the rest of his kinsmen. In practice Azande do not subscribe to these commonsense implications of inheritance rules. It is of greater commonsense concern to them to know whether a particular person is bewitching another at a particular moment (pp. 24, 25). 'Hence the doctrine of hereditary witchcraft probably has little influence towards indicating to a man his possession of witchcraft', even to the extent that an accusation has no significance to the sons or other relatives of the accused (p. 127). If Azande followed the implications of the doctrine of hereditary the situation would arise where the attention would be focused on witchcraft in the abstract, unrelated to particular persons, and large numbers of clansmen would become involved immediately whenever an accusation was to be made. Inheritance of witchcraft explains how persons come to possess it, but the belief that it can lie dormant, or 'cool', in a person limits the extension of the doctrine to particular persons at specific moments, and this connects it to social relations between a victim and an accused: 'witchcraft is a social fact, a person' (p. 73). Social relationships between two people come first, and when the state of these relationships calls for it an accusation is made, and not the other way about. 'Witchcraft does not make a person commit adultery' (p. 74); it is the knowledge or suspicion of adultery which leads a person to accuse another, not a suspicion that a person is a witch in a general sense. It is of the utmost significance that this order of precedence is always kept in mind, otherwise confusion is likely to occur between the occasion which permits an accusation to be made and the social relationships which prompt a person to a public condemnation of another.

Social relationships, left undefined, constitute too broad a category to make meaningful what witchcraft is all about. It is now necessary to attempt to specify more precisely the social relationships which are susceptible to control by accusations of witchcraft. Several explicit statements by Evans-Pritchard assist the narrowing of the field. Thus 'I am not here concerned with crime that can be brought before the courts and penalized, nor with civil offences for which compensation can be exacted by legal suits'[35] excludes the clearly legal aspects of jural relationships, but it does not exclude the sentiments which people hold about litigants, nor the general evaluation of the rightness or wrongness of a person's action in taking a matter to court. This rider is added because witchcraft deals largely with people's evaluation of their fellow men, as the following statement shows: 'the drive behind all acts of witchcraft is to be looked for in emotions and sentiments common to all men—malice, jealousy, greed, envy, backbiting, slander, and so on' (p. 170). When, therefore, a person is successfully accused of witchcraft the condemnation is of an act or acts lying in the general field of morality. Before making an accusation a man first considers who among his neighbours bears him ill-will, so that when an accusation is made it is tantamount to saying that this man's envy, malice, greed, and so on, is adversely affecting the social well-being of his fellow men; 'moral condemnation is predetermined' (pp. 107, 109). While it is a useful step forward to identify the field of action of witchcraft as linked to morality, the diffuseness of this field gives it an expanse sufficient to incorporate such a range of activities as to raise doubts about its utility. The danger of an institutional mode of control which considers everything is that it might fail to decide anything. Since witchcraft provides clear decisions, it is necessary to attempt to characterize further those social relationships to which its decisions relate.

As far as I am able to discover, the most frequently mentioned breach in social relationships cited by Evans-Pritchard is adultery. It is referred to on at least eighteen separate occasions,[36] and this does not include references to love affairs and the like which are not specifically designated as adultery. Scattered throughout the book are many remarks suggesting the nature of social relationships preceding the resort to witchcraft and, since so much interest has been shown in the misfortunes which a person uses to justify an oracular consultation, it is of importance in the context of this essay to weight the social relationships which are prior to both misfortune and consultation.

One case details the sickness afflicting a man who spurned a woman's invitation to have sex relations with her in the bush, and of his wife's counter-action (pp. 53, 54). A second case tells of a man wishing to marry consulting the poison oracle to find out whether the girl he has chosen is the right one (p. 88). And in a third case, where intent to marry is again the reason for a consultation, the man addresses the oracle saying, among other things, 'you are marrying her to me' (p. 298), although the course of action should the answer be negative is not given. But in another section, where a man has made his choice only to find that it is a wrong choice, it is clear there would be grounds for an accusation of witchcraft (p. 341). In a fourth case a man who is betrothed begins paying bride-spears to her father, on the verdict of a single oracle test to be followed by a confirmatory test later (p. 301). Consultations concerning the suitability of the girl are only part of the point of enquiries conducted in advance of marriage; a man is also curious to know whether relationships with his affines will prosper—but, of course, since the oracle cannot in fact foretell the future, these tests are attempts to deal with information or suspicions about present relationships.

The oracle can be used to break off a betrothal when one of the parties decides that the match is undesirable (p. 350), or if a man's intended parents-in-law wish to thwart his advances, or if both parties are in agreement but both wish to ensure that they will not suffer interference from others (p. 344). Men previously joined as affines, but between whom relations have deteriorated to the extent of breaking the marriage, interpret these relationships as the breeding ground for witchcraft (p. 301). After marriage, affinity still presents problems, and witchcraft can be evoked to deal with them; some of the questions in poison oracle seances detailed by Evans-Pritchard include questions about affinal interference in the relationships between a man and his wife (pp. 104, 304, 305).

In the more restricted range of relationships between a man and his wife, witchcraft appears as a means of allaying suspicions by bringing them to public notice and designating an offender. The question 'Will my wife die?' asked of an oracle, is only another way of stating that an intruder is interfering (p. 88). A man, after consulting his 'rubbing-board oracle about myself and my wife' (p. 94) exhorts his neighbours to listen to his warning lest either he or his wife suffer misfortune, necessitating a direct confrontation with the witch through the use of the poison oracle. Quarrels between husband and wife, stress and strains between co-wives, a wife's relationships with neighbours, are all matters which in one way or another are delegated to the oracles for adjudication, judgment and regulation.

In this examination of the social relationships which lie concealed at the root of witchcraft accusations, overlain with a thick layer of the misfortunes which are used as promptings for consultations, the following categories appear to be significant: sexual intercourse in the form of adultery or illicit love affairs, the selection of wives (and the control of marriage implied by it), affinal relationships, social relationships between husband and wives, the condition of co-wives and the relation of spouses to their neighbours. In short, the range of relationships, beginning with the wide span of any relationships falling outside the strictly jural field which required the application of a sense of fairness, first contracted to a general area of morality; and morality has now been further circumscribed to leave only that kind of morality which springs from sex differentiation, sometimes with specific reference to sex relations, not by any means confined to them, but always emphasizing the social rather than the physically sexual component in them.

Other than the social relationships discussed here, there are many other events which take a man to the poison oracle. Indeed, in a catalogue of 'causes' for consultation the actual social relationships between the victim and the accused would be obscured by the more immediate misfortunes. Evans-Pritchard's analysis is mainly of a mode of thought, and for this reason he gives stress to misfortunes,

'It is only in matters affecting his health and in his more serious social and economic ventures that he consults oracles and witch-doctors about witchcraft. Generally he consults them about possible misfortunes in the future . . .' (p. 88). Witchcraft is 'a function of misfortune and of personal relationships but also comprises a moral judgment' (p. 107). Discussing where Zande moral notions differ profoundly from our own, Evans-Pritchard claims that 'any misfortune evokes the notion of injury and the desire for retaliation', whereas 'in our society only certain misfortunes are believed to be due to the wickedness of other people, and it is only in these limited situations of misfortune that we can retaliate through prescribed channels upon the authors of them' (p. 113). Misfortunes in Azande witchcraft are as varied as they are many. Sometimes a man stubs his toe against a stump of a tree and it festers, a piece of wood cracks in a carver's hands, a pot breaks in the care of a skilful potter; sometimes a crop fails, a hunt is unsuccessful, a journey is inauspicious; sometimes a man is seriously sick, a child dies at birth, a woman suffers injury from a fall off a branch of a tree.

Whatever the misfortune, when an oracle is consulted a name has to be put to it, and the selection of names is determined by the social relationships between the person who selects and the person selected. Misfortune is haphazard; the selection of names is deliberate. It is the selection of names which relates to morality, not misfortune. The essence of consultation is that a person cannot seek verdicts about moral relationships, for these are of significance only when particularized in social relationships, otherwise the whole of society would be condemned at one stroke, since no one is perfect. But to particularize it becomes necessary to select among people. Adultery may be evil, but a man must be suspect of the act; philandering with women may be immoral but until circumstances lead to suspicion that a particular man is practising it he is free of fault. Granted the grounds for suspicion, a particular event is required to proceed with consultation because it is in relation to a known event, not to suspicions, that an accusation can be made. It is in this context that misfortune assumes some importance, although, since misfortunes of one kind or another are readily available, the selection of the misfortune to be used as validation of a consultation would appear to be as whimsical as the occurrence of misfortune itself. That misfortune is not the 'cause' of an accusation is clear from the fact that a ne'er-do-well who is disliked by his fellow men is given short shrift when he attempts an accusation, however well founded it may be in misfortune (p. 78).

Implicit in this argument is the view that it is not the oracle which gives a verdict but the community of people who use it. It is they who decide whether or not a person is justified in seeking a verdict against another, and this they do having regard to their assessment of social relationships obtaining between victim and accused. In order to deflect the attention away from the evils in social relationships which neither witchcraft nor anything else can eradicate, the particularity of a misfortune is used as the subterfuge, and the oracle is employed to conceal the fact that the decision is taken by a community of people. I turn now to the way in which a decision arises out of agreement among people of a community, and to the significance of oracles in this process.

There are five means of consultation for the purpose of finding witches among the Azande. They are the rubbing-board oracle and witch-doctors, the 'three sticks' oracle, the termites oracle, and the poison oracle, and they are rated in this ascending order of importance by Evans-Pritchard and the Azande (pp. 91, 92, 352, 353), with the rubbing-board oracle and witch-doctors equated as inferior, (pp. 149, 187, 188, 194, 360, 373), and the poison oracle as supreme (p. 260). This rating is drawn up largely in terms of reliability, the latter varying with the degree of human manipulation that is possible.

The rubbing-board oracle, consisting of a kind of wooden stool, the surface of which is smeared with plant juices, and a disc with a handle which is rubbed against the sticky surface of the stool, gives a verdict depending on whether the disc sticks or moves freely. Obviously, the operator can exert more or less force as he chooses, and since cheating is easy it is considered to be inferior. The witch-doctor is known locally and knows his client, as well as the members of the audience at a seance, and he is therefore too much influenced by the people concerned to be of any great reliability.

The three sticks oracle consists of three tubular pieces of wood or manioc stalk, two arranged side by side and the third on top. An answer to an enquiry is given by the sticks remaining in position, or if the top piece has dropped into a space created by the two side-by-side sticks rolling apart. The Azande appreciate that what happens to the sticks depends on how they are stacked by the operator, and this oracle is not, therefore, considered to be much more reliable than the rubbing-board oracle.

The termites oracle is thought to be very reliable (p. 353). It consists of two pieces of branches of a certain tree thrust into a termite mound, an oracular verdict being derived from the amount of wood, if any, the termites have eaten. Apart from the fact that the wood can be tougher or tenderer, answers to an enquirer depend on the way the question is phrased (p. 355), and since both pieces of wood might be eaten, left untouched, or only nibbled, or in one of a variety of conditions, there is plenty of scope for interpretation.

The poison oracle consists of administering poison to a chicken, the verdict depending on whether the chicken dies or survives, what its movements are, whether it seems to die and then revives, and so on. The supremacy of this oracle rests on the apparent freedom from human interference and the chance element of the chicken's survival or demise—Evans-Pritchard conducted probability tests in which twenty-two fowls died and twenty-seven recovered in a total of forty-nine tests which he recorded (p. 328). Excluding the quantity of poison used—this is irrelevant to the Azande, anyway, for the poison is ritualized and it is this ritual substance which conveys information through the fowl's movements, not poison—the oracle is subject to manipulation on two counts. The reactions of the chicken must be interpreted; and 'there is an art in questioning the oracle, for it must answer "yes" or "no" to a question and a man can therefore define the terms of the answer by stating them in the question' (p. 351).

Not one of the oracles is reliable, therefore, in any acceptable sense, although the skills required to elicit a preferred answer vary with the oracle used. A gradation of the oracles in a hierarchy of reliability is an irrelevance. If the use of the different oracles is not a matter of inferiority and superiority, or of unreliability and reliability, to what, then, do the different oracles relate? Why are there four means of finding a witch? The answers to these questions cannot be in terms of reliability or superiority, since two are thought to be quite unreliable and inferior by the Azande themselves, and only one is accorded the reliability of offering a truthful verdict. Moreover, it is hard to believe that the verdict of the poison oracle, consulted only in situations of stress, which is considered infallible, and whose decisions are more important and more far-reaching in their consequences than any of the other oracles, is free from human interference. It must be, surely, that the superiority and reliability of the poison oracle lie in the social importance of the matters put to it, and not in the nature of the oracle itself. Even stated in terms of the importance of the issues presented to the poison oracle, there is a danger of confusion in thinking about the problem, since the statement begs the question 'Important for what?'. It will now be argued that the several oracles serve disparate functions in relation to distinctively different groups.

The rubbing-board oracle is easily the most frequently used of all the oracles. It is transportable, expense is not incurred in its use, and it can be consulted without the fuss of rituals associated with the poison oracle. With regard to the use made of it, Evans-Pritchard writes that it is used 'in dozens of situations when the issues are of minor importance and hardly worthy of being presented to the poison oracle' (p. 360) and 'we may observe that this admission' (that it answers so many questions that it is bound to be wrong sometimes) 'can be made because situations of use are minor and do not involve social interrelations' (p. 361). On two counts this view that only minor issues are taken to the rubbing-board oracle appears ill-founded.

First, it is used for a preliminary selection of names before consulting the poison oracle (p. 91), so that some of the issues are the same for both oracles. Second, the details of consultations show that in many cases important issues are put to the rubbing-board oracle; for example, a daughter had run away from home after being beaten by her parents, and they wanted to know whether she had died, whether she was with relatives and whether she would return to them (p. 366); a man wishes to know whether his wife and unborn child will die during pregnancy; whether a wife is faithful to her husband; whether a witch has withdrawn his influence (pp. 368, 369). The importance of the rubbing-board oracle is not that only minor issues are dealt with, but that trivial and important matters are referred to it. And when important matters are afoot, a man can use the verdict of a rubbing-board oracle to give a public warning of witchcraft without identifying the witch: 'I have consulted the rubbing-board oracle about myself and my wife, and without hesitation it foretold misfortune to us. Therefore I said I would tell it to you that you might hear it . . .' (p. 94). This public declaration was made to neighbours, and in this fact lies the significance of the rubbing-board oracle: a man chooses the public to which he wishes to divulge his information. Selection is also present in the people who gather for a consultation, for a man can consult it alone in the privacy of his home, or in the company of a small number of friends of his choosing (pp. 366, 368). Suspicions are aired when the rubbing-board oracle is used. Confirmation of these suspicions encourages a man to seek, if he wishes, the assent of his chosen friends and neighbours. Therefore this is the oracle a man can use as a first test and consultation of opinion other than his own before proceeding with a charge against an enemy.

The three sticks oracle cannot be used as privately as the rubbing-board oracle because it is placed where it can be seen by passers by 'in a clearing at the edge of the garden where it borders the homestead or at the back of a hut' (p. 358) and it must be left there overnight. That is, the user cannot conceal from people the fact that he is consulting as effectively as he can when using the rubbing-board oracle. Significantly, Evans-Pritchard reports that the three sticks oracle is not often employed by men, and that it 'is considered especially the oracle of women and children' (p. 358). The implication is that if men do not wish to reveal the fact of consultation to inquisitive neighbours—possibly hostile neighbours—they can parry probing of this sort by claiming that either one of the womenfolk or one of the children is using the oracle. In either case, the ethos of the status of women and children being what it is, a man can avoid committing himself semi-publicly to a course of oracular enquiry which if revealed prematurely might damage his aim—rallying public opinion—quite seriously in its early stages. Thus although the range of people who can come to know about consultation of the three sticks oracle is greater than in the case of the rubbing-board oracle, it is still relatively restricted, and represents a test of public reaction of a tentative kind which allows the user to desist from further enquiries or pursue them with more determined purpose, depending on his judgment of the movement of public opinion.

The sticks of the three sticks oracle can be put in a more or less conspicuous place as the user wishes. He does not have the same liberty of choice with the termites oracle, for termite mounds are not always located to suit his convenience. Moreover, some termites are thought to be more efficacious than others. Therefore before a consultation a person must find a mound composed of the right sort of termites. A mound on the edge of his own homestead garden might meet his needs, but he might have to ask his neighbour for the use of his. Prior to a consultation a person must observe certain taboos, the mound must be prepared in a prescribed fashion, and a speech is made (pp. 354, 355). In all these details there is clear indication of a greater degree of publicity than is necessary in the use of either the rubbing-board or three sticks oracles. The use of the termites oracle, in other words, gives a person the opportunity of sounding out the opinions of people lying outside the range of small, selected groups of people whose reactions he has tested with the other two oracles. In using the termites oracle a person purposely moves into an area of social relationships among his fellow men over which he has less control but which he must capture if his final step is to be successful.

Although Evans-Pritchard places the witch-doctor on a par with the rubbing-board oracle in his estimation of their oracular status and accords both an inferior position in the hierarchy of oracles, of the 367 pages of his book directly concerned with witchcraft 110 pages, or nearly a third, are devoted specifically to witch-doctors. The extent of the interest indicated by this volume of writing is, in my opinion, much more in keeping with the importance of witch-doctors than any evaluation of their status in terms of their relation to the situations in which they operate. For a witch-doctoring seance brings together a public which is quite different in composition to that involved with any of the oracles previously considered, and at which it becomes possible to guage the public opinion of a relatively large number of people without yet pressing a matter to the point of demanding a consensus of opinion.

A seance is held at the request of a householder, and the question will be asked presently, why a person should find it necessary to make this request; for the preliminaries to a seance require that the householder accepts inconvenience. There may be several witch-doctors—as many as six sometimes (p. 155)—to whom gifts have to be made, and who require to be fed and entertained, and a few of the more influential spectators will, perhaps, be invited as well (p. 159). Throughout the morning of the seance the householder has to gather the pieces of apparatus necessary for it, and this usually means begging them from neighbours. If a man goes to this amount of trouble it cannot be merely for the witch-doctor to tell him what he wants to hear (p. 170). If the householder's interest is only in a confirmation of his suspicions, he could get this with much less trouble by consulting the rubbing-board oracle, whose verdict is as good as a witch-doctor's, or the three sticks or termites oracles, both of which are better, according to Evans-Pritchard's rating. In any case, before the seance takes place the witch-doctors spend some time with their client and some of the more influential spectators, and between them they come to have a fair idea of the names the client has in mind. A witch-doctor is an intelligent man of the locality, familiar with the gossip, the squabbles and the enmities among people, and if he happens to be of another locality he will take the advice of his colleagues from his client's locality. During a seance the witch-doctors are able, in various ways, in particular by watching the congregation's reaction to their remarks, to arrive at a precise idea of the person who both the client and members of the congregation think is the witch.

In answer to the question why a man should choose a witch-doctor rather than one of the three lesser oracles, Evans-Pritchard gives the opinion that 'the desire to enhance one's reputation by giving a public entertainment is the most important' (p. 163) reason. The social kudos to be derived from 'throwing open his house to the countryside and by employing performers' (p. 164) is the sort of element in ceremonial which Evans-Pritchard is quick to seize,[37] but while this kind of social advantage is the likely windfall of most ceremonial gatherings, there is always a significance related to the purpose of the gathering. The witch-doctors' seance is of consequence in terms of the nature of the congregation and what they are able to do with it on behalf of their client.

The number of people at a seance appears to be large. Evans-Pritchard refers to a 'crowd of spectators' (p. 160), including both males and females, and drummers and a chorus made up of local boys and youths. The witch-doctor threatens his audience even before the seance properly begins (p. 161); he cajoles its members into receiving his revelations (pp. 171, 178), peering inquisitively at a person in the congregation (p. 178); he might shoot witchcraft at someone whom he feels is causing him annoyance (pp. 179, 190); and while he manages his audience in this way, at the same time he carries on with the business of ferreting out the witch, carefully couching his revelations in innuendoes, astutely alive to the mood and reactions of his audience, and skilfully marshalling opinion to move in the direction he wishes to take it. A man employs the services of witch-doctors not for the flush of pleasure to be gained from transitory prestige or 'gaining public support and recognition of his difficulties' (p. 164)—although this is undoubtedly a most important contributory factor of the witch-doctor's role—but to proselytize for a client's cause, to play the piper and lead his client's co-residents towards a concensus of support for one man against another of the same community. If, after testing the opinion of different ranges of neighbours, a man still doubts whether he has sufficient strength of backing to stage a public attack on one of his named fellow men, the witch-doctor is instrumental in removing these last doubts from his mind.

Although this analysis of the role of witch-doctors is based on Evans-Pritchard's own data, his conclusions about them are somewhat different to mine, for he sees them as 'sleuths' who 'clear the atmosphere of witchcraft' and as diviners who 'are not regarded as furnishing more than preliminary evidence' (p. 258). My argument is that witch-doctors constitute an important part in the process of moulding a consensus of public opinion, since they and all the oracles deal with shifts in social relationships among the people who use them. Indeed, the thread which runs throughout Evans-Pritchard's work is this very thread of social relationships; the use of oracles and the witch-doctors represents the culturally legitimate way of dealing with certain sets of social relationships. When an Azande suffers misfortune this may manifest the fact that the natural order of things has been disturbed, and the disturbance is within the realm of relationships comprehensible to a human being—social relationships. No amount of ritual can cure a misfortune, since it is a finite experience: a cracked bowl is irreparable, a ruined crop is an irrevocable loss, a festering toe is not cured by a witchcraft accusation, nor is miscarriage averted in this way. But social relationships can be controlled by the licence ritual permits a person to accuse another of immoral behaviour.

Oracles do not provide merely for successive confirmatory verdicts. This would mean an unnecessary reduplication of effort, at some cost to the enquirer; and, since each consultation is likely to add complexities when clarity exists at the outset, the result would be the uncontrolled spread of ambiguities at a time when the person initiating an enquiry is seeking to bring his fellow men to declare publicly against one of them. Consultation is an enquiry designed to ascertain the support available in a community for the condemnation of a co-resident in connection with social relationships which lie outside the formality of axiomatic jural relationships, but about which the general sense of fairness must be given institutionalized expression if the relationships of people who perforce live cheek-by-jowl are to remain tolerable. Each enquiry addressed to the oracles is therefore a test of the views of selected groups in a local population, and in this scheme of things the poison oracle stands as the instrument which gives public declaration to a consensus of view reached after controlled manipulation of a population by other oracles and the witch-doctors. In short, the argument is that the power of the poison oracle is not a function of its ability to deal with a misfortune which occasions a consultation, but is a function of the dimension of social relationships it comprehends.

The poison oracle is costly (p. 282). Chickens are one item of expense, but their value is very small when set against the cost of the poison. The poison creeper grows in what used to be the Belgian Congo, and to procure it involves 'a dangerous journey, rendered more arduous by irksome taboos, for more than 200 kilometres' (p. 271), and although Azande were expressly forbidden to cross the political border into the Belgian Congo (for fear of re-introducing sleeping sickness into the Sudan), they 'gladly risk imprisonment to procure it' (p. 278) because the poison is so necessary to them. Some of the poison is acquired as part of barter exchanges across the border, or in return for gifts, but the most reliable poison is that gathered by the Azande themselves (p. 279). After the poison has reached its destination it must be treated with the utmost care, and anyone handling it must observe strict taboos. The cost, danger, care and attention associated with the poison are indicative of the importance with which Azande view its use, and of the gravity of the social situations its use is designed to regulate. At an oracular seance 'the operator performs in public' (p. 323) and everyone in a community knows the identity of the accuser and the accused, unlike the more restricted groups of people involved in the consultation of other oracles. When, therefore, the poison oracle gives a verdict against a particular person, it is a ritual manner of registering public interference in the social relationships obtaining between two persons, and this interference is expressed positively as support for one of them and a denunciation of the other.

It needs to be stressed again that the oracle is not in fact giving a verdict, since, although its answers appear to rely heavily on chance, it can only answer to questions put to it, to names advanced to it, and the twin arts of putting questions (which themselves go a long way to eliminating the chance element) and interpreting answers ensure that the desired result of a consultation will ensue. In any event, the public decide whether to take an enquiry seriously (p. 78). An unpopular enquirer, however serious a misfortune he might have suffered, would be given short shrift if he attempted to rely merely on the ritual mechanics of the poison oracle to achieve a public condemnation of a neighbour. Charges considered to be spurious meet, not with support, but with public ridicule. The poison oracle lacks meaning without a public backing to support its verdict. It does not exist in Azandeland to censure behaviour in whimsical fashion, but to manifest the considered judgment of a community in such a manner that blame for this judgment cannot be apportioned, and that its verdict is accepted with the good grace appropriate to its ritual pronouncement. All that is left for an accuser to do is to concede the charge, acquiesce in the verdict and promise to improve his behaviour. There is nothing else he can do, for although Evans-Pritchard argues that acceptance of a verdict by blowing water onto a dead chicken's wing (pp. 95, 97, 98, 123, 124, 125) itself nullifies any further argument, argument is futile anyway because the chicken's wing is the symbol of a common consensus of opinion. The ritual of the chicken's wing is only the local cultural mode of handling the delicate matter of highly sensitive moral relationships, when confrontations between protagonists would rob the community of its control over an area of social relationships as ambiguous as they are urgent.

After the Anglo-Egyptian occupation of the Sudan in 1905 witchcraft beliefs and practices persisted while other indigenous institutions disappeared or crumbled beyond the point of recognition. The new legal codes refused 'to admit witchcraft as a reality' (p. 18) and affected, no doubt, the jural standing of the poison oracle in particular, but the changes which occurred did not expunge witchcraft ideas from people's minds, nor did they efface the areas of ineradicable social relationships to which these ideas relate and which must always be controlled, whatever the cultural specifics at any given time. It is interesting that in a situation of change the cultural paraphernalia of witchcraft were not dismantled but stood virtually intact as a bunch of beliefs and practices, albeit in a new social context. Parts of the beliefs and practices came to be endowed with a different analytic significance because the general configuration of their context had altered, but far from impeding change these existing beliefs and practices were used as tools with which to fashion it.

One element in the changed situation is worth noting. Prior to European conquest it was always possible to check an oracular verdict of guilt after a person's death by autopsy—witchcraft is thought to be a physical substance in the body, and in the body of a man declared to be a witch an autopsy should reveal its presence. King Gbudwe, who ruled before the European occupation, appears to have been strong enough politically to suppress the practice of appealing to an autopsy, and if it was used by someone 'no official cognisance was taken' of it (p. 40). He had good reason to adopt this stance. The poison oracle is thought to be infallible always, but commoners cannot be trusted to observe the various taboos of consultation meticulously, or they might omit one of the many necessary rituals. The poison oracle of a king or a prince is not only infallible but also invariably gives correct answers, because special care is taken to secure the observance of taboos and the performance of rituals. If, therefore, a man who dies condemned as a witch is shown by autopsy not to possess witchcraft substance in him, then it can only be the king or the prince who is at fault, not the oracle. King Gbudwe was powerful enough to counter this challenge to his authority. With the advent of the British district commissioner, an additional and superior authority became available to the Azande. Consequently the appeal to an autopsy 'reappeared with its old vigour after European conquest' (p. 40). Autopsy necessarily reveals an absence of witchcraft substance in the body. The reappearance of the autopsy denotes the curtailment of princely power by commoners, who with each appeal to autopsy nibbled away their authority. Customs are not curios which block change; they are stepping stones which mark out its direction.

There is no necessity to summarize the conclusions that can be drawn from the analysis of Azande witchcraft beliefs and practices, since its purpose is to show how it can be used comparatively, and this can best be done by a brief exposition of the points of social anthropological similarity between the actions of the Welsh youth groups and the use made of Azande oracles.

1. The essential problem in both cases is that of controlling an aspect of morality related to the differentiation which arises between the sexes, whether as a result of their sexual marital courtship or

domestic affairs. It is an ambiguous area of morality in as much as it defies comprehension by clearly stated rules. In this area law is incapacitated because the evidence is often highly circumstantial and includes people's opinions about the facts as much as the facts themselves. The judgments on which the Welsh youths act, and which the oracles proclaim, represent the mood of a people towards particular persons, of particular circumstances, at particular times.

2. Both the Welsh youths and Azande oracles function in a number of other situations as well. In this context they both appear to be acting haphazardly, so that the serious and the trivial are seen to be juxtaposed: at their meeting place near the shop the youths pick on anyone for anything, and the Azande use their rubbing-board oracle to answer any sort of problem they choose to put to it. Both means of control are thus given a kind of characterization, while the characterization of the behaviour against which they strike is shrouded in the obscurity of the general image derived from the ability they possess to penetrate any relationships.

3. Much of the effect of both is to constrain behaviour. The evidence for both is that sometimes the action is premeditated and sometimes unplanned. In either case, whether the victim suffers the penalty of an accusation of witchcraft or physical assault, or merely a warning or minor embarrassment, the control is restrictive. But this negative effect sometimes achieves positive results. Conspicuous as an instance of this is the control exerted over the choice of marriage partners, for while both obstructed—if only temporarily—the progress of marriage plans, they are also interfering in the selection of marriage partners, and thereby assisting in shaping the design of marriage patterns.

4. The suggestion that interference in courtships or betrothals may be only temporary is intended to indicate another feature of this type of control. While it may scar a person it does not maim permanently. If an offender desists he need no longer fear an accusation of witchcraft among the Azande, or further penalty in the Welsh countryside. In neither case is the punishment a permanent degradation of status. The concern is always with a person who is practising evil *now*. It could hardly be otherwise, since everyone at some time is good and at other times bad, and were the punishment permanent then entire communities, in both cases, would stand condemned. Control of morality does not eradicate immorality or attempt to do so, but it meets its challenge whenever it appears.

Moreover, this form of control is limited to the person of the offender, and does not extend to include his kin or neighbours. For, it needs to be stressed, this form of control is directed against the specific acts of particular offenders and not concerned with an expanded domain of persons connected to the offender.

5. An expansion of the range of people subject to control at a given time is made impossible also by the nature of relationships within the moral community. Both in Zandeland and in the Welsh countryside the modes of control govern people with a history of social relations and a population of restricted span. The poverty of circumstances in both cases heightens the intensity of relationships, and in neither is there sufficient wealth to divert interests away from these relationships. The very density of such relationships necessarily implies that the span of morality is a small locality, whether of people or of geographical area, since such density of relationships would become reduced to a casual interest in incidental gossip if spread to cover a large population or area. With these kinds of relationship obtaining, control must perforce be specifically directed and ephemeral in its effect.

6. Implicit in what has been said about both cases is the important fact that these kinds of relationship are between people who are social equals, at least to the extent that differentiation is not an impediment to sociability. Rank appears in both areas, but in both its forms it is, so to speak, disinterested. It concerns the people of both areas in some matters, but it lacks the capability to decide the issues of morality to which their relationships give rise. It is the absence of rank, as defined earlier, which gives consensus its significance as an agent of moral control.

7. Consensus, if it is to assume the responsibility for making decisions about the character of people, cannot be either instant or spontaneous. Before they take premeditated actions the Welsh youths secure the maximum support of their community by a lengthy process of sifting information from a wide spectrum of the population. The Azande, before they make a public charge of witchcraft, use various oracles to test opinion and their witch-doctors to rally support. Neither could be effective without the backing of a consensus. Without it, both communities would fragment into entities of enmity.

8. In both cases the instruments of control are guarded from attack. The youth group is protected by the anonymity bestowed on

it by adults. Oracles are surrounded by ritual and taboo. Both are free from retaliation. Why control should be vested in a youth group in Wales, and in a ritual object among the Azande, is a major problem on its own, requiring separate treatment.

9. In the sense that neither the youth group nor the oracles are participants in the situations they control—the youth group because it is composed of minors and the oracles because they are ritual objects—both are endowed with the fiction of externality. Thus endowed, both can carry the responsibilities of the moral problems arising out of the relationships among adults. A semblance of externality, it seems, is given to the agent onto whom or which the insoluble problems of intimate social relationships are deflected. But this externality is illusory, for in both cases it is nothing more than the common consensus of those among whom the problems arise. A pattern cut in a cornfield is not the prank of irresponsible youths; an accusation of witchcraft is only peripherally related to the poison oracle. Both represent the condemnation of the behaviour of an individual by his fellow men, not by boys and poisoned chickens. The externality of Welsh youths and Azande oracles is the externality of an emblem.

10 Both in the Welsh countryside and in Azandeland changes have occurred, but the cultural familiars have withstood the challenge, and, moreover, have assisted the process of change. Welsh youth groups act to re-shape the map of morality. Azande oracles share in the re-casting of political relations. Changed circumstances may not bring about the collapse of indigenous cultural forms, but the changed contexts of forms alter their social anthropological content.

The pleasure of exploring the work of Evans-Pritchard lies in the generality to be found in it. It is this which enables one to lift his findings out of their cultural contexts and apply them to the activities of people in other parts of the world. The explanation thus achieved brings behaviour, so strangely different in its local cultural clothing, within the bounds of comparative comprehension.

[1970]

Notes

1 Originally the title of this paper was 'Group joking relationships', and although it has already been quoted thus it is so inadequate a title that I have decided to abandon it.

This article began as an informal talk to a gathering of staff and students at the Department of Social Anthropology in the University of Manchester in 1962. During the discussion that followed, Dr R. P. Werbner made comments which caused me to limit the range of cultural comparison I had initially included, and since then we have discussed the various problems contained in this article so often that I am no longer sure which ideas are his and which mine. I am most grateful to him for this intellectual camaraderie—and, while I am about it, I wish also to thank him for the chore he so willingly undertakes of reading my typescripts.

2 Since such frequent reference will be made to Mr Rees' work, in subsequent references I give only the page number of this particular book. The relevant chapter of the book, entitled 'Youth', consists of eight pages (pp. 82–90), but I draw on data from all its parts for this analysis.

3 Rees, p. 75, although he has little to say about the pattern of marriage, clearly implies that marriage links cross the administrative divide when he says '. . . one must try to visualise the kinship network extending continuously across the artificial boundary of the parish . . .'

4 The ethnography contained in this paragraph up to this point can be found in Rees, pp. 82–4.

5 I make this deduction on the basis of Rees' table 'Age and marital condition, 1940' (p. 172, table (*b*)), and my own information.

6 Rees, p. 172. I arrive at the approximate figure of fifty-five as follows: the number of bachelors in the 20–29 age group is thirty-five, and all these are included; the number in the 30–39 age group is seventeen, from which I subtract seven to allow for those who have ceased to be members, as they move into the status of confirmed bachelors, leaving ten recruits from this age group; the number in the 10–19 age group is fifty, of which I take only one third, since youths are not admitted to the group until they are over 16 years, leaving seventeen recruits from this age group; the total number of possible recruits, on this estimate, is sixty-two.

7 The figure of twenty-seven is arrived at as follows: on 104 smallholdings there are sixty youths of the right age and status for recruitment purposes; this gives a ratio of 1 youth to 1·7 farms, and, since it is estimated that two border groups attract sixteen youths, they will, therefore, be drawn off twenty-seven farms.

8 Rees, p. 70, and also the table on p. 178.

9 Rees, pp. 74–8, especially fig. 28, p. 76.

10 Rees, p. 100, refers to the view that this area of Wales lacks 'visible signs of community life' but partly disclaims the view when he proceeds to argue that 'a diffused form of society' exists.

11 See, for example Evans-Pritchard, *The Nuer* (1940), pp. 216–25, Frankenberg, *Village on the Border* (1957), pp. 78*ff* and pp. 118*ff*, and Peters, 'The tied and the free' (1968).
12 Cf. Rees, p. 89, where he suggests that disputed paternity might be a matter for the courts.
13 Rees, p. 87: 'During each decennial period from 1890 onwards the number of illegitimate births per thousand live births in Llanfihangel was more than twice the number for England and Wales, while figures for 1931–9 show a gradual increase as the area becomes more rural.' Also, p. 180, chapter VII, note 10.
14 Rees, p. 78: 'The question "Who is he?" is interpreted as "To whom does he belong?".'
15 Rees, p. 173. The table showing size of holdings including rough grazing, gives thirty-two farms of 1–20 acres, twenty-one of 21–50 acres, eighteen of 51–100 acres, thirty-four of 101–200 acres, eight of 201–400 acres, and one over 600 acres.
16 Rees, p. 76. See map of kinship, fig. 28.
17 This remark is not intended to be pejorative in any sense. Rees was not concerned with pursuing my problems, and therefore I would not expect him to provide all the information for an analysis different to his own. It is to his great credit that the wealth of data he provided permits considerable accuracy on matters which did not directly concern him.
18 Since Rees does not show compass points on any of his maps, the directions I give are approximate only, and they are based on the assumption that north lies at right angles to the horizontal axis of the parish.
19 Peters, 'Aspects of rank and status' (1963).
20 I say this not only on the basis of the information from Rees and my own work in south Lebanon, but also in reference to a village in central Lebanon where most of the population belong to the highly authoritarian Maronite Church. It is a most interesting feature of this latter village that matters relating to moral relations between the sexes are first adjudicated by the community and afterwards taken to the Church for validation.
21 This statement refers to the period before August 1969. A military coup occurred at that time, and since then Colonel Qadafi, the head of state, has sequestrated Italian holdings. In all probability the remaining Italian families have left.
22 I hasten to add here that while I have sought to single out critical points in the behaviour of youth groups, I have not sought to reduce it to a few necessary prerequisites. Human behaviour is always too complex to yield to such facile over-simplification. The analytic characteristics I have shown are so numerous as to negate that kind of quest, anyway.
23 See Colson, 'Clans and the joking relationship . . .' (1962).

24 Radcliffe-Brown, 'On joking relationships', in *Structure and Function in Primitive Society* (1952), pp. 90–104; 'A further note on joking relationships', *op. cit.*, pp. 105–16.
25 Radcliffe-Brown, 'On joking relationships', p. 101.
26 Radcliffe-Brown, 'On joking relationships', p. 98: 'Thus the joking relationship with the uncle does not merely annul the usual relationship between the two generations, it reverses it.'
27 Radcliffe-Brown, 'On joking relationships', p. 98.
28 Radcliffe-Brown, 'The mother's brother in South Africa', *op. cit.*, p. 28.
29 Radcliffe-Brown, 'On joking relationships', p. 103.
30 Radcliffe-Brown, 'A further note on joking relationships', p. 108.
31 'L'Alliance Cathartique'.
32 Radcliffe-Brown, 'A further note on joking relationships', p. 113.
33 Since I shall be referring to this book frequently, hereafter, for convenience, I give only the page number in subsequent references to it.
34 Evans-Pritchard, pp. 32, 33. Here the separation of commoners from their social superiors is made specifically clear in the important passage which sets the social limits to commoners' witchcraft accusations by indicating those social statuses which are immune. See also p. 75, where it is argued that the social situation of ranked differences excludes witchcraft. An explicit statement on this point appears on p. 104 also.
35 Evans-Pritchard, p. 85. See also p. 268, where Evans-Pritchard points out that courts 'do not admit the only evidence which is really relevant to the cases which come before them'.
36 Evans-Pritchard, pp. 16, 25, 31, 63, 74, 77, 78, 93, 107, 216, 267, 268, 269, 282, 299, 300, 307, 342. I do not claim that this list is exhaustive, since I did not set out with the intention of picking out every reference, but the list is sufficient, quantitatively and qualitatively, to show how large the subject looms in Azande minds, both when discussing witchcraft and when providing instances of accusations.
37 Compare with his foreword to J. W. McPherson, *The Moulids of Egypt* (1941).

Bibliography

Colson, E., 'Clans and the joking relationship among the Plateau Tonga of Northern Rhodesia' in *The Plateau Tonga of Northern Rhodesia*, Manchester: Manchester University Press (1962).
Evans-Pritchard, E. E., *The Nuer*, Oxford: Clarendon Press (1940).
— *Witchcraft, Oracles and Magic among the Azande*, Oxford: Clarendon Press (1937).
Frankenberg, R., *Village on the Border*, London: Cohen & West (1957).

Fortes, M., *The Dynamics of Clanship among the Tallensi*, London: Oxford University Press (1945).
Goody, J., 'The mother's brother and sister's son in West Africa', *Journal of the Royal Anthropological Institute*, vol. 89 (1959).
Griaule, M., 'L'Alliance cathartique', *Africa*, vol. 18 (1948).
McPherson, J. W., *The Moulids of Egypt,* Cairo: N. M. Press (1941).
Peters, E. L., 'Aspects of rank and status among Muslims in a Lebanese village' in *Mediterranean Countrymen*, ed. J. Pitt-Rivers, Paris: Mouton (1963).
— 'The tied and the free' in *Contributions to Mediterranean Sociology*, ed. J. G. Peristiany, Paris: Mouton (1968).
— 'No time for the supernatural', a review of P. Bohannan's *Social Anthropology, New Society*, 19 December 1963. (I disclaim any responsibility for the title of the review.)
Pitt-Rivers, J., *The People of the Sierra*, London: Weidenfeld & Nicolson (1954).
Radcliffe-Brown, A. R., *Structure and Function in Primitive Society*, London: Cohen & West (1952).
Rees, A., *Life in a Welsh Countryside*, Cardiff: University of Wales Press (1961).

4

Absence makes the heart grow fonder

Some suggestions why witchcraft accusations are rare among East African pastoralists

P. T. W. Baxter

Douglas[1] has recently pointed to the 'marked variability in the degree to which witch-beliefs are favoured explanations of misfortune'. She suggests that they appear to be a dominant mode of explanation in those Central African societies 'in which authority is asserted by senior kinsmen over members of local corporate matrilineal descent groups'. Following Gluckman and others, she points out that witchcraft operates 'only in the cracks and crevices' of most social systems—that is, 'in the range of small-scale, ambiguously defined, strictly local relationships'. She also assumes that there is a relation between the expression of belief and social structure and suggests that 'The distinction between blame-pinning and non-blame-pinning explanations of misfortune will surely produce sociological correlations.'

One of the means of stressing the moral responsibility of persons connected socially for the maintenance of each other's connected fortunes is by accusation of witchcraft and sorcery against those supposed delinquents who bring evil mischance. Among East African pastoralists such accusations are rare despite a widespread belief in witches. After establishing that such accusations are rare, I continue to a discussion of why this should be so. Marwick[2] has suggested that a task for sociological analysis is 'to explain why witchcraft or sorcery took on in some societies and not in others to which they became known'. To which he cautiously conjoins the *caveat*: 'No easy explanations for their absence can be put forward.'

The peoples to whom I refer are the Nandi, Mandari, Dinka, Nuer, Turkana, Karimojong, Samburu, Somali and, most particularly, the Boran; but I think the points I make are applicable more widely and fit, for example, our data on the Baggara, Fulani and Tuareg. I limit my examination to the beliefs in, and supposed activities of, witches and sorcerers, and I ignore tutelary spirits, ghosts and other agencies which may also be utilized as occult pointers to those responsible for the suffering of others.

I do this for simplicity and economy, firstly, because it may be possible, as among the Yakö, for beliefs concerning supernatural beings and entities to be 'conceptually independent and unintegrated'.[3] Secondly, I am not arguing that among these societies misfortune is never, nor even only rarely, attributed (by occult connection) to people's failure to sustain their moral responsibilities to each other; but I am arguing that misfortune is only very rarely attributed to the aggressive and malevolent wishes or occult actions of others. Accusations attributing blame or responsibility, whether the mechanism utilized is accusation of witchcraft or sorcery, neglected ancestors or offended tutelary spirits, occur in social situations in which the actors are bound together in such a web of ties that escape from them seems scarcely imaginable without recourse to some form of physical, psychical or moral violence. As Gluckman puts it, such a 'view of the universe is a small-scale view, appropriate to a small-scale society'.[4] It is a view which did not disappear until such patterns of relationship had been eliminated by 'the full flowering of the industrial revolution'[5] or, as Marwick puts it:

> The point in history when beliefs in witchcraft and sorcery begin to decline seems to have been when small scale, intricate communities began to be displaced by large, impersonal urban complexes.[6]

I suggest, tentatively, that an examination of non-industrialized, non-urban societies, in which responsibility for individual misfortune is only rarely attributed to occult forces activated by the specified malice or culpable neglect of moral obligations, should also help to diminish the implication, carried by any evolutionary hypothesis, that there is a gap in intellectual sophistication between ourselves in industrial society and people in non-industrial societies.

Belief in witches is found among each of the nine peoples listed above, but the information published about their activities and characteristics varies considerably. The fullest accounts of witches we have are for the more settled Dinka, Mandari and Nandi, while descriptions from the nomadic pastoralists are slight. Indeed the words 'witch' and 'sorcerer' do not appear in the indexes of some of the monographs. The differences in the amount of published information could be due to the chances of publication or merely be a reflection of the differing interests of the ethnographers, but they more probably do indicate that witchcraft beliefs are of little importance among 'religious' beliefs for the explanation of why the misfortunes of life strike whom they do or of social processes in pastoral societies. Certainly both Boran social relationships and their religious beliefs can be fully discussed without reference to witches.

Stereotypes of witches, in very broad terms, share many similarities across the African continent.[7] Witches are selfish people. A summary of their characteristics is a résumé of the dark side of the psyche and lists those human traits which, if not restrained by respect for others, would destroy the delicate balance of mutual obligation which makes up daily social intercourse. Witches are sly and are associated with the dark, bestial lusts and habits, possession of the Evil Eye, bitter tongues and envious longings. They are poor, to some extent socially unfortunate, and they could therefore be expected to harbour jealousy and spite. Similar clusters of notions occur among Dinka, Mandari, Nandi and Boran; it is likely that similar notions also exist among the other peoples.

Among the nine peoples accusations of witchcraft—especially direct accusations—are rare, though not equally so. I proceed now to examine the relation between the degree of dependence on pastoralism and the incidence of accusations.

Of the peoples selected the Mandari and Nandi are, I think significantly, those amongst whom pastoralism is economically least important and accusations would appear to be most frequent. Of the Mandari Buxton writes: 'Sickness is believed to come from many sources, and witchcraft is not by any means the most commonly diagnosed.'[8] But where witches are blamed they are usually mistrusted immigrants who are said, because they are destitute (or are supposed to be so), to be attempting to acquire land illegitimately. Motivated by greed and envy, they harm their land-owning patrons by 'trying to restrict fertility and expansion',[9] as well as by causing illness and death. They are clients who, though attached to their patrons by pseudo-kinship, are nevertheless, in specified respects, outsiders. In another paper she states that their social position is 'full of ambiguity'.[10] She also reports that land-owners expect clients to act viciously and enviously, 'because in a similar position they would have like human feelings'.[11] Only when they were accused of causing 'death and persistent illness was action taken against them'.[12] Among the Nandi, according to Huntingford, witches are associated with 'interlopers' and, though beliefs are 'widespread', only a proportion of misfortunes are attributed to witches; frequently the witch is 'untouched and no action taken when his identity is known'.[13] But among both the Nandi and Mandari, witches may be identified, accused and subjected to punitive sanctions, among the Mandari even to the extent of being roasted like a bush-pig. Those most likely to be accused—and certain people 'become a continual focus for suspicions'—are persons with tainted pedigrees rather than particular categories of kin or neighbours.[14] That is, witches are likely to be selected from within a distinct and identifiable social grouping, defined by descent or place of origin, and not from categories of persons in ego-centred action-sets, as has frequently been demonstrated to be the case in other societies. Witches are identified by their social antecedents rather than in a specific social situation. It would seem that there is a general consensus as to who are witches, or likely to be witches, and Huntingford suggests that among Nandi divination only occurs when no obvious witch springs to a victim's mind.[15] I do not wish to exaggerate the incidence of appeals to witch beliefs or of accusations among Nandi and Mandari, for indeed Huntingford comments that a stranger might be excused for thinking there was no witchcraft in Nandi, but it is clear that the prominence of beliefs and the incidence of accusations is more marked among these two peoples than it is in the other selected peoples. Both Mandari and Nandi, though valuing pastoral activities highly, fall in the economic category 'pastoral with agriculture'.[16]

Lienhardt writes that among the Dinka, even though every child knows something about witches, it is nevertheless 'a concept in some ways marginal',[17] and that he came across but two accusations, only one of which was 'a really serious accusation of witchcraft between people meeting face to face'[18]—i.e. generated in a context of strained close social relationships. (They were, in fact, quarrelling co-wives, and in each of the few cases recorded among the other peoples discussed, co-resident women were accused and accuser, i.e. persons both connected through a highly valued link with a third, such as a husband.) Yet, despite (or perhaps because of) the paucity of accusations, the Dinka talk, sing and even joke about witches, although these embody all those false-faced characteristics which Dinka profess to hate. Lienhardt[19] also describes, but dismisses 'as marginal', magical practitioners whose powers reside in their possession of fetish bundles, called *ran wal*, between whom and witches the line is 'often not very clearly drawn'. The medicine they use is primarily directed to enforce the payment of cattle debts. The medicine is said to come from non-Dinka and sometimes from the Nuer; whereas Nuer, who also know it, 'trace it to the Dinka'. A *ran wal* 'is usually a visitor, perhaps an itinerant Nuer or Dinka'.

Evans-Pritchard[20] hardly mentions witches, *peth*, among the Nuer, though he discusses medicines, fetishes and wizards, all of which are said to be recent introductions from outside Nuerland. He knew only one wizard, and he states he had to depend on 'hear-say' for his information: it is clear that though witches are greedy, malevolent and feared, their activities do not enter into intimate social relationships. Cattle husbandry is more important economically to the Nuer and Dinka than to the Mandari and Nandi.

Among the Turkana cattle husbandry has much greater economic importance than cultivation. The Gullivers[21] write that 'despite a general belief in witches' (who operate through possession of the Evil Eye, and even children know of them), Turkana 'are as a rule prosaic . . . When they can find a rational explanation they will accept it, and in the main their beliefs do not enter into *social relationships* or *economic activities*.' Sorcerers are rare. While Spencer[22] writes of the Samburu, who do not cultivate at all, 'only a few men known to have Turkana ancestry are believed to be witches, and hence accusations of witchcraft within the tribe itself are infrequent'. A man who wishes to injure another by sorcery 'usually goes to the Dorobo or Tiamus' to seek out and employ an expert. Clearly, as among Turkana, witchcraft accusations do not enter into localized or intimate social relationships. Accusations appear to be negligible among Karimojong.

Lewis[23] reports similarly of the northern, nomadic Somali: 'In contrast to the power of religion, magic, witchcraft and sorcery play minor roles.' The few persons accused of 'ill-wishing' are either socially peripheral and kinless widows 'credited with a general grievance against society' or the weak and scorned, but protected, Yibir bondsmen 'who stand furthest outside Somali society'.[24] Clearly, amongst Somali also, accusations do not intrude into close social relationships. I myself found that Boran, almost all of whom depend entirely on their herds and flocks, believe in witches, sometimes speak fearfully of them, and have a set of notions about them comparable in variety and in content to those described by Lienhardt for the Dinka; but I have no record of a public accusation, nor even insinuation, against a named person and I recorded only a very few covert insinuations made to me in private. Only one of these intruded into the area of close social relationships. It was made by a sick man against one of his four wives who had deserted him to live with her lover. Even this was a suggestion rather than an accusation, and the maker was groping for any possible explanation for his continuing sickness, for which he had tried Islamic, traditional and modern hospital treatments. Moreover, at the moment he made it he was particularly dejected. He was squatting in the bush with racking diarrhoea, after having drunk about four gallons of water in which the stomach of a bullock and its contents had been soaked for a day and a night. He did not repeat the veiled accusation and, as far as I know, did nothing further against the errant wife (there was little he could do), about whom his usual comment was 'good riddance'.

Before continuing my general argument I interpolate a brief account of Boran possessors of the Evil Eye. The Borana word *buuda* is used both as a noun to describe the possessor of the Evil Eye (*iila hama*) and the activity itself. A person can be a *buuda* or be afflicted by *buuda*. Boran talk of 'families' who 'have' the Evil Eye (particularly smiths), a characteristic which they share with owls, hyenas and some other bush creatures. There is some ambiguity about whether its activation is entirely in the control of its possessor, because it is perceived as an inherited characteristic. But its use is considered to be at least semi-deliberate. But for Boran the question whether the possessor is morally responsible for his act is not an important one, because the misfortunes it causes are not major and possessors are defined not so much by intention as by their membership of the category of possessors who, by definition, are 'bad'. But, as will be clear from what follows, not all persons who could possess the Eye are accused of using it.

'Eyers' are said to be poor in stock and largely dependent on sheep and goats for their subsistence. This dependence means that they are persons who follow particularly isolated and wandering grazing circuits. Wealthy and influential men are by this same definition excluded. But certainly not all poor herders of sheep and goats are Eyers and I was assured that in Marsabit District all the 'families' who had this disability had withdrawn from the fully pastoral economy and settled on maize plots either at the mission or in the settlement controlled by the Administration. Some were named on confidential enquiry. Only a few of the cultivators were thought of as possessing the Eye. Most of, and probably all, the cultivating Boran families (about twenty) possess some stock which they keep with them at the government-supervised settlement and have other stock herded for them by pastoral kin or friends. Mutual visiting is maintained between cultivators and pastoralists, and I have no evidence which suggests that Eyers were avoided in any way. Pastoralists valued connections with cultivators, particularly for their hospitality when they visited the station, and a few men valued them as sources of illicit gin. But to cultivate is in itself deviant behaviour to Boran, and is looked down on. Cultivators, who are very few, are themselves apologetic about their mode of life, and are referred to by both pastoralists and themselves as being 'only part Boran'.

In pre-colonial days, when the alternative of settling as a cultivator did not exist, pernicious Eyers were said to have been driven out to become herdsmen or concubines of Rendile or Somali. Whatever the historical truth of this assertion, what is sociologically important is that there exists a pool of persons on whose generalized spite certain types of affliction can be blamed, without specifically pinning responsibility on the victim himself or any of his fellow herders. The types of affliction attributed to the Eye are inexplicable and annoying, but non-lethal, complaints which strike sporadically and which are likely to clear up of themselves. Examples are an itchy type of scabies which is endemic but which does not occur in epidemics, bouts of tetchiness, listlessness and lack of appetite in children, and the appearance of blood in the milk of otherwise fit cows.[25] I have never heard of any death of people or stock attributed to the Eye, but stock straying or general bad luck might be attributed to the Eye of persons or of bush creatures. Visitors and travellers pass through villages daily, and owls and hyenas are commonplace. But all the attributions I heard were general, and frequently semi-jocular. Although Eyers were ascribed nightmarish abilities and qualities in general conversation, examples of their evil were relatively innocuous. Many children, and some adults and animals, wear protective amulets against the Eye. My recollection is that these were more common among Muslims than among traditionalists, but Boran were not much preoccupied by protective devices[26]—whereas all men prayed daily for God's help.

Before making some suggestions about possible connections

between the social consequences of a pastoral economy and the absence of accusations of witchcraft, I comment briefly on two explanations for the absence of accusations among pastoralists.[27] The first usually appears as an implication rather than an explanation and, I suspect, would not be seriously defended by those who give it. But it is so pervasive that it merits dismissal in passing. I quote only from the Gullivers and Lewis. The Gullivers are quoted above as calling the Turkana 'prosaic' and favouring 'rational explanation'. Lewis suggests that Somali 'excel' in 'eminently practical reasoning . . . [as against] many other African peoples'.[28] This type of explanation, I think, only illustrates the fascination that nomads and pastoralists seem to exert over all who have been fortunate enough to live amongst them. Evans-Pritchard, in his publications on the Azande which are the inspiration of all our studies in the field of witchcraft, clearly demonstrated that the Azande acted practically and rationally, and regarded witchcraft as 'normal' and 'ordinary'. Fortes writes of the witchcraft-free Tallensi, whose 'thought is dominated by the belief in the supremacy of departed ancestors', that nevertheless 'their culture is fundamentally mundane'.[29] Asserting the normality of the people they study seems to be a constant, if irrational, need of ethnographers. There are no reasons for believing that prosaicism or rationality vary tribally or ethnically.

Lewis also hazards a tentative but interesting sociological explanation for the absence of acusations among Somali: that 'where tensions are resolved freely by fighting, as they are in Somaliland, there is little need for witchcraft . . . where sorcery and witchcraft occur it is usually between people who, for one reason or another, are prevented from fighting'.[30] Marwick[31] also suggests similarly, but more generally, that 'the presence of alternative forms of expression, such as singing contests, slanging matches, feuds, war, actual homicide' may explain the absence of witchcraft accusations in some societies.

These are primarily hypotheses about political or inter-group relationships rather than small-scale and intra-group relationships, and are not immediately or closely relevant to my theme. But, in so far as they are, I must reject them. Among Boran any fighting between members of the nation is the most heinous of sins. Certainly between elders, at least of the same major political unit, it is also reprehensible and rare among other pastoralists.

This ethnographic helter-skelter has, I hope, established for the nine selected pastoral societies that:

1. Although beliefs in witches are widespread, the attribution of affliction and misfortune to witchcraft is not frequent.
2. Accusations are rare and very seldom intrude into the cracks and crevices of close social relationships.
3. Accusations appear to be most frequent where cultivation is essential to subsistence and rights over land have economic importance.
4. Such accusation as do occur are likely to be directed against 'outsiders' or 'strangers', that is, persons identifiable by their peripheral status and lowly economic positions.

Among pastoralists the 'why' of serious misfortune or affliction is most frequently attributed to agencies other than witches. These may be various. The most frequent are: the commission of a personal fault or sin; breaches of a ritual prohibition; an offence against God or one of his 'refractions'; or an unknowable whim of God or one of his 'refractions'. But, of especial importance, they may be attributed either to the withdrawal of the protection of a senior's 'blessing' or 'men's blessings', or the active intervention of a senior's 'curse' or of 'men's curses'. Though all these agencies may be set in a context of disturbed social relationships and may be manipulable by the actors (or at least variously interpreted by them), they are seldom, if ever, secretive or considered to be activated by immoral, anti-social or bestial malevolence. So that the attribution of responsibility for a misfortune is not an accusation of the type which either dramatically 'blasts' existing social relationships apart or legitimizes their re-structuring. Where mystical agencies of the type I have just listed above are utilized, and a failure in fulfilment of social and moral obligations is diagnosed as the precipitating cause of a misfortune, the person responsible for triggering the misfortune may be judged harsh and unbending, but not promiscuously malevolent. An elder who curses is a reluctant agent. There is also little room for the variable and manipulative interpretation of the sources of misfortune by persons occupying competing social positions of the type, for example, so graphically described by Middleton in *Lugbara Religion* (1960—see Gluckman's article).

Obviously, there is no reason why men and women who depend for their subsistence on animal products should hate one another less than those depending on cereals or vegetables. But I suggest that the hazards and hardships of a pastoral life, the extended range of links needed to sustain herds and flocks in a hostile environment, and the necessities of efficient stock management, *combine* to impose a pattern of social relationships and a consequent world view, or set of 'cognitive maps',[32] that are incompatible with the widespread use of witchcraft-type accusations.

I consider that there are several interconnected reasons why this should be so. The first is difficult to demonstrate succinctly because it is an explanation partly in terms of ethos, and contains the dangers of obfuscation by the generation of a romantic pastoral mystique. But I have the advantage that part of that type of explanation—though in a different context—has been argued before by Gluckman and by Foster.[33] Further, though its acceptance supports my argument, its rejection does not controvert it. I take as given the pervasiveness in pastoral societies of what Evans-Pritchard has called 'a bovine idiom' and the mutual dependence and identification of men with their cattle, identification which is present economically, in the context of social relationships, and mystically in their relationships with God. These do not need demonstration. It follows that a consideration of the role of stock must be central to any discussion of moral responsibility for misfortune because social relationships are enmeshed in the context of stock husbandry, as also are the social personality and social position of a stock-owner. Men and animals are in many contexts, as Evans-Pritchard has demonstrated, interchangeable.

William Hazlitt wrote of settled peasants: 'All country people hate each other, they have so little comfort that they envy their neighbours the smallest pleasure or advantage and nearly grudge themselves the necessaries of life.' Subsistence-cultivating economies are stationary. Even where land is plentiful the production of a surplus over subsistence needs is limited by the amount of work that can be performed by the hands of the cultivator and his dependants. Cultivators, indeed, commonly see themselves in competition for a common and limited pool of resources; so that one man's gain inevitably involves another man's loss, and a type of occult mercantilism prevails.[34] A man is in 'competition with his own kinsmen for position and property' in what is, or at least is perceived to be, a 'limited' economic system. Frequently economic success is attributed to the selfish misuse of occult forces, while a primary responsibility of elders is to protect from such depredations the health, property, fertility and welfare of their dependants. This may require them to take aggressive counter-action, or to be interpreted as taking such action. Such power to defend and to attack occultly is ambivalent, and demarcation between its legitimate and illegitimate use is open to variable interpretations.[35]

Cows, camels, sheep and goats, on the other hand, visibly breed and multiply, and a herd which increases brings dependants and affines. Surplus milk and meat, where there is no market, have to be distributed. Grazing and water are limited but title to their use, with negligible exceptions, is open to all members of the political community and is not vested in individuals. Boran, for example, speak of both as belonging to God. With care, and the linked blessings of God and men, every boy who has a heifer has the source of a herd, which, in its turn, over time should produce herds for his sons. This is symbolically and materially expressed at the naming ceremony for every Boran infant boy. At this ceremony the boy is presented with a heifer, which is called his navel (*handuura*) and forms the nucleus of his own independent herd. The navel of another beast which has been sacrificed at the ceremony is slit and placed around his wrist while God's blessing is prayed for. Boran, I judge, perceive their herds, given good management and God's blessing, as always containing the potentiality of increase which is not at the expense of other Boran but depends, rather, on their active and amicable co-operation. The activities of elders are constantly directed to maintaining those co-operative social relationships which are subsumed in 'the peace of the Boran', which is an expression of God's peace visible in active economic and social co-operation.[36]

Elders in these societies have mystical power 'to bless' and 'to curse' and are responsible for the ritual which maintains health and fertility, but their actions are open and not covert, public and not private, and do not involve taking aggressive occult action designed to deprive others of the natural increase of their herds. That cattle diseases are contagious and not isolable, any more than is drought, also makes particularization of misfortune difficult empirically. Misfortune in the form of pestilence or raiders, it is true—at any rate in folk belief—may eliminate a herd and reduce a man from prosperity to beggary over night.[37] But such an individual tragedy is too overwhelming to be attributed to human malevolence, or even to the righteous wrath of offended neighbours and kin. Such Jobian afflictions could come only from God. I suggest, for reasons which I shall give below, that extreme reversals of fortune are, moreover, very remarkable, although they feature prominently in the cautionary tales which are the currency of folk morality. Exemplary tales depend for their dramatic force on the fusion of possibility, rarity and enormity. The first long dry season I spent in Borana was a year of death-dealing drought but I have no record of a stock-owner being reduced to beggary, even though some villages lost all the herds they tended and the Administration had to organize emergency relief. Though there were widespread losses, as far as I am aware these involved few variations in the relative wealth and status position of individual homestead heads or in their dependant's access to milk. If there had been, I am sure that I should at least have heard talk of them, because one of the most widely repeated stories in the area was the following. It concerned a young Muslim of Isiolo District named Hapi.

The long dry season of 1949 was hard, and for some months everyone was hungry. Then, after the rains broke, there was more milk than even the young men could get through. Hapi took a full milk-pot, emptied it into a milking bucket, and staged the following scene. (In some versions he laid out a row of full milk-pots.) Hapi played both parts.

Hapi. Where have you been to all this long time Hunger has been killing us.
Milk. In the stomach of God [or 'In the sky'].
Hapi. Return to God then! ['To the sky' i.e. the source of rain.]

With which remark Hapi kicked over the bucket and beat the milk with a stick, 'as if it were a man', while it drained away into the sand.

During the next dry season all Hapi's stock perished and he was said to be a wanderer begging for his daily milk. His sacrilegious stupidity deterred others from assisting him to form a new herd which, it was argued, would surely suffer the fate of the first.

I do not know if the dramatic scene ever took place or if it was invented as a cautionary tale to explain the singularity of Hapi's plight. I never met Hapi, nor, as far as I know, anyone with whom he shared stock rights, and I do not even know if Hapi suffered as extensively as reported. But the story demonstrates the uniqueness of

Hapi's offence and divine punishment; it has the qualities of myth in its narrative simplicity, dramatic reversal of fortune, and symbolic resonances. Epidemics or raiders usually strike more diffusely. As is well known, many pastoral people (and also mixed economy stock-owners) distribute their stock among the herds of other men. One of the reasons given for this is to spread the risk of loss.[38] A consequence is that the herd a homestead feeds off is made up of the stock of different owners, and conversely the herd a man 'owns' is distributed and provides subsistence for many different homesteads.

God (*Waaḳa*) or Fortune (*Iyaana*) are blamed for major misfortunes, such as the death or serious illness of people, children and stock. God may strike from wrath, as at Hapi, or from mere whim; but by and large he hears the prayers of the good and strikes down the wicked. Neither God nor Fortune have refractions. But among settled Galla who have a mixed economy, such as the Macha, God has many spirit refractions or aspects. Knuttson reports that these manifest themselves by possessing leaders of localized social groupings at various levels. Shamanistic leaders diagnose sickness and misfortunes which are caused by breaches of social obligations and attribute moral responsibility.[39] My own recent observations on Arussi Galla, who now have a mixed economy, shows that they possess a set of witch beliefs which are very similar to those of the Boran, and they similarly do not make specific witchcraft accusations. But, unlike the Boran, they do sometimes attribute misfortune to angry spirits (*jaari*) who have been offended by social and moral lapses which are revealed by mediums. Elderly Arussi informants stated that such spirits have increased in number and in activity during their lifetimes—that is, since the Arussi became more settled and more dependent on crop production.

Lienhardt[40] notes that among the Dinka attempts to count children or cattle—that is, especially to single out, mark and direct attention to them—are likely to result 'in suggestions that the assessor has the evil eye', and perceptively that 'in the field of mystical action *individual* action is witchcraft and sorcery'. But if I have established that actual accusations—the most striking possible singlings out of an individual—are few, why then should the field of 'individual actions' be so limited? Why should the permitted arena for particularized action, either aggressive by witchcraft or defensive by accusation, be so restricted?

The answer lies partially, I suggest, in some of the attributes of cattle as property. Cattle are productive capital which provides subsistence. Neither the beasts nor their owners are tied to a fixed place. Most animals represent a bundle of rights, and only rarely are all the rights over the animal held by one person. If one asks any Boran who 'owns' the herd or flock which he tends and from which he and his dependants subsist, he will answer, 'It is mine.' But, as I pointed out above, men distribute their stock partly to spread their risks, partly to meet the differing grazing needs of different types of stock, and partly to create social links. So that in that herd or flock there will certainly be some beasts which other men could, and would, legitimately point to as theirs. Most animals are held in 'multiple ownership'. In the field I was constantly stumbling across strands of ownership connecting men to herds and to individual beasts cared for by others. Also Boran, like other pastoralists, identify with their cattle (though they rarely dedicate specific beasts to God); cattle are attributes and extensions of their owners as well as being their primary source of subsistence and equivalents for wives and children. Any stock-holder who accused another of attacking his stock would perforce involve his co-holders, as co-accusers, in an accusation which might be embarrassing to them. Equally, he would have to be prepared to face unknown co-holders in the herd of the accused. The moral aura of the accusation could be diffused and extended beyond the cracks and crevices, the areas of moral ambiguity, into an open and uncontrollable field of relationships, because property holding, property tending and residential groupings are not co-terminous. Eyers, it will be recalled, were said to be found among poor sheep and goat herders who graze the desert margins, the least likely people on whose assistance a cattle or camel owner would be likely to need to call.

This leads on to a related point. It is well established, as Evans-Pritchard pointed out for the Azande, that people 'are most likely to quarrel with those with whom they come into closest contact'. In his first Marett lecture, after analysing why 'accusations are the outcome of profound moral crises in relationships within the group',[41] Gluckman asks the question 'Why cannot those who wish to do so simply move away?' Sometimes cultivators do split, and witch beliefs are called on to legitimize the breach of residential and kin solidarity. But, frequently, physical movement is inhibited because those in dispute are bound to one another by interests in joint, immovable or indivisible property; and they are tied by growing crops and investments of toil in land, or because physical departure involves jumping from the frying pan into the fire. Moving away, in itself, is tantamount to an absolute rift in relationships. These considerations do not apply to free-ranging pastoralists. They and their animals can, and do, simply move away. Moreover, frequent territorial mobility is a customary feature of their lives as an integral part of the pastoral mode of life. Men who like living close to each other, and are reluctant to part, are frequently called upon to separate because of the exigencies of their stock. Remaining together implies mutual satisfaction, not just mutual tolerance. I suggest that there is an inverse relationship between ease of homestead movements (that is, when these cause little economic or social dislocation) and accusations of malevolent occult action.

In pastoral areas, density of population is low and people are usually very mobile. But I am not arguing that a low rate of accusation is a simple function of a low density of population. Indeed, shamanistic divination which points to individual responsibility for misfortune is a feature of some societies of hunters,[42] while among the Ibo, who have a high density of settlement, withcraft and sorcery allegations are reported to be rare. Indeed, Green[43] argues that that very density would make searching for witches 'a menace to their social stability' and therefore it is 'eliminated as far as possible'. Ibo diviners attribute the responsibility for death and sickness 'to offended ancestors, a deceased kinsman or the sufferer himself'. It is the type of moral, rather than demographic, density which is relevant.

Nandi, who are 'pastoral with agriculture', do not make seasonal movements and place 'strong ritual value' on ancestral land. 'The economic unit is the family, working its own cultivated plot.'[44] Mandari practise shifting agriculture, but are 'pastoralists by inclination' and 'part of the population of each chiefship is almost continually on the move'. The needs of cattle enforce 'co-operation between isolated chiefdoms' but the 'boundaries of the main land-owning groups' are seen as set and unchanging.[45] A man can only hold full rights of land ownership 'in the country where his clan have this status'. But any village or cattle camp contains representatives of several property-holding groups, settlers and clients, while 'a number of cattle at any time belong to maternal or affinal kin'.[46] Pastoralists appear to accuse immigrant cultivators but not each other.

The Dinka 'know themselves free to move away from each other' and consist of 'relatively mobile groups of herdsmen, who have behind them old traditions of migration and separation from each other'.[47] 'The wandering habits' of the Nuer are well known.[48]

Of the Turkana the Gullivers write that there is 'frequent change-over of the human population of the homesteads due to individual requirements' and the 'needs of the stock dictate that a man's family should be divided between two, three or four homesteads at the height of the dry season'. And, importantly, 'in all his movements the Turkana is guided by the needs of his stock'.[49] Because of the

> particular type of the nomadic system few inter-personal contacts are continuous. Each stock-owning unit [nuclear family] is a self-determinant pastoral unit, moving more or less independently of like units, and there is no fixed community life anywhere . . . There are only exiguous temporary connections with relatively fortuitous neighbours. A man's category of stock associates is spread over a wide, irregular area, and spatial relations frequently change.[50]

Dyson-Hudson[51] writes similarly of the Karimojong, and quotes a proverb which graphically expresses their dry-season dispersals: 'The sun mixes us.' He also notes that 'the men of a camp unit are friends' and the 'dissolution of a camp unit has normally only ecological causes and is a completely neutral occurrence'. Spencer reports similarly of the Samburu that 'associations in one settlement are in a continual state of flux'[52] and, as among the Karimojong, if a man has quarrelsome wives he may split his homestead, 'in order to keep them at a greater distance from one another'.[53] An 'elder is ideally free to migrate and manage his homestead as he pleases'.[54]

Somali hamlets are 'not firm local units but merely ephemeral aggregations of people and stock' and 'a man may live with his wife and children and his flocks far from the pastures where his sons and young brothers graze his camels'.[55]

It appears, then, that people who are likely to be involved in relationships of moral ambiguity of the type which are believed to be prone to lead to destructive malevolence (i.e. those in competition for property rights, resources or influence over people of a type which cannot by custom be openly expressed or adjudicated) are frequently dispersed because of their herding duties. Or, if they are not, each can appeal to the needs of his stock—an indisputable claim—as a reason for separating. Those who have reason to dislike or envy each other do not have to live and work together nursing their ill-will into hate or fear, but may legitimately separate, easily justifying their removal in terms of good stock management.[56] Men who have excellent relationships may and do separate simply because they arrive at different assessments of grazing and the likelihood of rain and the needs of the herds for which they care.

Dramatic blasting away of more or less permanent social, including residential, ties would be redundant. Men do not have, like Tiv and other cultivators, to get along with their 'agnates or become expatriates'. I have few examples in my notebooks of enduring jealousies and tensions between co-resident Boran. Boran villages which depend on 'dry' cows, or camels, or sheep and goats move frequently and, though most have a core of close friends who try to keep together (or at least coincide often), a village move frequently results in the separation or addition of a homestead or homesteads. Villages which depend on lactating cows tend to be both less mobile and more stable in homestead composition. The following example describes a situation in a particularly stable cow-village in which two men in rivalry continued to co-exist without any open breach.

J. had superabundant energy, was ambitious, and had the attributes traditionally required for recognition as a leading elder. He was the eldest of several sons of a distinguished deceased father. In his youth he had acquired a reputation for valour and he had a quick mind, good words and a generous disposition. (Personally I liked and respected him immensely.) His herds prospered, which was an indication of God's blessing. He was a sort of auxiliary government headman for the cattle grazing area in which he mainly resided and in which he was registered for taxation. After I had left the field he became, as was anticipated, official government headman on the death of the incumbent. Not surprisingly, J. had rivals who coveted his position for themselves and who frequently, but privately, accused him of self-seeking and ambition and, both publicly and privately, argued that he did not represent the Boran case against grazing controls to the Administration with sufficient force. J. himself was aware that he was the victim of backbiting but was not perturbed by it. He suffered, moreover, from a deformed and staring eye and was often referred to, in a jocular and punning fashion, as the man with 'the bad eye'—*ila-hama*. *Hama*, like the English word 'bad', has multiple meanings, such as 'defective quality', 'disliked', 'wicked', 'evil', 'offensive', 'dangerous', and it is used to describe comparatively a degree of ill-health. I never heard it suggested seriously that J. caused any individual any harm, nor that he had either the propensity or capability of doing so. He was a prosperous and senior cow herder, so it was unthinkable that he should be an 'Eyer'.

For purposes of stock management Boran divide their cattle, camels, sheep and goats into herds and flocks according to their grazing and watering needs. One member of a stock-owning group, usually a father and his sons or a set of siblings, lives with and manages one type of herd or flock. The herd of cows in milk is the most valued. It is kept on the best grazing land, is the least arduous to care for, and is usually managed by the senior owner. Villages therefore consist of herds or flocks of similar type managed by men who, from the point of view of stock management and ownership, are of approximately similar status.

J. was about forty-two years old and 'father' of a village of herders of cows in milk. His deceased father had also been father of a village, and J. perceived himself, and was perceived by others, as his father's successor. His younger brothers lived dispersed in other villages, managing other types of stock. J. had one living wife, and his children were infants. The herd he managed, and off which his family subsisted, was tended by himself, his wife, a client (an ex-slave of his father's), his client's herd-boy son, and the son of a 'best friend' who lived in the same village. During the rains two (and sometimes even one) homesteads have sufficient labour to care for their stock independently, but in the dry season the co-operative labour of several homesteads is required for watering at deep wells.

J.'s village moved less and was more stable in its composition than most. The Administration had recently introduced a stock limitation policy in the grazing area which J. used during the dry season. This had several consequences. The size of the herd allowed there was limited, so a brother of J. tended another herd of cows in milk in a different, uncontrolled area. As the total of stock allowed in the grazing area was small, pasture was plentiful, so movement in search of pasture was diminished. The grazing supply was further increased because several homesteads with their herds had left J.'s village (and others in the area) rather than submit to governmental supervision. J. liked to live within walking distance of the district commissioner's office. If he had left rather than submit to stock control he would have had to abandon his ambition to become headman.

J.'s village, at the time I first knew it, consisted of eight homesteads. None of the homesteads' fathers was a close kinsman of J. About two hundred yards away were a couple of homesteads headed by a man who, when he used the same wells as J., usually built near him, but always a little separately. Sometimes his homesteads were referred to as part of J.'s village, sometimes as a village on their own. During the period of my observations they moved off immediately the first short rains came, before J. was ready to move. In the event the rains failed, so J. did not move, but the two homesteads did not return to build near him. There had been neither quarrel nor dispute of which I could learn, but merely different assessments by homestead heads of what would be best for their herds.

About two miles away was a village of only two homesteads, but both had large herds. Its 'father' had formerly had a large village but it had dwindled. This 'father', W.G., was a man regarded as one who had had undeserved bad luck. The fathers of W.G. and J. had been great friends and W.G. clearly regarded J. in a fatherly manner, and J. equally clearly regarded W.G. with warm affection. The old man liked to build near J. and spent a good deal of his spare time in J.'s village. But the two villages grazed separately, though they co-operated for watering at deep wells; W.G.'s village would have been very hard put to it to water its cattle without assistance from members of J.'s village. W.G. did move off quite separately during one rains, but rebuilt near J.'s village in the following dry season. Excluding the two homesteads which had built two hundred yards from J.'s village during the dry season before my observations commenced, over a period of eighteen months, three homesteads appeared to have detached themselves, though one returned after an absence of a year. No homestead father died during the period, so no rearrangement of kin, for stock management purposes, was required within any of the stock-owning groups.

The two homesteads which partly detached themselves were headed by an old and wealthy man, B.J., and his friend G. G. was a jolly old man who seemed in everything to follow the lead of B.J., alongside whom he had built since they were young men. Throughout the following incidents G. constantly tried to smooth things over but, as far as I know, initiated nothing. He clearly had nothing to gain by detaching his herd from J.'s village; such a move could only have resulted in more work and less daily company for him. B.J. was in his seventies, fit enough around the homestead and byre, as was demonstrated by the immaculate condition in which he maintained his cattle and calf pens, but was unable to walk far from home and showed little interest in public affairs. He had built alongside J.'s father, his contemporary, for very many years. To me, at any rate, he explained any present difficulties as a consequence of the general decline of the world, like the imposition of grazing controls, but always did so in the most cheerful and hearty manner. Decisions about stock management he claimed, and appeared, to leave to his eldest son, H. His younger sons lived with other stock elsewhere.

H. was about thirty-five years old, had two wives, but like J. had only infant children. Both J. and H. led wealthy homesteads. H. was used to playing the role of elder. Initially my impression was that H. and J. were close. But, later, either as the differences between them widened or as I got to know them better, H. expressed clearly to me in private his resentment at the respect in which J. was generally held. If the resentment had not been accompanied by ambition the solution was obvious; H. could merely have gone his own way during the rains and joined another village for the succeeding dry season. But if he wanted to become in effect a 'father' to a village of his own, he needed others to join him. (During the lifetime of his father, who depended on him, a new village would have been known as that of his father. But a son can become 'father' of a village during the lifetime of his own father, providing they are territorially quite distinct, and two brothers can each be 'fathers' to separate villages.)

Within a short interval of each other, both J. and H. held a naming ceremony for a child. These are great festivals, and in beasts sacrificed, meat distributed and meticulous observation of tradition H. was held to outshine J. J. shrugged off the matter condescendingly, commenting that H. had been rather ostentatious for a man who had killed neither a man nor a lion, both of which J. had done in his youth. In the following short rains H., his father B.J., and his father's friend G., moved off and grazed separately from J. They joined up again for the next dry season and co-operated over watering, except that they built a little apart. To the eye they could have been either one or separate, but H. asked me to pitch my tent in 'his father's village'. Then H. himself went off for three months to visit his stock and kin in Ethiopia. On his return he set to work to get a new well dug in the valley, where there was a short string of wells at which many villages watered during the dry season.

The well was to provide an extra outlet, and was a watering convenience rather than an addition to the total supply. Chances of it filling were estimated to be about even, for several dry holes interspersed the existing wells. The labour was arduous because the hole had to be cut in part through rock, which involved building a series of fires over the rock and then pouring cold water over the heated rock to crack it. H. enterprisingly obtained a 'loan' of government tools through a private arrangement with a foreman. At one time or another most men in the area, including J., put in a stint at the digging. The well did fill at the next rains and was blessed at a solemn ceremony at which H. sacrificed a beast, and in which J. participated. According to custom all men who have participated in the digging, or eaten of the sacrificed beast, and their patrilineal descendants are entitled to water stock at that well. H. did not acquire any exclusive rights in the well. But he achieved a public reputation as a benefactor, an organizer, and a man of judgment, and by right of his 'fatherhood' of the well he obtained a respected voice in the deliberations which would be held to decide watering rotas at it. His success also clearly indicated that his work was blessed by God. Unfortunately, my field work concluded shortly after the well blessing, and I only know that H. and the 'village' of his father went off separately during the next rains. I do not know if H. and his father rejoined J.'s village again or not.

I have considered witch beliefs and witchcraft accusations in nine rather arbitrarily selected transhumant or nomadic East African societies, but I think the following general proposition may have less limited application:

Where property rights are not particularized and access to prosperity appears to be open though dependent on wide co-operation, and men are not impelled to work with and reside in close proximity to their rivals, then:

1. Witch beliefs are peripheral to explanations of misfortune; and
2. Direct accusations of occult meddling couched in terms of personal responsibility are few.

I do not suggest that the factors outlined above are the only ones which may be relevant to an explanation of a low rate of witchcraft or blame-pinning accusations. (One which would seem to merit further examination, for example, is the mode of controlling sexual competition for women.) But the suggestions I have proposed might be further generalized, for example to the urban situation, because in one respect pastoralist and townsman are comparable. Only rarely is either forced to live in such morally dense situations that the only method of separation is through a violent breach. In Central African towns people 'are thrown higgledy-piggledy together'; the conditions of their employment and the availability of housing 'mixes' them. In such urban industrial situations, as in pastoral societies, the attribution of misfortunes to the malevolent manipulation of the occult by persons with whom responsibilities are shared can be inappropriate. Mitchell,[57] in an article on 'The meaning of misfortune for urban Africans', concludes that:

> Social separation is a feature of urban societies so that tensions that arise in towns do not call for a catalytic agent such as witchcraft accusations to provide justification for segmentations . . . To see the hand of witchcraft in misfortune may be the first reaction of a townsman, but it is an interpretation which in terms of the social and administrative structure of the urban community allows him no direct retributive action,

so that he has to cast explanations in other terms in which 'there is something he can do about it'. For a pastoralist, 'doing something about' misfortune in terms of witchcraft accusations would do more harm than good, because it would disrupt the network of multiplex ties, active or potential, on which a herdsman's very subsistence depends. But Mitchell's townsmen and pastoralists are comparable only in the respect that neither are normally forced by ecological and economic circumstances to live, to pray and to work with those with whom they are in rivalry. When townsmen are involved in competitive and close relationships, as Kapferer[58] has recently shown, then accusations continue to be made in the idiom of witchcraft. The comparison can be only tentative and tenuous. Early in this paper I quoted statements by both Gluckman and Marwick which related the decline in blame-pinning accusations to the flowering of the industrial revolution and the growth of impersonal urban complexes. Clearly, such a decline is gradual and not an immediate and dramatic withering away—indeed, in Europe the economic changes were accompanied by a last florescence of accusations.

New townsmen, then, seeking for an explanation in familiar terms when in an unfamiliar situation, tend to attribute their misfortunes to the intervention of ancestor spirits or to blame rural kinsmen, even ones they have never met. Mitchell argues that they are forced to seek for socially distant attributions because ones made nearer home would either provide explanations which were clearly inadequate or would scatter the blame too confusingly wide.

Early in this paper I noted that references to witchcraft accusations in the ethnography of East African pastoralists are sparse. Interestingly, however, references to blessings and curses abound. Certainly the daily social intercourse of Boran floats on a stream of blessings, even the daily passing of greetings is an exchange of blessings. The withholding or withdrawal of blessings is one of the major controls which seniors have over juniors. Harsh words, abuse and vituperation provoke widespread alarm and can be cancelled only by their withdrawal followed by an exchange of blessings. Curses are so dreadful that they are invoked only as an ultimate sanction, and feature more prominently in myth than in life.[59] A comparative examination of blessings and curses and their intermediate forms is beyond the scope of this article, but one general point which connects with my theme can be made summarily. Evans-Pritchard states that, among the Nuer, 'if a man wishes to be right with God he must be in the right with men'.[60] Blessings and curses are spoken by men to men but they are addressed, explicitly or implicitly, to God. They are either appeals for the good and ordered to be maintained or for the bad and disturbed to be put to rights again. They are mediatory because, almost invariably, they are not automatic in their consequences but are conditional—conditional, that is, in that they depend for their efficacy on the moral and spiritual conditions and social positions of both the utterer and the receiver. So that the boundary between blessings and curses is not always clear, and one is capable of transformation into the other.[61] Curses are also a form of oath in so far as they bind the curser and the cursed to accept the judgment of God. Allocation of responsibility is transferred out of the particular and immediate level of the relationships between the offender and the offended, from which it arises and which is open to manipulation by occult means, to a mystical and societal level in which judgment is God's. Boran recognize, as it seems do most pastoralists, that God is capricious and acts in ways that are hard for men to understand, so, when confronted by misfortune, they examine their own conduct, offer prayer and sacrifice and beg for blessing and the withholding of wrath. The intervention of God in human affairs is recognized especially when men act badly, as Hapi the milk waster acted, but men do not malignantly manipulate the occult for their personal advantage. The nexus of widespread interdependencies on which the maintenance of their herds depends could not bear the strains which such actions might generate.

[1970]

Notes

1 'Witch beliefs in Central Africa' (1967), pp. 77–8.
2 *Sorcery in its Social Setting* (1965), p. 295. Douglas's comments above were made in a review of this book.
3 Forde, 'Spirits, witches and sorcerers in the supernatural economy of the Yakö' (1958).
4 *Custom and Conflict in Africa* (1955), p. 94.
5 *Politics, Law and Ritual in Tribal Society* (1965), p. 218.
6 Marwick, *Sorcery in its Social Setting* (1965), p. 295.
7 See P. Mayer, *Witches* (1954). I do not suggest that differences of belief are not present, or are unrelated to other aspects of culture or social structure, but my data are insufficient for an examination of differences of witch belief. See M. Wilson's 'Witch beliefs and social structure' (1951), and Nadel's 'Witchcraft in four African societies' (1952).
8 'Mandari witchcraft' (1963), p. 102.
9 *Ibid.*, p. 108.
10 'The Mandari of the southern Sudan' (1958), p. 86.
11 'Mandari Witchcraft' (1963), p. 108.
12 *Chiefs and Strangers* (1963), p. 134.
13 Huntingford, 'Nandi witchcraft' (1963), pp. 176–80.
14 'Mandari witchcraft' (1963), pp. 111 and 109. See especially the case of the motherless child of Mojut who stayed out after dark (pp. 118–19).
15 Huntingford, 'Nandi witchcraft' (1963), pp. 182–3.
16 Huntingford, *The Southern Nilo-Hamites* (1953), p. 26.
17 'Some notions of witchcraft among the Dinka' (1951), p. 304.
18 *Ibid.*, p. 315.
19 *Divinity and Experience* (1961), pp. 64–7.
20 *Nuer Religion* (1965), pp. 94–104: *peth* is also the Nuer term for the

'evil eye'—'an act of covetousness or envy' (p. 15)—and would appear to approximate closely to Galla notions of the evil eye.

21 *The Central Nilo-Hamites* (1953), p. 86.
22 *The Samburu* (1965), pp. 185–6.
23 *A Pastoral Democracy* (1961), p. 26. See also p. 258.
24 *Ibid.*, p. 263.
25 Cf. Buxton, *Chiefs and Strangers* (1963), p. 116: she states that Mandari most frequently attribute 'undiagnosed illness and petty annoyances of everyday life' to Eyers. Similar categories of Eyers are a feature of Cushitic cultures (both Amhara and Gurage also use the word *buuda*, and both associate its possession with craftsmen. Amhara use the term *buuda* also and associate it particularly with necrophagy (e.g. Shack, *The Gurage* (1966), p. 9). The type of scabies which brings up grey patches on the body skin is, I have been informed, contracted from the cows, particularly by sweaty contact with the hides used as sleeping mats.
26 See Marwick, 'The sociology of sorcery in an African tribe' (1963), p. 7.
27 Marwick, *Sorcery in its Social Setting* (1965), suggests, and Turner states explicitly in 'Witchcraft and sorcery: taxonomy *versus* dynamics' (1964), that 'witch beliefs are associated with the high rate of morbidity and mortality that afflict most tribal societies'. I have no reason to think that either is relatively low in pastoral societies: indeed, they are probably both high.
28 *A Pastoral Democracy* (1961), p. 28.
29 'Psychosis and social change among the Tallensi of northern Ghana' (1966), p. 11.
30 *A Pastoral Democracy* (1961), p. 263. Lewis's suggestion merits further discussion. It seems a tenable hypothesis that within the pastoral complex, in which most major political units, whether Somali lineages or the Boran or Samburu nation, were in constant hostility with one another, that the necessity for maintaining mutual dependencies within the units inhibited divisive accusations, particularly as one accusation tends to generate another: cf. Gluckman, *Politics, Law and Ritual in Tribal Society* (1965), pp. 305–13.
31 *Sorcery in its Social Setting* (1965), p. 295.
32 Bailey, 'The peasant view of the bad life' (1966), p. 2.
33 Especially Gluckman in *Politics, Law and Ritual in Tribal Society* (1965), chapter 11; see also Foster, 'Peasant society and the idea of the limited good' (1965).
34 Fortune, *Sorcerers of Dobu* (1932), describes a magical method for 'seducing yams from a neighbour's garden into one's own' and argues: 'It is assumed throughout that social success is necessarily gained at the expense of others' (p. 135).

35 See especially M. Wilson *Divine Kings and the Breath of Men* (1959).
36 Baxter, 'Stock management and the diffusion of property rights among the Boran' (1966). Mpaayei writes: 'The Maasai say that the cow is the head of a man—that is, a man can build up a home by the good care of one cow'—*Inkuti Pukunot oo Llamaasai* (1954), p. 39. Spencer, *The Samburu* (1965), writes that 'Mystical beliefs which suggest a certain tension between brothers among the Rendile are not shared by Samburu' (p. 294). He suggests that this may be because the longer gestation period of camels (main stock of Rendile), as compared to cows (main stock of Samburu), means a slower rate of herd growth, stock shortage and a prolonged dependence of younger brothers on their elder brothers.

Cattle of other peoples are, of course, fair game; e.g. 'The Masai believe that in the beginning God gave them all the cattle in the world, and therefore nobody else has a right to possess any': Huntingford, *The Southern Nilo-Hamites* (1953), p. 107.
37 The nearest thing to a case of witchcraft described for the Karimojong, in which 'a spiteful tongue and a fierce temper' are mentioned, followed some time after the loss by an unfortunate of 'most of his cattle' to Pokot raiders. A quarrelsome woman who spoke 'bitter words' kept two mutually dependent herdsmen apart in separate, though nearby, settlements.
38 Cf. Buxton, 'The Mandari of the southern Sudan' (1958), p. 90: 'People like to separate their herds as a safeguard against disease and raiding.'
39 *Authority and Change* (1967).
40 *Divinity and Experience* (1961), p. 22 and p. 247.
41 See Gluckman's essay in this book. I was privileged to see the manuscript of Gluckman's Marret lecture, from which I quote here.
42 For a summary see Service, *The Hunters* (1966), pp. 66–70. Though Lorna Marshall, 'Sharing, talking and giving: relief of social tensions among !Kung Bushmen' notes of the harmless Bushmen that 'Occasions when tempers have got out of control are remembered with awe' (p. 231) and that 'bad words make them uneasy. Bushmen attribute most sickness and misfortune to God', E. M. Marshall writes of them in *The Harmless People* (1959): 'without very rigid co-operation Bushmen would not survive the famines and droughts the Kalahari offers them' (p. 33).
43 *Ibo Village Affairs* (1947), p. 95.
44 Huntingford, *The Southern Nilo-Hamites* (1953), p. 23.
45 Buxton, *The Mandari of the Southern Sudan* (1958), pp. 69–72.
46 *Ibid.*, p. 90.
47 Lienhardt, *The Western Dinka* (1958), pp. 114 and 132.
48 Evans-Pritchard, *Kinship and Marriage among the Nuer* (1951), p. 1.

49 The *Central Nilo-Hamites* (1953), pp. 63–5.
50 *The Family Herds* (1955), p. 252.
51 *Karimojong Politics* (1966), pp. 45, 50–1, 63 and 71.
52 *The Samburu* (1965), p. 16.
53 *Ibid.*, p. 11.
54 *Ibid.*, p. 175.
55 Andrzejewski and Lewis, *Somali Poetry* (1964), pp. 18–20. Dr Y. Eilam informs me that witchcraft and sorcery accusations are absent among the BaHima of Ankole and that Stanley's observation (*In Darkest Africa*, vol. 1, p. 363) is correct that 'they settle down whenever they are tempted [by pasture] and when there [is trouble] they build a house on another spot'.
56 Marwick, *Sorcery in its Social Setting* (1965), p. 17, attributes the low frequency of believed attacks between Cewa spouses to the 'easy and frequent divorce' so that 'if tension develops between them, they can easily part before it reaches a dangerous level'.
57 (1965), pp. 201–3.
58 'Norms and the manipulation of relationships in a work context' (1969), especially p. 203.
59 This would also seem to be so among the Nuer, see *Nuer Religion* (1956) pp. 165–76.
60 *Nuer Religion* (1956), p. 18.
61 *Nuer Religion* (1956), p. 170; see the discussion of *biit*.

Bibliography

Andrzejewski, B. W., and Lewis, I. M., *Somali Poetry*, Oxford: Clarendon Press (1964).

Bailey, F. G., 'The peasant view of the bad life', *The Advancement of Science*, vol. XXIII (1966), pp. 1–11.

Baxter, P. T. W., 'Repetition in certain Boran ceremonies' in *African Systems of Thought*, ed. M. Fortes and C. Dieterlen, London: Oxford University Press for the International African Institute (1965).

— 'Stock management and the diffusion of property rights among the Boran', *Proceedings of the Third International Congress of Ethiopian Studies*, 1966 (forthcoming).

Buxton, Jean, 'The Mandari of the southern Sudan' in *Tribes without Rulers*, ed. John Middleton and David Tait, London: Routledge & Kegan Paul (1958).

— 'Mandari Witchcraft' in *Witchcraft and Sorcery in East Africa*, ed. John Middleton and E. H. Winter, London: Routledge & Kegan Paul (1963).

Buxton, J. C., *Chiefs and Strangers: a Study of Political Assimilation among the Mandari*, Oxford: Clarendon Press (1963).

Douglas, Mary, 'Witch beliefs in Central Africa', *Africa*, vol. XXXVII, No. 1 (January 1967), pp. 72–80.
Dyson-Hudson, Neville, *Karimojong Politics*, Oxford: Clarendon Press (1966).
Evans-Pritchard, E. E., *Kinship and Marriage among the Nuer*, Oxford: Clarendon Press (1951).
— *Nuer Religion*, Oxford: Clarendon Press (1956).
Forde, Daryll, 'Spirits, witches and sorcerers in the supernatural economy of the Yakö', *Journal of the Royal Anthropological Institute*, vol. 88, II (1958), pp. 165–78. Reprinted in *Yakö Studies*, London: Oxford University Press for the International African Institute (1964).
Fortes, Meyer, and Mayer, Doris Y., 'Psychosis and social change among the Tallensi of northern Ghana', *Cahiers d'Etudes Africaines*, 21, vol. VI (1966), pp. 5–40.
Fortune, R. F., *Sorcerers of Dobu*, London: Routledge (1932).
Foster, George, 'Peasant society and the idea of the limited good', *American Anthropologist*, 67, 2 (April 1965), pp. 293–315.
Gluckman, M., *Politics, Law and Ritual in Tribal Society*, Oxford: Blackwell (1965).
Green, M. M., *Ibo Village Affairs*, London: Sidgwick & Jackson (1947).
Gulliver, Pamela and P. H., *The Central Nilo-Hamites*, London: International African Institute (1953).
Gulliver, P. H., *The Family Herds*, London: Routledge & Kegan Paul (1955).
Huntingford, G. W. B., *The Southern Nilo-Hamites*, London: International African Institute (1953).
— 'Nandi witchcraft' in *Witchcraft and Sorcery in East Africa*, ed. John Middleton and E. H. Winter, London: Routledge & Kegan Paul (1963).
Kapferer, B., 'Norms and manipulation of relationships in a work context' in *Social Networks in Urban Situations*, ed. J. Clyde Mitchell, Manchester: Manchester University Press (1969).
Knutsson, Karl Eric, *Authority and Change: a Study of the Kallu Institution among the Macha Galla of Ethiopia*. Etnologiska Studier 29. Goteberg: Etnografiska Museet (1967).
Lewis, I. M., *A Pastoral Democracy: a Study of Pastoralism among the Northern Somali of the Horn of Africa*. London: Oxford University Press for the International African Institute (1961).
Lienhardt, Godfrey, 'Some notions of witchcraft among the Dinka', *Africa*, vol. XXI, No. 4 (December 1951), pp. 303–15.
— 'The western Dinka' in *Tribes Without Rulers*, ed. John Middleton and David Tait, London: Routledge & Kegan Paul (1958).

— *Divinity and Experience: the Religion of the Dinka*, Oxford: Clarendon Press (1961).
Marshall, E. M., *The Harmless People*, New York: Knopf (1959).
Marshall, Lorna, 'Sharing, talking, and giving: relief of social tensions among Kung Bushmen', *Africa*, vol. xxxi, No. 3 (1961), pp. 231–249.
Marwick, M. G., 'The sociology of sorcery in an African tribe', *African Studies*, vol. 22, No. 1 (1963), pp. 1–21.
— *Sorcery in its Social Setting: a Study of the Northern Rhodesian Cewa*, Manchester: Manchester University Press (1965).
Mayer, Phillip, *Witches*, inaugural lecture, Grahamstown: Rhodes University (1954).
Mitchell, J. C., 'The meaning in misfortune for urban Africans' in *African Systems of Thought*, ed. M. Fortes and G. Dieterlen, London: Oxford University Press for the International African Institute.
Mpaayei, John Tompo Ole, *Inkuti Pukunot oo Llmaasai*, London: Oxford University Press for the School of African and Oriental Studies (1954).
Nadel, S. F., 'Witchcraft in four African societies: an essay in comparison', *American Anthropologist*, vol. 54 (1952), pp. 18–29.
Service, Elman R., *The Hunters*, Engelwood Cliffs, N.J.: Prentice-Hall (1966).
Shack, William A., *The Gurage: a People of the Ensete Culture*, London: Oxford University Press for the International African Institute (1966).
Spencer, P., *The Samburu*, London: Routledge & Kegan Paul (1965).
Turner, V. W., 'Witchcraft and sorcery: taxonomy *versus* dynamics', *Africa*, vol. xxxiv, No. 4 (1964), pp. 314–25; reprinted in *The Forest of Symbols: Aspects of Ndembu Ritual*, Ithaca, N.Y.: Cornell University Press (1967).
Wilson, Monica H., 'Witch belief and social structure', *American Journal of Sociology*, vol. 56, No. 4 (1951), pp. 307–13.
— *Divine Kings and the Breath of Men*, Frazer lecture, Cambridge: Cambridge University Press (1959).

5
When witches are not named

Basil Sansom

The Pedi of Megwang chiefdom, Transvaal, Sekhukhuneland, South Africa, believe in witches and witchcraft. They spend time, effort and cash in attempts to counter the malevolence of witches. Local doctors are paid to divine and diagnose malign influences. They are paid again to supply the medicines of protection or revenge. In Pedi law witchcraft is an actionable wrong and culprits could be paraded and punished in Pedi courts. Nonetheless, Pedi of Megwang do not try to identify and stigmatize witches before an audience. While witch beliefs are prevalent, accusation, in the full sense of public denunciation, hardly ever occurs.

Faced with misfortune, a Pedi may see its genesis in witchcraft. He may also believe that he can name the culpable witch. His culture provides the preconditions for accusations of witchcraft. There are witchcraft beliefs that are unquestioned. There are known forms for denunciation. Yet Pedi *choose* not to accuse.

This is my initial puzzle: why is accusation of witchcraft a rejected alternative for the people I studied?

At the outset a facile and apparently obvious answer must be discounted utterly. In South Africa it is an illegal and criminal act for one person to accuse another of witchcraft. But this law is one that Pedi tribesmen can ignore with impunity. Pedi have a compact with their local Bantu Affairs Commissioners. Though vested with powers to intervene, the commissioner leaves the internal affairs of chiefdoms alone. For their part, the Pedi do not bring white administrators into local affairs. Chiefdoms are insulated. In Sekhukhuneland it is unthinkable for a man to visit the consequences of a white man's law on a fellow Pedi. This defines the greatest treason. Its consequence is social annihilation by ostracism. White laws do not prevent the naming of witches.[1]

An accusation of witchcraft is an attempt to modify a set of social relationships relevant to an accuser, to an accused and to certain others who are potential parties to the accusation. The charge is that the accused used illegitimate magical or supernatural means to accomplish an end. His use of such means establishes him as a witch. As a witch, he is estranged from his accuser and from those witnesses who have accepted his guilt. An accusation of witchcraft is work carried out before, and upon, an audience. The accuser presses the charge: a convinced audience fixes guilt. When unconvinced, the audience absolves. The attempt may thus succeed or fail.

I argue that the sets of social relationships in which Pedi are involved cannot sustain accusations of witchcraft. These relationships dictate an accuser's inability to mobilize the support necessary for an accusation to succeed. A second strand of argument is that, in Megwang chiefdom, witchcraft as a charge is inappropriate. If relationships are to be modified by estranging an individual from others, witchcraft is the wrong charge to make.

These arguments subserve a general proposition. Accusation of witchcraft introduces ambiguity into constituted relationships; it is most effective in modifying relationships in a field that is characterized by relative certainty about patterns of sociation. Conversely, where future patterns of sociation are uncertain, accusation of witchcraft will fail to alter a given situation. Seen as an element of strategy, accusation of witchcraft should be put aside when actors work in conditions of uncertainty. Pedi data illustrate these conditions.

Successful accusation: its context and effects

An accusation of witchcraft is a charge imposed on an already existing set of relationships. Its formulation, progress and effects are conditioned by them. Seen thus, witchcraft accusation is structurally dependent. Its incidence reflects the social processes on which it is imposed. In Marwick's catch phrase, it is 'a social strain gauge'.[2] Since the Pedi do not accuse, evidence from other places must be examined to show the effects of the transmutation of the accused into a witch.

I begin by citing Central African studies in which witchcraft accusation is part of local-level politics. Mitchell, Marwick and others have shown how accusations of witchcraft serve political ends.[3] Accusations mark competition for headmanship when a man consciously tries to discredit rivals in order to attain office. Schism of local groups is also a typical occasion for accusation. Douglas[4] labels this the 'obstetric' function of accusation because the accusation acts as midwife to the birth of a new group out of an old. Again, movements of individuals from one group to another can be justified in terms of witchcraft. Accusations of witchcraft are used as part of attempts to modify incumbency of office or the size and composition of local groups. The issues are membership, leadership and support.

Secondly, accusation of witchcraft can be assimilated to procedures of self-help where there is no accepted central authority to administer justice. In traditional times, accusation of witchcraft among the Lele of the Kasai can be described as continuing the feud by other means.[5] Homicide and killing by witchcraft were socially equated. If a man was guilty of killing by witchcraft, his kinship group had to pay blood money as if he had speared his victim. The groups mobilized by homicide and witchcraft accusation were identical. Accusations could culminate in a lethal poison ordeal. If a man died by the poison his guilt was established. Surviving kin shared his guilt and had to compensate the accusers for the loss that had instigated the charge of witchcraft. There was redistribution of wealth. The defeated group lost on the political front as well. In the small, contained Lele village which provided the usual arena for accusation, witchcraft accusation thus dramatically brought political crises to a head and forced a decision about the distribution of property and power.

Nash[6] reports the association of witchcraft and self-help in a Mexican *pueblo*. The *inditos* of the *pueblo* keep the representatives of the government out of local affairs. Resolution of internal feuds can involve killing, and homicides are frequent. Accusation of witchcraft is used as a *post factum* justification for killing. A gang of men fall on an enemy, preferably when he is drunk and helpless. Later the body is discovered. Everyone knows the identity of the killers, but the killers must establish that the killing was just according to local standards. They acted as executioners, not as murderers. By the killing the *pueblo* was rid of a witch. The *pueblo* has the power to make this discrimination, for the *pueblo* controls the witnesses and hence the evidence about the killing. A post-mortem definition of the victim as a witch establishes the killers as representatives of the community. When the police arrive they will be unable to glean evidence to form the basis of a criminal charge. The homicide becomes virtuous. The removal of the witch involves realignment in social relationships.

A case of the victimization of a washerman in the Indian village of Bisipara reported by Bailey provides an instance of the economic competition in a caste structure.[7] The local washerman was enjoying property above the standard commensurate with his status. This was due to the fortunes of his sons, who had found employment outside the village. The villagers had no control over these outside sources of income. The washerman could not be reduced in the normal manner, simply by paying him less for his services. Instead, he was accused of harbouring a spirit which was blamed for causing several deaths. He was heavily fined. In Bailey's analysis the consciously directed nature of the attack by the clean castes on this untouchable is patent. The washerman offended by having too much cash, and he was deprived of cash.

Another Indian example illustrates a more subtle transformation in relationships. Epstein has described accusations of witchcraft within the peasant caste in Wangala, a Mysore village.[8] In Wangala only women among the peasants can be accused of witchcraft—men do not harbour the type of spirit-familiar that instigates mystical attacks. To explain this categorical limitation Epstein proffers the same interpretation as that given by Gluckman to account for a similar restriction among the patrilineal Zulu.[9] Wives are outsiders in an exogamous patrilineage. They represent points of differentiation in the lineage, which, ideally, should be united. In Epstein's phrase, men 'project their guilt'[10] onto women.

Now, Wangala women trade and contract debts to finance their petty trading. Their financial arrangements are largely segregated from those of men. In the case in question a woman became indebted to another, who charged the usual high interest rate of the region. Unable to redeem her increasing debt, the debtor accused her creditor of witchcraft. Further, she assaulted the 'witch' and the village council ordered her to recompense the assailed woman by paying damages, thus compounding the indebtedness. The creditor was paid in full—but only because the kinsmen of the debtor provided the cash.

My interpretation of this event is that the debtor established herself as a victim in the eyes of her kinsmen. As a victim of witchcraft she faced a special crisis. Normally people are personally accountable for their debts. Kinsmen cannot generally be held responsible for the trading debts of female relatives; this would enable women to put men in pawn. However, in times of crisis, illness, bereavement, etc, kin should rally to rescue or sustain their relatives. By turning the relationship between debtor and creditor into one of victim *vis-à-vis* witch, the debtor–victim turned her personal indebtedness into a family crisis. She shifted responsibility from herself onto a wider circle of kinsmen. A personal problem in Wangala kin groups involves defining the boundary between kinship obligation and individual accountability. In accusation the debtor found a device for crossing this divide.

These examples show strategic implications in accusation. Fixing accusation allows relationships around perpetrator and denouncer to be modified. To catalogue, witchcraft can provide the occasion for inevitable schism, the idiom of a smear campaign, the justification for breaking a relationship, a form for prosecuting the feud, justification of homicide, an excuse for expropriation, the operator that transforms a debtor into a case for charity.

In each instance accusation is a move in a game played for the stakes of social status. Accusation is an attempt to degrade another so that one's own position may be redefined in terms of the others' degradation. The rules of this game are the rules that govern degradation of status.

Witchcraft and degradation of status

Here witchcraft is treated as a member of a class of events defined by Garfinkel.[11] An accusation of witchcraft is an attempt to achieve a ceremony of status degradation. In this formulation, accusation of witchcraft is an instrumental act. It can be compared with other instrumental alternatives and evaluated against them. One can then describe what is entailed when a man decides whether to accuse or to refrain from levelling a charge of witchcraft.

For Garfinkel, a ceremony of degradation is 'Any communicative work between persons, whereby the public identity of an actor is transformed into something lower in the local scheme of social types.' He adds that 'these identities must refer to persons as "motivational types", not to what a person may be expected to have done or do (in Parsons' term, to his "performances") but to what the group hold to be the "ultimate grounds" or "reasons" for his performance'.[12]

Denunciation of total identity mobilizes moral indignation. Its force is evident in its consequences. The person denounced is transformed and perceived anew: 'He is not changed, he is reconstituted. The former identity, at best, receives the accent of mere appearance . . . the new identity is the basic reality. What he is now is what, "after all", he was all along.'[13]

To exemplify, Coke's raging prosecution of Sir Walter Raleigh turned that knight inside out and made his career a sham:

> I will prove you to be the most notorious traitor that ever came to the bar! . . . Thou art a monster! Thou hast an English face but a Spanish heart . . . thou viper! . . . Thou art thyself a spider of hell. Thou art the most vile and execrable traitor that ever lived . . . Then let all that heard you this day judge what you are, and what a traitors heart you bear, *whatever you pretended* . . .[14]

The public English face all the time hid the private Spanish heart. 'Viper' expresses the righteous indignation of the deceived persecutor who speaks for king and people. Raleigh is declared traitor and his total identity is transformed.

In the incumbency of the new type, the subject is made strange, set apart from the moral community which granted him mistaken membership.

The effects of accusation of witchcraft accord so well with Garfinkel's scheme that they could well have served as its prototype. The primary image of the witch is of one who abrogates claim to fellow-feeling because he has worked outside the permitted range of human activity. Further, imputation of inhuman acts—bestiality, incest, necrophagy—repeat, amplify and dramatize the primary image. The stereotype of the witch provides legitimation for action. Those denounced in its terms are estranged, removed by their special trespass. Attribution of witchcraft entails a moral lowering, the ascription of abominable motives, a degradation of total identity.

Yet, although an instance of status degradation, witchcraft entails accusation of an imagined crime. Degradation *via* witchcraft is peculiar. Imagined crimes must be attributed rather than proven: their perpetrators have equivocal status. It is difficult to quell reasonable doubt about their guilt. Nor need one question the sincerity of local beliefs in witchcraft to note the perpetual ambiguity of the status of witch. These beliefs themselves create ambiguity. Witches are prone to choose victims when others are likely to appear culpable (Cewa).[15] They can interfere with the devices used to indicate guilt (Azande).[16]

Accusations of witchcraft evoke a plot with a 'whodunit' structure. It opens with an established misfortune, often a death, the *corpus delicti*. Belief in witchcraft allows men to ask who was responsible for the misfortune. While the misfortune is evident, the link between perpetrator and event is obscure.

Witches are condemned on evidence that is, and always must be, circumstantial. If proof is to be produced, it is the manufactured proof of an ordeal or the equivocal indications of divination. Pinning the accusation is difficult because of inherent doubt and ambiguity.

To clinch any denunciation, Garfinkel shows that the denouncer must establish a triangle of identities and relationships. This triangle links the denouncer to the perpetrator, and both of them to an event.[17] A man becomes a proper denouncer by establishing his credentials as a representative of community values. The event for which responsibility is to be allocated belongs to a special class. Its commission automatically condemns its perpetrator on motivational grounds. The audience must accept event, denouncer and perpetrator as proper representatives of their types, just as they must judge the unsuccessful accuser to be unqualified to denounce and denied the right to stand for group values. The event may be questioned—was it witchcraft or the will of the gods? Or a qualified denouncer may deal with a misfortune but accuse the wrong person.

While all elements and links in the triangle can be questioned, certain types of accusation put greater stress on different parts of this model. Arguments about heresy, for instance, centre on the interpretation of the event(s). The words and actions of the accused must be shown to be at variance with orthodox belief. Because heresy is pre-eminently about belief, its ambiguities arise in the counter-position of dogma and alleged antithesis. Do these acts indeed constitute heresy?

In contrast, witchcraft accusation, with its 'whodunit' plot, puts the greatest strain on the link between perpetrator and event: is this man indeed the witch in question?

Accusations of witchcraft, then, have a special kind of ambiguity.

Witnesses are asked to identify a witch on grounds that are always uncertain.

Accusations of witchcraft have other signal attributes that derive from the character and motivation of 'communicative work'. First, accusation is effective: the accuser is 'doing something to' a named person. Second, the accusation is prompted by a set of prior events. These include not only the misfortune but the behaviour that leads to the identification of a suspect. The accuser is 'doing something about' a predicament. Finally, communicative work demands an audience of witnesses. It succeeds when at least some onlookers are brought to accept the transformation of accused into witch.

When the work of denunciation is initiated the accuser pits himself against the accused in the face of the audience. The progress of the work is measured by the differentiation of roles within the audience. Its members may support either the accuser or accused, or they may opt out and establish their neutrality. The criterion for success in the work of degradation is that 'the denunciation must re-define the situation of those that are witnesses to the denunciation work'.[18]

One further point may be made. Garfinkel posits that only in a state of anomie will there be no forms and ceremonies for degradation of status.[19] This implies that in rejecting witchcraft as an idiom for degradation the Pedi must adopt something else. Also, their current forms of degradation must be more suitable to present conditions than accusations of witchcraft. Why this should be so is foreshadowed by the above discussion. Specifically, the inherent ambiguity in the process of accusation is inappropriate in social relationships in Megwang chiefdom.

The range of local possibilities

Accusations of witchcraft always occur within a range of possibilities that are locally defined. There are three sources of social limitation on accusations of witchcraft. It is as if three types of censor were at work, each eliminating the attribution of witchcraft from social categories or relationships on his own particular grounds. Witchcraft allegations may be variously banned by ideological censorship, institutional censorship or self-censorship.

Ideological censorship occurs when accusations between certain categories of person are inconceivable. They would entail contradictions that cannot be entertained in local conceptions. For example, an Azande cannot accuse a fellow member of his patrilineage. If he did so he would implicate himself in witchcraft and lower his stock. Azande believe that the substance of witchcraft is hereditable and that it is transmitted in the patriline.[20] Limitation of witch identity to women in Wangala (Mysore) or in Zululand is of the same order. The diacritic of ideological censorship is that it is categorical and absolute.

Institutional censorship is the denial of the possibility of accusation between persons linked in specific status relationships. Thus the Kriges report that a Lovedu commoner would not accuse a chief of witchcraft.[21] The accusation is incompatible with this status relationship.

Finally, self-censorship occurs when accusation of witchcraft is eliminated in specific relationships because those who participate in them reject the possibility of accusation as an appropriate course of action. Here no ideological censor prohibits. Individuals could accuse certain others, but, generally, do not. Self-censorship is a matter of choice. It can be wholly explained only if notions of decision-making and rationality feature in the analysis.

The causes of misfortune

Pedi can invoke the supernatural to account for the particularity of misfortune in a plurality of ways. Misfortune can be an act of God or an act of the ancestor spirits. It can be due to the inherent power that enables senior agnates to harm their juniors, or due to one of three kinds of witchcraft. In addition, breach of taboo (and there are various types), ritual contagion due to contact with persons in the dangerous state of impurity (e.g. a recent widow) and the effects of anti-witchcraft or anti-theft magic can all take their toll. A list of all agencies of misfortune, their means and their most likely effects is not important here. One need only note the marked redundancy of possible supernatural causes. Pedi do not 'need' witchcraft to account for the general category of misfortune, nor do they 'need' witchcraft when dealing with one of its alleged instances. Without belief in witchcraft, Pedi would not be bereft of explanation. The possible agencies of misfortune are manifold.[22]

Pedi are thus supplied with the ideological requisites for questioning particular witchcraft allegations.

In practice, individuals do not favour the notion of plural mystical causation when considering an instance of misfortune. Opting for one cause eliminates other hypotheses: if it is witchcraft it is not God and the rest. Among men viewing an event opinion may be divided. But each man holds one opinion at a time. Arriving at a consensus about causation means that the members of the relevant group each overtly, though they may have private reservations, opt for the same verdict.

At one remove, argument about causes is an argument about persons. Witchcraft as a cause posits a witch. For the afflicted, misfortune is due to another. In contrast, breach of taboo turns the cause back onto a man who has suffered reverse of fortune. This is now a consequence of his own action (though breach of taboo—like the marriage of Oedipus—can be an unconscious act).

During beer-drink Ntake was grumbling about deaths in his herds. He suggested witchcraft. With increasing animation he began to cite the unusual circumstances in which his goats had died. Quietly, Mafiri interposed: 'Ntake, why don't you pray to your ancestors?' Ntake subsided. We talked of other things.

Attribution of an event to witchcraft is logically prior to the accusation of a witch. In the circumstances of Pedi life, this attribution must be made in the face of any competing alternatives that find exponents.

Yet, in a crucial way, witchcraft is distinctive. It is the one mystical cause of misfortune, experienced singularly by individuals, that allows ego to lay misfortune at the door of a culpable other. The causes of misfortune are of three kinds:

1. Acts of supernatural beings and forces that are whimsical though they can take some account of the moral status of persons when determining the direction of harm. God and the ancestors belong to this group. In face of these beings and forces, men can only lead the good life, hope, pray and sacrifice. Responsibility is supernatural.
2. Forces that are triggered by individual error, conscious or unconscious. Breaking taboos, contact with ritual impurity and the anger of senior agnates are examples. The individual is not freed of personal responsibility: he knows what to avoid

and he knows the actions required to remedy those breaches of which he is conscious.

3. Witchcraft, for which others are responsible.

Here the anger of senior agnates merits discussion because it is removed from witchcraft only in that it is not culpable. Pedi inherit patrilineally and say that agnates should live and work together. A patrilineage is made up of ranked lines whose seniority originates in the birth order of brothers and the rank of their mothers in a polygynous household. A lineage, therefore, is a grouping of seniors and juniors in which no two members have equal rank. Rank is recognized by deference and, ideally, positions of authority are held by seniors who command juniors. This authority is buttressed by an occult mystical power (*kgabe*). If a senior agnate is offended by a junior 'his heart darkens', and that junior is liable to suffer misfortune. This occurs whether or not seniors consciously wish misfortune on juniors. Hence anger should be neither nursed nor provoked within a lineage because it is destructive.

The power of agnates is, in one respect, like Azande witchcraft. It is inherent and may work without the knowledge of its possessor.[23] A senior agnate who is asked to rub medicine on the ailing child of his junior cannot refuse. Once this treatment is performed the power of the senior is cooled and the child should recover.

Though the power of agnates works so that one man's anger visits misfortune on another, the senior agnate who projects it is not culpable. *Kgabe* is like the power of ancestors: people live with it, and—if they divine evidence of its working—conduct an appropriate ritual placation. *Kgabe* is linked with ancestor worship in another way. Senior agnates are, in one sense, living ancestors. Still, *kgabe* can kill if it is not diagnosed and treated. But a senior agnate who *wants* to kill will resort to witchcraft. A reputation for being the source of *kgabe* attacks marks a man as a likely witch. He has more than the normal quota of malice. Witchcraft accusations between agnates can thus be entertained.

Witchcraft beliefs

The Pedi witch, as the only culpable other who directs misfortune onto chosen victims, may achieve his ends in one of three ways: the use of inherent power to bewitch, the utterance of malediction, or the use of medicines and spells.

The Pedi distinguish between 'witchcraft of the day' and 'witchcraft of the night'. Night witches are usually women, who are possessors of inherent evil which they can pass on to their children. Night witches test their babies by tossing them against the hut wall. If the infant clings like a bat, he has inherited his mother's ability. Perhaps this functions as a survival test, eliminating normal children from witches' homes. Night witches belong to a secret society of witches and have familiars who do their bidding. Finally, and most significantly, night witches bring harm to communities rather than to individuals.

Day witches bring harm through the use of medicines over which spells may be said. Alternatively, they can be guilty of *boloi bja molomo*, witchcraft by malediction. Schapera has translated this phrase as 'oral sorcery' in his discussion of Kgatla belief.[24] The dread Sotho–Tswana formula for uttering oral sorcery is the phrase 'You will see' and the direction of this malediction is indicated with a pointing index finger. Other threats are also recognized. For instance, to call a woman barren (*mopa*) is a grave insult in itself but it is also a malediction in the sense of oral sorcery. All Sotho–Tswana peoples seem to believe that the verbal power in certain voiced maledictions is sufficient to bewitch. I tried to press informants on the distinction between 'oral sorcerers' and 'sorcerers by medicine'. What, for me, is a final verdict was delivered by one man who said, 'What does it matter whether he uses words only or medicines as well? If a man says these things you know you are bewitched.'

For my analysis the distinctions between witchcraft by activating inherent evil, by the use of familiars, by the use of magic or by the power of words is not crucial. Those who have studied the Sotho–Tswana peoples have all provided observations to the effect that these distinctions are only 'theoretical'. Informative to the study of cosmology, they are irrelevant to accusations. No one is named 'night witch' as against 'day witch'. Pedi act in terms of witchcraft as something undifferentiated.

Persons as possible witches

Pedi and other Sotho–Tswana peoples are distinctive in Africa because the ideological censor eliminates only a few persons from the category of possible witches. Children of the same mother cannot bewitch one another, though half-siblings may. Nor can there be witchcraft attacks between mother and child. The only general ban is that which limits responsibility for the act of bewitching to adults.

Radcliffe-Brown noted that Sotho–Tswana 'are decidedly exceptional in Africa' for another reason.[25] This branch of the Southern Bantu have notably few restrictions on choice of marriage partner. As Shapera writes for Tswana, a man 'is not allowed to marry his own mother, sister, daughter, father's sister, or mother's sister . . . Cohabitation with any of the women he is forbidden to marry constitutes incest.'[25] Sotho–Tswana have prohibitions of incest but no rule of exogamy.

I posit that there is a necessary congruence between lack of ideological limitation on the identity of either marriage partner or witch. Limitations in either field are ideological, things of the same order. Ideology limits by defining categories of the permitted and the forbidden.

In other African societies (particularly those with unilineal descent groups) the categories of non-witch are normally defined in terms of kinship or of opposition of the sexes. Where this occurs the category of non-witches is generally clear and unambiguous.[27] But Pedi kinship does not yield the unequivocal category. Instead, lack of a rule of exogamy confounds kinship and affinity, 'our women' with 'their women'. Further, close kin are preferred marriage partners. Preference increases the likelihood that agnates will, at the same time, be affines. The relationship between men and women is also affected. Women as wives are not inevitably outsiders, commodities exchanged between exogamous lineages or clans.

It is necessary to reassert the distinctiveness of Sotho-Tswana in these respects because Douglas, in an important and stimulating paper, has ignored it. Concerned with definition of the areas to which accusation of witchcraft is confined among different African peoples, she classifies the Southern Bantu as 'societies in which witch accusations attack women'.[28] This is a patent error. If it were not, I would have only to ask why present-day Pedi no longer accuse their women.

Investigating the source of Douglas's mistake demonstrates my proposition about the operation of the ideological censor: Douglas applied too widely Gluckman's interpretation of accusation among

Zulu. Zulu have patrilineal, exogamous lineages. Women born in one lineage enter another as wives. 'They are regarded as bringing quarrels into the ideally united patrilineal groups'.[29] Zulu wives are the focus of a conflict, the 'incompatibility and inconsistency between the duty of a wife to be fruitful and to strengthen her husband's group, and the actual divisiveness of her fruitfulness'.[30]

Wives of Zulu agnates, by their diverse origin, differentiate brother from brother, half-brother from half-brother, agnate from agnate.[31]

Some marriages among Sotho–Tswana can have precisely the opposite effect. Marriage with father's brother's daughter is the most dramatic example. There is structural variety to Sotho–Tswana marriages. Zulu exogamy uses variety of origin to make all wives the same—strangers in their husbands' homes. Sotho–Tswana kinship does not yield unambiguous categories of sameness. These

Sex of witch among the Lovedu

Category of accusation	*Male witches*	*Female witches*	*Total*
1. Accusations between 'relatives'	10 (20%)	25 (50%)	35 (70%)
2. Accusations between 'strangers'	11 (22%)	4 (8%)	15 (30%)
3. *Totals*	21 (42%)	29 (58%)	50 (100%)

peoples cannot simply conceive a monstrous category of women. Nor can they envisage other kinship categories that include only kin defined in terms of a single unambiguous principle. Hence categorical limitation of witchcraft is not part of Sotho–Tswana ideology.

The Kriges, writing about the Transvaal Lovedu in the 1930's, provide some statistics about the sex of accused witches. They distinguish two kinds of accusations of witchcraft, those between (1) relatives and (2) strangers. The distribution in the table is of fifty cases that came before the Lovedu courts. I have summarized the Kriges' information and classified witches according to sex.[32] Though Lovedu women were accused somewhat more frequently than men, men were regularly accused. On this score the Kriges comment that 'both men and women are equally liable to harm either men or women'.[33] One may note, too, that male witches victimized 'strangers' more frequently than did women.

There is another aspect to Sotho–Tswana witchcraft. Accusations can be part of political competition between men fighting for office. 'Thus, in 1928, the Kwena, after a long hearing in the *kgotla* [tribal court], were apparently all satisfied that Sebele II's uncle Kebohula had been trying to bewitch him.'[34] This is an accusation between a chief and one of his 'natural uncles' in the chiefly house.

Consideration of Pedi belief places emphasis on the optative elements in the formulation of accusations. In the sphere of belief about causation, witchcraft is only one possible cause of misfortune. In the sphere of social action, the choice of witch is not limited by the ideological censor. Hence the whole range of relationships in which men come into close contact is open to the possibility of witchcraft. Unsurprisingly, Pedi place stress on the work of diviners who help them to identify the cause of trouble and, when witchcraft is divined, the identity of the attacker.

The work of diviners

Recourse to a diviner is a response to the suspicion that misfortune is due to mystical causation. The diviner must first divine the nature of the cause. If he confirms the suspicion of witchcraft, he must further indicate the direction whence witchcraft has come. Diviners do not name witches: they indicate totem, sex and personal characteristics. The diviner's client directs the beam of suspicion to a pinpoint that strikes a single person. In form and method Pedi divination has not changed since Junod described it in 1925.[35] What has changed is the total sequence of events in which divination is set. Divination is no longer a prelude to denunciation. In the absence of open accusations the existence of diviners is even more important. Their wealth and their relationships with tribesmen are the two visible indications of Pedi concern with witchcraft.

While I cannot hazard its frequency, I posit that accusation of witchcraft was a feature of traditional Pedi life. Comparative evidence supports this, as does informants' knowledge of the proceedings for accusation and their knowledge about traditional punishment of witches. Again, Pedi say that witchcraft is on the increase because witches are not checked any longer.

The most popular diviner is still the *ngaka* or doctor who combines the roles of diviner, herbalist and magician. He can both diagnose the cause of sickness, etc, and prescribe and supply remedies.

Part of his work is the ritual and medicine of prevention. He is enriched when people either anticipate or experience attack. The *materia medica* of the diviner have been expanded through contact with the outside world. Medicines from Nigeria reach Sekhukhuneland. Pedi are prepared to spend large amounts on medicines that either prevent or cure. In view of Pedi poverty, the amounts that are spent are sometimes spectacular. Medicines are now more varied, and this permits a wider range of price. While there has been innovation in medicines and treatments, the most popular method of divination is still by casting and interpreting a fall of lots.

The doctor is a confidence man. His client comes to him in trouble and doubt, and a satisfied client must leave more sure of himself. In consultations the doctor's performance is crucial. He uses his instruments of divination both to diagnose and to inspire confidence. Thus a session does not begin with a client's statement of troubles. Instead, the doctor casts in order to find out about his client. He tells him about his movements, his friends, his relatives, and finally tries to say what brought the client to the consultation. Thus the client is first presented with statements he can verify. He either affirms or denies them, providing clues for the diviner's further investigation. In this first phase the diviner is on test. For 'heavy' matters, or when the client indicates ability to pay well, the first phase is lengthy. Men sometimes take minor matters to diviners just to test them. Diviners try, over time, to build a regular clientele who are confident of their ability. Here success breeds success.[36]

Failure in a particular case does not kill the doctor's reputation. Pedi have a theory of compatibility; some doctors suit a man, others do not. The relationship that doctors establish with clients is symbolized in the first acts of divination. The client, after sitting in the correct position, must blow into the skin bag that holds the lots. The doctor then cuts two slivers of skin from the bag. The client slowly chews one while the doctor eats the other. This is a communion which relates doctor and client to each other and to the bag of lots. Regular consultation of one diviner repeats this communion, which becomes deeper and more permanent. The client strikes a lasting alliance with a man who can mediate in the business of supernatural causation. A client judges his diviner by the results of both diagnosis and medicines supplied. Diagnosis and remedy are separate, each has its own price. Hence one doctor can be used for diagnosis and another for remedy. When Pedi go far afield to consult doctors, it is for remedy rather than diagnosis. They seek the power of foreign medicine rather than the diagnostic insight of stranger-doctors.

The session with a doctor is characteristically private or held before a very small audience. It parallels consultation with a Western medical practitioner, priest or lawyer. It is privileged. A diviner cannot be called before a Pedi court to give evidence about a normal consultation. Only if doctor or patient are accused as witches ('unprofessional conduct') is this permitted. Secrecy of consultation is routine, and a general suspicion that doctors seduce female patients, accepting sexual favours as payment, is a product of secrecy.[37]

Just as consultation is covert, imputation of witchcraft is today a personal conviction, or a secret shared only by close associates. The discretion of diviners and the privacy of consultations are not innovations. It has always been the diviner's function to establish a relationship of confidence with his client. This has two aspects: confidence in integrity and confidence in the diviner's performances. Because a trusted diviner equips a man with the knowledge and the means to deal with uncertainty, confidence in the diviner is transmuted into confidence in self.

In general, then, diviners equip men to deal with vicissitudes that are beyond secular remedy. In particular, they supply anti-witchcraft medicine and magic that may purge the effects of witchcraft, strike back at the witch, or prevent his depredations.

The Pedi response to suspicion of witchcraft is thus to enter into secret alliance with a professional and direct the aggression of medicine-magic against the witch. This does have an effect on social relationships in so far as degrees of self-confidence influence action. Further, men define their special enemies in non-secular terms. The divination of a witch can supply a personal rationale that justifies bold secular action. 'For me he is a witch, therefore I will terminate our relationship/be ruthless towards him,' etc.

Where I was able to extract witchcraft imputations from informants, these were usually confided after time had made them irrelevant. Witchcraft imputation is not part of tactics in social relationships. It is a *post factum* justification of accomplished deeds. Recourse to a doctor is the single course of action generally open to those who hold that they are victims of witchcraft. This is why I suppose that the doctor's role has changed. In the old days a doctor's verdict could inspire a man to voice an accusation. Today he is deflected from this path and his response limited to magical retaliation.

In this section Pedi response to witchcraft has been described as a private response that may alter an individual's inner state. Later I shall show how it can, in the name of witchcraft, re-define a situation for other actors.

The accusing coalition and the tempo of sociation

Failure to communicate and generalize the definition of specific witches implies the anticipation of an operational failure. Individuals know that they cannot mobilize support to form a coalition of men who will join to call the accuser's enemy an enemy of group values.

The basis for such predicated failure lies in expectations about the general nature of social relationships in Megwang. An individual's sociation with others is, in many significant instances, of relatively short duration. The field from which he chooses his associates is extensive. It corresponds with the total population of the chiefdom rather than being confined to a smaller and more manageable sub-set within it. There is a tendency towards the minimum of overlap and coincidence between the social network of one individual and another.

These abstractions define the converse of situations which have been seen to yield successful accusation. The traditional Lele and the Cewa, for instance, are members of groupings in which membership is in the long term. The groupings are, to a degree, corporate. Incorporation demands a coincidence of interests and networks of relationships. When either a Cewa or a Lele was accused, there was a proto-coalition to which the accuser appealed. Accusers are emboldened to accusation by the knowledge that accusation demands a response that will be made in terms of existing alliances.

I propose the most telling indicator of the types of relationship that will not sustain accusation is a measure of the tempo of sociation in a specified population. The tempo of sociation is a measure of the rate at which relationships of various types are struck and broken within a particular social universe. Its prototype is the divorce rate expressed as a ratio of newly contracted relationships to terminated relationships over a given period of time. This measure can be made whenever relationships can be defined in a manner that allows them to be commensurate. A quick tempo of sociation indicates inconstancy of inter-personal linkages. A slow tempo indicates continuity in sociation.

A quick tempo of sociation implies uncertainty about the future of social relationships. In formulating strategies one cannot assume the permanency of A's relationship with B. For a field of social relationships, one cannot assume the constancy of group formation. A quick tempo of sociation implies that every task for which men must be mobilized requires a task-specific coalition. A slow tempo of sociation presents suitable sets of stable relationships. Appeals are made to proto-coalitions pre-constituted in the local structure of relationships.

A quick tempo of sociation, with its correlate of uncertainty about the future of relationships, vitiates the possibility of degradation of witches at Megwang. I briefly indicate the social conditions that produce this result.

Domestic units in the chiefdom are stable. The composition of domestic groups relates directly to the facts of breeding and ageing and marriage. Megwang households generally contain nuclear families at various stages of development. Nuclear families are, from time to time, expanded to include other kin. Apart from the complication introduced by the possibility of polygyny, the kin added to expanded families are remnants from other incomplete households —widows, orphans, etc. Marriage in the chiefdom is highly stable.

Each man, woman and child in Megwang is a member of a relatively stable household grouping. Ideally, each house has a male head, though in the event of widowhood some women 'act like men' and do not accept the direction of a deceased husband's kinsman. The domestic ambit exhausts the store of stable and predictable relationships.

Members of separate households are linked in various relationships of co-operation and support. In this field there is an overall constancy of pattern but an inconstancy of personnel. The most significant social grouping above the level of the household is the set of men who are the clients and followers of a local leader. Relationships between followers, and between followers and leaders, are crucial because this set has relevance for most activities pursued by men and women in the chiefdom. The pattern of relationships in leader–follower groupings *is* the pattern of association at Megwang.

Megwang leaders have no titles, and their position is unprecedented in the traditional structure of Pedi administration. They are described as stay-at-homes, *bashalagae*. The name points to a leader's distinguishing characteristic: he is a man gainfully employed within the chiefdom. He does not have to migrate to urban centres in order to find work. Stay-at-homes are highly distinguished in a South African Reserve, where poverty of local resources forces most able-bodied men to make the cyclical movements of the labour migrant. While he is thus distinguished the leader's position is extremely insecure. He is leader only so long as he can live in his chiefdom: his leadership ends if he goes to town or has to retire as an older man who becomes dependent on the earnings of youngsters. The rate of turnover of leaders is high. When leaders fall, their groupings of followers fragment. Further, during a leader's incumbency the personnel of his group alters from month to month. His followers are not a constant body. Men in the chiefdom move from one leader to another.

Leadership in Megwang must be seen in the context of South Africa and *apartheid*. The Sekhukhune Reserve does not have enough land to enable its people to eke a subsistence by their rural pursuits of farming and herding. Cash cropping is out of the question. Labour migration is the necessary answer to the need for extra income to supplement Reserve resources.

Poverty of Reserve resources is coupled with restrictions on mobility imposed by law. Unlike the anti-witchcraft laws, which have no bite in the Reserve, the laws that control African movement are rigorously enforced. Megwang men can establish themselves in South African towns only if they meet onerous conditions for qualification as urban residents. The Reserve man most likely to establish himself in town is one who has some education and can command something better than a labourer's job. Megwang men are uneducated because in the past they rejected Christianity. Confessional rejection entailed rejection of mission schools. Megwang is a tribal, non-Christian, uneducated chiefdom.

Men from Megwang can go to town as migrant workers but they must leave their families at home. Typically they travel between 200 and 300 miles to the work place—too far to permit weekend visits home. Their work stints are long, lasting a year or more. Thus labour migration brings with it a division of labour between town and country. The country remains a place of domicile, where a married man's family lives and where the unmarried man will seek his bride. Broadly, division of labour corresponds with the distinction between wages and investment. The worker earns wages in town and invests what he can save in Reserve people and resources.

Megwang leaders exist to bridge the gap between town and country. The migrant in town has left family and fields behind. People and resources demand proper attention and management during his absence. Before leaving home for town the migrant contracts with a local leader who undertakes to plough his fields and help the members of the migrant's household should they require assistance. This assistance is primarily construed as financial aid.

The leadership of Megwang stay-at-homes is built on economic success. Analysis of their achievement shows why a strategy of action that favours a rapid tempo of association is generally favoured at Megwang. Each Megwang man has three possible sources of income. These are land and cattle in the Reserve; income gained for performing services for other Reserve people; and wages earned in town. There is this universal dilemma: urban wages are gained at the cost of absence from the rural area. The demand for services in the Reserve is created by the absence of migrants. It is the absentees who need such service in order that their Reserve resources can provide some income.

For obvious reasons there is a surplus of labour in the Reserve. Hence labour service in the Reserve commands little reward. However, in conditions of poverty, capital resources are difficult to accumulate. Thus service that demands prior capital investment is highly rewarded. The stay-at-homes are all men with ploughs and plough-teams. Ploughing is normally done with oxen. The plough-herd demands attention, and stay-at-homes try to assemble complete herds. Some of the animals they care for belong to other men. Stay-at-homes command plough fees and profit from herding arrangements.

About eight or ten plough teams can cope with all the land owned by Megwang people. Thus Megwang does not provide an unlimited market for ploughmen and there is intense competition for plough contracts. These contracts justify capital investment in animals and ploughs. Without them, ownership of oxen would be less profitable. A plough contract is struck for one season. These annually reconstituted relationships are important. Ploughing for a man who is away normally implies taking care of his economic interests during his absence. The ploughman–leader must have capital available. What distinguishes him from kinsmen who might be expected to look after a migrant's home affairs is that the stay-at-home can supply deficiencies of cash. A migrant makes arrangements for the running expenses of his household. But, removed from home, he cannot cope with crises and contingencies that demand an unusual outlay of cash. Nor can he expect that kinsmen who happen to be at home will have cash available. It is a leader's task to be ready to supply loans that will be redeemed when the migrant returns. His reward is the constancy of the migrant's custom.

The leaders in Megwang are involved in two other types of dealing. They are brokers in land and financial intermediaries to marriage negotiations.

Land in Megwang is in short supply. However, customary law has provided that each man has the right to land that is attached to the house established for his wife on marriage. Rights in land are inherited in the patriline. But no man can expect that his mother's house fields be divided or made over to him before her death. The result is that most new marriages provide the occasion for a series of deals. Some land has to be given up to supply the new bride with land. The leaders who, as ploughmen, know the fields well contrive to carve out a new field for the bride. This is achieved by arranging a complicated series of pay-offs to those who relinquish strips of arable land. This relinquishing of local capital resources may be wondered at. However, there are always land-owners whose need for ready cash is sufficiently acute to force them to part with a fraction of their holding.

Marriage negotiations involve the transfer of large capital sums in bride-wealth as well as the redistribution of rights in land. Today a large proportion of the amount of bride-wealth is paid in cash. However, at least one beast must be provided for the marriage feast.

Bride-wealth transactions create local demand for cattle for exchange and for consumption. Those who demand the cattle are normally younger men who migrate to earn cash. The stay-at-homes are herd-owners and benefit from these transactions. Further, stay-at-homes can become involved in lending arrangements with young men who wish to hasten into marriage before they have saved the required sum.

A successful Megwang leader is a man who accumulates capital by migrating and saving part of his wages over a long period. Supplied with capital, he makes a bid for leadership. He buys a plough and a team to draw it; then he solicits contracts.

At least half the bids for this status fail. I have a record of the careers of stay-at-homes in Megwang over a five-year period. Nearly all the men who make the bid stay at home for one or two years. Entering a third year as stay-at-home is the criterion of success. It marks a new phase. The initial capital invested has been expended and the stay-at-home must now live off the profits of investment. He has no fund for contingencies that dates back to his career of migrancy. The story is thus one of ambition that ends for contenders as they fail the three-year test.

Since they stay at home only because others migrate, the chiefdom can afford only a small number of these leaders. There are 960 people in the chiefdom. At any one time about 120, or 42 per cent, of adult men are working in towns. At any one time over the five-year period examined there were between ten and sixteen men either established as leaders or making bids for this status. My records showed that there was less than a fifty–fifty chance of passing the three-year test. Those who succeeded held their positions over a period by maintaining followings. Successful men have always had followers but the identity of followers changes over the years. From one year to another the rate of turnover in a stay-at-home's following usually exceeds 50 per cent.

This rise and fall of leaders, coupled with frequent movement of followers between groups, is an expression of what I call a quick tempo of sociation.

Given the number of adults at Megwang, it is no exaggeration to say that for ego any man has the potential to be a relevant other in important economic transactions. The chiefdom is the field in which men strike and break relationships. Because social relationships outside the household are discontinuous, the chiefdom provides a social field characterized by uncertainty about the future of relationships. A high degree of individual competition with money as focus is also part of the situation.

Competition plus uncertainty about the identity of future associates are the characteristics that account for the absence of accusations of witchcraft. The open economic strategy demanded by the situation means that economic relationships are pervasive. It would be extremely difficult to seal off groupings defined, say, on kinship principles that would be immune from the pervasive uncertainty engendered by economic considerations.

Specifically, two effects of a rapid tempo of sociation may be noted. Discontinuity of relationships maintains overweening emphasis on questions of performance rather than motivation. The leaders of Megwang are insecure and highly sensitive to the moves of followers. Renegue on a promised plough contract and the *moshalagae* leader is put at risk. Shift from one group to another and encourage a friend to do likewise and the position of the leader is substantially imperilled. Leaders contract yearly with between fourteen and twenty-five men. They depend on custom. Deprivation of custom has immediate effects. What applies to leaders applies in various ways to other extra-domestic relationships. Short-term associations are associations for a purpose. They are instrumental and do not accrete notions of trust and loyalty among a large membership. To contemporary Pedi, friendship, the trust of a particular other, is more important than incorporation and the mutual loyalty of group members.

The second point is that the locus of total identity is extensive in these conditions. If a Pedi is to be degraded at all he must be degraded as a tribesman, a member of a chiefdom. He cannot be degraded as member of a small group equivalent to a local descent group in, say, Cewa country. Between household and chiefdom there are no stable groupings strong enough to hold a man's identity.

The Pedi response to witchcraft is an individual response that matches the individualism of Pedi economic life.

Alternative forms of degradation

In Megwang, while accusation of witchcraft is rejected, any court case can turn into a degradation ceremony. The court is constituted as an arena for community action. Its authority and function is co-extensive with the group that holds the total identity of Megwang tribesmen. This qualifies the court to degrade. Secondly, the court considers questions of performance and, predictably, degradation in Megwang is degradation which imputes motives on grounds of specific and revealed performance. The emphasis is not on 'whodunit' but on what was done. I cite an example.

A youth called Matenge was accused of seducing an uninitiated girl. Because the girl was uninitiated the offence of seduction was compounded: what Matenge committed was both a wrong and a sin. In Pedi terms the uninitiated are ignorant and cannot have sexual knowledge, licit or illicit. The girl, after pressure from her female kin, had named Matenge as responsible for her pregnancy. The heinousness of the crime may be judged from informants' allegations that in the old days both parties would have been killed. Matenge confessed his guilt, but this did not satisfy the court. He was made to recount the details of his relationship with the girl. They used to meet in the veld where, among other things, they would drink milk straight from the cow's udder. Matenge became the 'milk drinker', *senwa maswi*. Now the Pedi word for sin is *maswe*, while milk is *maswi*. The possibilities did not escape the court. 'Milk drinker' now stands in the local vocabulary for sin, and, more generally, for sexual misconduct. Girl songsters composed lyrics in which the misdemeanour was celebrated. Matenge, *alias* 'Milk Drinker', and his family still suffer degradation, and special degradation was inflicted in addition to the fine paid by the youth's father and the corporal punishment meted out to him. This event is too well fixed in public memory for people to forget it easily. Most 'interesting' court cases yield permanent possibilities, e.g. when a prominent man is branded adulterer or constitutionally mean—a stinger.

In the courts, men hearing the case look for possibilities in evidence. Although most cases are brought before the courts for arbitration on evidence of performance, attacks on identity can emerge. One is alerted to an attack on identity when court members begin to 'chew' the evidence. They solicit more and more facts about the relationships of those concerned and seize on facts that are startling or peculiar, or can be made to appear so. Adulterers are given a particularly rough passage. This is understandable, for adultery is a problem due to male absenteeism.

Court cases are not as flexible as accusations of witchcraft. The court is biased in favour of consideration of evidence of performance. It must be diverted in order to degrade. But when the work of degradation is done, interlocutors ferret in areas of privacy. The courts can open a person to public gaze. When a fact is established in the context of providing evidence it becomes public property. Even though people may have whispered it before, they are now free to proclaim it.

Talking about court evidence after a case is over is mere gossip and not scandal. The more evidence yielded by a case, the more material people have to discuss and re-formulate. A court case leads to two verdicts. One, on the issue, is always given in the court. The second, on the persons involved, can be formulated both in court and out of it.

The girl songsters of Megwang are important because their songs carry the message of degradation. They pay a great deal of attention to court cases, gleaning the facts from local gossip because as girls they cannot attend the court. The songsters have the licence of the irresponsible and youthful to sing in collective anonymity. They dare to sing what adults would not singly dare to say. In the way that the Spanish *vito* or the Welsh youth group mete out punishment to offenders against morality, Pedi girls provide lyrical commentaries on the established peccadilloes of their elders.[38]

Court evidence provides more appropriate grounds for degradation than accusation of witchcraft in Megwang because of two factors: uncertainty and privacy. I have shown that relationships outside the domestic group are of uncertain duration. In addition, contracts between men and details of monetary negotiation are kept as private as possible. Men try to conceal not only what they own but also what they owe and are owed. Megwang is a place of rumours, of uncertainty of information about persons and their commitments. Court evidence, in this context, is information of a special kind. It is a public statement with pretensions to truth. In court, interlocutors are allowed to ask questions which they could not otherwise ask. The event which the court considers becomes established as an official happening. It is an item of property created by work in the court and owned by the community. At Megwang an accusation of witchcraft is as uncertain in its form as the relationships on which it would have to be imposed. An accusation in which there is ambiguity about a perpetrator's identity cannot be imposed on relationships which themselves have an uncertain future.

Witchcraft as degradation: its general import

Finally, I comment on the general implication of defining accusation of witchcraft as an attempt to mount a ceremony of status degradation. Accusation of witchcraft is not in a class of its own. It is a peculiar representative of a general type of procedure. Thus defined, its parallels are manifest. One can seek similar and equivalent types of action elsewhere. As status degradation, accusation of witchcraft is rendered comparable with other performances that share its form.

In addition, a refinement can be introduced into the explanations for the incidence of accusation advanced by social strain theorists. In his analysis of Cewa witchcraft, Marwick saw accusation of witchcraft as one possible mode of coping with strain in social relationships. He presents a 'last resort' theory in which accusation of witchcraft is voiced when other means fail or are unavailable. A residual category is situations of intense competition when highly motivated actors seek the same indivisible goal.[39]

Marwick's signal contribution is to set accusation of witchcraft against alternative means. In his analysis he does not, however, distinguish social degradation as a means. He merely separates accusation of witchcraft from all other means locally available. In his formulation something is lost. If or when the choice is between accusations of witchcraft and a second form of degradation, it is of one order. If or when the choice is between a form of degradation and a second means that does not involve degradation, the choice is of a second and different order. If this distinction were maintained, formulations about responsibility in the tradition of social strain theory would be more incisive.

I illustrate my point with reference to Epstein's account of the peasant witches of Wangala. Epstein follows Marwick closely in the trend of her argument. Witchcraft is a last resort.

> In a small-scale community such as that of Wangala Peasants, in which people live face to face, tensions are bound to occur in their everyday relations. But not all tensions find expression in accusation of witchcraft; only tensions which have no other outlet lead to such accusations. Wherever a judicial mechanism exists to settle questions between individuals or groups, tensions in their social relations can be brought out into the open and therefore will not be channelled into witchcraft accusations.'[40]

The emphasis here is on the deviousness of the charge of witchcraft. In court cases, whether degradation is involved or not, the accusation concerns alleged wrongs that are not imaginary. But this is a sidetrack, because the similarity of the results of accusation of witchcraft and the results of judicial degradation are obscured by it. I show how.

Epstein has to explain why only women are accused of witchcraft among the Wangala peasants. She presents the argument already referred to. The peasant caste is made up of exogamous patrilineages. Women as wives are divisive strangers in the patrilineage and disrupt its unity. They are blamed for conflict inherent in structure; men 'project their guilt'.

An additional reason can be advocated for the Wangala limitation. In the word 'outcaste' India has provided the West with a term that denotes ultimate degradation. Indian men are judicially responsible for maintaining their own caste and that of their families. Men are blamed for their dependants. Men are particularly vulnerable to charges of breaking caste, for there are a plethora of caste observances and prohibitions. Further, caste ideals are always more demanding than caste practice—the performance and the ideals are highly discrepant. Everyone does, and is liable to, infringe prohibitions. Given the right climate of opinion about a fellow caste member, it should be easy to 'make him polluting' and hence degrade him. There is sufficient ambiguity in caste observance to proclaim a man's shame, not because he is less meticulous in caste observances than others, but because he is unpopular.

One can now advance a more general proposition about degradation alternatives in Wangala. Accusations of witchcraft take the focus of degradation away from caste and hence make it independent of caste behaviour *per se*. To accuse a Wangala woman of breaches of caste etiquette or ritual, etc, may impugn her father and brothers and sully relationships between affines. Caste charges, seen tactically, may evoke the wrong parties.

In her book about economic relationships in Wangala Epstein presents some material on the work of the caste council.[41] She shows that the council does degrade men and declare them polluting. To redeem himself, a polluted man must go to trouble and expense, re-entering caste relationships when he performs cleansing rituals and feasts his caste-fellows. All this gives plausibility to the reinterpretation.

Only women in Wangala are accused of witchcraft, because men are accused of sins of pollution. Making women witches achieves a degradation of women as women and not as members of a caste. This avoids implicating men in the guilt of female transgression. Do men, in fact, project guilt onto women as Epstein alleges? Men are highly susceptible to the sullying and degrading charge of pollution. Accusations of witchcraft against men are redundant.

Conclusion

My argument amounts to this: it is too dangerous for a man to set about the task of degrading another by levelling an accusation of witchcraft in the social circumstances of Megwang. The form of procedure required to do this work is that of a status degradation ceremony. In mounting such a ceremony the accuser puts himself at risk. The risk might be worth taking if there were some chance of achievement. But the volatile social relationships in the chiefdom work against the formation of structured groupings that endure in time. The accuser will not address himself to an audience already divided into familiar factions or parties. He can have no surety of support and, without support, his accusations become but a personal declaration of belief in another's enmity towards him. At best, the accuser is judged unwise to have ventured the accusation. Otherwise, he is seen as mischievous, vindictive or unbalanced. When degradation of status is achieved at Megwang the means towards this end are not thus fraught with individual risk. The chief's court and the girl's song group provide immunities. The girls are wrapt in collective anonymity, and furthermore, as girls, are irresponsible. Officials of the court come to decisions in accordance with local canons of justice and the work of judgment is public and collective. Judgment is finally uttered by the chief or his representative, figures secure in legitimate authority.

This essay has been about the social incidence of accusations of witchcraft in a Pedi chiefdom. Its interest is that it presents a null case, an instance in which witches are not named. The progress of my argument has paralleled a discussion by Professor Evans-Pritchard, who in a pioneering article dealt with the social incidence of magic in Africa and Melanesia. In analysing 'The morphology and function of magic' Evans-Pritchard first defined the elements of the act of magic—'the rite, the spell, the condition of the performer, and the tradition of the magic'.[42] Correspondingly, by drawing on Garfinkel's work I was able to anatomize the act of accusation. Secondly, Evans-Pritchard related the morphology of magic to local social structures, an exercise that has been undertaken here for Pedi acts of accusation. Finally, Evans-Pritchard turned his attention to the 'functional occasions of magic',[43] showing that these occasions are determined by the social structure. In the null case considered here, features of social structure account for the non-occurrence of accusations of witchcraft between Pedi tribesmen. But the final link between my own essay and that of Evans-Pritchard is substantive rather than formal. In 1929 he provided the framework of analysis within which Pedi recourse to the magic of the *ngaka* can be explained.

When a Pedi approaches his *ngaka* or 'doctor' in order to resolve problems of inter-personal relationships, he consults, in private, with a reputable practitioner who draws on a pharmacopoeia of medicines that has been enlarged by the addition of novel items imported from other tribes and places. As Evans-Pritchard remarks of the Azande, 'new magic is constantly being created, and . . . it is created by successful men influenced by the rumours of magic which attend their success.'[43] The power of Pedi magic derives from its exclusiveness; knowledge of its properties and nature is esoteric, the *ngaka's* possession: 'the more the performance of magic becomes public property, the less social utility it possesses'.[44] As a specialist, the Pedi *ngaka* has the character of a powerful practitioner.

In Megwang the fact that any man has consulted an *ngaka* is normally public knowledge. However, the particular concern that occasioned his consultation is a matter for speculation. Also, the *ngaka's* diagnosis and his prescription—if any—are a secret between him and his client. What is known therefore, is that a certain man has been to a particular practitioner and that he has come away again. The 'client' of the *ngaka* could divulge his affairs to others, but without witnesses to his private session with the 'doctor' he may be telling in part, or in full. He could be lying. The point is that secrecy, if maintained, transfers the esoteric and therefore potent powers of the *ngaka* to his client. The medicines received (and were any medicines bought?) become multivalent. They could be anything from substances effective against thieves to those potent against the man who would cuckold the client. The medicines might not be designed to affect others at all, for the *ngaka* dispenses curative substances which a client takes to cure his bodily ills. The client therefore makes his medicines multivalent by keeping them to himself. Although a common man without special craft, he becomes as powerful as the doctors. He has had access to the doctor's store, and who knows what he has taken from it?

I suggested that the would-be accuser is deterred from naming those whom he believes to have bewitched him because his accusation of witchcraft might end up as an unsupported and therefore personal declaration of enmity. He might well be left to face his adversary alone. In the secrecy that surrounds consultation, one can say that such solitary antagonism, devoid of friendly alliance, is anticipated. Consultation of the *ngaka* on the one hand, and mounting a public attack by naming a witch on the other, are two procedures that in one aspect are inversely related. In the first case, secrecy, the absence of 'communicative work', gives strength. In the second, the criterion of a success is the convincing communication of a charge. Convincing public communication is set against abstinence from any announcement. Opposites, harnessed to the appropriate forms of procedure, work similar effects. One man's visit to the *ngaka* can make another uneasy. In the last analysis, the visit can be construed as an attack, especially when a third party knows that he has wronged the first.

Consultation of *ngakas* and mounting accusations of witchcraft involve procedures that are known as possible courses of action whose forms are explicit in Pedi culture. They can be used in attempts to redress the same real or imagined wrongs; they are alternative courses of action. In my experience Pedi eschewed accusation of witchcraft. Where the courts would not serve them, they turned to the *ngaka*. My last word is this: Pedi medicines, secretly dispensed, do not merely work on the individual psychology of the *ngaka's* client to give him confidence. The client emerges armed. He will know the nature of any purchased specific but, to the world, his acquisition is not a specific unless the client reveals it as such. Under cover, the medicine is multivalent and the client bristles as if with protective quills. After all, the porcupine is the praise animal or totem of the Pedi.

[1970]

Notes

1 For confirmation of this description of Pedi immunity on this score see Mönnig, *The Pedi* (1967), p. 252.
2 Marwick, *Sorcery in its Social Setting* (1965).
3 See Mitchell, *The Yao Village* (1956), and Marwick, *Sorcery in its Social Setting* (1965).
4 Douglas, 'Techniques of sorcery control' (1963), p. 141.
5 *Loc. cit.*

6 Described by Nash in 'Witchcraft as a social process in a Tzeltal community' (1961).
7 This case is presented by Bailey in *Caste and the Economic Frontier* (1957), pp. 166*f*.
8 Epstein, 'A sociological analysis of witchcraft beliefs in a Mysore village' (1967).
9 Gluckman, *Politics, Law and Ritual in Tribal Society* (1965), p. 222.
10 Epstein, 'A sociological analysis of witchcraft beliefs in a Mysore village (1967), p. 150.
11 Garfinkel, 'Conditions of successful degradation ceremonies' (1956).
12 *Ibid*., p. 420. On 'performances', Garfinkel cites Parsons and Shils, 'Values, motives and systems of action' (1951).
13 *Ibid*., pp. 421–2.
14 Cited in Bowen, *The Lion and the Throne* (1957), ch. 15.
15 Marwick, *Sorcery in its Social Setting* (1965), p. 74.
16 Evans-Pritchard, *Witchcraft, Oracles and Magic among the Azande of the Anglo-Egyptian Sudan* (1937), p. 330.
17 Garfinkel, 'Conditions of successful degradation ceremonies' (1956), pp. 422*f*.
18 *Ibid*., p. 424.
19 *Ibid*., p. 240.
20 Evans-Pritchard, *Witchcraft, Oracles and Magic* (1937), pp. 21–39.
21 E. J. and J. D. Krige, *The Realm of a Rain-queen* (1942), p. 268.
22 A full account of Pedi beliefs is presented in Mönnig, *The Pedi* (1967), ch. 2.
23 Evans-Pritchard, *Witchcraft, Oracles and Magic* (1937), p. 33.
24 Schapera, 'Oral sorcery among the natives of Bechuanaland' (1934).
25 Introduction to *African Systems of Kinship and Marriage* (1950), p. 69.
26 Schapera, *Handbook of Tswana Law and Custom* (1938, 1955), p. 127.
27 On this point see the discussion by Gray in 'Some structural aspects of Mbugwe witchcraft' (1963).
28 Douglas, 'Witch beliefs in Central Africa' (1967), p. 78.
29 Gluckman, *Politics, Law and Ritual in Tribal Society* (1965), p. 223.
30 *Ibid*., p. 224.
31 Gluckman, 'Kinship and marriage among the Lozi of Northern Rhodesia and the Zulu of Natal' (1950).
32 These data are abstracted from *The Realm of a Rain-queen* (1942), pp. 264*ff*.
33 *Ibid*., p. 263.
34 Schapera, '*Handbook of Tswana Law and Custom* (1938, 1955), p. 278.
35 Junod, 'La Divination au moyen de tablettes d'ivorie chez les Pédis' (1925).

36 Ashton has emphasized these aspects of divination among the Southern Sotho in *The Basuto* (1952), pp. 296*ff*.
37 Cf. Mönnig, *The Pedi* (1967), pp. 81–8.
38 The *vito* is described in Pitt-Rivers, *The People of the Sierra* (1961) and the Welsh youth group by Rees in *Life in a Welsh Countryside* (1961).
39 *Sorcery in its Social Setting* (1965), ch. 11.
40 'A sociological analysis of witchcraft beliefs in a Mysore village' (1967), p. 153.
41 *Economic Development and Social Change in South India* (1962), pp. 116–19.
42 'The morphology and function of Witchcraft' (1929), p. 5.
43 *Ibid.*, p. 19.
44 *Ibid.*, p. 17.

Bibliography

Ashton, H., *The Basuto*, London: Oxford University Press for the International African Institute (1952).
Bailey, F. G., *Caste and the Economic Frontier*, Manchester: Manchester University Press (1957).
Bowen, C. D., *The Lion and the Throne*, London: Hamish Hamilton (1957).
Douglas, M., 'Techniques of sorcery control' in *Witchcraft and Sorcery in East Africa*, ed. J. F. M. Middleton and E. H. Winter, London: Routledge & Kegan Paul (1963).
— 'Witch beliefs in Central Africa', *Africa*, vol. 37 (1967), pp. 72–80.
Epstein, S., *Economic Development and Social Change in South India*, Manchester: Manchester University Press (1962).
— 'A sociological analysis of witchcraft beliefs in a Mysore village', *Eastern Anthropologist*, vol. 12 (1959), pp. 234–51; reprinted in *Magic, Witchcraft and Curing*, ed. J. Middleton, New York: Natural History Press (1967).
Evans-Pritchard, E. E., 'The morphology and function of witchcraft: a comparative study of Trobriand and Zande ritual and spells', *American Anthropologist*, vol. 31 (1929), pp. 619–41; reprinted in *Magic, Witchcraft and Curing*, ed. J. Middleton, New York: Natural History Press (1967).
—*Witchcraft, Oracles and Magic among the Azande*, Oxford: Clarendon Press (1937).
Garfinkel, H., 'Conditions of successful degradation ceremonies', *American Journal of Sociology*, vol. 61 (1956), pp. 420–4.
Gluckman, M., 'Kinship and marriage among the Lozi of Northern Rhodesia and the Zulu of Natal' in *African Systems of Kinship and*

Marriage, ed. A. R. Radcliffe-Brown and C. D. Forde, London: Oxford University Press for the International African Institute (1950).
— *Politics, Law and Ritual in Tribal Society*, Oxford: Blackwell (1965).
Gray, R. F., 'Some structural aspects of Mbugwe witchcraft' in *Witchcraft and Sorcery in East Africa*, ed. J. Middleton and E. H. Winter, London: Routledge & Kegan Paul (1963).
Junod, H. A., 'La Divination au moyen de tablettes d'ivoire chez les Pédis', *Neuchateloise de Geographie*, vol. 29 (1925).
Krige, E. J. and J. D., *The Realm of a Rain Queen: a Study of the Patterns of Lovedu Society*, London: Oxford University Press for the International African Institute (1942).
Marwick, M. G., 'Witchcraft as a social strain gauge', *Australian Journal of Science*, vol. 26 (1964), pp. 263–8.
— *Sorcery in its Social Setting*, Manchester: Manchester University Press (1965).
Mitchell, J. C., *The Yao Village*, Manchester: Manchester University Press (1956).
Mönnig, H. O., *The Pedi*, Pretoria: Van Schaik (1967).
Nash, M., 'Witchcraft as a social process in a Tzeltal community', *American Indigena*, vol. 20 (1961), pp. 121–6.
Pitt-Rivers, J. H., *The People of the Sierra*, London: Wiedenfeld & Nicolson (1961).
Radcliffe-Brown, A. R., introduction to *African Systems of Kinship and Marriage*, London: Oxford University Press for the International African Institute (1950).
Rees, A., *Life in a Welsh Countryside*, Cardiff: University of Wales Press (1961).
Schapera, I., 'Oral sorcery among the natives of Bechuanaland' in *Essays presented to C. G. Seligman*, ed. E. E. Evans-Pritchard *et al.*, London: Kegan Paul (1934).
— *Handbook of Tswana Law and Custom*, London: Oxford University Press for the International African Institute, second edition (1955).

6
Sin, blame and ritual mediation[1]

Richard P. Werbner

How blame is fixed on individuals is a problem which Evans-Pritchard illuminated when he considered the morality of witchcraft and the bias of patterns of accusation in *Witchcraft, Oracles and Magic among the Azande* (1937). Evans-Pritchard showed that Azande fix blame according to cultural stereotypes of sin. For a distinct realm of moral rules concerns Azande when they accuse others of witchcraft. The realm which Evans-Pritchard observed is this: 'It is in the idiom of witchcraft that Azande express moral rules which mostly lie outside criminal and civil law.'[2] Such expression, occurring between some persons and not all, is limited and biased. It is only in close, personal relationships that Azande use the idiom of witchcraft to hold men responsible for their conduct and their sentiments. Thus oracles which Azande consult if misfortune strikes or is expected are primarily consulted about the anti-social sentiments and conduct of neighbours. The personal relationships whose histories are then set forth and coloured during consultations are mainly relationships other than those of kin. While these consultations locate blame for misfortune, they do so without placing ultimate responsibility on ancestors. Such an appeal to the authority of the dead would require that kinsmen be at fault. Evans-Pritchard considered that 'The ghosts of the dead cannot be appealed to as arbiters of morals and sanctions of conduct, because the ghosts are members of kinship groups and only exercise authority within these groups among the same people over whom they exercised authority when alive.'[3] The very appeal to ancestral spirits restricts ritual, necessarily, so that, unlike accusations of sorcery or witchcraft, it cannot cope with a realm of morality where individual responsibility prevails—that is, in close relationships between neighbours who are not kin and thus not jointly responsible for one another. In his study of witchcraft, therefore, Evans-Pritchard gave his main attention to problems of responsibility and moral regulation among persons other than relatives. The questions he asked, however, call for further understanding of the sinful concerns of kin.

Evidence from Kalanga of eastern Botswana suggests the importance of analysing how distinctly ritualized modes of fixing moral responsibility for illness, such as sorcery accusations and invocations of spirits, are interconnected. The pressures which relatives and neighbours direct when they ritually re-define their relationships in domestic rituals of possession by demons of the wild, *mazenge*, are compounded by sorcery accusations. Moreover, for both modes, within a definable range of close kinship and affinal relationships, joint responsibility and an absence of a segregation of interests are essential. To demonstrate this is to analyse the significance of property relations and economic obligations and debts among relatives, and to examine the relatives' jural bonds along with their interests in personal transactions, goods and services. I give most attention in my analysis to the roles women play in fixing responsibility for misfortune, because they mediate, in various senses, both in ritual and apart from it. Reciprocity in kind or on similar occasions sponsored by a closed circle of donors, distributors, receivers and consumers of ritual goods need not occur among Kalanga. Instead, a regular and controllable disposal of goods takes place. This obligates others within a pre-selected set of relatives and neighbours. For Kalanga a kinswoman, in the role of possessed initiate in the domestic cult of affliction—in the role of host[4]—is the cardinal subject around whom her relatives, men or women, may mobilize narrow or restricted congregations of neighbours and relatives. Where competing obligations exist, declarations are made, both of priorities and of rights, and these are warranted through the rituals of demonic possession. A host's ritual mediation, directing members of the congregation to fulfil obligations, is necessary to compel declarations of responsibility to be made. Various relatives are able to act as closed congregations, without involving outsiders, because they appeal to arbiters of morals that are hereditary demons of the bush rather than shades of ancestors. Indeed, the very crux of ritual mediation through a host is mutual negotiation of their disparate affairs by interested and jointly responsible relatives who are variable sets rather than a fixed group.

Though an account of divination would document in detail how the metaphysical sense in a personal predicament must be grasped in order to treat it among Kalanga, such an account is beyond the scope of this essay. Similarly, because sorcery accusations vary, a full discussion of them would clarify the interconnection between seemingly disparate modes of fixing blame. As a beginning, however, I contrast accusations according to how they are made—by baiting privately, by insinuation in gossip, by denunciation in public, or by charging in a legal suit.

Before examining the evidence from Kalanga, a comparative discussion of a nexus between social separation, accusations of sorcery, and rituals by kinsmen appeasing spirits, is useful. Recently Mitchell has shown that some urban Africans in Salisbury give misfortune a double meaning.[5] First, they may blame it on unrelated rivals or enemies practising sorcery. Second, or later, they may refer it back to rural kinship relationships, the sufferer being held accountable or punished for a past breach of kinship morality, not necessarily his own. There is a bounded range of sorcery accusations. They are kept out of a set of relationships—for some of these townsmen, familial and kinship ones—and raised elsewhere, in relationships that are close and personal yet characterized by rivalry for success and advancement, and by sexual and economic competition. In town, when such kinsmen rally to the afflicted and placate their ancestral spirits, they may meet free of sorcery charges against one another. Theirs is a congregation supporting, affirming and generating duties among themselves and towards other kin.

Mitchell's suggestion is twofold: on the one hand, the organization of urban administration does not admit legal charges and direct denunciations of sorcery, for it is a criminal offence to make such accusations; and, on the other hand, the accusations have an effectiveness in rural areas like that of 'catalysts' in a process of segmentation. Mitchell's reasoning refers to public action. He keeps in view public and direct accusations which, he implies, can be made in rural areas and not in towns. However, in both areas, various ways of making accusations are possible, each having its own effectiveness.

In both urban and rural areas of Southern Rhodesia the colonial law penalizing witch-finders, accusers and professional wizards is so administered that it does not suppress all accusations of sorcery or witchcraft. This leeway is clear in case reports from the urban police of Salisbury. Accusations are there distinguished, in legal practice, from abuse, though the Witchcraft Suppression Act provides no explicit basis for this distinction. In practice, a criminal case is dismissed when remarks alleging sorcery or witchcraft are held to be 'more in the nature of abuse than a definite accusation'.[6] Moreover, Crawford, a barrister, records an informant's perception that 'where wizardry allegations (accusations of either sorcery or witchcraft) are made in town they are often by innuendo . . .'[7] This and other evidence[8] suggests that account must be taken of how people make various kinds of accusation of sorcery in towns, how they bait one another, insinuate, and perhaps also make denunciations; and it suggests, moreover, that the 'catalyst' view needs rethinking also.

A second caution about Mitchell's suggestion is this. He calls attention to the double interpretation of misfortune, without seeing simultaneity. He argues, tellingly, against the conventional view that kinship rituals or ancestral cults are less adaptable to town life than is sorcery. But arguing against this view, he misses the several fronts of action that are encountered together, and are not in series as successive alternatives. Townsmen need not proceed alternatively from one divination to another, replacing the less 'effective'—sorcery accusation, according to Mitchell—by the more satisfying and 'effective'—invocation of the punitive spirits of dead relatives. Rather, a single divination discriminates a multiple set of agents, causes and relationships. This the fullest of Mitchell's cases[9] shows pointedly; a man's death was divined to be due not solely to the sorcery of a co-worker and other rivals. Simultaneously this cause was recognized along with faults within the family—its members had failed to fulfil their kinship obligations at various mortuary rites.

Mitchell's essay is terse, in terms of its appearance within a symposium. Moreover, it centres on problems which do not require him to give much evidence about the redress of grievances or the re-establishment of relationships at sacrificial feasts and through ritualized offerings to living and dead kin. Yet one conventional aim of the sacrificers in town is to conciliate afflicting spirits and expiate wrongs to kinsmen. Significantly, on the occasions Mitchell sketches only long-standing faults towards remote or absent relatives were divined. I suggest that ritual action towards the spirits of deceased kin has its special importance in a town precisely because it does not reach to the rawest grievances, and need not involve difficult new issues in an immediate personal crisis. The ministering of relatives at expiatory feasts in a town is an aspect of their bids for mutual support in the midst of potentially hostile strangers. Similarly, accusations of sorcery against unrelated persons are an aspect of appeals against intimates who, at their expense, stand to gain in ill-defined relationships full of uncertainty.

The determination of one cause or another—either this responsible agent or that—is not always the outcome of a divination. A combination of interpretations may be divined, each partial interpretation requiring action. Such a combination may reflect diversity within the divining congregation. It may also indicate a single party's attempts to handle, at once, its disparate spheres of involvement. Indeed, the party, as in a case I discuss later,[10] may be one person alone at a seance with a diviner.

Turner, in his recent studies, makes a similar point.[11] In his earlier work, developing Mitchell's arguments about Yao seances,[12] Turner considers the divining congregation sharply divided into hostile parties who need the mediation of a distant diviner. In this discussion Turner disregards the congregation that is a partisan cabal. He generalizes about seances primarily in terms of the contradictory theories put forward by rival partisans whose interests in a patient are opposed. Unfortunately, Turner's study of basket divination is based on texts from diviners, since he was unable to attend a seance. This, in part, is why he considers, at first, the contradictory theories exclusively, without discussing also the composite interpretations of a single party. In his more recent account of 'A Ndembu doctor in practice', however, he gives evidence supporting my immediate point, and he comes near to stating it, when he writes, '. . . when misfortune is attributed to mystical causes in Ndembu society, it is common for many sets of disturbed social relations to be scrutinized by interested parties.'[13]

Various ritualized modes of fixing moral responsibility for illness—such as sorcery accusations and invocations of spirits—are interconnected, because, in at least two respects, the consequences of each may be modified by those of the other. First, both accusations and invocations may be made, simultaneously or sequentially. Second, both may converge: that is, both may operate in one range of relationships, though sorcery accusations, as among Kalanga, may span a wider range also.

A narrow range of close relationships is the one where both operate among Kalanga. To be a mother, a sister, a mother's sister or a father's sister is, among Kalanga, to be exposed to accusations of sorcery. Such a kinswoman is not immune, and there is a bias towards accusations of the old by the young, of seniors by their juniors, or between members of the same generation. Accusations thrust into the closest of a woman's kinship relationships, with a possible exception: I know of no instance of a daughter accusing her mother. So too the confines of the domestic rituals in which demons, *mazenge*, are invoked are the closest relationships of kin and affines. The affliction of own kin—uterine siblings, their children and their grandchildren—is ritualized in the cult of possession by *mazenge* demons. It requires these relatives and their spouses to act dutifully; they must demonstrate their amity towards the hosts of demons, towards possessed women, who, like their patients, may be the accusers of other kin or themselves be the accused. Thus the rituals reach through relationships laden with sorcery accusations.

This is readily understood when pairs of roles are considered, first for the accused and second for the accuser of sorcery. Other pairs exist, but these, often observed, pairs are crucially relevant here. In one pair a woman is a victim of accusation and an intercessor in ritual. But her roles do not merge; they are kept apart by her relatives, according to their residence and their personal involvement with her. Intercessor is the single role which she usually has for relatives beyond the immediate vicinity of her hamlet. For relatives within this vicinity she may have one or the other of the paired roles. She may be accused by some nearby kin or affines—say her brother or brother's wife—and not be suspected or accused by others—such as her sister's son or sister's daughter. Relatives sponsor a ritual, approach her piously, and seek to appease the demons whose wrath they admit they themselves aroused, only if they do not blame her for bringing them illness by sorcery. Thus even nearby in her vicinity different relatives cast her in each role, and she may play an active part at the centre of strife between sets of her close kin.

Another pair of roles is that of sponsor or patient of a ritual of possession and accuser of sorcery. The relative whom the sponsor or patient accuses of sorcery is usually absent from the ritual and, of course, is never the kinswoman whose demon is invoked and propitiated. The accuser who is also a sponsor or patient is thus able to compel kinsmen to rally around as a congregation declaring their mutual interdependence and accountability for sin, but to the exclusion of the accuser's personal enemy or rival. I shall show this in detail later, when I examine an instance of this kind.[14]

Only women, whether young girls[15] or adults, become hosts of *mazenge* demons. This fact, taken in isolation, immediately conjures up recently fashionable explanations of spirit possession in terms of an escape from inferiority of status, or a compensation for 'peripherality' or a redress for a lack of rights.[16] But among Kalanga, to put it briefly, where there are no rights there can be no spirit possession; and once relationships are reduced, full of rights and little else, spirit possession is irrelevant.

A host's part in the regulation of moral responsibility fits her importance for a flow of goods and services between relatives. This can be grasped, once it is seen who requires her ritual services, where, and when. Again, a set of roles must be considered. These hold between the principals—the host, her patient, the sponsor of the ritual, its convener (the head of the hamlet where it is held)—and others in the congregation or excluded during a performance. One false impression is easily recognized: the mistaken notion that women ritually fleece their kin for luxuries not due to them. To consider rituals of possession as if these were occasions for extortion is to misunderstand the symbolic nature of ritual giving. Applied to Kalanga, in particular, the notion of ritual blackmail can only distort the offering of sacrifices. The notion is wrong because it suggests hostility, the opposite of what actually holds between a host and the sponsor of a ritual; and also because it must obscure the connection between a mediatory role in ritual and in transactions apart from ritual.

The various relatives who find fault and blame in themselves and seek to appease a woman's *zenge* (singular form) with sacrifices of meat and offerings of cash, beer, beads, blankets, leg rattles and livestock are not blackmailed by her. Rather, her unwillingness to accept any offering, any token of responsibility and mutual goodwill, is a sanction she may apply against her kin; it is the leverage she exerts. She may withhold her ritual services entirely, or delay giving them, when she is grieved and feels mistreated by her relatives. Above all, theirs is an act of devotion and piety. They seek ritual services from a host, whom they trust, and in a place where they know there is benevolence towards them. They avoid a host or convener whose sorcery they fear. Moreover, they so divine in selecting the venue of the ritual and its central actor, the host, as to avoid a context merely of jural relations.

Between a sponsor, a host and a convener, the relationships which are usually found are of a distinct type that is shaped by personal transactions over productive goods and basic services. Ritual mediation is possible—nay, vital—because joint responsibility for faults and sins constrains the diverse kinds of kin who are so crucially interdependent. Thus the woman who is a host is the focus of a defined set of potential patients. These are the woman herself, her own brothers and sisters, and their offspring. Some of these, along with the wives of kinsmen, she may admit to be her juniors in the cult, for payment; but her kinsmen or the daughters of sons are patients whom she never initiates into the cult. Nevertheless, she represents their joint responsibility; and the belief is that her *zenge* can afflict a sinner or innocent children and grandchildren, not necessarily the sinner's own. All these close kin and their spouses are bound both by obligation towards her and by need of her ritual services. Therefore pressures can be brought to bear from one set of her relationships to another. For example, when a relative from a remote locality sponsors a performance ostensibly in order to treat a fault in one relationship, he also provides an occasion for a dialogue about faults in other relationships important to the congregation at the convener's locality.

Negotiation is involved, which does not occur in all types of relationship. It does not occur where a flow of mutual and personal investment is not admitted. Such relationships are simply restricted. They are so dominated by jural regulation that the relatives do not look to each other for reciprocal or conditional co-operation in production and in sharing basic resources. Apart from an immediate family, such are the usual patrilineal relationships among men classed as 'fathers', 'brothers', 'sons'. They have a right and a duty to speak for one another in a legal dispute, for example; they also have claims on heirs of major estates which have passed from father to son. Rarely, however, do they give or lend each other primary assets, and it is also rare for them to be close neighbours as heads of independent hamlets. Avoidance holds between them, because their jural relations and various personal transactions which arise out of neighbourliness are, ordinarily, incompatible. Consequently, a man avoids the hamlet of his father's brother as a ritual venue for possession, along with that of others such as his classificatory brothers, his patrilineal cousins. The place where a man usually sponsors a ritual with his father's sister as the host is at the hamlet of her children, his cross-cousins. There she mediates for him as she does not in a hamlet of their patrikin. Significantly, a woman's role in transactions is not the same as a man's, so that she can expect goods and services from male patrilineal relatives which a man neither expects nor gets. It follows that a woman sponsoring a ritual is not bound to avoid the same places as a man: the relationships differ for her, and she may be a sponsor at her father's brother's hamlet. Nevertheless, whether the sponsor is a man or a woman, the basic context is constant in that ritual occurs when mediation is required between persons whose mutual interests are not regulated solely (or primarily) by jural rights and duties—that is, between persons who can and do turn to each other for a variety of personal and economic services and for gifts of productive resources, such as land and livestock.

The power of women as hosts is not the power of the weak. Nor is it a blackmail by otherwise passive inferiors or nascent suffragettes, as has been suggested for various cults of possession. A host mediates and makes her demands as a relative—a kinswoman or an affine—and she may make these demands, during spirit possession, only in a residential context clearly defined according to kinship.[17] No principal in the rituals of possession—no convener, sponsor, patient or possessed host—makes demands indiscriminately against a category, such as males or females; demands are always made in respect of specific relationships. A host's immediate vicinity is the sphere where her various roles, ritual and otherwise, connect together to the greatest extent and are the least sealed off from one another. Around her there, relatives are neighbours in whose internal affairs she can exercise her right to a voice, more or less influential according to her status. The interplay of sorcery accusations and spirit invocations, in an immediate vicinity, depends greatly on the way kinswomen actively assert their rights and promote their individual interests.

This interconnection, between invoking a spirit and accusing a sorceress, relates to an absence of segregation within a single range of close kinship. For many Kalanga, competition at home and in town involves their kin. For these men and women, becoming a labour migrant does not mean co-operating and competing solely with unrelated persons. Relatives can be of crucial importance both at their places of labour migration and at home. At some time in their working careers many Kalanga call on relatives to help them find a job or a place to live in town while unemployed, to keep them informed of events in the rural area or in town, and to act as go-betweens carrying money, goods and messages. Relatively few jobs are available nearby on ranches or in the trading towns, Francistown and Plumtree. Most jobs are found hundreds of miles away in South Africa or, to a lesser extent, in Southern Rhodesia. The distance of these places contributes to the development of multiplex relationships with kin in the urban and rural areas (rather

The distribution of women according to visits to town

	Number of women
No visits	85
Working visits	34
Other visits	89
Total	208

than acting as a bar). Nevertheless, if women were excluded from urban relationships, there could be a segregation of interests that would be reflected in sorcery accusations and the cult of possession. Women, however, actively bridge both areas.[18]

In the four wards best known to me, most women, roughly 60 per cent have visited towns for periods of varying lengths, and this includes roughly 16 per cent who have worked in urban areas, most as domestic servants and a few as hospital nurses. The remaining minority, about 40 per cent, have never been to town. The distribution is shown in the table. These visits by the majority of women do not mean that many come to know towns well. Perhaps to most men far less of town life remains unknown or unfamiliar than to most women. Yet the visits of women enable them to share in more than mere superficial experience of towns. Women communicate the needs and demands of distant relatives. Women are aware that they must sometimes go directly to the wage-earners if their own claims and those of other rural kin are to be met. When men are too long absent from home, women sometimes go to their places of work to bring them back. In various ways, therefore, women participate crucially in the linking of the urban and rural sectors of the economy.

Their various ritual roles relate to differences in women's participation in labour migration. Once a migrant worker, never a novice host, seems to be the rule. In the four wards of my census and elsewhere, to my knowledge, no women have become initiated into the status of host after a period of work in town. Some women, initiated before working in town, returned home for a visit, or permanently, and resumed the role of host in rituals of possession. Other roles among the principals are played by previously uninitiated women who work away from their rural homes (excepting perhaps the convener's role). Such women are prominent among the patients and sponsors of the rituals. They are not required to take on the host's roles of intercessor and representative of occult authority. They are the ones who ritually pass property or on whose behalf it is passed to other women.

A general point for comparative analysis must be raised, because a woman's structural importance is not summed up by her jural status as a legal dependent of a man, or by the determination of her residence by her husband's. Being a legal dependant of a man entitles a woman to rights. These, like a woman's interests, vary from one society to another and, within a single society, vary from one status or phase in her life to the next. She need not be barred, because she is the legal dependant of one man, from having a cluster of rights and interests in sets of other men and their goods. Indeed, her structural importance may be great precisely because it is only through her that such a cluster may be combined with the different rights and interests of a legal ward. Thus among Kalanga a woman is not merely involved in various estates, since she may inherit as a wife, a daughter and in some circumstances as a sister also. Even more, she canalizes a flow of property in the form of bridewealth, gifts and loans as well as inheritance. At stake in a woman's rights and interests are those of her male guardian, who may prevent her from alienating her property. His, however, are not the only ones at stake—indeed, in some respects, others' rights and interests compete with his. Therefore when a woman makes demands as a host, calling for the passage of ritual tokens of responsibility, she does so because she mediates other transactions as well.

These suggestions about mediatory roles, personal transactions and interconnected modes of fixing individual blame along with joint responsibility for illness or affliction are best seen by examining an instance of ritual action. I recorded the one shown in Fig. 1 during my field work in 1964–5. Baka Siya,[19] a labour migrant and not herself a host, sponsored a ritual on her own behalf. She was patient and sponsor. Her father's sister was the possessed host. Along with Baka Siya and the host, Baka Siya's mother, her

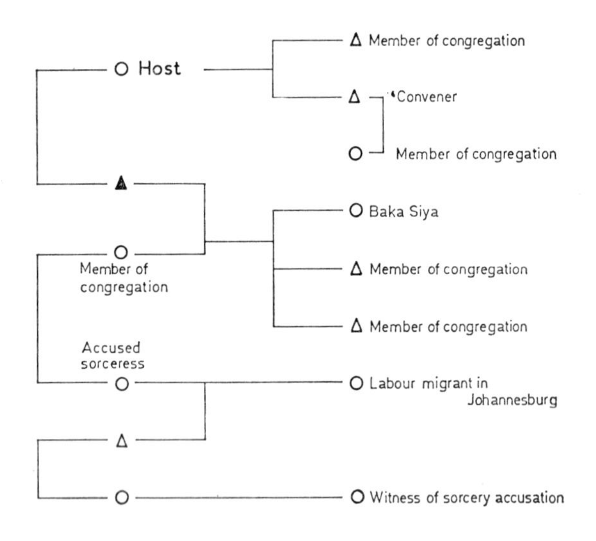

Fig. 1 Congregation at a ritual and witness at a sorcery accusation

brothers, the sons of the host (Baka Siya's paternal cross-cousins) and one of their wives met as the congregation at the most exclusive events of the ritual. Baka Siya's offerings included a red, white and black mantle to cover the possessed host, beer and a goat for sacrifice. She had consulted a diviner in Johannesburg while she was ill and after her loss of employment as a cook and nursemaid. She went to several diviners, she told me, to some alone and to others with her boy-friend, a Kalanga. 'They all said I don't give anything to the father's sister. I was so ill my ears couldn't hear well. But when I remembered that I ought to go home, my ears were opened.' She also divined that her mother's younger sister and her daughter had practised sorcery against her.

Shortly before the ritual this mother's sister caught Baka Siya visiting me. Baka Siya tried to hide by my hut; her mother's sister pursued her, ostensibly to greet me, and surprised her. The mother's sister began a little homily after the pleasantries of welcoming Baka Siya home, and spoke allusively through proverbs, the most choice of which was 'The going, going jackal returns with a brace of hounds.' The mother's sister drew out the meaning: 'The great traveller comes home with faults, *milandu*.' After this she got up to go, but as she rounded the enclosure outside my hut she began to complain that Baka Siya had excused herself from coming to visit in her hamlet, yet had gone much farther to her mother's brother's hamlet (Baka Siya had sent her brother to say her feet ached too much for her to travel and visit). Baka Siya replied, sadly but sharply, 'Well, I fear you.' ('Gala *ndomucya*'.) Her mother's sister continued, 'Yes,[20] is it so? Then why have you not come to my hamlet, since you were sick?' Baka Siya responded, 'I fear, when I reflect on many things.' There was a pause, then a few words of seemingly trivial banter were exchanged, and the mother's sister left at a dignified and unhurried pace. Baka Siya remained with me, complaining about her feet and telling me of her mother's sister.

Baka Siya's neighbours expected her to do more on her return home than sponsor a ritual. They spoke of this meeting and another, and, as one said, 'Ah you see, she's telling her now; she cannot go and not tell her plainly' (*pacena*, 'in the bare'). However, on both these occasions there was innuendo, the allusions were veiled, and the mother's sister gave as much as she got. The suspicion was spread, however, to enough neighbours, the right ones for the mother's sister to hear of it, and try to clear herself, as she repeated, against a 'going, going jackal'.

The force of such suspicion is that it does spread, and can corrupt the closest relationships, so long as it remains ambiguous, not overt and yet not fully convert. Suspicion is forceful and threatening, particularly where no relationship is immune, where an accusation raised in one relationship can be taken up in others, until filling a bundle of these and becoming direct accusations. One of my closest neighbours was such a suspect, and accused; her sister-in-law, her brother, her daughter-in-law, her son and others had all accused her on occasion, and they continued to do so, to the day her mother died, and then the scandal of blame for this rocked the vicinity where I lived. During the time of Baka Siya's brief visit her suspect's son refused to remain in their hamlet with her, and went to the hamlet of the woman who became the witness of Baka Siya's accusation; he told me in confidence of his fears of what his mother and his sister (the labour migrant) might be doing, and that it would come back to them in the lightning of vengeance.

The suspect, for her part, tried to provoke Baka Siya into a direct accusation in front of responsible witnesses, who could later testify without supporting Baka Siya at a moot. Suspicion and insinuation would then have been turned into an actionable charge and slander. There is a procedure for combating this; it is a hearing within the kin group after, or followed by, a divination with a congregation representative of the interested parties and the responsible kin. Baka Siya was not ready for this, and the suspect knew it. Baka Siya told me that she intended to pursue the matter in the future. 'Some day I will go with her to a diviner and we will see together.'

Within her kin group, where a moot would have been held first, Baka Siya could not rely on agreement about her mother's sister. This suspect of hers was the most trusted of sisters for her mother's brother, trusted especially by contrast to Baka Siya's mother. Her mother had been held to blame for the death of this kinsman's wife some twenty years before, and been beaten severely by him with a stool a few years earlier; after Baka Siya left she was suspected once more of causing him a lingering illness, through sorcery. The brother then showed his trust in Baka Siya's suspect by leaving his own hamlet to seek refuge while recuperating in this sister's hamlet. Just as neighbours gossiped about her mother's sister in relation to Baka Siya, so too they gossiped about a counter-accusation against Baka Siya's mother and another sister, that they were trying to make 'dolts' (*cihema*) out of their brother's children in order to inherit all their mother's goats as well as his property.

The first ritual action Baka Siya took on her return from work was to bring her natal family, her mother and brothers, to a hamlet of her close paternal kin where her father's sister lived. This paternal kinswoman was not related by kinship, directly, to the suspected sorceress, who, along with other maternal kin of Baka Siya's, was neither invited to attend nor came to the ritual. Before Baka Siya returned to Johannesburg, shortly after the ritual, she accused her mother's sister of sorcery. Baka Siya accused her victim directly in private, baiting her. I was told that none of the congregation at the ritual was present at the baiting. The only witness was another woman, a close friend of Baka Siya's and an affine of the accused who also blamed her for other acts of sorcery. Other neighbours and kin considered this accusation, as they told me, 'an affair of the women'.

Baiting—I stress that this was the mode of accusation, direct and private, because it is essential to distinguish one mode from another; sociologically, each differs. An accuser need not bait her victim with the accusation of sorcery, as did Baka Siya. She may insinuate sorcery, or denounce, or sue on a charge.[21] When an accusation is made indirectly in gossip it is an insinuation; made directly in public, it is a denunciation; and raised in a legal or forensic context, it is a charge. For purposes of comparison such distinctions are revealing, as I have suggested earlier, when discussing the accusations that are made in towns.

Baka Siya's choice of a ritual venue effectively excluded the mother's sister, whom she suspected, from the congregation. An alternative choice, which Baka Siya could have divined, would not have achieved this exclusion. Her mother's other sister was a host, living in a nearby hamlet in the same ward as Baka Siya's natal family, and belonging to the same local kin group under the leadership of Baka Siya's mother's brother. If Baka Siya's divination had fixed on this host the mother's sister would have been able to join the congregation and raise her complaints against Baka Siya for neglecting her in the past and avoiding her, a 'junior mother' with a claim to attention and a visit from her nearby 'child'. In a similar case Kalanga explained to me that 'the lions [*shumba*, the ritual guise of a host] of that place have been defeated long ago by her'.

Instead, Baka Siya got the sanction of occult authority for her appeal to assert the priority of dues owed paternal kin, and thus re-defined her present relationships. Her sponsorship compelled her natal family to meet as a congregation outside their own ward and apart from the rest of their local kin group. Only an external relative, her father's sister, could, as a host, have furthered Baka Siya's campaign to separate her natal family from her local kin group. This host alone could act as the ritual focus that Baka Siya required. In her father's sister Baka Siya secured an intercessor, indebted and grateful to her, and without cause for blaming her. Moreover, limiting the composition of the congregation to some of

Baka Siya's paternal kin and her natal family assured that grievances against Baka Siya within her local kin group were not raised during the ritual. Thus her divinatory choice anticipated crucial consequences for relationships with her close kin.

Her own fault for neglecting a duty of kinship was central in Baka Siya's divinations. If she had needed to gift her kinsmen in the congregation excessively, to compensate for a past lack of generosity, her sponsorship of the ritual would have been an investment of another kind. But it is no paradox that her acceptance of responsibility meant both a declaration of her dutifulness and an assertion of obligations owed to her. In one respect she had in the past neglected none of the principals in the congregation, including her father's sister. All were obligated to her for the money, blankets, clothing and other goods that she gave them each time she returned on her vacation from work. In time of scarcity she was the mainstay of her natal family; her brothers largely depended on her cattle and goats, and prided themselves on her bank account in Francistown. What she divined she owed her father's sister was a ritual offering, and giving it was not a substitute for other dutiful acts, within the congregation. It was the binding quintessence of these acts.

A threat to Baka Siya's standing within her local kin group came from her parallel cousin, the daughter of the suspected sorceress. This cousin was a potential rival. Baka Siya had got her young cousin a job in Johannesburg several years earlier, and the cousin was beginning to prosper while Baka Siya, now reaching the end of her career, had trouble finding work. The cousin, unlike Baka Siya, had yet to invest substantially at home. In saving from her earnings, the cousin did not try to sustain her natal family. When Baka Siya sent bags of grain home during the drought the cousin did not; the cousin's family battened on Baka Siya's and, Baka Siya's family believed, occasionally pilfered from them. Thus in effect the claims of Baka Siya's kinsmen forced Baka Siya into an indirect subsidy of her rival. As Baka Siya saw it, her mother's sister was envious of her and wanted her daughter to 'surpass' (*pinda*) Baka Siya.

Baiting her mother's sister enabled Baka Siya to reject kinship obligations to this kinswoman without compelling Baka Siya's natal family publicly to be parties to the accusation, or involving others of the local kin group. At the same time, invoking the *zenge* demon of her father's sister publicly rallied her natal family and other kin around her and promoted her own cause.

So far I have discussed pressures generated by ritual action and but briefly considered Kalanga concepts of the demons or the relation between the demonic order and various moral rules. A second illustration is necessary to show how the demons are appealed to as arbiters of morals and also to show a prevailing concern of kin about obligations that are due to a host in her own and not in an inherited status. Baka Fupi (G on Fig. 2), a patient who was not

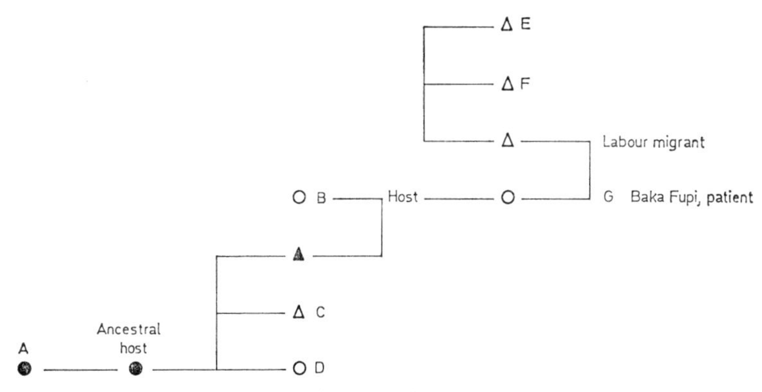

Fig. 2 Congregation at a divination for Baka Fupi

herself a host, divined along with representatives of both her marital family (E and F, her husband's brothers) and her natal family (B, her mother, and C, her father's brother). They agreed to call a sister of her father (D) and propitiate this host while she was to be possessed by her *zenge*.

Wrongdoing against the father's sister was part of the blame for the patient's illness: the kin had not paid the father's sister her share in the bride-wealth of the patient, to which she was entitled. The patient told me, 'The spirits are demanding the cattle of the father's sister, because I have not been *lobogwa*, married by the passage of bridewealth. The spirits say we have no child for whom bride-wealth is not given, for whom we do not eat.' Long ago the father's sister, the host (D), had received her *zenge* from the deceased (A), her maternal grandmother, but the divining congregation did not refer to (A) nor to a relationship to her. They referred to the host (D) and her kinship position only.

In Baka Fupi's case the fault was not a disturbance requiring a re-establishment of the relationships of the principals present at the ritual or the divination. Indeed, the defaulter whom the congregation believed primarily responsible—Baka Fupi's husband—was absent on both occasions. He had paid no *malobola*, and this fault, held to have aroused *mazenge* demons, lay primarily with him, for he had earned enough to pay bride-wealth, while his wife, after several miscarriages, had borne him a son. His brothers accepted that he could claim a contribution from them. In his absence as a labour migrant, they acknowledged their responsibility for their kinsman and showed their agreement with their affines by providing a goat for sacrifice and a shawl for the host when she was possessed. So long as he resisted their appeal he had to share in the blame for the illnesses of his wife and his son.

This bare account springs beyond my immediate point to several others about property relationships,[22] and these are best considered closely elsewhere. However, to complete the illustration I must resume, briefly, a discussion of jural rights and personal transactions. The passage of bride-wealth is not, ordinarily, the subject of litigation in the courts of chiefs and headmen, except in a paternity suit or, rarely, at a divorce. Moots of affines or their intermediaries bargain, initially, about the amount of the wife-receiver's debt. Payment of most of it is usually deferred, however. The legal token of marriage is a payment, *bukwe*, by which the spouses' conjugal rights are contracted. It is usually paid, along with some of a series of marriage payments, prior to *malobola*. But *malobola*—the payments which entitle a husband to be pater of all children his wife bears until she dies or is divorced—are rarely, if ever, transferred at once and in the full amounts promised. Many marriages are fruitful, ending with old age or death of the spouses, without much or any of the paternity payments being paid; the debt remains.

This deferment of marriage payments does not mean a lack of rights or of various sanctions to sustain the rights. A father, or, failing him, a woman's own brother, is entitled to receive whatever bride-wealth is paid; in turn, he must give a greater or lesser share, according to right, to the woman herself and to her close paternal and maternal kin (her mother, an own brother and sister of her father and of her mother, her surviving grandparents and the adults among her own siblings).[23] A wife has the right to return to her natal kin when her husband maltreats her, and then demands are made for further payment of bride-wealth. Moreover, if the maltreatment is gross, even when no large amount of bride-wealth is outstanding, the wife's kin may impose a fine on her husband. Usually what is exacted is partial, or a further promise rather than its fulfilment. Kalanga speak of this as *rapelana*[24] or *ḳumbilana*, 'entreating' one another. Conduct in these close relationships is praised by saying that a man has *ngoni*, 'pity, compassion, mercifulness', and trying to force rights may be condemned as more disruptive than dragging out payment or avoiding payment in the agreed form.

To marry is, among other things, to incur long-term indebtedness to various close relatives and affines. Such indebtedness looms large in much of their divination and talk about what arouses *mazenge* spirits to send affliction. Courts and other forensic institutions are not excluded, by definition, from deciding disputes which arise out of this indebtedness. But they rarely do so. In this respect, *mazenge* spirits are treated as arbiters of moral relationships where the sanctions of forensic institutions little apply.

When Kalanga appeal in domestic ritual for the well-being of their children and themselves, the ritual makes them recognize a dangerous resemblance. It is a resemblance to non-human virtue: where they have failed their kin, they have acted as becomes creatures of other orders, not men. They must face, even seek blame for, sins. What they desire is relief from personal suffering, such as loss of employment, and they come to appease afflicting demons, *mazenge* (the hereditary demons which are outside guardians and not the shades of the dead). They beg to be freed from a wide variety of afflictions, from minor ills and aches to chronic and paralysing diseases, severe pains during pregnancy, and childlessness. Their concern is the failure of kin 'to act with humanity' (*tama buthu*), their failure to meet their obligations under—to use Evans-Pritchard's phrase—'moral rules which mostly lie outside criminal and civil law'.

Their faults, Kalanga believe, arouse various spirits such as the hereditary demons of the bush, *mazenge*, and the shades of ancestors, *midzimu ye bobatategulu*, and the Creator, Mwali. In accord with each variety of spirit there is a cult, interconnected with the other cults and centred in an order of moral relationships. *Mazenge* are the subject of the cult which is centred on domestic morality in close relationships. They are guardian demons whose worship calls for women to be possessed at the homes of their close relatives and nowhere else.

The symbolic coherence between their cult of affliction and their other cults, such as that of the ancestors and of the land shrines, is mapped for Kalanga by a conceptual scheme which is bound by their division of the space within and about their homes. Each cult has its own characteristic space. This is conceptually oriented along co-ordinate axes of location: a public–private axis (corresponding with a division of space from the front to the back of a hamlet) is co-ordinated with an external–internal axis (corresponding to the outside and inside of a hamlet). Moreover, a sexual division is included, and its axis co-ordinated with the others. The woman's side is the private and domestic place to the rear of a hamlet. The public and court place to the front is the man's. So too, in ritual, relationships through females are oriented in space directly behind and opposite those through males. Primacy in public is placed where the legal and public authority over a man and his hamlet lies: with his patrilineal kinsmen. Other kinship relationships are located in the meeting-place that is private and either external or internal. Thus in ritual a variety of kinship relationships are represented spatially as apart and even counterposed to patrilineal relationships and descent; but the place of one is recognized relative to that of the others, and the orientation is complementary.

Mazenge, spoken of as spirits of the living, are believed to dwell in the east, directly opposite the shades of the dead in the west. Their libation is the reverse of that for the shades. It is poured in the east, behind and outside the hamlet. At dawn, when the sun is low and red, the possessed women and their kin ladle white beer from a red pot of fired clay still unblackened by soot from cooking. They pour in the veld to the east, behind a towering tree which bears fruit or pods (a marulla or winter thorn) and never in the tree's shadows to the west. By contrast, a libation for the patrilineal shades is poured to the west from a black pot (the colour of the shades) and within the hamlet at the front, in the shadows, by posts of hardwood from a tree which, though fruitless, may flow with ant honey.

The epithets of *mazenge* demons condense meanings which are expanded in the acts, metaphors and stylized cliches of the ritual. These epithets convey remoteness, contrariness. They convey a paradoxical purpose of the demons. From a distant grassland near plentiful water, where they eat their prey without want, the demons come in order that they should deceive or mock (*tsetse*) 'cramping, oppression, pinching' (*mana*).[25] The epithets are:

Crushers of Meat	*Pondha Nyama*
They of the Great River	*Baḳa Gwizi Luḳulu*
They prey at the Tall Grass	*Banodja ḳu Mpumbu*
Of snatching without shortcoming	*Wa hweze usinga pelevule*
They came from far, far	*Baḳadha ḳule, ḳule*
They should mock cramping	*Baḳa Tsetse mana*

There is an ambiguity, which is extended, and not resolved in the ritual. The use of an infinitive—*mana*, 'to cramp or oppress'—in the last epithet allows it to mean that they should mock vice and also to mean that they should deceive to be vicious.

Mazenge are conceived of as capricious spirits, and a woman, while possessed, may sing of herself as 'carrying an evil' (*senga mbimbi*). These afflicting demons, unlike mankind, are not bound to act according to specific ethical rules. Their demonic order represents disproportion, rapacity, and chaos for mankind. It is in their nature to act according to *lunya*, 'peevishness, spite, antipathy to children'.[26] Their viciousness and contrariness resembles human contradiction, it represents the derangement of human morality, for through the cult congregations obtain 'a glimpse of the kind of world they could anticipate when evil triumphs'.[27]

In the ritual of affliction a woman, a cult host, is possessed and lionized. She ceases to be herself, becoming a 'lion' (*shumba*). She is told of the affliction and pollution, the 'dirt' (*shamwa*) and 'rubbish' which concern members of the congregation. She is asked what faults have brought on affliction and treats her patients with herbs which she digs up while she is possessed. A host is believed to be like a pursuer of animals, scenting them from afar by their dung; she is required to convey what cannot be seen because it is hidden in 'dirt'. She is expected to feel, and be seen to feel, overcome by awe and enacting human vice, or rather animal virtue. Through her symbolic acts she grapples ritually with the sins which caused *mazenge* demons to send affliction: denying relatives the share which they are to 'eat' (for example, cattle of inheritance, bride-wealth, or slaughter at a feast); failing to feed relatives and give them their dues from one's earnings; favouring some kin at the expense of others; stealing a kinsman's wife through adultery—in brief, exacting for oneself the lion's share. A host appears to grapple with selfishness and rapacity which cheat and dispossess close relatives of what should be theirs.

In the ritual an order of rightful sharing and enduring geronto cratic authority is symbolized. But the order is set forth within the compound and kitchen, the setting of the ritual and the symbol of the closest relationships of kin and affines. Gerontocratic authority is also symbolized at an ancestral shrine, known as a 'great lion' (*shumba wulu*). However, to emphasize the domestic aspect of this authority Kalanga speak of *mazenge* and the cult of affliction as 'offering to the spirits of the hut' (*pa midzimu ye ngumba*).

A brief sketch shows the primary focus of the cult of *mazenge*. At one performance a possessed woman mimed a man as if he were a boy cleaning a loinskin, with lewd innuendo enjoyed by all with peals of laughter. The host began her take-off, holding the gourd round the bowl and pointing its long curved neck (a phallic symbol?) at other women:

Soloist [in high-pitched boy's voice]. My loinskin, my loinskin.
Soloist [in second voice]. I am going to give you *my* loinskin.
Chorus. Mine has been bitten by a dog.
Soloist [in second voice]. You were cleaning it to bring it where?
Soloist. To you, woman.
Soloist [own voice]. Ah, little man.

At this the soloist turned the gourd round by the neck, holding it like a hoe, and danced about miming a woman at the early weeding (*shakula*) of a garden. In other performances an elder's staff was the main and focal prop of the act.

At this performance members of the congregation drew my attention to the culmination in regular production—*shakula*, the early weeding. They did not comment explicitly on any sexual innuendo in the take-off. In the cliches of the cult, however, allusions to the loinskin, baring it or 'cleaning' it (which is an act of occult significance also: cleansing from the wrath of the spirits) are usually references to adultery or incest and its consequences. Kalanga explained that children are warned to fear and respect the loinskins of their fathers and avoid adultery and incest. In dramatizing this, women do not play-act at being men because of some deprivation or envy of masculinity: they ridicule. Their act is satire, enlivened by laughter, for they enjoy the ridiculousness of men and also of other women tempted to transgress with men.

A sexual division of labour, involving a sharing of work, is ritualized here, not as if the job of weeding were the affair solely of women. A great burden of work belongs to men. This is one of the tasks for which helping parties of adults or children of both sexes are called. These parties do the heaviest part, leaving maintenance for women. When they boast of their roles, as they sometimes do, in a jesting fashion, a favourite theme is the irregularity of much of a man's work. Baka Nyaka, a neighbour of mine, bragged to me, 'We women, ah, we work all year long. Men only work when it is a matter of cutting and clearing, in summer or in winter, to cut beams for hamlets. Ah, but our work goes on every day.' Thus in domestic ritual women display and celebrate where they rule like the cock (an important figure and a regulator of time in the idiom of the ritual)—that is, in the daily and continuous devotion to a task. 'Preen yourself, preen yourself,' runs a song of the hosts, and they do. Their act with a gourd is a comic take-off, proceeding through the caricaturing of a man in the guise of a boy and a woman in the guise of a man, uniting male and female, culminating in the exposure of disguise—as a woman assumes the agricultural task in which she devotes herself to a routine of rising, long before the cock crows, to prepare a meal for her household, then rushing to catch the dew on their gardens before the ground grows hard, as the dawn breaks. For comedy lies in the routine of life if anywhere.

When she mediates and intercedes ritually a woman acts in a representative, not a personal, capacity. During the dance of a ritual, plaints are chanted about suffering from neglect, from old age, from the meanness of relatives, their mocking, backbiting and ingratitude. These plaints are addressed to a high place, 'a knoll that has in it *mazenge* demons' (*dombo ladzina mazenge*), which is a ritual phrase for the possessed woman. In her role as host she must appear as other than herself. The spirit 'come from far, far' is believed to be performing her ritual acts. Its souls, the wind (*pehpo*) and the air (*mea*), 'arrive' (*svika*) to her, then 'go forward' and 'return backwards whence they came'. At night she rushes forward out of a hut which faces west (as do all except the south-facing huts of a land shrine)[28] and runs back to the east, to the rear of a hamlet, when she falls possessed (*wa shumba*, 'fall a lion'). Thus she maintains her personal freedom from responsibility while she intercedes or finds fault as a host; it is her hereditary spirit of the bush which appears to have intervened.[29] Moreover, a denial should be a host's first reply when the innermost congregation tell her that they have called the lion to appease her afflicting spirit. They say 'We called you ourselves. We report suffering to you. We divined and we caught you.'[30] She replies, 'It is not of mine, it is of those surrounding, and of the old, and of great mother.'[31]

Close relatives are coerced ritually. However, they are not involved in a widening circle of external or disinterested persons. The congregation at a Kalanga ritual of affliction is, at its widest, a body of kin and neighbours. It is not a casual assembly. It is a congregation of persons brought together because of their specific interests in one another. As members of a congregation they act parts symbolically dramatizing their roles towards one another.[32] Outsiders do not take part, and ordinarily they are absent when a cult host—the possessed kinswoman—reveals the faults that are being punished by her guardian demon, when she whispers the demands of demons, or when relatives voice grievances and rebuke one another for conduct liable to cause affliction. To have 'care, heedfulness, concern' (*hanya*) for a kinswoman is a moral responsibility which relatives share. They are compelled to regulate this responsibility among themselves because they appeal, as a closed congregation, to arbiters of morals and sanctions of conduct which are at once hereditary and outside spirits (*midzimu ye shango*, 'spirits of the veld').

In the domestic ritual externality is important for special roles within a narrow circle of relatives—for example, for the host's representative role in which she acts the intervention of an outside spirit. Externality is thus selectively significant, because the kin vary in their involvement with one another from one set of relationships to the next, and also because the kin are marked apart in particular affairs, though not in all. Moreover, if a host performed for a fixed group and her role were restricted, her spirit could be the shade of an ancestor of the group. In fact she takes part in the ritual regulation of moral responsibility among persons closely related in various ways, including kin and affines. This part calls for an outside demon, because the host mediates on behalf of variable sets of interested and jointly responsible relatives.

Evans-Pritchard's work on sin and blame for misfortune raised a constellation of problems. To pursue the subject calls for a more comprehensive analysis of ritual among Kalanga, including other modes of ritual action, such as those at the shrines of kin[33] or spraying water by senior kin to 'cool' ancestral wrath.[34] I have discussed how some modes of ritual action involving accusation and expiation operate in relation to each other. The evidence suggests that of all possible repercussions, re-establishment after ritual is the most superficial. It is also the one that strains our gullibility, as observers, the most. If sorcery accusations did no more than catalyse, ease or accelerate constant reactions, rituals of affliction too could be reduced, in analysis, to restorative remedies.[35] There is power in an accusation, as there is in a piacular sacrifice. Neither is an automatic trigger for the inexorable,[36] for splits or joinings that must be unmasked as aspects of more fundamental processes. Nor does one compensate for disturbances the other carries forward. Each caters to the tactics and the strategy of kin urging demands on one another, whether uncalculated or deliberate. Relative to the relationships at stake, kin can advance their interests through the leverage of sorcery accusations and rituals of affliction, sloughing away demands or promoting them dutifully. Only in the context of specific conditions can analysis reveal what the urgency of the pressures may be or how and where their repercussions are directed.

[1969]

Notes

1 I am grateful to the Social Science Research Council for Grant HR 790/1 and to the University of Manchester for supporting my research in Botswana among Western Kalanga during a fifteen-month period in 1964–5 and a three-month period in the summer of 1969. I wish to thank also Professor Emrys Peters, Dr Emanuel Marx, Professor Max Gluckman, and Dr Paul Baxter, who criticized earlier drafts of this essay. I mention Eastern Kalanga of Southern Rhodesia, among whom I worked in 1960–1; but, apart from such specific mention, my reference in this essay is to Western Kalanga of eastern Botswana.

2 Evans-Pritchard, *Witchcraft, Oracles and Magic among the Azande* 1937), p. 110.

3 *Loc. cit.*
4 The term ***host*** refers to a status and its role, that of a woman who has been initiated into the cult of possession by *mazenge* demons. 'Host' does not refer to the woman's *zenge* (singular) or *mazenge* (plural; she may have more than one). This demon is her hereditary and capricious tutelary.
5 Mitchell, 'The meaning in misfortune for urban Africans' (1965).
6 CR 102/11/59 dated 4 November 1959, heard at Harare police station and summarily digested in Appendix B of Gelfgand, *The African Witch* (1967), p. 224. In this case a woman hurled the abuse at her neighbour and alleged that she killed and then practised necrophagy.
7 Crawford, *Witchcraft and Sorcery in Rhodesia* (1967), Appendix i, and pp. 159–60, 169–70, 172–3. The text of the Act is Appendix ii. Crawford also shows the comparative rarity in Southern Rhodesia townships of prosecutions before magistrates under the Witchcraft Suppression Act. Out of his sample of 103 criminal cases involving allegations of sorcery or witchcraft during 1956–62, no more than three cases were urban ones, two of these being prosecutions for homicide also. Serious offences and crimes of violence are prosecuted more commonly along with sorcery or witchcraft accusations in rural areas: see p. 169*f*.
8 See Kapferer, 'Norms and the manipulation of relationships in a work context' (1969), especially pp. 202–7.
9 Mitchell, 'The meaning in misfortune for urban Africans' (1965), pp. 198–201.
10 See below, pp. 238*f*.
11 Turner, *The Forest of Symbols* (1967), pp. 359–93, and *The Drums of Affliction* (1968), pp. 125–6.
12 Mitchell, *The Yao Village* (1956), pp. 165–75.
13 Turner, *The Forest of Symbols* (1967), pp. 376–7. See also Bohannan, *Justice and Judgment among the Tiv* (1951). Turner reports villagers' composite interpretations and a diviner's confidential diagnosis to him, after a divination, of sorcery and ancestral affliction, in *The Forest of Symbols* (1967), pp. 375 and 386 respectively. The diviner told Turner that 'he had mentioned the name of (the sorcerer) to no one except myself, for he did not want to be said to have caused trouble in the village'—*The Drums of Affliction* (1968), p. 126.
14 See below, pp. 238*f*.
15 I saw no young girls in full ritual costume and possessed; I was told that a host performs regularly only after becoming an adult. However, the following are the details told to me on the recruitment of hosts in the four wards which I know best: recruited before marriage, ten hosts; after marriage, eighteen; recruitment unknown to me,

fourteen. These forty-two hosts represent roughly twenty per cent of the 208 adult women in the four wards.

16 See Wilson, 'Spirit possession and status ambiguity' (1967), for a recent and critical review of the literature on this theme. Evidence from Kalanga does not sustain Wilson's view that men, as sponsors of ritual, are 'tools' of the possessed, women.

17 The *mazenge* of a host may be invoked only at the home of her own kinsman or her husband, once he has made a marriage payment to her senior host.

18 I am grateful to Dr Bruce Kapferer for describing his evidence on labour migration in Zambia and pointing out to me the great significance of women's visits there also.

19 In this illustration and in all others, I respect the privacy of individuals and use fictitious names, following a Kalanga convention by which a man is called Ta . . . , 'Father of', and a woman Baka . . . , 'Mother of' . . .

20 To 'fear' is to 'respect', and the mother's sister turned the remark about, so that she could challenge her sister's daughter with failing to show respect in a visit.

21 For an analysis of charges as distinct from other accusations see Schapera, 'Witchcraft beyond reasonable doubt (1955) and 'The Crime of Sorcery' (1969). Magistrates' records of sorcery charges involving Kalanga of Southern Rhodesia are examined in Crawford, *Witchcraft and Sorcery in Rhodesia* (1967).

22 I am grateful to Dr Y. Eilam for helpful criticism here.

23 The only named portions are of the woman, her mother's brother, her mother, father, and his siblings; the rest of her close kin have a right to 'eat' of a portion, known as 'the wetting of the mouth'.

24 In Tswana *rapela* means 'pray, entreat, soothe'—Brown, *Secwana* Dictionary (1962), p. 259. In Shona, *rapa* means 'cure, heal'—Hannan, *Standard Shona Dictionary* (1959), p. 256.

25 '*Mana*' also has the sense of forcing disproportion, squeezing a misfit.

26 See Hannan, *Standard Shona Dictionary* (1959), p. 548.

27 Peters, 'Aspects of rank and status among Muslims in a Lebanese village' (1963), p. 198. Peters' view that authority is not flouted or reversed in certain types of ritual illuminates the Kalanga cult.

28 A sexual orientation of space is unvaried. The shrine faces the male deity, the Father of Mwali, in the south; its back is to the female, the Mother of Mwali, in the north. Between them lies the path of a shooting star, whereas the path of the sun goes from *mazenge* (the demons of the rising sun, *midzimu ye buda huba*) to the shades of the dead (the spirits of the setting sun, *midzimu ye ngina huba*).

29 See Firth's discussion of the role of mediator and his suggestions, which

evidence from Kalanga sustains, 'that externalization of responsibility is an important function of spirit possession': 'Social organization and social change' (1964), p. 64.

30 *Isvi tamudana. Tomubikila zvogwadza. Takandila tibata imwi. Ndimwi munomusila kaba, ndiko timudana wali.*

31 *Hateli imi, nde zve bawumbe ne bacembere na me gulu.* Such words as *bawumbe, bacembere* are used in Shona but in Kalanga are peculiar to the ritual of *mazenge*. The term for wrath, *kaba*, is said to be borrowed from Tswana, and some Kalanga substitute for *kaba* the word for spirits, *midzimu*.

32 See Bateson, *Naven* (1936), *passim*.

33 A description of such ritual among Western Kalanga is given by Willoughby, *The Soul of the Bantu* (1928), p. 224 and pp. 273–5. My own observations correspond with his description.

34 For an account of a similar mode among the Kgatla, who are distantly south of Kalanga in Botswana, see Schapera, 'Oral sorcery among the natives of Bechuanaland' (1934), pp. 293–305.

35 This and other points about cults of affliction are developed further in a comparison of Ndembu and Kalanga cults which I make in 'Symbolic dialogue and personal transactions' (1971).

36 The need to reconsider the 'obstetric view of witchcraft and sorcery' is shown by Douglas, 'Techniques of sorcery control in central Africa' (1963), pp. 123–41.

Bibliography.

Bateson, G., *Naven*, Cambridge: Cambridge University Press (1936).

Bohannan, P., *Justice and Judgment among the Tiv*, London: Oxford University Press for the International African Institute (1951).

Brown, J. T., *Secwana Dictionary*, Lobatsi: Bechuanaland Book Centre (1962).

Crawford, J. R., *Witchcraft and Sorcery in Rhodesia*, London: Oxford University Press for the International African Institute (1967).

Douglas, M., *Purity and Danger—an Analysis of Concepts of Pollution and Taboo*, London: Routledge & Kegan Paul (1966).

— 'Techniques of sorcery control in Central Africa' in *Witchcraft and Sorcery in East Africa*, ed. J. Middleton and E. H. Winter, London: Routledge & Kegan Paul (1963).

Evans-Pritchard, E. E., *Witchcraft, Oracles and Magic among the Azande*, Oxford: Clarendon Press (1937).

Firth, R., 'Social organization and social change' in *Essays on Social Organization and Values*, London: Athlone Press (1964).

Gelfand, M., *The African Witch*, Edinburgh and London: E. & S. Livingstone (1967).

Goody, J., *Death, Property and the Ancestors*, Stanford: Stanford University Press (1962).
Hannan, M., *Standard Shona Dictionary*, London: Macmillan (1959).
Kapferer, B., 'Norms and the manipulation of relationships in a work context' in *Social Networks in Urban Situations*, ed. J. C. Mitchell, Manchester: Manchester University Press for the Institute for Social Research, University of Zambia (1969).
Krige, E. J. and J. D., *The Realm of a Rain-queen*, London: Oxford University Press for the International African Institute (1943).
Mitchell, J. C., 'The meaning in misfortune for urban Africans' in *African Systems of Thought*, ed. M. Fortes and G. Dieterlen, London: Oxford University Press for International African Institute (1965).
— *The Yao Village*, Manchester: Manchester University Press for the Rhodes-Livingstone Institute (1956).
Peters, E. L., 'Aspects of rank and status among Muslims in a Lebanese village' in *Mediterranean Countrymen*, ed. J. Pitt-Rivers, Paris: Mouton (1963), pp. 159–200.
Schapera, I., 'Oral sorcery among the natives of Bechuanaland' in *Essays presented to C. G. Seligman*, ed. E. E. Evans-Pritchard, *London:* Routledge (1934), pp. 293–305.
— 'The crime of sorcery', *Proceedings of the Royal Anthropological Institute* (1969), pp. 15–23.
— 'Witchcraft beyond reasonable doubt', *Man* 55, 80 (1955), p. 7.
Snaith, N. H., *The Distinctive Ideas of the Old Testament*, London: Epworth Press (1945).
Turner, V. W., *Chihamba the White Spirit*, Rhodes-Livingstone Paper No. 33, Manchester: Manchester University Press for the Rhodes-Livingstone Institute (1962).
— *The Drums of Affliction*, Oxford: Clarendon Press for the International African Institute (1968).
— *The Forest of Symbols*, Ithaca, N.Y.: Cornell University Press (1967).
— *Lunda Rites and Ceremonies*, Rhodes-Livingstone Museum occasional paper No. 10, Livingstone.
— *Schism and Continuity in an African Society*, Manchester: Manchester University Press for the Rhodes-Livingstone Institute (1957).
Werbner, R. P., 'Atonement ritual and guardian-spirit possession among Kalanga', *Africa*, xxxiv, 3 (1964), pp. 206–23.
— 'Guardian spirits', *Man, Myth and Magic*, 42 (1970), pp. 1183–7.
— 'Symbolic dialogue and personal transactions', *Ethnology* (July 1971).
Willoughby, W. C., *The Soul of the Bantu*, London: Student Christian Movement (1928).
Wilson, P. J., 'Status ambiguity and spirit possession', *Man*, 2 (1967), 3, pp. 366–78.

7

Taking the blame and passing the buck, or, The carpet of Agamemnon[1]

An essay on the problems of responsibility, legitimation and triviality

Ronald J. Frankenberg

1. *Introduction*

All absolute ethical systems, so called, erected on the basis of supposedly eternal and immutable moral truths, are helpless before the problems occurring most often in life, namely, situations of conflict in which doing what is thought to be right brings about evil consequences. Uncertainty here does not arise because the so-called sinner is ignorant of the moral norm obligatory for him in the given situation; the moralist may come forward with his pompous commandments and prohibitions, but that does not help, because the situation is connected with a clash of contradictory standards and the poor sinner cannot decide which has priority. This may be called an 'Orestes' situation. Such situations confound all 'absolute' moral systems, religious or lay.'[2]

In *Agamemnon*, the first play of the Oresteian trilogy, Aeschylus describes how Clytemnestra tricks Agamemnon into the seemingly trivial act of entering his palace by walking over a purple carpet. Her motive in so doing is to legitimate the murder she is about to commit by transforming Agamemnon's misdemeanours within the family, the sacrifice of his daughter and the taking of Cassandra as his mistress, into an insult to the gods. She is, in fact, engineering a change from the trivial to the cosmic so that relatively petty motives of jealousy and revenge are transformed into world-shaking events. Alternatively, world-shaking events are diminished to the trivial.

The basic problem of responsibility which I wish to discuss in this paper is more than an academic point of who or what is responsible for the disturbance of social relationships. I am here asking the further questions of how responsibility is attributed and what social action follows. Gluckman, in his Marett lectures,[3] suggested that in tribal society the social action that followed disturbance was based on the principle of magnifying the wickedness of the disturber.

By contrast, he suggested, in advanced modern urban industrial society the aim of divination (in the person of outside consultants) was to diminish individual responsibility within a specific social situation by relating crises to the wider social situation. Either 'It's all the fault of the system' or, I may add, 'It's that chap out there who is at fault; we are all guiltless here.'

In this essay I shall first argue that certain structural principles are common to two widely divergent spheres of decision-taking within British society—the village, and a wartime Cabinet sub-committee, the Chiefs of Staff. Secondly, I shall suggest that the same principles can be seen operating in other spheres of responsibility. These are the family firm, described in Cyril Sofer's *The Organisation from Within* (1961), the relationship of the psychiatrist to the law courts discussed by Barbara Wootton in her Winchester lecture (1963), and even the situation of Cyril, the rate-fixer at an engineering factory in the north of England, described by Lupton in *On the Shop Floor* (1963). If I were concerned with the concept of responsibility and how it is to be defined, class and social strata would be essential variables. If, however, as I intend, I confine my analysis to the social actions involved in the attribution of responsibility, I can discuss processes independently of their content. This, incidentally, may be upsetting, as when a Polish sociologist objected to my comparing the Polish United Workers' Party to the Rotary Club in a Middle Western American town, and as a lawyer might object to my comparison of Welsh rowdies with High Court judges.

The paper is partly polemical since, as in previous publications,[4] I am arguing for a methodology in which the discussion of small segments of society in great detail is used to throw light on the general. It is my firm view that only the particularistic can illuminate the universalistic. I take comfort from the fact that it was evidently a view shared by Aeschylus. The cases with which I deal in this paper have a number of things in common. Firstly, the relevant actors at the relevant times are either equal to one another or consider themselves so to be. It follows from this that the problem of responsibility cannot be shelved by appeal to authority.

Secondly, in each case (as in Tallensi divinations),[5] decisions are seen not merely being taken but also being legitimated. Thirdly, in each case disputing parties, while in conflict in one system, have in common membership of an overriding, more encompassing system about which there is consensus. These systems are respectively the village, the war and victory in it, the firm, the law, and production.

Fourthly, in each case someone who is both within the sub-system and within the overriding system has attributed to him the responsibility for actions within the sub-system. This has the effect of shifting outside the system the consequence in social action of the attribution of responsibility within the system.

Experts, consultants, lawyers, psychiatrists, jurors and rate-fixers are seen as being used—but this does not imply that experts are never genuinely experts, that consultants are never advisers, that psychiatrists are never doctors, or that rate-fixers never genuinely fix rates. Another important qualification is that it must be recognized that there is often a choice of several overriding systems. The consultant in the family firm could have chosen to support (or confront his client with the realities of) the profession, the family, the firm or the nation.

2. *The controversy over the strategic air offensive against Germany*

This is a modern tragedy, every bit as moving as *Oedipus* and *Agamemnon*, and one of which the last act has not yet unfolded. Like Greek tragedy, it unfolds at every level and the trivial decision has great consequences, while the great decisions operate at trivial levels.

In his Godkin lectures on *Science and Government*, published in 1961, Sir Charles Snow turned temporarily from the writing of fiction to the chronicling and analysis of fact. He offered an analysis of decision-making processes in the application of science by wartime government.

In his own words, in a postscript to the lectures,

> Quite a number of critics—most of them not familiar with these events and not committed to either side in any of these controversies—have scolded me, good-temperedly and charitably, for setting the issue in terms too black and white. They conclude—and in many cases this has been intended as an excuse for me—that the imagination of a novelist had been too strong.[6]

In this paper I am going to argue that in his interpretation of these events Snow reveals too weak a use of his imagination as a sociological novelist. Closeness to the situations he describes has misled him into over-emphasizing the influence of the personal attributes and under-estimating the significance of underlying social process. My argument will involve a discussion of the legitimation of decision-taking processes in the football committee of a remote Welsh village.

Snow himself provides authority for this apparently bizarre comparison:

> In the Tizard–Lindemann story we saw three of the characteristic forms of closed politics. These three forms are not often completely separable, and usually fuse into each other, but they are perhaps worth defining. The first is committee politics, and everyone who has ever lived in any society, in a tennis club, a factory dramatic group, a college faculty, has witnessed some of its expressions. The archetype of all these is that kind of committee where each member speaks with his individual voice, depends upon his personality alone for his influence, and in the long run votes with an equal vote.[7]

Snow's other forms of closed politics are the *hierarchical*, 'the politics of a chain of command, of the services, of a bureaucracy, of a large industry, and *court politics*, 'attempts to exert power through a man who possesses a concentration of power. The Lindemann–Churchill relation is the purest example possible of court politics.'[8]

Like Snow himself I shall concentrate on committee politics while remembering, as he does, that hierarchical and court politics are not so simple as they sound. The controllers of courts and both controllers and administrators of hierarchies have to be convinced that the decisions of committees are legitimate.

The Chiefs of Staff committee. Of the particular incidents which Snow describes, I shall concentrate on one—the 1942 controversy on the future of strategic bombing. I give my own account of this controversy. Its life history is complicated and woven from many strands.

Firstly there is what I shall call the metastrategical element. As soon as the aeroplane was invented and its use in war foreseen, argument began as to whether the strategy of air warfare should be *sui generis* or whether the aeroplane should be regarded as an auxiliary to naval and land power. Sociologically one would expect, and one finds, that Chiefs of Naval Staff and army officers tended to the second view and airmen to the first. This conflict is inherent in the situation created by the very existence of the aeroplane and is continuous throughout the story.

Secondly there is the grand strategical element. How stood the war in 1942? The stage set is described by Webster and Frankland.[9] Europe had been evacuated in front of the advancing German armies. The British empire in the Far East was melting away before the advance of the Japanese. The Germans had been brought to a standstill at the gates of Moscow. During 1941

> . . . Astounding changes had taken place in the general war situation. Hitler's summer *Blitzkrieg* in Russia had failed. The wound had been deep, but not mortal. In the winter it was the turn of the German army to suffer deprivations and its first important defeats of the second world war. While these gigantic events were being unfolded in Russia, Japan attacked the American fleet at Pearl Harbour and Hitler declared war on the United States of America.

They go on to quote Churchill:

> In the days when we were fighting alone, we answered the question: 'How are you going to win the war?' by saying: 'We will shatter Germany by bombing.' Since then the enormous injuries inflicted on the German army and manpower by the Russians, and the accession of the manpower and munitions of the United States, have rendered other possibilities open.[10]

Thirdly there was the *narrow* strategical setting revealed in the distinction made between operational targets and tactical targets—which can be roughly translated as targets that bombers could hit and targets they would have liked to hit. Night precision bombing had proved an expensive failure.

It was in the light of this background that a new bombing directive was issued in February 1942. It was directed towards area bombing, 'the primary object' of which, the directive continued, '. . . should now be focused on the morale of the enemy civil population and, in particular, of the industrial workers'.[11] The point was underlined in a pencilled minute by Sir Charles Portal, Chief of Air Staff to Air Vice-Marshal Bottomley:

> Ref the new bombing directive: I suppose it is clear that the aiming points are to be the built-up areas, not, for instance, the dockyards or aircraft factories where these are mentioned in Appendix A.
>
> This must be made quite clear if it is not already understood.[12]

The Navy was expected to oppose the policy.

> The naval staff clearly thought that increasing numbers of long-range bombers should be tactically committed to the actual zones of encounter, and that this should be done regardless of the effect which it might have upon the strategic air offensive against Germany . . .
>
> The Air Staff . . . believed that the diversion and dispersal of heavy bombers to the struggle at sea should be kept to the absolute minimum consistent with survival.
>
> . . . certainly the Air Staff could never have justified to themselves a policy of removing the heavy bombers from an activity in which they believed they could succeed, that is, the strategic attack on Germany, and introducing them to another in which they thought they would fail, that is, the destruction of surface and submarine vessels at sea.

There are added complications to the story arising from relationships with the United States and with the Soviet Union, but I have said enough to show the historical complexity of the situation into which Professor Lindemann, later Lord Cherwell, on 30 March 1942 introduced his minute to Churchill on the effects of strategic bombing. To this Tizard replied; and it is this which provides Snow with one of his parables on scientific overlordship. The clash between Tizard and Cherwell was not, of course, their first clash. Snow summarizes their previous relationships—A is Tizard, B is Cherwell:

> Once they were bosom friends. They were associated in great hazards in the 1914–18 war. Afterwards they advanced each other's careers, were allies at the university, were linked by family life. Suddenly, without A's knowing it, B's feeling changes. He begins to talk of A as that 'wretched little man'. They are brought together as members of a committee, in a task on which the safety of the country may depend. B abuses A, in front of the committee, in terms of uncontrolled violence. Other members force B off the committee. A has a period of great influence. Again a twist of fortune: B is given the authority. The time is the summer of 1940, the country is in danger, A sends a message through a common friend: can't they patch up the quarrel and work together? B returns the answer: 'Now that I am in a position of power, a lot of my old friends have come sniffing around.'[13]

Thus the actual minute with its attendant controversy is an incident in two social processes: (1) a continuing relationship between Cherwell and Tizard, and (2) the continuing process of decision-taking concerning the conduct of wars in general and the second world war in particular.

Snow is arguing about the impact of (1) upon (2). Cherwell, he argues, was in a position of great power. This arose from his personal friendship with Churchill, and from the fact that he was a scientist among non-scientists. It was dangerous to everyone else because (1) Cherwell was vindictive, (2) Cherwell's scientific and military judgment was bad, and (3) in any case single scientists, however able, should not be given great power.

Snow's analysis falls down in my view because he does not see Cherwell's minute as an event at the intersection of a number of processes. The personal relationships of Cherwell and Tizard are out of perspective.

The football club. The village events, although very different in content, can also be seen in terms of strategy and tactics, and the independent or auxiliary roles of a social activity.[14] The village had a football club to which the men and women inhabitants had different attitudes.

To the men, football was a game that they themselves had played and enjoyed. The organization of the football club was a means to provide football as an independent activity for village boys. The men also worked outside the village and wanted, by its football success, to bring the village prestige in the outside world.

The women were separately organized into a football supporters' club. They organized dances, whist drives and eventually a carnival—the proceeds of all of which social activity normally went to pay the costs of the football team. For the women, football was a means to an end, an excuse to carry on other activities they enjoyed. Puritan village norms required that concerts, dances and social activities must have an ultimate purpose—they must be in aid of something. Football also gave the women the opportunity of seeing their own sons and husbands play. The women derived prestige from invidious comparison. They were housewives and sought to raise their prestige with reference groups within the village. The men, commuters, looked outwards. Thus although both men and women were interested in the success of village football *in general*, their *particular* interests differed.

A situation arose in 1953 which made these contradictions appear as irreconcilable antagonisms. I have analysed this situation and its effects in detail elsewhere. Here I can summarize briefly.

The village was a small one and by 1953 had run through its

footballing talent. If it was to maintain its place in the North Wales League, as the men wished, it would have to import outsiders to play for it. This the women felt to be against their interests. Importing outsiders added to expenses. The need to raise revenue and the desire for a better pitch on which outsiders would be prepared to come to play caused a move from the easily overlooked field in the middle of the village to the outskirts. Now watching a game became a deliberate act, not a casual occupation to be indulged in by women on their way to and from the shops on a Saturday afternoon.

The conflicting interests of men and women had been brought into the open. An open dispute started between the women's supporters' club and the men's football club. Should the proceeds of a carnival the former were organizing be devoted to football or not? There were other strands to the tangle. Family enmities were carried over from other situations. There was a long-standing grievance amongst the women that the men violated the norms of reciprocity by failing to attend whist drives and dances.

Most important of all, the disunity was emphasized by a fundamental unity. Men and women were all villagers—they all wanted what was good for the village. In other situations they were related as husbands and wives, mothers and sons. They could not allow their real differences of opinion permanently to divide them and still remain villagers and families.

In the course of my analysis of how such totally disruptive disputes were avoided I mentioned several devices familiar to students of politics, local and national—failure to keep minutes, and the appeal to authority or precedent are examples.

I laid most emphasis, however, on the use of strangers. I argued that in any social group, however homogeneous it might appear, there were odd men out who were in some ways different from the rest and in one sense therefore protected from the informal pressures which restrained the majority from taking actions which would make divisions in the group overt. Thus the supporters' club committee consisted of women, with a man as a chairman. The parish council had a majority of Baptists, but its three successive chairmen were the only three non-Baptists. In the football committee there were three outsiders, an English miner, a dog breeder from Lancashire, and myself.

I suggested that in situations where an appeal to higher authority was not possible such strangers (who might also be outsiders but did not necessarily have to be) were made to appear to take decisions which otherwise would cause serious dissension among the group of insiders. Another way of putting this might be to say that decisions were legitimated in the eyes of village non-committee members by committee members saying, 'It's not our fault; we agree with you. It was the strangers on the committee.'

When the women supporters who were on the carnival committee wanted to deny the proceeds of the carnival itself to the football club, they tried to organize the discussions so that strangers should move the controversial resolutions. In their counter-attacks the football committee behaved similarly. The result was that the strangers behaved inconsistently, pushed hither and thither by the manipulation of first one and then another section of public opinion. Village unity was maintained even if ethnographers and other (permanently or temporarily) marginal men and women were made uncomfortable. The substance of the matter—and this is an important point—was settled by related external events, namely the football team's lack of success. In my book I suggested that the role of the stranger in this North Wales village was not unique. I there cited the leopard-skin chief amongst the Nuer, the Sanusi of Cyrenaica, the Tallensi shrines and divinations and the monastic settlements in early Wales as structurally similar examples within very different cultural contexts.

The direction in which I am expanding the idea in this essay is by now, I hope, apparent. Let me summarize the analogies I am putting forward. The village had to maintain unity. There were divided interests within it. The principal division in this context was men *versus* women. The men's interest was in football as an independent activity which by its external success brought prestige to each as a representative of the village. The women's interest was in football as an auxiliary activity within the village which brought prestige to the individual through son or husband who acquitted himself well. When events outside committees made the recognition of this conflict of interests unavoidable, decisions were taken which threatened the interest of one group. They were legitimated by blaming them on strangers.

The Chiefs of Staff committee was responsible to the Prime Minister for the overall conduct of the war. It had to maintain unity and co-operation between the services. There were divided interests within it. The principal division in this context is Air Staff *versus* Naval Staff. The Air Staff are in favour of the use of independent air power for a strategic offensive. The Naval Staff are convinced that the most valuable use of air power is as a tactical auxiliary in the sea battle of the Atlantic. When situations arise where this conflict comes into the open, Sir Dudley Pound, representing the Admiralty, and Lord Portal, representing the Air Ministry, use 'stranger' scientists and mathematical myths to express viewpoints and legitimate decisions which in fact are largely affected by the relative political power of Air Ministry and Admiralty and by external events. It is not merely chance, as the official historians point out, that the first thousand-bomber raid (on Cologne, 13 March 1942) and the destruction of the Renault works and of Lübeck occurred while the vital discussions were going on.[15]

If my argument is correct, *in the particular case which Snow cites*, the scientists are being manipulated by events and institutions more than they are influencing them. What is the evidence for this view?

While we cannot know from the published literature whether Portal and Cherwell discussed the issue informally, the crucial directive changing bombing policy from precision to area bombing was issued on 14 February 1942. Portal's pencilled minute already referred to was dated 15 February. Cherwell's minute to the Prime Minister was not sent until 30 March, six weeks later. The reaction of Sir Archibald Sinclair, Air Minister, and Sir Charles Portal, Chief of Air Staff, was that Cherwell's arguments were 'simple, clear and convincing'.

Sir Henry Tizard questioned Lord Cherwell's calculations. The original Cherwell minute and Tizard's rejoinder are quoted in full from the official history by Snow in his *Postcript to Science and Government* (1962). His concern with personality, however, has led him to omit a page and a half of the narrative which is very relevant to the theme. I set it out here in full, with those parts I consider most significant italicized:

Lord Cherwell clearly felt that his calculations had been taken too literally. 'My paper,' he told Sir Henry Tizard, 'was intended to show that we really can do a lot of damage by bombing built-up areas with the sort of air force which should be available.' As to the size of the bomber force, he said that he had used 'the round figure of 10,000' partly because in March, when he wrote his minute, the Ministry of Aircraft Production had been somewhat more optimistic than it was in April when Sir Henry

Tizard wrote his, and 'partly to save the Prime Minister the trouble of making arithmetical calculations'. Even, however, if Sir Henry Tizard's expectations proved to be more realistic than his own and, in the event, it was only possible to subject the leading German towns to a weight of attack three or four times as heavy as that which had fallen on Hull and Birmingham, Lord Cherwell remained convinced that the effects would be 'catastrophic' (letter, Cherwell to Tizard, 22 April 1942).

Sir Henry Tizard had never denied this, but he had sought to show that there might be a great difference between 'catastrophic' and 'decisive' results: 'I should like to make it clear,' he told Sir Archibald Sinclair on 20 April 1942, 'that I don't disagree fundamentally with the bombing policy, but I do think that it is only likely to be decisive if carried out on the scale envisaged by the Air Staff, which, if I remember rightly, contemplated a front-line strength of 4,000 aircraft and a rate of reinforcement of 1,000 heavy bombers a month. We cannot achieve this,' he continued, 'this year, or even until next year, so if we try to carry out the policy with a much smaller force it will not be decisive, and we may lose the war in other ways' (letter, Tizard to Sinclair, 20 April 1942).

In other words, Sir Henry Tizard's objections were really founded upon the fear that by concentrating Bomber Command upon an offensive which, in view of its limited size and rate of expansion, he thought would not be decisive, the war might be lost by failure to attend adequately to defensive measures. 'You know,' he told Sir Archibald Sinclair, 'that I am very keen about the greater and better use of the Air Force against enemy ships of war . . .' (letter, Tizard to Sinclair, 20 April 1942). *The differences between Sir Henry Tizard and Lord Cherwell were the same as those at issue between the Naval Staff and the Air Staff. The fact that Sir Henry Tizard had been able to point out fallacies in Lord Cherwell's calculations, fallacies which Lord Cherwell scarcely denied, was relatively unimportant. After all, these calculations, like those made by Sir Henry Tizard, were extremely approximate and were only used to make the case presented more graphic.*

These calculations, indeed, depended upon factors which could not be measured and scarcely guessed. It was difficult to work out the number of bombers which the British aircraft industry could produce. It was still more difficult to estimate the speed at which the Germans would be able to shoot them down. The ultimate role and size of the American bomber force was still unknown. Even so, these matters comprised the simpler parts of the calculations. The problem of trying to estimate the consequences to Germany of the offensive was infinitely more complex. It was still possible to arrive at widely different opinions as to the effects of the German attacks on British towns. It was impossible to know how much more effort the Germans would have had to make in order to produce decisive effects. Similarly, it was impossible to calculate the size and duration of attack which would be necessary to reduce Germany to the point of capitulation. It was possible only to guess. As Mr Churchill wrote, 'experience shows that forecasts are usually falsified and preparations always in arrears' (*The Second World War*, vol. III, p. 583). *The difference of opinion between Lord Cherwell and Sir Henry Tizard was, therefore, really no more than an illustrative reflection, in somewhat more scientific terms, of the issues which divided the counsels of the Air and Naval Staffs.*

It is only fair to add that the official historians consider that Cherwell, because of his direct personal influence on Churchill, 'exerted a much greater influence upon the Prime Minister than did Sir Henry Tizard'. They conclude,

Nevertheless, the conflict of opinion which revealed itself over the acceptance of the February directive and the Cherwell minute was never resolved and was never far beneath the surface.[16]

Snow's final comment bears upon the occasion in the autumn of 1942, when Sir Dudley Pound raised the issue again, calling for a scientific committee to look into the effects of the bombing offensive. Portal referred him to Lord Cherwell, 'who should be asked to give or obtain an authoritative opinion'. Snow writes:

Those are terrifying words. Not terrifying because Lindemann was Lindemann, though that gives them an added twist. They would be just as terrifying if, for Lord Cherwell as the source of authoritative opinion, we read Bush or Compton or Tizard or any scientist whose judgment has been proved unusually good. For the terrifying thing is, not who issues this authoritative opinion, but that intelligent and high placed non-scientists should believe that it exists.[17]

There is no evidence, in fact, that any 'high placed non-scientist' did believe any such thing. It is evident from a full consideration of Portal's note that he was under no such illusions, he merely knew which scientists were on which side.[18] Churchill listened to Cherwell, but he also used his judgment and was influenced by the events of the war. Indeed, Portal's curt reply was far from closing the issue. The CIGS, Sir Alan Brooke, intervened on the side of the Admiralty, and, in the words of the official history, 'Sir Charles Portal was compelled . . . to give much ground'.[19]

Cherwell's special position as a personal friend of the Prime Minister gave him particular importance, but this was obviously a personal 'court' position which owed little to his role as scientist. Part of the resentment he engendered arose from the fact that he could thus sometimes play the game outside the rules. Tizard had to play to the rules and appears to have been very adept at it, and, as Snow says, 'They often thought of putting him in uniform: but that would have defeated his whole virtue as an interpreter between the two sides. "I utterly refuse to wear a busby", he used to say.'[20]

Indeed, both Tizard and Blackett—who came independently to the same conclusion on bombing—were perfect in the role of stranger of the kind I have been describing. Both had experience in the first world war as officers, Tizard in the Royal Flying Corps and Blackett in the Royal Navy. Tizard, in addition, came from a naval family and but for poor eyesight would himself have been a regular naval officer. Both made major contributions to the application of science to warfare. They were thus both, in a sense, of the services but not in them and both had the added qualification of scientific knowledge. Their views carried weight, and Snow tells us that 'In fact, with the exception of those concerned with bombing policy, the senior officers were ready to be convinced as soon as Tizard started to talk.'[20]

Yet, as Blackett recalls,

> By this time a certain allergy to arithmetic was spreading in Whitehall, and our numerical forebodings went unheeded: the Air Ministry agreed with the Cabinet Office paper, and the policy of dehousing the German working-class population, with the object of lowering its morale and will to fight, became a major part of the British war effort.
>
> The story goes that at that time in the Air Ministry it was said of anyone who added two and two together to make four, 'he is not to be trusted; he has been talking to Tizard and Blackett'.[21]

While in matters of scientific policy all three men were innovators, their views on other controversial policies were only as effective as the political backing they enjoyed.

In this scientists are not alone in administration. Professor Ely Devons has analysed the use of statisticians and statistics in a similar way in the Ministry of Aircraft Production (1950). In the bombing controversy itself a lawyer, Mr Justice Singleton, was called in in April 1942, apparently at the suggestion of Sir Charles Portal. He came near to my village stranger who supported both sides at different times. However, he went one better and supported both sides at once:

> The vague language of the Singleton Report, so far from resulting in any firm conclusions, merely tended to exacerbate the dispute about bombing policy which continued to divide the counsels of the Chiefs of Staff Committee. It was impossible to summarize the findings of the Report, but it was easy to draw quotations from it which could be used to illustrate almost any argument.[22]

This, of course, Sir Charles Portal and Sir Dudley Pound proceeded to do. In the view of the official historians, however,

> . . . the Singleton Report did perform one valuable service. It showed that a decision about bombing policy could not be arrived at on the basis of academic investigations into the prospects of the strategic bombing offensive. Whether these investigations were statistical or juridical they could, because of the nature of the evidence, prove nothing. The solution of the problem did not lie in further research or in further argument. It lay in the field of action.[23]

It was accordingly in the field of action that Air Marshal Harris, commander of RAF Bomber Command, set out to prove his point, and to some extent he succeeded.

Webster and Frankland conclude part of their discussion of this controversy by saying:

> The conduct of the bombing offensive was always either to a greater or less extent the product of compromise between the demands of offence and defence, of the strategic and tactical roles of the force and between the independent and auxiliary applications of bombing.

I have suggested that it was also the product of a political decision-making process in which equals—the Chiefs of Staff—legitimated their views to one another by calling in the evidence of 'strangers' (experts).

But the equals were also part of a hierarchy, and the final appeal was to the higher authority of the Prime Minister. The game, however, did not stop there. There were international complications. Professor Blackett recalls that during the winter of 1942–43

> . . . the Admiralty had to enlist President Roosevelt's personal influence to ensure that a squadron of that admirable anti-submarine aircraft, the B24, was allocated to Coastal Command, where they were brilliantly

successful, and not, as the Air Staff wanted, sent to Berlin, for which they were not very suitable.[24]

The family firm

In this essay I have argued, not that the village is a microcosm of the nation, nor a football club of the defence forces, but that sometimes similar social mechanisms meet similar social situations arising in very different surroundings. There are general principles involving the allocation of responsibility in decision-taking processes as well as specific complications. It is perhaps both alarming and encouraging to discover that the basic processes of political decision-making are similar whether the outcome is a lower place in the local football league or the destruction of cities, the loss of lives and the defeat of nations. It is even more alarming, and encouraging, to carry the argument further into firm, forensic arena and factory.

Sofer (1961) in the book cited by Gluckman, deals with a case study of Tavistock Institute action as a consultant in a firm known as Davidson's. The facts, briefly, are these. The Institute was called in by the home sales manager, Mr E. Adams, ostensibly to advise on a selection procedure for a new company secretary. It asked what had happened to the old one, and was told that he was going to Australia. He was Mr E. Adams's sister's husband. Faced with this extra information, Tavistock agreed to act only as full consultants, and in due course Sofer went in to meet the full board, who were all five descendants of the original chairman. The younger brother of one of them was also in the company and the departing secretary, as we have seen, was married to their sister. It was a public company with 500 employees (350 works, 150 staff) and 40 per cent of the share capital in the hands of the family. Sofer suggests that it was a family firm in more ways than one. Twenty per cent of the employees had been there more than twenty-five years.

The directors said the new appointment was made necessary by 'modernised and mechanised accounting procedures which they had just introduced with the aid of management consultants'. I do not wish here to go into the rather tortuous details of this case study. The salient facts are that:

1. The leading personnel were all related as kin.
2. They were divided between a younger element who wanted to

change the firm in the direction of economic efficiency and older conservatives.

3. The younger members were themselves divided because they were competing with one another for scarce board places and top managerial jobs.
4. These divisions were concealed by patterns of work that had developed (e.g. buying was a function of a junior clerk in the manufacturing department).
5. The division led to a crisis when a vacancy on the board was about to arise.
6. The crisis was partly resolved by bringing in Sofer as a consultant and allotting responsibility for upsetting changes to him. There had been a previous attempt using management consultants. Once the crisis was past, he was not exactly jettisoned but put into the background.

In Sofer's own words,

Since the events reported in this account, contact with the Davidson company has greatly lessened. We have helped the Davidsons on several occasions with selection and appraisal matters, and in connection with the psychological health of executives. The persons involved have usually been in positions below management committee level, and, by what seems to have been a tacit agreement, neither the company nor we have tried to stimulate more frequent or higher-level meetings. We have not been involved with the board in top-level policy consideration. On their side, they have presumably preferred to continue with the current equilibrium as long as it could be maintained without dismissals, resignations, or overt and manifest damage to the business. In these circumstances there has not been a significant role for the Institute to play. An additional factor reducing the amount of contact might be inferred to be the wish of the new professional managers to show how much they could contribute to effective organizational functioning. And it must have been seen at the Davidson end that we regarded the protracted discussions that were developing with us over management traineeships, training methods, and so on, as diversions from their central needs (additional commercial effort and fuller rationalization of senior management structure), and that we wished to avoid supporting such diversions.

Nevertheless, our contacts with the company have been sufficient to keep the relationship alive, and to carry with them the communication that the facilities of the Institute remain available if these are again found necessary.[25]

Psychiatrists and the law courts

The case of the psychiatrists in the courts is not documented in such detail (but see Wootton's paper on 'The law, the doctor, and the deviant' [1963]). In most judicial procedures there is an element of ambiguity and discretion by which justice is tempered with mercy. Judges, counsel and jury are able simultaneously to uphold the law in the letter and administer it in the spirit. Before the 1957 Homicide Act, in cases of murder, however, judges were left without discretion. Once the facts were proved to the satisfaction of a jury a death sentence was inevitable. Before 1957 in the defence of insanity, and afterwards in the defence of diminished responsibility, psychiatrists came most fully into their own. As Wootton pointed out, they did not have the expected function of deciding what treatment should be given after the facts were established but were asked to pronounce in advance on the responsibility of the accused. In Wootton's trenchant words, 'the doctor (along with everybody else except the Almighty) is not well cast as an authority on responsibility'. If the courts, by use of outside medical experts, can find diminished responsibility, the culprit can be spared, the law still be upheld and yet justice be done.

This was shown most sharply in a case not involving homicide, namely the Pedrini part of the Challenor affair.[26] Riccardo Pedrini was arrested in Soho on the night of 21 September 1962, in company with a number of other men, by Detective-Sergeant Harry Challenor. He was convicted at the Old Bailey in December the same year of various offences, including the possession of an iron bar—an offensive weapon. He was sentenced to seven years' imprisonment. His solicitors advised him that there was no ground for reversing the conviction, but he appealed against sentence to the Court of Criminal Appeal, and his appeal was rejected. His highly respectable, middle-class Italian family did not let the matter drop but appealed to the Home Office to re-consider the case, which it did in May 1963.

On 11 July 1963 Detective-Sergeant Challenor arrested two boys at a demonstration against Queen Frederika of Greece outside Claridge's Hotel. It was subsequently found that half-bricks—offensive weapons—had been planted on these boys. The discovery led to a series of events which culminated in November 1963 in an internal police inquiry into Challenor's behaviour. This was brought to public notice by a television programme in the same month, and shortly afterwards the Court of Criminal Appeal allowed Pedrini and his associates to appeal out of time and granted him legal aid for this purpose.

Before the appeal came up, however, Challenor, who had been languishing in Netherne Psychiatric Hospital in Surrey, was brought from it and charged in connection with the arrests of 11 July 1963. The court of summary jurisdiction in March 1964 committed him to the Old Bailey where, on 4 June in the same year, he was found unfit to plead and returned to psychiatric hospital. Three other police constables associated with him in these events were sentenced to terms of imprisonment. These convictions were followed in July by a further police inquiry and by a public inquiry into Challenor's conduct over an extended period of time. This was held at the end of September. Meanwhile Pedrini's appeal came, once more, in July 1964, to the Court of Criminal Appeal.

It is in fact the function of the Court of Criminal Appeal to rectify specific mistakes or omissions in lower courts. It has not the power itself to try the case again. It can quash convictions on points of law but it cannot question the decisions of juries unless the jury has been misdirected by the judge or unless fresh evidence is available. In July 1964 a recent change in procedure had given the Court power to order a re-trial. I continue the story in Miss Grigg's own words:

It seemed to the judges at first that this was the kind of case in which their new powers ought to be used. But it was a difficult situation. The Home Secretary had not wanted to make a decision on the case and had passed it on to the Court of Criminal Appeal. Could it be the right thing to pass it back to a jury? What did the prosecution think? The prosecution counsel told the Lord Chief Justice that he had been instructed to be 'neutral'. He implied, however, that the Crown was not in favour of re-trial and that the matter should be dealt with finally by the Court of Appeal.

This re-introduced the problem of fresh evidence. The evidence the court felt would be relevant was that relating to Challenor's insanity. Three doctors were called. Two of them said that they were unable to trace the officer's illness any further back than May of 1963. One, however, said that in his opinion Challenor could have been sick in 1962. There was no proof that he *was* insane when the Pedrini group were brought to trial, yet this medical evidence was considered sufficient for their convictions to be quashed. In another case, in different circumstances, the judges might quite properly have decided that such evidence was too flimsy to allow for the release of men who had been found guilty.

This seems to me to be an unusually sharp case in which the kind of psychiatric role I have been discussing is most clearly displayed. It does, however, raise another point which is so obvious that I myself completely overlooked it until my attention was drawn to it by an eminent lawyer. This is, of course, that the position of the jury in the English and American courts is precisely of the kind that I have been describing for scientists, psychiatrists and strangers. Judges are required to take impossible decisions. They must decide who, of equally plausible or implausible litigants, they are to believe, and they must decide within a very short time or else the machinery of justice will come to a standstill. In such a situation the law has recourse to juries whose very qualification is their lack of qualification but who represent the overriding system of the people. Their reasons for their decisions are not merely completely ignored but there are positive injunctions against exploring them. Their existence as groups is totally ephemeral, and when they have carried out their impossible and irrational task they disappear back into the people from which they came, impervious to criticism and too evanescent for revenge.

On the shop floor

Finally, I wish to turn to the realm of industrial sociology, to the shop floor and to the factory described by Lupton and called Jay's. Lupton describes the position of the rate-fixer in the following terms:

> Cyril, the rate-fixer, figured much more prominently in the life of the shop than either Jim or Slim [store-keeper and floor controller respectively]. He was employed in the Planning and Rate-fixing Department, where he spent most of his time getting out requisitions, job instruction sheets, etc., for the section. But he was also responsible for fixing rates for all tasks performed on the section. When new designs were introduced, or modifications were made to old designs, Cyril would time-study the tasks and fix rates for them. And when workers claimed compensation for delays, amendments, repair jobs and the like, Cyril would negotiate the rates with them. Most days of the week Cyril spent between ten minutes and one hour in the section negotiating allowances. From time to time he would spend a whole day, and on occasion two or three days, in the shop making

time studies. Of all the representatives of management who were known to the workers or who had contact with them, Cyril was the one whose activities stimulated their liveliest interest. Cyril had been an erector himself. He had no special qualifications in industrial engineering, but he possessed a good knowledge of transformer erection and was not easily fooled. He was also skilled in argument, and his job offered him opportunities in abundance to exercise his skill.[27]

We see, then, that the rate-fixer is a member of management who has, however, also been an erector and who mixes on equal, if uneasy, terms with other erectors. Lupton describes this in his episode, 'Cyril exposed',[28] and he makes the facts of this clear:

But the rate-fixer, in pursuing the ideal of a rational incentive system, was beset by many social pressures. If he pursued too rigorously his quest to abolish loose times and make all times keen enough to call for an all-out effort, he evoked the displeasure not only of the workers but also of the shop management and supervision. The workers, in their attempt to preserve their area of control over the system, which they felt to be necessary to handle the situation of uneven work flow and the effects of bad design and mismanagement, resisted the attempt to tighten up times. When the technique of cross-booking to cover losses failed, they used the power of the union to prevent effective downward pressure on rates. This procedure involved shop management in long negotiations with the steward, the rate-fixer and the men immediately concerned. Since shop managers and supervisors had to live at close quarters with the men from day to day, they did not like to be constantly bickering about rates. A rate-fixer who was continually 'in the office' was regarded as a bit of a nuisance, interfering with the smooth running of the shop. But the rate-fixer was also dealing with the operatives every day in face-to-face relationships and was subject to pressure to conform to the easy-going informality of workshop relations, of which Episode 4 is a good example. Thus, if the rate-fixer wanted to have a comfortable existence he soon found that this was inconsistent with the single-minded pursuit of his ideal of a rational incentive scheme. These pressures transformed him from a pure representative of management into a kind of arbitrator. He was induced to work in terms of what was acceptable, given existing relationships.[29]

It does not surprise us, after this, that a manager should comment on the dog-in-the-manger attitude of rate-fixers, and add: 'I often find myself in sympathy with the men but in view of the attitude of the rate-fixers in their calculations—they won't shift—I am placed in a difficult position.' Nor should we be surprised that workers criticize rate-fixers rather than higher managers.[30] Workers see themselves (often realistically) and the firm as trying to achieve common goals and as frustrated by the unreasonable behaviour of rate-fixers.

This analysis is necessarily crude. It could be related to insights of Weber on the social origins of charisma and Ramsöy on the relations of systems and sub-systems.[31] I think, however, it does two things. Firstly, it brings out similarities in diverse processes. In each of the cases we have considered there are opposing systems united in a common overall system—men's group and women's group united in the village, Air Staff and Naval Staff united in the Chiefs of Staff, family-oriented and efficiency-oriented united in the firm, strict law maintainers and humanitarians united in the preservation of the legal system, and management and men united in the goal of production. In each case the two sub-systems are able to co-exist because of the activity of roles which exist in the overlapping parts of the system. Such a role is *in* one or both of the sub-systems but in one sense not *of* them. In each case the actions of the incumbents of such roles serve (*a*) to legitimate decisions, (*b*) to accept responsibility for the disturbance of the social order, and (*c*) to represent the interests of the wider, more inclusive system. In each case, I suggest, we add a dimension lacking to a merely commonsense view and achieve a new understanding of the implications of social positions.

Finally, we have begun to explore what I believe to be one of the many ways in which small-scale empirical studies can be treated comparatively without, at the same time, forsaking a dynamic view of the study of process for a more static structuralism. I think this is most important because, as Laslett (1956) and others have pointed out, political large-scale decisions are still of necessity taken in small groups of equals. Despite those philosophers criticized by Schaff in the opening quotation of this paper, the grand concept of responsibility in taking major decisions which settle the fate of the world may in fact always be subordinate to responsibility to the small group of close and equal associates with whom open dispute must be avoided.

Agamemnon submitted to Clytemnestra's cajolements knowing that to do so was wrong. He was not alone in taking the short-term, small-scale view that temporary harmony in the face-to-face group now is cheaply bought at the price of eternal chaos to come.

[1967]

Notes

1 Completed in 1967, this paper was originally read to my colleagues in the Sociology and Social Anthropology seminar in the University of Manchester and owes much to their discussion and comments. It was then presented for the first time at the British Association in Aberdeen on 4 September 1963. Yet another version of it was read at a conference at Caius College, Cambridge, in September 1966 (see Introduction to this book). I am most grateful to all the scholars who attended for the most stimulating discussion. I am especially grateful for specific points to Professor Moses Finley and M. Vernant, who drew my attention to the carpet of Agamemnon, and to Professor Charles Black, who drew my attention to the role of the jury in legal systems. It goes without saying that in this, as in other writings, I have to thank Professor Gluckman for guiding my footsteps towards the consideration of this kind of problem. Professor Thomas Lupton was not present at this particular conference but my use of his material is informed by discussions that he and I had together some years ago when he was on the staff of the Department of Social Anthropology at Manchester University. Readers of other papers at the British Association were Dr Martin Southwold and Professor W. J. M. Mackenzie, to whom I am grateful for many helpful discussions before and since. I am grateful for the generosity of the Wenner-Gren Foundation and of the University of Manchester, which made it possible for me to attend the Cambridge conference at a time when I had already taken up the post of Professor of Sociology at the University of Zambia.

2 Schaff, *A Philosophy of Man* (1963), p. 33.

3 Available in manuscript in 1965, published herein.

4 Frankenberg, 'British communities' (1965) and *Communities in Britain* (1966).

5 Fortes, *The Dynamics of Clanship among the Tallensi* (1945).

6 *A Postscript to 'Science and Government'* (1962).

7 *Science and Government* (1961), p. 59.

8 *Ibid.*, p. 63.

9 *The Strategic Air Offensive against Germany* (1961), p. 319.

10 *Ibid.*, p. 783.

11 *Ibid.*, p. 323.

12 *Ibid.*, p. 324.

13 *Science and Government* (1961), p. 12.

14 Frankenberg, *Village on the Border* (1957), *passim*.

15 Webster and Frankland, *The Strategic Air Offensive against Germany* (1961), p. 310.

16 Webster and Frankland, *The Strategic Air Offensive against Germany* (1961), p. 336.

17 *Science and Government* (1961), p. 36.
18 Webster and Frankland, *The Strategic Air Offensive against Germany* (1961), p. 371.
19 See *ibid*., pp. 373*f*.
20 Snow, *Science and Government* (1961), p. 29.
21 Blackett, *Studies of War* (1962), p. 110.
22 Webster and Frankland, *The Strategic Air Offensive against Germany* (1961), p. 338.
23 *Ibid*., p. 339.
24 *Studies of War* (1962), p. 125.
25 *The Organization from Within* (1961), pp. 39–40.
26 Grigg, *The Challenor Case* (1965).
27 *On the Shop Floor* (1963), p. 124.
28 *Ibid*., p. 148.
29 *Ibid*., p. 151.
30 *Ibid*., p. 165.
31 Gerth and Mills, *From Max Weber* (1948), *passim*; Ramsöy, *Social Groups as Systems and Sub-systems* (1965).

Bibliography

Birkenhead, Lord, *The Prof. in Two Worlds*, London: Collins (1961).
Blackett, P. M. S., *Studies of War*, Edinburgh: Oliver & Boyd (1962).
Christie, A., *The Moving Finger*, London: Collins (1943).
Churchill, W. S., *The Second World War*, vol. III: *The Grand Alliance*, London: Cassell (1950).
Devons, E., *Planning in Practice*, Cambridge: Cambridge University Press (1950).
Fortes, M., *The Dynamics of Clanship among the Tallensi*, Oxford: University Press for the International African Institute (1945).
Frankenberg, R., *Village on the Border*, London: Cohen & West (1957).
— 'British communities: problems of synthesis' *The Social Anthropology of Complex Societies. A.S.A. Monographs* No. 4, London: Tavistock (1965).
— *Communities in Britain*, Harmondsworth: Penguin Books (1966).
Gerth, H. H., and Wright Mills, C. (ed.), *From Max Weber*, London: Routledge & Kegan Paul (1948).
Grigg, M., *The Challenor Case*, Harmondsworth: Penguin Books (1965).
Harrod, R., *The Prof.*, London: Macmillan (1959).
Irving, D., *The Destruction of Dresden*, London: Kimber (1963).
Laslett, P., *Philosophy, Politics and Society*, Oxford: Blackwell (1956).
Lupton, T., *On the Shop Floor*, London: Pergamon (1963).

Ramsöy, Odd, *Social Groups as Systems and Sub-systems*, New York: Free Press (1963).
Schaff, A., *A Philosophy of Man*, London: Lawrence & Wishart (1963).
Snow, C. P., *Science and Government*, London: Oxford University Press (1961).
— *A Postscript to 'Science and Government'*, London: Oxford University Press (1962).
Sofer, C., *The Organisation from Within*, London: Tavistock (1961).
Webster, Sir Charles and Frankland, M., *The Strategic Air Offensive against Germany*, London: HMSO (1961).
Wootton, B., 'The law, the doctor and the deviant', *British Medical Journal*, vol. 2 (27 July 1963), pp. 197–202.

8
Some social contexts of personal violence

Emanuel Marx

Coercion is so common in daily life that it often tends to escape our notice unless it is applied forcefully. I shall discuss some of the more extreme forms of coercion, commonly subsumed under the heading 'violence', as observed in Maaloth,[1] an ordinary small Israeli town. I am in full agreement with Bienen, that 'to treat violence . . . as pathological phenomena does hinder analysis. Yet much of the literature . . . does treat violence as a phenomenon outside of a "normal" social process.'[2] I shall therefore treat various types of violence as normal events, and shall explain them, just like other social facts, within their social context. Many violent acts can be shown to be 'rational' in a Weberian sense, i.e. designed by the actor to achieve a social aim. Others are irrational from the actor's viewpoint because unlikely to succeed; nevertheless they too may be amenable to sociological interpretation. In a comparative examination of my case material I shall try to reach some conclusions about the causes and effects of violence in a complex, highly bureaucratic society.

I

Maaloth is situated in the mountains of western Galilee. It was established in 1956 and almost all its 3,000 inhabitants are immigrants from various parts of Morocco. They were settled there by the Absorption Department[3] immediately upon arrival in Israel. The new immigrants were mostly destitute; among them were many large families as well as many elderly and sickly individuals. Each family was provided with a flat, and for this purpose nuclear families were counted. They were also given some household equipment and essential furniture and some cash to support them during their initial three months in the country. From then on the Absorbtion Department's responsibility to maintain the new immigrants ceased and he had to deal directly with the various bureaucratic agencies running Maaloth, of which the Absorption Department was merely one. Many people found it hard to cope with these agencies and became discouraged and resentful.

Maaloth is a law-abiding community. Its crime statistics for 1963, as prepared by the police, compare favourably with official crime figures for the whole country (see table). In most respects crime rates in Maaloth are relatively low. The numbers of the non-serious violent offences, as shown in the categories 'Assault' and 'Damage to property', are however, rather above the national average. These crime figures may be inflated, because inhabitants have little hesitation about contacting the police. No fewer than fifteen policemen live in the town. They are all stationed outside it, and the nearest police station is two kilometres away. Policemen are officials who do not participate in the running of the town. They are considered to be neighbours and acquaintances to whom one can turn for advice and with whom one can lodge complaints. Inhabitants therefore approach them unhesitatingly, and as equals.

Criminal offences dealt with by the police in Maaloth in 1963, and comparative figures for the whole country*

Type of offence	*Maaloth*† *Cases*	*Rates*§	*Whole country*‡ *Cases*	*Rates*
Assault	22	71	7,191	29
Damage to property	16	52	5,552	23
Housebreaking	6	19	11,705	48
Theft	19	61	28,936	119
Others	9	29	13,864	57
All offences	72	232	72,604	299

* As no serious violent crimes, such as murder and manslaughter, and no sexual offences were committed in Maaloth, figures on these have been omitted from the table.

† Information cited by Police Inspector Shoshani, Nahariah.

‡ Israel Central Bureau of Statistics, *Statistical Abstract of Israel, 1964* (1965), p. 545.

§ As crime rates are calculated per 10,000 of the total population, they do not take into account the size and specific demographic factors of Maaloth. They can therefore only roughly indicate trends.

Maaloth is a town only in the administrative sense. It is so small that it cannot develop the complex division of labour associated with town life. There is very little industry in the town, and there are few businesses and no places of entertainment. But it is not a village, for its inhabitants do not own or cultivate land. Official statistics put the number of unemployed, and employed on relief work, at about half the working population,[4] a figure which still understates reality.[5]

Maaloth is located in an area of relative unemployment. The inhabitants are, however, restricted in their search for work to the area under the jurisdiction of their local labour exchange. They would be entitled to work in another town only by moving there. Such a step is out of the question for most of the inhabitants, who cannot collect the amount of money needed to acquire a flat or rent accommodation and to maintain themselves during a transitional period. This applies especially to large families, which, therefore, are seldom able to move away from Maaloth.

Relief work is supplied by the Ministry of Labour, or by the Jewish National Fund (KKL) acting as its agency. The work mainly goes to men, and only when there is no able-bodied man in the family will a woman be employed. The income of many families is supplemented by grants from the Ministry of Social Welfare, and about half the town's families are on its lists of recipients of aid. The majority of Maaloth's inhabitants thus become entirely dependent on the various administrative agencies supplying them with work and welfare services. The combined income from these services and the additional services supplied gratis are just enough to give people a decent standard of living and provide in addition a modicum of security. While all the industries hitherto established in Maaloth have closed down after a short time, relief work and welfare assistance payments have continued regularly over the years. People realize that, on balance, dependence on the State may be as good as a job in industry and they express this insight in a frequently quoted equation: Welfare and relief work = Isasbest.[6] Economic entrepreneurship is at a disadvantage in these conditions. The local council sees to it that traders and artisans set up only in suitable premises. As the housing authorities did not include enough facilities in their plans and the potential entrepreneurs do not possess the necessary capital to buy them (according to the rules, commercial premises are only to be sold, not to be let), anyone who sets up in business has to do so illegally. One man hawks his wares on the pavement, another sets up a wooden shack next to his house, and all become involved in litigation with the local authority. Only a few have the perseverance to fight it out with the authorities.

Thus many people feel they fare best by staying in regular relief work and supplementing it by welfare assistance. This applies particularly to middle-aged men supporting large families, most of whose children still attend school. In families such as these, relationships are affected by the dependence on bureaucratic agencies: the number of primary relationships is reduced; relationships among even close kinsmen, such as brothers, become dormant and ineffective; even the obligations between parents and children are limited.

The situation is well illustrated by the customs of marriage. As a rule, young people themselves choose their partners for marriage. An engagement is celebrated, at which the bridegroom presents the bride with a set of clothing, mainly bought out of his savings. After the engagement the groom is supposed to work hard and save money so that he can buy furniture and put down the initial payment on a flat. This may take a year or even eighteen months,[7] and during that time he lives and eats with his parents, so that he can save money. But they do not contribute directly to his savings. Only when the bridegroom has collected the necessary amount is the wedding celebrated. After that, his becomes a separate family and neither he nor his parents are expected to support one another. People often stated that 'among us Moroccans [i.e. in Maaloth today] children do not support their parents'. If parents are in need, their children ask the welfare office to support them regularly, and as a rule the office obliges.

The assistance meted out by the bureaucratic agencies is by necessity limited and hedged in by rules and regulations demanding equal treatment for all applicants. Thus the welfare office deals regularly with 340 families and the official of the housing corporation deals with all Maaloth's 620 families. As there are so many people requiring assistance, the officials cannot possibly attend to each case in detail. Most decisions must be made according to formal prescriptions, and only a limited number of decisions are made to fit individual requirements. Special treatment can, however, be obtained by repeated and insistent pleading. Knowledge of this tends to increase people's reliance on assistance and induce them to exert heavy pressure on officials. Sometimes this leads to excesses and threats of violence. I shall discuss such cases below. Under certain conditions, however, men may despair of obtaining official succour.

When this happens, violent marital disputes may ensue. I shall examine several such cases.

Before entering on a detailed examination of violence in Maaloth, some observations on the place of physical coercion in various political systems will be made in the following section. I shall show that 'violence' is a concept peculiar to modern society, and that only here do certain sectors of society hold individual violence to be intrinsically immoral and, partly for that reason, to be essentially irrational. Many simpler societies do not share that attitude. There men may employ various degrees of coercion rationally and with the support of public opinion. Some Stateless societies do not make a clear distinction between non-violent and violent modes of coercion, and even those that do will not consider violence to be immoral or irrational.

II

Not all societies are equally averse to violence. The Nuer of the southern Sudan, for instance, even appear to encourage it. The Nuer nation comprises about 200,000 persons who live, according to Evans-Pritchard, in a state of 'ordered anarchy'.[8] They have evolved neither government nor regular political leadership, and have neither army nor courts of justice. Their patrilineages are, according to the accounts of native informants, corporately organized, but in reality their members live widely dispersed and thus assemble only rarely and under extreme provocation for joint action.

The Nuer's habitat is the flood plains of the White Nile and its tributaries. Natural conditions there constrain them to subsist on a combination of farming, pastoralism and fishing, and to make numerous seasonal moves. When the Nile rises in July and inundates the plain, the Nuer retreat to sandy ridges and small hillocks, scattered over the plain. On each small ridge a number of families, usually connected by kinship and affinity, gather and engage in farming. As the floods subside the villages gradually become deserted. Their inhabitants divide into small clusters of kinsmen herding their cattle and moving their camps in various directions in search of pasture and water. Water supplies dwindle towards the end of the dry season, and the Nuer congregate in large groups around the perennial pools and rivers. There they remain until the beginning of the wet season, when they begin another cycle of movements.

Thus every once in a while the Nuer finds himself in different company. As the extent of the inundation varies from year to year, the Nuer never knows whether in any year he can observe his accustomed cycle of movements and remain with the same sets of people. Nuer claim that they usually live with kinsmen, but not permanently with any one kinsman. They feel free to move all over Nuerland and to attach themselves to any kinsman or affine.[9] Freedom of movement is a fundamental need for the Nuer. In his résumé of Nuer political organization, Gluckman concludes that 'it is therefore essential for these groups to be on some sort of friendly terms with one another if they are to maintain their cattle and themselves alive. These ecological necessities force people to co-operate and this helps to explain how the Nuer can be organized in tribes of 60,000 people or more, without any kind of instituted authority.'[10]

The Nuer must also insure himself against seasonal shortages of food and against violent attacks. Therefore he always lives in a cluster of families. He shares food and co-operates politically with the members of the community he happens to live in, and in particular with those closely related to him.

The Nuer is reported to be fierce and independent and quick to take offence. But he does not lightly employ force to obtain his ends, for he knows that if he indulges in unnecessary violence he will lose the support of his friends, on whom he depends in all his affairs.[11] Yet frequent disputes occur. Some erupt spontaneously. 'It sometimes happens that when dancing parties of different villages duel, their play passes into fighting.'[12] Even two dancers bumping into each other may spark off a dispute. First they exchange angry words and curses, and then they get at each other's throats and blood may be spilt. But violence may also be premeditated. The Nuer explained to the anthropologist that they fight whenever they consider they have been insulted: 'When a man feels that he has suffered an injury there is no authority to whom he can make a complaint, so he at once challenges the man who has wronged him to a duel . . . There is no other way of settling a dispute, and a man's courage is his only immediate protection.'[13] Nuer cite various causes for fighting: disputes about property or rights to pasturage, borrowing objects without asking the owner's permission, adultery, and so on.[13] Evans-Pritchard was also told that 'from their earliest years children are encouraged by their elders to settle all disputes by fighting, and they grow up to regard skill in fighting the most neccessary accomplishment'.[13]

Nevertheless, there is good reason to believe that Nuer will not resort to violence at the slightest provocation in his daily life. 'Within a village,' we are told, 'differences between persons are discussed by the elders of the village and agreement is generally and easily reached . . . Disputes between members of nearby villages . . . can also be settled by agreement . . .'[14] Only where the social and physical distance between the disputing sides is great does it become harder to reach agreement by peaceful means. But even then a Nuer will not lightly fight, as the results may be disastrous. He will do so only if his kin feel that he is in the right,[15] i.e. that he has exhausted every peaceful means of obtaining satisfaction. Thus he gradually enlists the moral support of his kinsmen up to the point where they are prepared to use force in his aid.[16]

It will be seen that the Nuer tries to obtain satisfaction by agreement and persuasion, and only if these gentle means fail will he employ stronger pressures and, in the end, use violence. Violence itself has to the Nuer various degrees: 'Boys fight with spiked bracelets. Men of the same village or camp fight with clubs, for it is a convention that spears must not be used between close neighbours lest one of them be killed . . . When a fight starts between persons of different villages it is with the spear . . . and it cannot be stopped before considerable loss of life has ensued.[17] This is the Nuer's way of saying that there are various degrees of violence, and that one should exercise considerable restraint when fighting closely associated persons.

The Nuer will thus employ various degrees of coercion to achieve his aims. The means of coercion range from verbal persuasion to brute force. If slight pressures do not produce the desired results, he will employ stronger and harsher ones. The Nuer does not distinguish between non-violent and violent means of coercion; there is no point of transition from one to the other. The various pressures constitute so many degrees on a single scale, and he will go as far as the situation requires, always provided that he gains the support of his village or camp. His society, far from objecting to his use of self-help, may insist on his demanding his rights, even if it calls for violence, for only thus can the common values be safeguarded and publicly reasserted.

The approach to violence as a political tool differs fundamentally in societies that are able to activate their corporate groups at all times. Even where these societies lack centralized direction, they discourage individuals from using violence. Whenever a man becomes involved in a situation requiring more than common pressure, his associates intervene and jointly decide on a course of action. The Bedouin of the eastern Negev are a society of this kind.[18] The Israeli authorities rule them indirectly through chiefs chosen by the members of each tribe. At the same time the authorities try to gain control over part of the Bedouin's land, which is legally State domain, and one of the main tasks of Bedouin political organization is to resist restriction of their traditional tenure. The chief is usually a relatively affluent member of the largest land-owning group in the territorial division called 'the tribe'. Although he is formally the representative of government in the tribe, it is in his interest, and in that of the land-owning groups, to circumscribe government surveillance.

Thus these Bedouin maintain their indigenous political organization, in spite of constituting part of a centralized modern State. Within a tribe there is a fundamental cleavage between land-owners, who consider themselves 'real Bedouin', and landless persons (whom the real Bedouin consider to be 'peasants'), who gain a livelihood share-cropping for the land-owners. Both sectors of Bedouin society defend their contrasting interests through a political organization whose basic units are corporate groups composed of one or more clusters of agnates. These clusters of men usually, but not always, claim patrilineal descent from a common patronymic ancestor. Such groups can formally admit new members, but do so only rarely. For the land-owning groups are aligned on a territorial basis, as tribes and groups of tribes, so as to maintain their supremacy over the peasants and to prevent the peasants from forming larger groups and from acquiring control over more land. The peasants occasionally attempt to increase the size and effectiveness of their political groups, whose main task is to resist further pressure, but Bedouin usually prevent this effectively.

Members of a group also act jointly when the interests of one among their number have been infringed. It can be seen that the agnatic groups in Bedouin society serve numerous ends. It cannot always be clear to members when they ought to mobilize, and especially are they uncertain under which circumstances they should extend help to an individual engaged in a private dispute. A group must thus settle on a predetermined cue for its activation. It has to agree at which point a dispute should be considered serious enough to oblige the group to take over. Bedouin draw the line at the point where blood is spilt. A dispute which has reached that stage is considered a 'blood dispute' and concerns the corporate group. This line is not drawn in arbitrary fashion. It is connected to the ideology of corporate organization: membership of the group is defined in terms of consanguinity, and thus the conditions for the mobilization can be defined on the same principle. The group fights for its blood. When Bedouin describe the group as composed of those who 'contribute to the payment of blood' (*ḥaṭṭin qirsh al-damm*) they refer to these two aspects of their union of blood.

In practice the group interprets the meaning of 'blood' rather liberally; when disputants come to blows, this automatically constitutes a case of blood, and the corporate group goes into action. When such a dispute comes up for settlement the negotiators try to establish that blood has been spilled even if the contention is very doubtful. This can best be seen in a border-line case, such as the following. In the 1961 parliamentary elections, members of two corporate groups came to blows at a polling station.[19] The group who came out worst in the scuffle claimed the blood of one of its men. A month later, when negotiations had reached the stage of direct confrontation of the sides to the dispute, the chief of a tribe not involved in the case, who had negotiated the agreement, was asked to assess the severity of the injury. The elders of the claimant's group pointed out the exact spot on his cheek where he had sustained injury. The assessor was unable to find any trace of it; it could have only been a superficial abrasion or cut. But in order to fix the indemnity and to settle the case he pretended to see the scar. While the group initiated joint action as soon as its members exchanged blows, in the settlement of the dispute the spilling of blood was brought in so that the factual situation should be in accord with the tenets of coporate organization.

The parties to the dispute reiterated, incidentally, the precise point at which a group is to take over from a member in a dispute. The boundary was staked at the point where, in Western cultural idiom, violence begins. The distinction between non-violent and violent action is, then, the almost arbitrary outcome of an organizational principle.

Bedouin corporate organization protects the individual from violence and, if a violent dispute has erupted, localizes its effects and settles it peacefully. As soon as a fight breaks out, a machinery of negotiation is set in motion: third parties interpose their 'face' (*wijh*) and arrange for a truce (*ʿaṭwah*). Then a notable acceptable to both sides takes over negotiations and carries communications from one to the other until direct relationships can be re-established and a formal reconciliation (*ṣulḥah*) be staged. Bedouin know and admit that corporate organization not only works towards settlement of disputes, but also engenders violence and perpetuates disputes. The local concentration of agnates is not only very reassuring to Bedouin:[20] but it also often tempts individual members to apply more than the required amount of pressure.

A man knows that, in the event of a 'spontaneous' quarrel, all the available members of the corporate group will rush to his aid. Therefore when he exploits a momentary numerical advantage over his opponent a man may well end up by embroiling his whole group in a blood dispute. The group will take up the dispute, however unwillingly, because refusal would sap its foundations, for it can only function while all its members adhere faithfully to its ideology. On the other hand, in the name of this same ideology, collective pressure will often be put on an individual to pursue personal matters that fall within the corporate group's competence, so that it can take action. This is particularly true for land-owning groups, which put considerable pressure on members to avenge real or supposed affronts.

In Bedouin society, then, corporate groups tend to intervene in matters which, on their accepted definition, involve bloodshed. Although one of the group's *raisons d'être* is to localize and settle disputes, it does not shrink from the use of violence. It pre-empts for itself violent action, but does not voice any moral objections to individual violence. The individual has a right to use violence in self-help, and it is the group's duty to lend him its full support. Accordingly, in Bedouin usage an authorised application of physical force has no opprobrium attached to it.

In the modern State the rulers assume the exclusive right to use organized force.[21] It is vested in bureaucratic organizations specializing in the application of force, such as armies and police forces, which are directed by the rulers. Governments do not lightly delegate authority to such agencies. There always lurks a fear that some of their constituent groups will get out of hand or will even arrogate authority to themselves. To reduce this risk military organizations always stress a strict hierarchy, a chain of command culminating in the holders of authority, and their members are trained to discipline and blind obedience by such means as uniforms and drills, deference to formal insignia of rank, and drastic penalties. Independent thought is discouraged. Other administrative agencies are, just like ordinary citizens, legally entitled to use force only in self-defence. When such situations arise, however, they tend to call in the police, to be legally on the safe side. In other conditions, administrative agencies cannot employ force themselves[22] and cannot even use police forces unless authorized by a law court to do so. This constraint applies to a certain extent even to police forces; only in specific situations may they initiate the use of force, in others they respond to demands by the public and the courts. This means that officials cannot usually respond directly and immediately when faced with strong pressures from clients. The State then delegates authority to its officials to act in a prescribed fashion, but a determined client can bring such heavy pressure to bear on officials as to obtain decisions in his favour and even to bend regulations. The State cannot effectively protect officials against violence; it can mainly impress on citizens the idea that violence is immoral and it can impose harsh penalties on offenders in order to deter others.

Rulers jealously guard their prerogative, and look askance at the use of force outside their own organizations. Not only physical force, but even the threat of it, is proscribed. Rulers are particularly sensitive to unauthorized use of force when it is directed against their representatives, less so to the use of force between private individuals, especially when not in public. The distinction is shown in the manner various cases are dealt with in a modern State like Israel: when the police are called in to handle a fight between spouses they hardly ever take legal action. Disputes between neighbours[23] or between dealers and customers are usually settled out of court or, in the latter case, as civil claims.

The modern State also defines legally which actions are violent and thus infringe its monopoly of power: '. . . in modern conditions . . . only certain political associations, designated as "States", may delegate to any other associations the exercise of "legitimate" physical coercion. For the exercise and threat of this coercion . . . a system of casuistic regulations is devised, to which "legitimacy" is attributed.'[24] That the State should specify the boundary between non-violent and permissible actions and forbidden, violent ones is often considered so self-evident that violence may be roundly defined as the illegal employment of methods of physical coercion.[25]

The statutes distinguish between two varieties of persuasion and usually place the boundary at the point where a 'breach of the peace' occurs, that is, where threats intermingle with physical coercion. Disputes that fall on one side of the boundary are dealt with by civil law and are thought to concern mainly the individuals directly involved, while those falling on the other side are criminal and call for intervention and, if necessary, punishment by the State. Physical coercion of any kind constitutes violence in the legal sense. It is significant that the boundary is placed at precisely this point. Verbal persuasion, even where it consists of dire threats, presupposes a specific relationship between the persons concerned. Physical coercion, however, is a universal means of persuasion. It is equally applicable to every individual and dispenses with the coerced person's consent. It is thus eminently suited to the requirements of rulers who must sway masses. This is particularly true for the modern State, with its cultural diversity. Here not every argument is accepted and understood by members of every sector in the population and, for some citizens, only the knowledge that the State's regulations are backed by physical force ensures compliance. The modern State, then, does not usually intervene when a person 'kills' another's reputation, or 'violates' agreements, although the semantic usage indicates the seriousness of such acts. But the State takes a grave view of violence, and when directed against its representatives even threats of violence are an offence.

The obverse of the State's monopolization of force is the aversion to its use inculcated in its citizens. In the home, at school and in play, violence is regarded as morally wrong. These attitudes are elaborated in associations for prevention of cruelty to children or animals. Sorel has trenchantly summarized one outcome of this training: ' . . . Middle-class cowardice . . . consists in always surrendering before the threat of violence.'[26] His dictum also draws attention to the fact that not all strata of society fear violence. It is likely that those most intimately exposed to the State's schools and oher services have a better chance to acquire a distaste for violence. These, then, are the people who consider individual violence as immoral, as something to be shunned.

Although States discourage violence and parts of the population consider it as immoral, some people will always resort to it. The likelihood of violence increases in certain conditions; some of these are found in Maaloth and will be discussed presently.

III

Various instances of violent behaviour observed in Maaloth can now be examined in the light of the foregoing discussion. These instances fall into two distinct categories: while some illustrate the premeditated, rational use of violence, others appear to be spontaneous, irrational outbursts, at first sight hardly amenable to sociological explanation.

First, there are threats of violence employed against local officials, by persons possessing certain social characteristics, which can be defined as rational. They are used as means to obtain concessions from bureaucratic agencies. Such threats may occasionally lead to physical violence but may even then be efficacious. Second, there occur instances of husbands beating their wives, or of women beating their husbands, which could be considered as irrational outbursts. Assaults by drunken persons, either on members of their families, or on others, might also be irrational. For these violent acts achieve no social aim, and the perpetrators themselves never claim that.

I shall argue, firstly, that the acts of violence observed in Maaloth are intimately related to prevailing local conditions. Secondly, I shall attempt a sociological interpretation of these acts of violence. And thirdly, I shall show that some of the seemingly irrational violence contains rational elements.

It is in the nature of violence that it occurs sporadically. It often strikes without visible warning. Therefore it can only rarely be observed at close range,[27] and then the observer may not be in a proper state of mind to stand aside and note all the details of the case. I shall therefore in each case indicate the sources of my information, whether it be personal observation or accounts obtained from direct participants. I tried to talk to the various persons involved in a case as soon as possible after it occurred. My argument is founded on a limited number of such cases. It does not depend on statistical regularities, but on the detailed analysis of each case within its social context and on the comparative study of the variations found from case to case.

Coser has pointed out that violence can become a means to attain goals in modern society when alternative avenues of achievement are barred: '. . . Certain categories of persons may find themselves in structural positions which effectively prevent them from utilizing not only legitimate channels of opportunity but criminal and illegitimate channels as well . . . when all such channels are barred, violence may offer alternative roads of achievement.'[28] In Maaloth most of the roads of achievement lead through officials, whose limited resources must be distributed among a large clientele according to defined rules. Each of the officials represents his particular department to the local inhabitants. He works in isolation from departmental colleagues; and as long as routine business is involved he has only limited contact with his direct superior, whose offices are located in other towns, such as Nahariah, Acre or Haifa. Within his competence he is free, and obliged, to make independent decisions, and will not refer them to colleagues. Clients requiring such routine services are often aware of the situation, and may feel that threats and violence are the only effective way to obtain preferential treatment from the local officials. Others may be ignorant of the hierarchical structure of the organization concerned, and therefore try all possible means of persuasion on their local official rather than turn to his superiors. These aspects of officialdom may be conducive to violence.

Immigrants coming from territories where the State has not completely taken over police functions may consider violence to be a legitimate means of gaining one's ends. Many of the inhabitants of Maaloth derive from rural areas of Morocco, where public security remained precarious even during the French protectorate (1912–56). In the mountainous, predominantly Berber-speaking regions, in particular, the central government only in recent years succeeded in establishing a firm hold.[29] In that environment, local corporate groups based on descent and ethnicity played an important part in maintaining public order. Immigrants from such areas were accustomed to help themselves and do not now disdain to use violence, for they have remained relatively isolated from other sectors of the population. Many of them do not fully realize how officials of a modern State look at the matter, as is evidenced by cases to be discussed below.

During the last decades many Moroccan Jews migrated from the mountains to lower-lying areas, and from villages to towns and thence to the larger cities. While thus enjoying the fruits of firmer government rule, many of these people were so preoccupied with the struggle to take roots in their new environment that they did not manage to absorb the norms associated with bureaucratic rule.[30]

I do not wish to assert that the inhabitants of Maaloth reveal violent propensities, but only that owing to their cultural background they may have fewer reservations against recourse to violence in personal relationships than people in whom norms of non-violence have been inculcated since early childhood.

This cultural background to violence in Maaloth can be summed up as follows. Violence may be employed in relationships with distant persons, when required, and against one's dependants, but not against other close kin and friends. The literature on Jewish family life in Morocco makes no mention of violence between spouses and other kin;[31] it is therefore likely that there was very little of it. Children were, however, punished physically by both parents and by teachers. In Maaloth the situation is similar. When spouses quarrel they raise their voices and exchange accusations and abusive language. Physical assault is rare, and when it does occur the victim is just as likely to be the husband as the wife. Children are still punished physically for even minor misdemeanours, sometimes with a strap or cane. When a child ignores the lesson he may be given a harsh reminder, a heated kitchen knife pressed against part of his body.

People with this cultural background may reluctantly, but rationally, resort to violence after peaceful means have failed to obtain concessions from one or the other of the bureaucratic agencies that run their lives. A commission set up by the Ministry of Social Welfare to enquire into the frequent violent assaults on its officials stated that 'most manifestations of violent behaviour in the [Welfare] bureaux have taken place in [development and immigrant] townships.'[32]

A fair proportion of the violent crimes reported to the police in Maaloth are assaults on local officials. The following examples will provide the material for an analysis.

Case 1. The widow who wanted to change her flat

Mrs Shuqrun's[33] husband died two years ago. Her son has done well for a Maaloth lad, and holds a secure government job. He is still unmarried, and lives with his mother and maintains her. Several daughters are married or work outside Maaloth. For over a year Mrs Shuqrun has tried to obtain a more comfortable flat, and the local representative of Amidar, the national housing corporation, landlord of practically all the real estate in Maaloth, had regularly refused her request, for according to the rules she was not entitled to better housing. One morning she entered the office and calmly told the official: 'I shall not beat you, I shall not overturn your desk, I shall just stay with you until you give me a good flat,' and proceeded to stage a sit-in. Squatting on the floor, she led a long and inconclusive discussion with the official, in which she stated her conviction that he had it in his power to procure another flat for her, while he insisted he was just an employee who carried out his instructions. Eventually he was able to turn the matter into a joke and, for the time being, persuaded her to leave the office.

Another inhabitant of Maaloth, aged thirty-five, is regularly employed at a Nahariah factory and thus provides reasonably well for his wife and four children. When his efforts to obtain a larger flat for his family proved unsuccessful he decided on a more threatening approach: he told the housing corporation's official that he was about to smash his skull, and raised a chair high over his head. Had the official made a counter-move he would almost certainly have brought the chair down on his head. The official did not budge and talked soothingly to him.

An official of the labour exchange stated that parents of unemployed youths tried on several occasions to break chairs over his head, and he added that 'it is especially hard to find suitable work for youths between fourteen and eighteen. About fifty boys have been registering for many months and there is no likelihood that jobs will become available.'

In these and in similar cases the attackers were people whose problems, they believed, could be solved. They had all tried to gain their ends by long and weary negotiations with officials until at last they became convinced that only violence could shake the officials. This was 'common knowledge' in Maaloth. Even a very gentle and polite woman waiting to see the mayor about a job maintained that 'here you can only achieve things by force or by patronage'. As she had none of the latter, she would create a row in the mayor's office. An angry man waiting to see the mayor about an increase in his welfare assistance spoke in plain terms: 'If you don't beat him up, you get no response, he just sends you away.'

Violence was in these cases not only a desperate attempt to attract the attention of an official where no other means were available, it was also an assertion of independence within the almost total dependence on officials. For once, people permitted themselves to defy officials on whom they depended for various benefits, and they stood a good chance of losing those benefits in future. This aspect of their assault was underlined by the fact that people so frequently employed chairs as weapons. One can, of course, attribute this to the availability of chairs in offices and to their handiness as weapons. In some of the premeditated attacks, however, assailants planned beforehand to use chairs. Chairs may thus have a special significance for them, and it is likely that the attackers associate chairs with officialdom and what it stands for in their minds: authority, smugness and callousness. To them, the official's chief preoccupation seems to be to remain secure in his office, and not to care about his clients or his duties. People often said, 'All the officials care for are their chairs.'[34] Fighting the official with a chair, then, signifies an attack on his bureaucratic status and practices.

Not just anybody can defy and try to coerce the officials. Men were often in such straitened circumstances that they were in no position to gamble on the benefits bestowed by the officials. Individuals who attacked officials were usually not quite destitute, and a few examples of the kinds of demand they made will show this: shop licences, permanent jobs, better flats, or transfer to other places.[35] They could take the risk attending such a course of action: they hoped to gain but could also afford to lose.[36]

My cases had another characteristic in common: people who cling so tenaciously to their local officials, and hope, by exerting various degrees of pressure on them, to make them go beyond their competence, are apparently ignorant of the nature of bureaucratic organizations. They do not know how competences are hierarchically distributed among various officials, for none of them made efforts to see the immediate superiors of the local officials. When they did appeal to higher authority they addressed letters to the President of the State, the Prime Minister, or the Minister concerned. They hoped to circumvent official red tape in this manner, chiefly because they did not know to whom, or how and where, to apply. This ignorance reduces a man's chance to approach the right officials and utilize the proper procedure, as well as his possibilities of exercising verbal persuasion. Accordingly, he soon reaches the stage where he considers violent action necessary. In this context, violence is to be thought of as an effective but risky means to achieve an end.

This ignorance may be due to lack of information or of communicative devices. It is often compounded of a limited acquaintance with the language ('All the officials at the main office speak Yiddish' is how one man put this point, quite contrary to fact. He implied that the officials were speaking a language he did not understand properly, and that they were ethnically different, so that it was difficult for him to communicate with them); limited previous experience in dealing with bureaucratic organizations and practices; and officials' withholding information pertaining to the clients' rights and to proper procedures (frequently their instructions were to withhold information).[37]

The assaults on officials rarely involved serious physical violence. The assailants generally merely swore and threatened violence and occasionally indulged in violent gestures like lifting a chair. Only rarely did they smash office furniture, overturn the official's desk, grasp his arm or slap his face. In the cases recorded only one of the officials attacked suffered physical damage. The assaults certainly constituted crimes in a legal sense, but they were not really violent to an objective observer. That assailants generally stopped short of physical violence, contrary to the uncontrollable outbursts of violence in the family disputes subsequently discussed, once more confirms that they employed violence rationally.

Assaults on officials did not usually yield immediate gains, where the satisfaction of the demands required prolonged procedures, such as change of flats, transfer to other towns (with retention of immigrants' privileges) or increases in social welfare grants. They were more effective where the benefit was minimal or could be granted on the spot and without complex procedures, such as employment chits. Here the official is more inclined to give in, as the issue of such a document is not likely to cause him embarrassment. All officials were keenly aware of the constant threat of violence hanging over their heads. One of them frankly admitted to me that he 'refused petitions in certain matters, except when faced with the threat of violence'. Some of these matters, it turned out, were within his own competence. In certain matters he had been instructed 'to remain adamant', so that he could act only if considerable pressure was brought to bear on him. The fact that threats of violence sometimes led to success confirmed the inhabitants of Maaloth in their belief that one could achieve results by violence.

Furthermore, the potential assailant knew from precedent that courts were lenient, so that even if he became involved with the law his risk of being sent to prison was negligible. Amir reports that out of 151 persons taken to court for violent behaviour in social welfare offices between 1960 and 1965, 'only forty-six, or thirty-one per cent, were so sentenced that actual punishment was involved. In twenty-six cases the sentence consisted of conditional arrest; fines —ten cases. In seven cases the accused was put under probation; only in two of the cases the accused were sentenced to imprisonment, and in one case only was hospitalization ordered.'[38] If there is a good chance of success and the results of failure are known to be tolerable, then it is only reasonable for people to use violence as a last resort.

Our analysis indicates that there are social environments conducive to particular kinds of violence. In Maaloth the heavy dependence of so many inhabitants on various bureaucratic agencies often creates competition among them for better deals. People who fail to achieve their ends by the use of moderate pressures may choose violence, or threats of violence, as efficacious but risky means to obtain results. There exist objective factors determining how soon a person will feel that he has to step up pressures, and how far he can go safely. Lack of patronage, limited knowledge of bureaucratic procedure, or difficulties in communication, were some of the factors leading to increased pressures. If he retains some freedom to manœuvre— for instance, if he can shoulder the risk of losing in a violent encounter with the official who represents the obstacle—a person can employ violence rationally. However, some people may be in such a precarious financial situation and be so isolated socially that they cannot take the risk involved in such rebellious behaviour against the official. In these circumstances they are likely, by a process of displacement, to become violent towards persons most closely connected with them.[39] Such violence holds no chance of a way out of the impasse, and thus constitutes irrational behaviour.

At this stage I should like to stress that this analysis is not psychological. It does not explain people's behaviour in terms of their personalities, their thoughts and feelings, and it does not consider violence due to personality disorders.

Even the seemingly irrational violent acts to be discussed below are determined by the social structure and contain elements of rationality. Violence was committed by people endowed with widely varying personalities, some excitable and some quiet and subdued, some quick-witted and some slow. Personality could be just one of the factors in a complex situation. It might conceivably be one of the factors determining how soon violence would erupt. People acted violently because a confluence of circumstances created an impasse for them, and these conditions also determined whom they would assault.

In more favourable conditions, then, the violent persons discussed here could become peaceful and sober citizens. This will become clearer in the following section, which will examine cases of violence not directed against officials.

IV

The following cases will concern 'irrational' violence, as actions which did not contribute to a desired end. I shall try to find out which social factors force some people to refrain from employing strong pressures against officials where others would use them, and why these pressures are deflected onto members of their immediate families.

The following case illustrates the process involved in a simple everyday occurrence.

Case 2. The stubborn child

A work-weary mother accompanied her little girl on her first day at school. The girl was afraid of the unaccustomed surroundings and begged her mother not to leave her alone. The mother reproached the child and tried to persuade her to stay with her age-mates. The harder she pressed, the more frightened the girl grew, till at last she burst into tears. The embarrassed mother then lost her temper and, in the presence of other parents and children, slapped the child furiously on her face and body. When another woman tried gently to restrain her she cried angrily, 'The girl is mine; I can do with her as I please.'

The mother had left several small children at home without proper supervision when she took her daughter to school. She probably expected to return home within a few minutes. Now the girl delayed her, and all her reproaches only intensified her fears. Nor could she take the girl home, for had not she herself brought her to school and thus publicly acknowledged that she wished her to attend? The mother found herself in an impasse, and in her rage she struck the child.

Her remark aptly expresses her predicament: the child was undeniably and irrevocably hers and she was responsible for it whether she liked it or not. Society expected her to make the child stay at school, but she could neither make her see reason nor had the time to stay on with her. If she could not make the girl do as she wished, at least she could do with her as she pleased. The beating did not make the child more compliant; only when a teacher talked soothingly to her and introduced her to her class-mates did she gradually calm down.

The mother's violent reaction did, in this case, solve the problem in an indirect, non-rational fashion. It communicated her despair to the public and thus constituted an apparently unintended appeal for help. The other parents did not intervene even then, and only the teacher felt duty bound to attend to the child. The teacher sought primarily to put an end to the child's maltreatment, but perhaps she realized vaguely that she was also helping the mother out of her difficulty. I would therefore hesitate to assert that there was not, after all, a trace of rationality in the mother's seemingly irrational, violent outburst. Perhaps she hoped that the bystanders would understand her plight and help to alter the situation. Though this be irrational behaviour, 'yet there is method in't'.

There are affinities between this case and that of the Andaman Islander, who in a quarrel 'may vent his ill-temper by destroying any property he can lay his hands on, including not only that of his enemy, but also that of other persons and even his own'.[40] He forces an indifferent public to take up his dispute, by antagonizing it if need be. By destroying his own property as well he indicates to his fellows that he is one with them. He has reached an impasse, reacts irrationally to it, yet appears at the same time to appeal for public help. His behaviour thus exhibits 'secondary rationality'.

The incident described above could have happened anywhere, and not just in Maaloth. Clashes between obligations occur in any society, and thwarted individuals express their exasperation often in a fashion approved or admitted by their culture, and sometimes in a form that is considered extreme. Although brought about by various factors affecting social life in Maaloth, the incident was the outcome of a haphazard, momentary and unique combination of circumstances. It was unlikely that the persons involved would find themselves in the same predicament another time. There may, however, occur outbreaks of violence caused by a combination of relatively constant structural factors. People may suffer permanent (and relative) deprivations which in themselves are hard to bear. Then only a slight additional difficulty is required to create an impasse and provoke a violent reaction. In such cases, violence can be expected to recur at frequent intervals. I shall now examine several cases of this kind. It will be my task not only to point out the structural discrepancies giving rise to violence, but also to examine which circumstances spark off the outbursts.

Case 3. The Ederi family dispute

Mr Ederi, a gentle, soft-spoken man, is the father of nine minor children, ranging in age from one to thirteen years. Since his arrival in Maaloth seven years ago he has only occasionally been employed in light part-time work as a watchman. He suffered pains in his legs, especially in cold wet weather, and claimed that he was not strong enough for relief work in forestry. He attended at the welfare office and the local council office very frequently and there tried to obtain various concessions and benefits. Mostly he was fobbed off with promises, but here and there he also succeeded in getting some money. This was on top of his monthly subvention from the welfare office. In addition, his wife held a regular part-time job charring for the local council. The family thus had a small and stable income, but it worked on a very tight budget; there was no margin for unforeseen expenses. The family also ran up debts with a local grocer and a haberdasher, and from time to time, when the sums owed had reached a dangerous level, the merchants threatened to stop their credit. On such occasions there was little Mr Ederi could do. There were no kinsmen or friends who would loan money to tide him over the difficult period, for most families were in a similar situation. They all looked to the State's agencies for help. Mr Ederi knew that he obtained all the aid to which he was entitled and that another visit to the welfare office or the mayor would not help him any more. At the same time, he was expected by the community—and this included the social worker—to dress and feed his children and to see that they attended school. When things became too much for him, Mr Ederi would beat his wife cruelly.

One such assault was precipitated when a shopkeeper requested Mr Ederi to settle a debt and he found out that his wife had paid off much less of it than he had thought. He ran home and accused his wife of wasting money. Without waiting for her reply, he pushed his flat palm against her face and bent back her head, a very insulting gesture in Moroccan cultural idiom. In rising anger, he then banged her head against the wall. Finally he picked up a cane and blindly lashed out at her till she ran out of the house, blood oozing from the back of her head. It never occurred to Mrs Ederi to hit back at her husband, and her children acted as impartial bystanders. One son informed me, in a matter-of-fact way and without any signs of distress, that his father had just hit his mother.

At that time Mrs Ederi suffered pains in her legs and found it very hard to run a large household and keep her job as well. She was near exhaustion and wished to give up her job. In these circumstances her husband became doubly anxious when he learned of the outstanding debt. While she had her wounds dressed, Mrs Ederi muttered under her breath, 'What he wants is that I go out [to work], so that he can stay at home and attend to the children.' She realized, then, that her husband's concern was not this particular debt, but the prospect of being unable to provide the family's minimum requirements in the near future.

Mrs Ederi was inured to such scenes, and told me that only the week before her husband had cruelly beaten her. But she was going to do something about it: 'I shall tell the Rabbi about this bastard and ask him to send him a harsh letter.'

This very mild reaction to such cruel treatment is founded on Mrs Ederi's realistic appraisal of her position: she has no relatives or friends who would take sides against her husband (and the following case will further illustrate this point). Were her marriage to break up, she could not count on the support of the welfare officials, who would find themselves saddled with so many children. Other families had tried this way out, and in despair had deposited their children at the welfare office or at the local council. In each such case the police had been called in and the parents warned that they would be charged with desertion of their children. And after more or less prolonged discussions they had always returned home with their offspring and hardly any improvement in their condition. In this case such a gesture was out of the question, as Mrs Ederi was herself employed by the local council and could not afford to incur the displeasure of its officials.

The spouses, then, are tightly bound to each other, and in the last resort they alone carry all the worries and responsibility for their children. There is no avenue of escape for either of them.

I know of no divorces among the large families in Maaloth. Each deterioration in their situation once more brings home to the spouses their irksome mutual dependence. As the husband is usually considered the provider, his wife can make demands on him, and, while he feels the full impact of the situation, he cannot rid himself of responsibility. There is no way out of the snare in which he is caught, and one way to express his helplessness is to resort to violence. As his wife is one of the causes of the dilemma (both as child-bearer and as spender of household money), as she is the person nearest to him; as, furthermore, the crisis is often precipitated by her reproaches, it is not surprising that she is the obvious victim of the attack. The wife usually submits meekly, and does not even attempt to escape from the situation. She knows there is neither help nor remedy for it.

The Ederis did not appeal to the public for help. The assault took place in the privacy of their home, and when Mrs Ederi escaped into the street her husband made no attempt to follow her. Although wounded, she did not approach neighbours for aid and while she stood helplessly in front of the house no crowd collected around her. There was no point in appealing to a public with whom the Ederis had no intimate ties. Outside their immediate family they had no kin, friends or other primary relationships. In their case irrational violence held out no hope of relief.

There is something very significant about the spouses' behaviour during the assaults in this and in other cases observed: they begin with reproaches, threats and curses, which then turn into physical attack. The assailant becomes more and more incensed as he (or she) continues to belabour the victim, until there seems no limit to his fury. Only physical exhaustion or a dramatic turn of events, such as profuse bleeding of the victim or the appearance of strangers on the scene, can stop the assault.

It appears as if the violent behaviour is accompanied by a constant awareness that it does not provide a way out of the impasse. Thus each violent act only demonstrates to its perpetrator more clearly his desperate position, and only serves to increase his annoyance, in turn impelling him to react even more violently. The assailant is often so absorbed in the circular processes intensifying his (or her) own helplessness that he little heeds the victim's reaction, and even the victim's submissiveness does not make the assailant relent.

In the Ederi case, violence was the outcome of structured and relatively static conditions. It is therefore a repetitive event, and this was admitted by the victim. The children too took it for granted that their father would from time to time beat up their mother. The Ederi family was not unique in this respect, for other instances were observed in several impoverished large families. The following two examples show similar patterns.

Case 4. The Ben-Harush family dispute

On Mr Ben-Harush's family quarrel I was able to obtain information from both husband and wife, which enables me to amplify some of the observations made on the preceding case. Mr and Mrs Ben-Harush, who now have eleven children, were married in their small native town in Morocco. Their first three years in Israel were spent in a communal settlement. When Mrs Ben-Harush's brother came to Maaloth seven years ago, the family decided to join him there. Considering the conditions in Maaloth, Mr Ben-Harush did not do badly. He maintained close contact with the various bureaucratic agencies active in Maaloth, always on the alert for any concession or favour to be gained. He employed every conventional and unconventional means to gain his ends, including threats, feigned epileptic seizures, and activities for political parties. On at least one occasion he abandoned his children in the welfare office in protest against what he considered insufficient assistance. He succeeded in capturing one of the major prizes in this game: in 1962 he was given one of the first six shops built in Maaloth, in preference to many competitors. Yet he continued his relief work and was also retained on the rolls of the welfare office. In spite of his several sources of income, which yielded an average of £I 600–700 a month, Mr Ben-Harush found it hard to make ends meet. Any unexpected expenditure could upset the balance. None of his children was old enough to work.

The Ben-Harush family lived frugally. Only on the Sabbath were some delicacies served at their table. This restraint was dropped twice a year; on new year's eve and Passover every member of the family received new clothes, and large sums were spent on food. In this the Ben-Harush acted like most other families in Maaloth, who found relief from the penury and monotony of daily life by spending liberally on these two major holidays of the year and also on the great days of their life: circumcision feasts, coming-of-age ceremonies, and weddings. Early in 1966, however, Mr Ben-Harush was very apprehensive about the approaching Passover. Owing to an accident he had for several months not gone on relief work, and his business had also suffered. And then several things happened that made him feel as if the whole world was combining against him: his wife had just told him that she was again pregnant; his fractured leg hurt and he feared that the doctors would not soon relieve him of his plaster cast (a fear that proved later to be well founded); and on Friday the grocer had refused to sell his wife provisions for the Sabbath because they already owed more than £I 600. His wife then demanded money from him, the breadwinner, but he could not satisfy her demand. He stalked out of the house and apparently remained overnight in his shop.

He explained later how he felt that night: 'A man is like a river-bed; sometimes it is dry and sometimes it carries water. I have all the time provided for the family, and now that I am dry because of my bad leg, the wife behaves as if I had never provided for the family.'

When he returned home the following morning, his wife continued nagging him for money and they began to quarrel; then he lost his temper, and beat her over the head with his crutch, the attribute of his helplessness. Blood streamed profusely out of a deep cut.

The children did not take sides in the quarrel, A sister of Mrs Ben-Harush and her husband from the city were staying with the family at the time as their guests; they did not intervene in any way. When she sustained the wound Mrs Ben-Harush told her eldest daughter to call her brother, who lives across the street. The brother would not come to her aid, and his wife explained later on that 'he did not want to interfere, for after the couple make it up, then he remains outside'; she meant that they would bear him a grudge if he dared come between them. Still, she found the courage to rush to her sister-in-law's aid, and had her taken to hospital.

The reluctance of Mrs Ben-Harush's brother to interfere was prompted by previous experience. He knew there had been family disputes before that and that the couple had every time patched up their quarrel. The spouses were so mutually dependent, and had so little support from kin and friends, and such a heavy burden to carry, that a dispute was extremely unlikely to endanger their marriage. This was clear to the spouses themselves, and Mr Ben-Harush explained to me a few days later that 'with a family of twelve children you are tied with chains to your wife. You cannot leave her. You quarrel and you make it up.'

Here I must briefly touch on the nature of the mutual dependence of the spouses. Their relative isolation from kinsmen and friends keeps them at each other's mercy and at the same time reduces some social pressures supporting the marriage. But it also brings to the fore other pressures, and families rarely break up. The chances of a husband getting away with desertion are very slim, as it is hard to maintain anonymity in a small country like Israel, whose borders, furthermore, are closed. Also, the bureaucratic agencies on whom people depend in so many ways—for work, housing, welfare and medical aid—require their clients to document their identity. A Maaloth man who left his family of seven after a domestic quarrel found that out to his discomfiture, and after drifting about for several months he preferred to return to his family. Formal separation would be even harder to obtain, as legal procedures are long-drawn-out[41] and involve considerable expenditure. The welfare authorities would refrain from helping the spouses to obtain a divorce, as in all likelihood this would leave those authorities responsible for the maintenance of the minor children.

All these are minor considerations when compared with the fundamental importance of the children. For while children are the immediate cause of the family's troubles, they also constitute a valuable asset. If at the moment they are only an expense, the parents hope that they will later on help to supplement the family's income and gradually become its main support. That this calculation is incorrect does not alter the position. Adolescents contribute to their parents' budget only up to the time they decide to get married. From then on they save up for their own wedding and household equipment, and do not expect their parents to contribute a major share. Even if the parents realize this—and apparently many of them do not—it will not reduce the value they put on children. Children are not just a financial asset but also a support in any eventuality. If the State's welfare services should cease one day to provide for their parents, then they would certainly assist them in every possible way. Thus, in addition to their mutual dependence, spouses are bound to each other through their children.

A number of facts indicate that the Ben-Harushes were sporadically slightly better off financially and somewhat less isolated from the community than the Ederis. Mr Ben-Harush did care about public opinion, and for a few days after the assault on his wife he tried to remain out of sight. For the same reason he would not at first allow her to obtain medical treatment. But in practice the public did hear about the incident and more people became involved in this case than in Ederi's. First, there was Mrs Ben-Harush's brother's wife, who came to her aid in spite of her husband's warning. Although Ben-Harush's eldest son stood aside while his mother was being maltreated, he took an active part in bringing about a reconciliation between his parents. Mrs Ben-Harush also brought in a local policeman, who talked to her husband but did not prefer a charge against him. And lastly, after he made it up with his wife, Mr Ben-Harush found a friend willing to loan him £I 500 to tide him over the difficult time.

Although Ben-Harush's wider connections were useful in helping him out, they also proved an embarrassment. He was ashamed of his outburst and withdrew from contact with a public that might have censured him. As he put it, 'For many days after the quarrel I did not live at home, but stayed in the locked-up shop. I hoped no one would know about me, and only the children came to see me.' During those days he even felt that his family had forsaken him. 'I cannot bear the suffering any longer. There is no one who understands. My wife does not understand, my eldest son just stands there and does not do anything. Yesterday I was close to throwing myself into the sea.' Here there may be a connection between Mr Ben-Harush's deeper involvement with the community, his more extreme withdrawal even from his closest relationships after the assault, and his hint at violence directed against himself. This connection will be investigated in the following case.

Case 5. Mr Fahimah's attempted suicide

The Fahimah family originates from one of the coastal towns of Morocco, whence it drifted to Casablanca. After having engaged in a variety of jobs, such as waiter, itinerant trader and tailor, which in his Moroccan environment were considered as demanding very little skill, Mr Fahimah finally became the owner of a stall in the Casablanca market. His wife contributed to the family's comfortable income by part-time work as a doctor's assistant. Both spouses are literate in French. In 1964 the family, with its ten children, emigrated to Israel and was sent to Maaloth, against its wishes. Mr Fahimah was no longer young and thus was relegated to the category of restricted relief workers. As such he was at first sent to sweep the streets and was ashamed to have sunk so low; later he became usher in one of the local council's offices. The welfare office extended regular financial assistance to the family, but both incomes combined did not satisfy its minimum requirements. Mr Fahimah tried his best to supplement the family's income: one day he sold home-made cakes at Maaloth's bus stop, another time he served drinks at a local council function. All these occasional jobs did not add up to much. His wife's efforts to find work of any kind were of no avail. The family was certainly not well off, and, to maintain a standard of living according to its expectations, from time to time sold some of the valuables it had brought from abroad. Still, a year after their arrival in the country, the Fahimahs were in a better economic position than many of Maaloth's families, as their eldest children were growing up. One or two were beginning to earn independent incomes and others were being taken off their hands. The eldest son got married and joined the police force. He was stationed in another town, worked hard to provide for his own growing family, and did not contribute to his parents' budget. Another son had been admitted to a residential school at no cost to his parents. A daughter had entered a nurses' training college, where the State paid for tuition and boarding. A second daughter had sat for the teachers' training college entrance examinations and was waiting for the results.

The family as a whole had begun to find its bearings. Only Mr Fahimah's present situation contrasted unfavourably with the past. Abroad he had been relatively successful in business, had provided well for a large family and had attended to his children's training. In Maaloth his efforts to earn a proper living were failing, he had lost his economic independence and he was becoming a burden to the welfare services. His elder children were already fending for themselves, and the State had taken charge of the training of others. He had lost control over his children: even those still at the primary school became unruly, and both parents frequently resorted to physical punishment. Under the prevailing economic conditions there was little Mr Fahimah himself could do to alleviate his situation, and the local officials on whom he had to rely were equally unable to help. He felt old and useless, failing in his duty towards his family. This reaction found expression in Mr Fahimah's attitude to his wife. He felt that she could not possibly wish to remain with him, and thus he constantly suspected her of marital infidelity. He jealously watched her behaviour and accused her of committing various indiscretions ranging from exposing her knee to a visitor to having a clandestine lover.

There occurred frequent noisy disputes between the spouses which always remained at the verbal level; Mr Fahimah never struck his wife. On such occasions neighbours would collect in Mr Fahimah's flat, relieve his fears and suspicions, and restore peace for a while.

More than once Mr Fahimah sought relief from his misery by attempting suicide. Here are details of one such attempt which I witnessed. It was Friday morning; Mr Fahimah had not been to work. His wife was staying over the weekend with a brother in a nearby town and one of the grown-up daughters took care of the household and the smaller children. The eldest daughter had been away for a week. That morning she returned home with the good news that she would be admitted to the teachers' training college. She also delivered a message from her mother, to bring the youngest child to her over the weekend, while the elder girls should attend to their father and the other children.

An hour or so after the daughter's arrival, fearful, incessant shrieks suddenly arose from Mr Fahimah's home. Rushing down to his flat, I found him lying on the floor in a pool of blood. He had slashed his belly several times with a razor blade, but, it turned out later, his wounds were only superficial and not dangerous. His two grown-up daughters and the other children, as well as a number of neighbours, mostly women, were standing around him, still screaming but doing nothing to help him. He was conscious, but seemed unconcerned with things going on around him. By the time the doctor and nurse arrived, he had slightly recovered. While they treated his wounds, Mr Fahimah murmured, 'I did it all for my children.'

Perhaps he meant that as he was unable to provide for his children he did not wish to become a burden to them. His daughter's announcement that she would attend teachers' training college made it clear to him that his children were getting on without him, that he was redundant; not only '*for* his children' was he committing suicide, but also *because* of them.

As in the two cases discussed above, so here too a structural situation without remedy provoked violence, and each assault was brought on by a combination of circumstances that exposed the impasse. In contrast to the former cases, here violence was directed not towards another person but against the self. Perhaps the specific elements of the situation can shed some light on the difference, always bearing in mind that I am not attempting to explain the causes of attempted suicide in general but only one particular set of conditions conducive to it.

First, Mr Fahimah's economic problem was quite different from that of Mr Ederi and Mr Ben-Harush. He was not in financial straits and did not run up debts with storekeepers. He had enough economic reserves to make up for deficits. As his family was older, he had fewer dependants. But unlike the others he had come down in the world and did not expect to regain economic independence.

The Fahimahs maintained friendly relations with their neighbours, and there was constant coming and going in their home. One of the neighbours, who was also related to the family, said she often got help and good advice from them. Relations with other kin were also kept up by the frequent exchanges of visits and mutual entertaining. The fact that so many spectators rushed to the scene of attempted suicide testifies to the fact that the Fahimahs possessed an active cluster of relationships in Maaloth.[42] Thus Mrs Fahimah is not the exclusive focus of her husband's social relationships. Both spouses, and each of them individually, have numerous relationships which reduce their dependence on each other. Therefore the wife does not necessarily precipitate a storm or have to bear its onus; she can seek the aid of her relatives or take refuge with them. Seen from Mr Fahimah's subjective viewpoint, this combination of factors has grave significance: he has lost his hold, economic or otherwise, over the adults in his family, whose new relationships take them more and more out of the family circle. His wife also maintains close links with friends and kin within and outside Maaloth. Mr Fahimah himself possesses a relatively extensive network of relationships, and accordingly he and his wife are no longer so exclusively and intimately dependent on each other as were the pairs of spouses previously discussed. He lacks the absorbing, intimate tie with a single person which could make him turn on her when he finds himself in an impasse. When despair overtakes him he considers himself alone and forsaken, and thus vents his violence on himself.

Mr Fahimah's attempted suicides took place in circumstances which indicate that he wished to mobilize his immediate family and other intimates in the hope that they would find a way out of his impasse. His appeal was heard by his kin, but they were powerless to help him. Neither they nor the bureaucratic agencies could remedy his plight; no employment suitable for him was available. Only with great difficulty would Mr Fahimah have found employment suited to his very poor qualifications anywhere; under conditions in Maaloth he was unemployable.

Stengel points out[43] that attempted suicide is often analytically distinct from suicide. In the literature, however, attempted and unsuccessful suicides are necessarily lumped together. Attempted suicide is very often a person's appeal to a public to find a solution to a fundamental problem with which he has not been able to cope. Such appeals for help therefore presuppose the presence of witnesses, as in Mr Fahimah's case. Stengel reports that 'of 147 unselected patients admitted to a mental observation ward after attempted suicide . . . only forty-four were alone during the attempt. The rest were together with or near people. Forty of the total moved towards people during the attempt.'[44] In many instances Stengel found that temporary or permanent hospitalization solved the patient's problem, or that relationships with his spouse or kinsmen improved after the attempted suicide.[45] In other cases the attempt failed to procure any change in the patient's situation, as is evidenced by the fact that of the 138 patients whose histories were followed up, twenty-two had made previous attempts and eighteen repeated their attempts within the following five years.[46]

Mr Fahimah's repeated attempts at suicide indicate, then, that the difficulties under which he labours are chronic and persistent. The very ineffectiveness of his attempts are pathetic proof of his inability to remedy his situation. He seems condemned to a life in which violence against himself becomes part of a repetitive sequence. A relative of his told me that about a year after the attempted suicide discussed above he insisted on undergoing an operation which the doctors considered unnecessary. Soon after he returned home from hospital he began to complain about pains and was re-admitted to hospital for observation. The doctors found that he was recuperating nicely, but when he was sent home the pains set in again. It is not impossible that both the desire to undergo the operation and the relapses are variations on the previous theme of violence directed against the self.

The study of violence in Maaloth was only incidental to a regular community study, and it has yielded a limited number of cases. I am aware that I have not covered the whole range of phenomena subsumed under the term 'violence'. Thus no cases of homicide or suicide were available. Nor have I discussed organized violence. On the other hand, this situation permitted me to study violence in its social context and at close range. To reach some understanding of the processes involved, I re-examined Evans-Pritchard's account of the Nuer and my own material on the Negev Bedouin,[47] which made me realize that violence is employed rationally in simpler societies and is often supported by public opinion. Some of the violence in Maaloth, it turned out, could also be explained as rational (but not necessarily as legitimate).

When people encountered obstacles which appeared to them insurmountable, they would often react violently in ways not designed to advance their aim. While such violence is an admission of defeat, it may also be an appeal to the public. When a willing public is found, it may be able to help. Irrational violence may thus contain traces of a secondary rationality. Where violence is repetitive, however, this is a clear indication that the difficulties which gave rise to it have not been solved.

The distinction between rational and irrational violence may have some heuristic value, but it should not be understood as a way of classifying acts of violence. In a modern State, violence seems to constitute a form of behaviour lying on the border of rationality. This is evidenced by the ease with which rational, controlled violence lapses into an uncontrolled outburst. It is shown also by the risks involved in most violence, where individual violence often invites strong reaction and sometimes collective retribution.

The persons who assaulted officials considered violence as the last and only course of action open to them. They embarked on it after careful consideration, and after having first tried various gentler means of persuasion. None of them employed violence right from the start, and all realized the risk involved and took it willingly. From their point of view, they acted rationally. Yet from the observer's viewpoint their behaviour is partly irrational, for they ignored alternative avenues of action that carried better chances of success, with no risk to themselves. Thus they could have approached officials indirectly, through patronage—for instance, by becoming active for a political party. In some matters they could have achieved results by petitioning the superiors of their local officials, for although by local standards they were demanding exceptional treatment their demands could have been reasonable by standards applied elsewhere. (It should be kept in mind that Maaloth is situated in an economically depressed region.) In this context it is immaterial whether the assailants knew about the alternatives at the time of attack, for even if they did not they could have consulted other people. Their rational action contained important elements of irrationality.

The same is true for the cases of 'irrational' violence; it is also made up of rational and irrational elements. Here people were getting all the official assistance they were entitled to and, being so completely dependent on officials, they could not use force to obtain special treatment. Yet their situation often became unbearable, and then they would violently assault members of their families. These attacks were interpreted as cries for help. The assailants managed to be heard and, at least in some cases, to be vaguely understood.

It has been shown that people attack the person closest to them because he or she is seen as one of the causes of the difficult situation, and because his or her complaints had made it an issue. The wife is attacked only in the cases where the many-stranded relationship with her is so binding that nothing can break it. The situation is the same, *mutatis mutandis*, where a wife attacks her husband. In the attack, not only is one spouse made to feel the pain and sorrow of the other, but is also sharply reminded that he or she is a full partner in the crisis. And indeed, in consequence of the attack, the spouse takes over his or her share in the burden. (Again, *mutatis mutandis*, there are similar elements in some parental beatings of children. While, before, the child had behaved obstructively, now he was forced to come to terms with the parent or teacher.) Before, the wives had blamed their husbands for the lack of money, whereas now each of them sought to help the family in her own way. Mrs Ederi first ran out into the street, not only to get away from her husband, but also hoping that help would come from some unknown quarter. Later on she got in touch with the town's rabbi. He was to write a sharp letter to the erring husband, but he could also take some steps to restore peace in the family. The rabbi is an official, and controls some resources of his own. Conceivably he might offer some material assistance or use his influence in the Ederis' favour. Mrs Ben-Harush was persuaded to accept her husband's temporary invalid state and inability to earn enough money for the family. She too was made to seek outside help, from her brother's family. The brother's reluctance to step into the breach may have been partly due to his realization that material assistance was required, which he was unable to provide. Mrs Ben-Harush's appeal to the policeman, unlike Mrs Ederi's to the rabbi, was not designed to obtain help. Hers was an assertion of the independence she had gained *vis-à-vis* her husband through her brother's help, however limited and short-lived that independence may have been. After the attempted suicide Mr Fahimah's wife and daughters rallied to him for a while and sought some solution to his difficulties. His hospitalization gave them all a short respite. In none of these cases was a solution found, but in each case the cry for help was heard and renewed attempts were made to solve pernicious problems.

All the violent acts observed, then, were compounded of both rational and irrational elements, from the actors' as well as from the observers' point of view.

For those of its inhabitants who live on relief work and welfare assistance, Maaloth provides an environment that permits them few choices. Not only are the economic resources very limited, but they are also mostly concentrated in the hands of a few officials. When many people compete for the resources, such as employment, housing and welfare, they must use ever stronger arguments to convince officials of the justice of their special demands. That leads some people to use threats and violence against officials and others to feel helpless, incapable of obtaining their requirements from the officials.

Against this background the cases discussed in this essay fall into two categories. On the one hand, there are attempts to coerce persons (in Maaloth, these persons were normally officials), by the deliberate and controlled use of threats and violence, to yield up their resources. On the other hand, there are ineffective violent assaults on persons (who were in Maaloth members of a person's family, or the person himself; in the Andaman Islands any members of a village might have been included) on whom no concrete demands are made. The basic distinctions between the two categories of violent person can be summed up thus:

1. In the first, the individual has some choice between various courses of action, in spite of a limiting environment. He employs violent coercion in order to achieve a clearly defined goal. He is willing to do so because he is in a position to risk loss of benefits and possible punishment, but he is prepared to assume full responsibility for his actions. He behaves in a restrained manner; he uses mainly strong language and threats, and hardly ever resorts to physical assault.

2. A person in the second category is constrained by circumstances to such an extent that he loses his freedom of action. As a result he is liable to find himself in difficulties that cannot be resolved. The term 'impasse' was used to denote such situations. This type of violent person appeals to others to act on his behalf. He has no clear notion of what exactly the others can do for him, but by a violent act he tries to thrust part of his onerous responsibility onto another person (or onto a group of persons). He seems to single out for assault a person who is both intimately associated with him and who, in the first place, held him responsible, and forces him to share his burden. His appeal is usually manifested in violent physical assault, and the victim is often wounded, though not seriously.

Finally, I wish to reiterate that my aim has been to examine certain social relationships that engendered violence. The cases discussed all occurred within a specific social context, and only certain types of violence were encountered. They can all be classified as minor personal violence, and my conclusions cannot be applied directly to other social contexts and other varieties of violence.

[1968]

Notes

1 Field work in Maaloth was carried out over a period of twenty-two months, between August 1964 and September 1966. The analysis refers to that period; since I left the field, conditions in Maaloth have changed considerably. The Maaloth study constitutes one of a series of researches on Israeli immigrants directed by Professor Max Gluckman and myself in the Department of Social Anthropology, University of Manchester, and financed by the Bernstein Israel Research Trust. I am very grateful to the scheme's trustees for their generous support.

Early versions of the paper were read at a seminar of the Institute of Criminology at the Hebrew University, Jerusalem in February 1967, and published in Hebrew as 'Some notes on violence' (*Delinquency and Society*, vol. 2, 1967); and at a meeting of the Association of Social Anthropologists of the Commonwealth held at Brantwood, Coniston, in September 1968. Professor J. Ben-David encouraged me to go into the subject at greater length. Drafts of the paper were read by Professor J. Ben-David, Dr S. Deshen, Professor Gluckman, Mrs B. Silberstein and Dr R. P. Werbner. I am very grateful for their detailed comments and have tried to meet their points in this revision. Dr M. Amir kindly put his expert knowledge of the literature on violence at my disposal.

2 Bienen, *Violence and Social Change* (1968), p. 6.

3 This is a division of the Jewish Agency, the semi-governmental organization carrying out functions considered as central to Zionist ideology, such as bringing in immigrants and settling the land.

4 Israel Ministry of Labour, Manpower Planning Authority: *Employment and Unemployment in Development Towns in August 1966* (1966), p. 73 (in Hebrew).

5 The official figures of unemployed have been calculated for a 'working population' comprising 17 per cent of the town's population, as against a working population of 37 per cent for the whole country (*ibid*., p. 3). The working population, in this and other publications of the Manpower Planning Authority, is defined as 'all those employed, engaged on relief work or unemployed', i.e., registered for at least seven days as such at a labour exchange (*ibid*., p. 114). It does not refer to persons capable of work.

6 A plant in Nahariah producing asbestos building material. After a series of strikes and clashes with the police in 1961, the Ministry of Labour made it possible for inhabitants of Maaloth to be employed at the plant. It used to employ up to sixty-five men from Maaloth and was considered the best possible place of employment for unskilled labour.

7 This contrasts sharply with former customs. Dr Y. Ben-Ami, who has investigated traditional marriage among Moroccan Jews, informs me

that in the Atlas mountains marriage was not usually preceded by an engagement. In other areas marriage took place between one week to three months after the engagement.

8 Evans-Pritchard, *The Nuer* (1940), p. 6.
9 Evans-Pritchard, *Kinship and Marriage among the Nuer* (1951), p. 24.
10 Gluckman, *Custom and Conflict in Africa* (1955), pp. 5–6.
11 Evans-Pritchard, *The Nuer* (1940), p. 171.
12 Evans-Pritchard, *Kinship and Marriage* (1951), p. 2.
13 Evans-Pritchard, *The Nuer* (1940), p. 151.
14 *Ibid.*, p. 169.
15 *Ibid.*, p. 171.
16 In the language of modern politicians the practice is termed 'escalation'. Disputes are allowed to build up gradually, through a series of acts which provoke reactions, and public opinion is goaded to support ever stronger measures.
17 *Ibid.*, pp. 151–2.
18 The situation described here is correct for 1960–61, and to some extent for 1963, when I did field work in the Negev under the auspices of the Department of Social Anthropology at the University of Manchester. See my *Bedouin of the Negev* (1967). Since then fundamental changes have taken place in the Negev.
19 Some aspects of this case are discussed in my *Bedouin of the Negev* (1967), pp. 183 and 239.
20 The institution of feuding, in the sense of an endless series of killings between two corporate groups, is peculiar to this kind of political organization. For a discussion of the ideology and practice of feuding see Peters, 'Some structural aspects of the feud among the camel-herding Bedouin of Cyrenaica' (1967), pp. 261–82.
21 Gluckman, 'Tribalism, ruralism and urbanism in South and Central Africa' (1970), shows that this neither was true for medieval European States nor is for the so-called developing States of our times. Only in States which have achieved 'a high degree of utilitarian organic interdependence' do rulers increasingly monopolize the right to use violence, and do men who command armed force not try to use that force to seize power. I should emphasize that nowhere has the State gone so far as to deny citizens the right to use violence in certain circumstances.
22 A notable exception is the bailiff.
23 Mr A. Shur, head of Israeli Police criminal investigations, states that disputes among neighbours are a frequent cause of violence and that the police hardly ever bring such cases to court. They make every effort to settle the differences peacefully. (Hebrew University, Institute of Criminology, *Proceedings of the Seminar on Violence in Israel* (1967), pp. 57–8.)

24 Weber, *Wirtschaft und Gesellschaft* (1964), vol. 2, p. 659. This is a free translation of the passage.
25 So in the article 'Violence' by Hook in *Encyclopaedia of the Social Sciences* (1930–35).
26 Sorel, *Reflections on Violence* (1908, 1961), p. 78.
27 Thus all the cases of homicide and suicide discussed in Bohannan (ed.), *African Homicide and Suicide* (1967), are second-hand accounts. The literature on violence is, as a rule, more concerned with statistical analysis or with conditions conducive to violence than with examining case material.
28 Coser, 'Some social functions of violence' (1966), p. 10.
29 The French authorities completed their conquest of the Atlas mountains only in 1934. See Bousquet, *Les Berbères* (1957), p. 71.
30 Chouraqui, *Marche vers l'Occident* (1952), pp. 164–7, provides data on this internal migration which indicate that male bread-winners moved first and were then followed by their families.
31 See, for instance, Jacobs, *A Study of Culture Stability and Change* (1956), and Donath, *L'évolution de la femme israëlite a Fès* (1962). Dr Donath states in a personal communication that she never found signs of violence between spouses.
32 Amir, *Report of the Commission on Violent Behaviour in Government Social Welfare Offices* (1967), p. 12.
33 All names, as well as other details, have been altered, to prevent the identification of individuals.
34 In Hebrew the word 'chair' is frequently used in the sense of 'seat of authority', 'office', much as in English.
35 The list of items demanded by assailants in the cases studied by Amir, *op. cit.*, pp. 19–20, shows many similarities.
36 Blau and Scott, *Formal Organizations* (1963), pp. 81–2, report a similar finding in a study by G. Almond and H. D. Lasswell on aggressiveness among recipients of unemployment insurance: 'In contrast to the non-aggressive clients, aggressive clients tended to come from higher-income and education groups.'
37 Thus before arrival in the country each immigrant family was given a green card entitling it to cheap, State-subventioned housing. The officials of the housing corporation had been instructed to secure these cards before showing immigrants to a new flat, so that in case they did not like it they would not be in a position to ask for other accommodation.
38 Amir, *op. cit.*, p. 35.
39 'Displacement' here refers to the relinquishing by a person of an instrumental aim, due to his reaching an impasse. He capitulates to adverse social conditions. A description of the process and its effects on

social relationships will be offered below. The process of displacement bears resemblance, on a different analytical level, to substitute formation for repressed instinctual impulses, as discussed in S. Freud, 'Repression', *Collected Papers* (London, 1925), vol. IV, pp. 84–97, and elsewhere.

40 Radcliffe-Brown, *The Andaman Islanders* (1922), p. 48. [*Editor's note:* See further the discussion of some forms of 'self-help' in Moore's article in this book.] P. L. Newman, ' "Wild man" behaviour in a New Guinea highlands community' (1964), pp. 1–19, shows how a Gururumba attracts the attention of fellow-villagers to his impossible position. He antagonizes them and steals openly from them. His behaviour is not considered as criminal, but as a call for help. In some cases the villagers respond by helping the 'wild man' economically and by reducing his social obligations.

41 The rabbinical courts, which in Israel are competent in matters of personal status, at first try to conciliate the spouses and only if their efforts have proved fruitless over several months do they agree to discuss a divorce.

42 Compare this to the two preceding cases, in one of which no one came to the aid of the women attacked, and, in the other, even close kin helped reluctantly.

43 Stengel, 'Enquiries into attempted suicide' (1952), p. 613.

44 Stengel, 'The social effects of attempted suicide' (1956), p. 118.

45 Stengel, 'Enquiries into attempted suicide' (1952), p. 618.

46 *Ibid.*, p. 617.

47 I turned to ethnographic studies chiefly because much of the sociological literature on violence was found irrelevant to my purposes.

Bibliography

Amir, M., *Report of the Commission on Violent Behaviour in Government Social Welfare Offices*, Jerusalem: Szold Institute (1967).

Blau, P. M., and Scott, W. R., *Formal Organizations: a Comparative Approach*, London: Routledge & Kegan Paul (1963).

Bienen, H., *Violence and Social Change*, Chicago: Chicago University Press (1968).

Bohannan, P. (ed.), *African Homicide and Suicide*, New York: Atheneum Press (1967).

Bousquet, G. H., *Les Berbères*, Paris: Presses Universitaires de France (1957).

Chouraqui, A., *Marche vers l'Occident; les Juifs d'Afrique du Nord*, Paris: Presses Universitaires de France (1952).

Coser, L. A., 'Some social functions of violence', *Annals of the American*

Academy of Political and Social Science, vol. 364 (March 1966), pp. 8–18.

Donath, D., *L'Evolution de la femme israëlite a Fès*, Aix-en-Provence: Faculté des lettres (1962).

Durkheim, E., *Suicide: a Study in Sociology*, London: Routledge & Kegan Paul (1952; translation from French edition of 1897).

Evans-Pritchard, E. E., *The Nuer: a Description of the Modes of Livelihood and Political Institutions of a Nilotic People*, Oxford: Clarendon Press (1940).

— *Kinship and Marriage Among the Nuer*, Oxford: Clarendon Press (1951).

Freud, S., 'Repression', *Collected Papers*, vol. 4, London: Hogarth Press, (1924–25), pp. 84–97.

Gluckman, M., *Custom and Conflict in Africa*, Oxford: Blackwell, (1955).

— 'Tribalism, ruralism and urbanism in South and Central Africa; in *Profiles of Change: The Impact of Colonialism in Africa*, ed. V. W. Turner, Cambridge: Cambridge University Press (1970).

Hebrew University Institute of Criminology, *Proceedings of the Seminar on Violence in Israel*, Jerusalem: Institute of Criminology (in Hebrew) (1967).

Hook, S., 'Violence', *Encyclopaedia of the Social Sciences*, vol. 15, New York: Macmillan (1930–35).

Israel, Central Bureau of Statistics, *Statistical Abstract of Israel, vol. 15, 1964*, Jerusalem: Central Bureau of Statistics (1965).

— Ministry of Labour, Manpower Planning Authority, *Employment and Unemployment in Development Towns in August 1966*, Jerusalem (in Hebrew) (1966).

Jacobs, M., *A Study of Culture Stability and Change: the Moroccan Jewess* (dissert.), Washington: Catholic University of America Press (1956).

Marx, E., *Bedouin of the Negev*, Manchester: Manchester University Press (1967).

— 'Some notes on violence,' *Delinquency and Society*, vol. 2 (1967), pp. 22–5 (in Hebrew).

Newman, P. L., ' "Wild man" behaviour in a New Guinea highlands Community,' *American Anthropologist*, vol. 66 (1964), pp. 1–19.

Peters, E. L., 'Some structural aspects of the feud among the camel-herding Bedouin of Cyrenaica', *Africa*, vol. 37 (1967), pp. 261–82.

Radcliffe-Brown, A. R., *The Andaman Islanders*, Cambridge: Cambridge University Press (1922).

Sorel, G., *Reflections on Violence*, New York: Collier (1961; translation from French edition of 1908).

Stengel, E., 'Enquiries into attempted suicide', *Proceedings of the Royal Society of Medicine*, vol. 45 (1952), pp. 613–20.

— 'The social effects of attempted suicide', *Canadian Medical Association Journal*, vo. 74 (1956), pp. 116–20.
Weber, M., *Wirtschaft und Gesellschaft: Grundriss der verstehenden Soziologie* (two vols.), Cologne: Kiepenheuer & Witsch (1964).
Wolfgang, M. E., and Ferracuti, F., *The Sub-culture of Violence: towards an Integrated Theory in Criminology*, London: Tavistock (1967).

Index

absence of accusation, 177, 194f; explanations of, 170f, 194ff; in pastoral societies, 171
accusations: legal, 133; modes of (Kalanga), 239–40; of sorcery (Kalanga), 228–53
accusations of sorcery: Azande, 227; crime of, 229–30, 252; domestic rituals (Kalanga), 228, 231, 235, 239–240, 251; Kalanga case, 239–41, 242; modes of (Kalanga), 229, 241, 242, 253; moral responsibility (Kalanga), 228, 231, 232, 252; Ndembu, 252; among urban Africans, 229, 230, 231
accusations of witchcraft: absence of, 177, 184, 194f; Azande restrictions, 9; and caste, 220; and co-wives, 166; definition of form, 194, 197ff; and economic success, 172–3; against errant wife, 168; incidence among pastoralists, 165–7; incidence of (Azande), 140–1, 143, 145–6; justifies separation, 16; psychological truth in, 18; relation to mobility, 177; and tempo of sociation, 210; among townsmen, 184ff; and uncertainty, 194, 211; Yao, 30
accused, in triad (Chewa), 31
accuser, in triad (Chewa), 31
administration, bureaucratic, 294
Admiralty, 266
adultery: amongst Bedouin, 132; in Lebanon, 130; in Tripolitania, 133; and witchcraft, 143, 145
adults, and youths, 112–15, 118–20
Aeschylus, 257–8
Agamemnon, 257, 259, 277
agnates, wrath of, 25, 203
Air Ministry: attitude to arithmetic, 269; represented by Lord Portal, 266
air raids, 266, 267
Air Staff, 266, 267, 271, 277; Chief of, 261; views of on strategic air offensive, 267
Almighty, 273
Almond, G., 318
Amhara, 'Eyers', 187
Amir, M., 295, 299
ancestral spirits: Azande, 227; female—capricious (Zulu), 13; Zulu—divine, 14
ancestral wrath, 23f; Lugbara, 25f
Andaman Islands, 301
Andrzejewski, B. W., 189
animosities, witchcraft not simple reflection, 9
anonymity, and youth group, 116–17
antagonisms, origin in contradictions, 263
Arussi, Galla, 175
Ashton, H., 225
Atlantic, battle of, 266
'audience', for decisions, xx
authority: of ancestral spirits (Azande), 227; delegation of, 290–1; of the demons (Kalanga), 228; domestic (Kalanga), 248; gerontocratic (Kalanga), 248; occult (Kalanga), 241
Azande: accusations of witchcraft, 140–1; blood-brother, 36–7; changed

Azande—*contd.*
residential pattern, 28; isolation of, 139; quarrels among, 176; ranks among, 139; rationality of, 170; types of oracle, 146–7; witchcraft, 6f, 139–158, witchcraft beliefs, 203

Baggara, 163
Bahima, 188
Bailey, F. G., 187, 196
Baldwin, E., acknowledgment to, 47
Baptub, 264
Bateson, G., 254
Baxter, P. T. W., 251; summarized, xx–xxi
Bechuana, *see* Tswana
Bedouin, 288–90; adultery amongst, 132; joking relationships, 135; and moral authority, 132; mother's brother, 135, 137
beliefs: decline of, 164; stability of, xiv–xvi
Bemba, on luck, 23
Ben-Ami, Y., 317
Bienen, H., 281
Birkenhead, Lord, 279
Birmingham, air raid on, 267
Black, Charles, 278
Blackett, P. M., 269, 270, 279
blame: individual, 227, 251; Kalanga, 238, 244–5, 247–8
blessings: Boran (*see* curses), 171, 173, 185–6; of well, 183
blood-brother, Azande, 36–7
Bohannan, P. J., 89, 252, 318; and L., 33f
Bomber Command, 267, 270
bombing directive, 261
bombing, effectiveness of, 261
Boran, 163, 165, 170, 176, 187; blessings, 171, 173, 185–6; curses, 173, 185–6; 'Eyers', 168–9, 176; fortune among, 175; mobility among, 177; naming ceremony, 172, 182; stock management, 180f; village composition, J's village, 179–83; witches, 167–8
Bott, E., on close-knit network, 47
Bottomley, Air Vice-Marshal, 261
Bousquet, G. H., 294
Bowen, C. D., 224
bridewealth, deferred payment (Kalanga), 243–5
Brooke, Sir Alan, 268
bureaucracy, 284–5, 294, 298; politics in, 260
Bush, 268
Bushmen, 188
Buxton, J., 165, 188

Calloway, Bishop, 14
carnival, 263, 264, 265
Cassandra, 257
caste, and witchcraft, 196, 219
cattle: husbandry and distribution, 175; identification with, 172, 176; management of (Boran), 180; and misfortune, 172; as property, 176
causation, witchcraft as theory of, 6
censorship, of accusations of witchcraft, 200–1
Central Africa, towns, 184
ceremonies, of status degradation, 197f
Challenor affair, 273, 274
changes, handled by ritual, 17
charisma, 277
cheating: genuine Lugbara fear, 26; against interests of sufferer, 15
Cherwell, Lord, 263, 266; calculations questioned by Tizard (1942), 266; clash with Tizard, 267; 'court' politician, 269; influence on Churchill, 268; minute of 30 March 1942, 262; views on air raid effects, 267
Chewa, 30f, 189
Chiefs of Staff, and village, compared, 258, 265
Chiefs of Staff Committee, 260, 270, 277
child-rearing, and violence, 286–7, 292, 295, 300–1, 308–10
Chinese: beliefs, 12; joint family, 12
Chouraqui, A., 318
Christie, Agatha, 279
Churchill, Sir Winston, 260, 261, 263,

279; influence of Cherwell on, 268; quoted, 268
Claridges Hotel, 273
class, 258
client, of diviner, 208, 222
Clytemnestra, 257, 277
Coastal Command, 270
collective responsibility: and corporateness, 79; and liability, 85, 89, 93, 99, 100; and self-help, 68, 80; as stage of legal evolution, 52–4, 56
Cologne, air raid on, 266
Colson, E., 135; plateau Tonga homicide, 87
community: verdict of, 146; and youth groups, 124–5
competition: among Lugbara elders, 25f; in village, 5; of Zulu wives, 12, 196
Compton, 268
conflicts: deep in structure, 12–13, 15, 22; degrees of awareness, 21; in kinship amity, 45; between men and women, 264; of moral principle and ritual, 18f; among Mpondo and Nyakyusa, 20–1; among Nupe, 19–20; provide moral crises, 33; and situations, 257; in structure of society, 18; of Yao principles, 29–30
consensus: conditions for, 157; about encompassing systems, 258; and witchcraft, 152; and youth group, 117–18, 120
consultants, choice of overriding systems, 259
contradictions, xiv–xvi; rationalizations of, 8; in village antagonisms, 263
control, of feelings, 9. *See also* social control *and* moral control
corporate groups: and collective responsibility, 79–93; definition of M. G. Smith, 58
corporateness, 288–90
corporation activities of, 132; and moral control, 132
Coser, L. A. 294
court cases, Pedi, 217
Court of Criminal Appeal, 273–4
courts, use of, 133
courtship: and social control, 156; and youth group, 112, 114, 121–2
co-wives, and accusations, 166
Crawford, J., 252, 253
crime: in Israel, 282, 295; of sorcery accusations, 229–30, 252
crises, related to wider social situation, 258
cults: of affliction (Kalanga), 228–54; ancestral (Kalanga), 230, 245; diverse (Kalanga), 245–6
curses, 171, 185; Boran (*see* blessings), 173
custom, constraint of, 2f
Cyrenaica, 265
Cyril, the rate-fixer, 258, 275, 276

debt, Tallensi self-help, 68, 69
decision making, basic similarity of, in all contexts, 271
decisions: Devons on, xiii–xiv; legitimation of, 258, 260, 265, 277; taking of xx
defence: of diminished responsibility, 273; of insanity, 273
degradation of status, as social form, 197f
demons: appeal to (Kalanga), 228, 243, 245, 249–50; concept of (Kalanga), 243, 246–7, 251, 252; and moral rules (Kalanga), 243; possession (Kalanga), 228. *See also mazenge*, spirits
dependence, and violence, 297, 301, 303–4, 306–7
destiny, pre-natal, 44
Devons, E., 269, 279; memorial to, xi; on taking decisions, xiii–xiv; and Gluckman, on Nupe witchcraft, 46
differentiation, of sexes, 155
Dinka, 163, 164, 165; fetish bundles, 166; mobility among, 177; witchcraft as individual action, 175; witches among, 166–7
disputes: among Bedouin, 288–90; containment of, 69, 70; expanding beyond original individuals, **67, 70,**

disputes—*contd.*
73–5; marital, 295, 302–12; among Nuer, 286–7; as symbols of structural relations, 97
divination: Azande, 7; in course group's development, 29–30; of the future, xiii; Kalanga, 228, 240–3, 245; Lugbara, 25f; mode-related group situation (Zulu), 15–16; in modern society, 258; Ndembu, 231, 252; Ndembu struggle over, 33; outcome (Kalanga), 231, 242; Pedi methods, 207–10; solves moral, not technical, problem, 21f; struggle to control, 15; among Tallensi, 265; urban Africans, 230; Yao struggle over, 29f; Zulu, 14f
diviners: among Pedi, 207–10, 222–3. *See also* witch-doctors
divining bones, resume of social order, 15
Dobu, 187
doctors: called to testify on insanity, 274; ill cast as authority on responsibility, 273
Donath, D., 318
Dorobo, 167
Douglas, M., 31–2, 163, 186f, 195, 205, 254
Durkheim, E., 2, 4, 42, 56
Dyson-Hudson, N., 178

economic relations, 119, 125
economic statistics, xiii–xiv
economic success, and accusations, 172–3
egalitarianism, 23
Eilam, Y., 189, 253
elections, Israel, 289
Elias, T. O.: *mens rea*, 60; strict liability, 55
Emmet, D., influence of Evans-Pritchard, xii
Epstein, A. L., on African 'reason', 45
Epstein, S., 196, 219
escalation, 87
Evans-Pritchard, E. E., 139–58, 161, 172, 176, 185, 188f, 285–7; on Azande, 201; on Azande, oracles, 146–50; on blood-brother, 36; on containment of disputes, 70; Kipsigis civil cases, 73; Kipsigis wrongdoers, 89; legal definition of 'tribe', 51; on morphology of magic, 221; on Nuer attitudes to fighting, 64; on Nuer witches, 167; on political ritual, 18f; on quarrels among Azande, 176; on rationality of Azande, 170; on social control and witchcraft/sorcery, 227, 245 251; theories of, 6f; tribute to, xf, xx, xxvi, 3f, 9
evidence: in Pedi courts, 217; of witchcraft, 199, 217
evil eye: Boran possessors of, 168–9; among Mandari, 165; among Nuer, 186–7; among Turkana, 167
exaggeration: of mutual responsibility, 18; of wickedness, 5
Exeter College, xxvii
exogamy: and witchcraft, 205; Zulu, 11
experiments: precluded for Azande, xv; precluded for Bechuana, xvi–xix
experts: as experts, 259; as strangers, 270
explanations of misfortunes, Douglas, M., 163
expulsion, from a social collectivity, 89–91
externality, 121, 123; fiction of, 158
'Eyers': Amhara, 187; Boran, 176; characteristics of, 168; Gurage, 187; Mandari, 187f; meaning of, 179–80

face-to-face group, harmony in, 277
failure, rationalization of, 8
family, Masloth, 284, 302–12
family firm, 37f, 258, 259, 271
farming: in Llan, 119, 128; in Tripolitania, 133–4
Fate, Greek, 44–5
feelings: control of, 9; exaggerated power in tribes, 41–2
feminity, inherent evil of, 13f
fertility: ambivalence and, 16–17; effects of female, 12

fetish bundles (Dinka), 166
Finley, M. I., 278
firm: as encompassing system, 259; family, 37f; village like, 5
Firth, R., on externalization of responsibility, 253–4
football, 260, 263–4; supporters' clubs, 263
Forde, C. D., 4, 186f
Fortes, M., 278–9; on conflicts in kinship amity, 45; on Greek and African Fate, 44; on ritual of polity, 18f; on Tallensi, 65, 68–9, 88, 170
fortune, among Boran, 175
Fortune, R. F., 187
Foster, George, 172
Frankenberg, R. J., 278, 279; summarized, xxv
Frederika, Queen of Greece, 273
Freud, S., 299
Friedson, E., xi
Fulani, 163
future, divination of, xiii

Galla, 175
Garfinkel, H., status degradation ceremony, 197f
Gelfand, M. 252
Gerth, K. K., and Wright Mills, C., 279
Gluckman, M., 163–4, 171–2, 176, 184, 205, 251, 257, 271, 278, 286; strict liability, 55, 60–3, 96
Godkin lectures, 259
golden mean, 23f, 33f
Gray, R. F., 224
Green, M. M., 177
Griaule, M., 138
Grigg, Miss Mary, 274, 279
Gulliver, P.: Arusha bloodwealth payments, 82; Arusha violence, 65; containment of dispute, 70; Jie and Turkana stock associates, 80; moral sanctions, 90; political function of dispute, 98
Gulliver, Pamela and P. H., 167, 178; explanations of absence of accusations, 170
Gurage, 'Eyers', 187

handuura, *see* naming ceremony, 173
Hannan, M., 253
Hapi, the milk waster, his misfortunes, 173–5, 186
Harris, Air Marshal, 270
Harris, R., collective responsibility of Mbembe, 88
Harrod, Roy, 279
Hart, H. L. A., on strict liability, 43
Hazlitt, W., on peasants, 172
Hoebel, E. A.: expanded dispute, 73; historical development of law, 54; private and public law, 57–9
Home Office, 273
homestead, South-eastern Bantu, 11
Homicide Act, 1957, 273
Hook, S., 292
Horton, R., theories of ritual, 45
host: and cases (Kalanga), 238, 241, 243; and externalized responsibility (Kalanga), 249–50; and labour migration (Kalanga), 237; role in cults (Kalanga), 228, 232–5, 249–51, 252; symbolic acts of (Kalanga), 247–9, 251; and transactions (Kalanga), 237. *See also* demons; spirit possession; women
'house–property' complex, 46
housing, in Israel, 281, 295–6
Howell, P. P., Nuer moral attitudes, 64
Hull, air raid on, 267
Huntingford, G. W. B., 165–6, 186, 188

Ibo, absence of accusations among, 177
identification, with cattle, 172, 176
identity: and anonymity, 116–17; locus of, 216; total, 198
ideology, of stationary societies, 17
independence, of man from wife (Zulu), 12
Indian joint family, 13
individual action, as witchcraft, 175
individual responsibility: in legal

individual responsibility—*contd.*
evolution, 55; and self-help, 68; inside a social collectivity, 93, 99
industrial consultants, 37f
industrial sociology, 275
insanity, 274; defence of, 273
Irving, David, 279
Islam: and protective devices, 169; regulation of marriage, 131

J., his village and its composition, 179, 183
Jacobs, M., 318
joking relationships, 135–9; and Bedouin, 135; Radcliffe-Brown on, 136–9; and social interest, 123; and Tonga, 135; types of, 136
judges, 273
judicial: action impossible in Tiv arises, 35; handling straightforward breaches, 17; Ndembu action, 32
judicial thinking, 3–5
Junod, H. A., 45, 207
jural: bonds (Kalanga), 228, 233; restriction and negotiation (Kalanga), 234–5; rights (Kalanga), 244; status of women (Kalanga), 237
jurorh, 259
jury, as stranger, 274–5, 278

Kalanga: of eastern Botswana, 228–9, 231–51; of Southern Rhodesia, 251, 253, 254
Kapferer, B.: on labour migration, 253; on urban accusations, 184, 52
Karimojong, 163; mobility among, 178; witches, 167
Kgabe, 203
Kgatla, 254
kin: and bridewealth rights (Kalanga), 243–5; conflicts in amity of, 45; co-operation among (Zulu), 11; economic transactions of (Kalanga), 233–5; joint responsibility of (Kalanga), 228, 234; mobilization of (Kalanga), 228, 235, 241–2, 249–50; mobilized in town (Shona), 231; not accused, Azande, 9; often accused witchcraft, 10; pressure on (Kalanga), 228, 234, 238–43, 245, 247–8, 250–1; quarrels between, 10; represented in ritual (Kalanga), 246; sorcery accusations between, 227, 229–31, 232, 235–6
kinship: in Llan, 119, 125–6; and social control, 126; and witchcraft, 143–4, 205
Knuttson, K. E., 175
Kopytoff, I., Suku lineage obligations, 82
Krige, E. J. and J. D., 206
Kuper, H., on Swazi, 45–6

labour migration: Kalanga, 236, 244; Pedi, 212; Zambian, 253
LaFontaine, J., Gisu bloodwealth, 89
Laslett, Peter, 277, 279
Lasswell, H. D., 318
law: as encompassing system, 259; and witchcraft, 154, 194
law courts: Israel, 290, 299, relation of psychiatrist to, 258, 273
lawyers, 259
Leach, E. R., on parental contributions to child, 46
leaders, among Pedi, 211–21
Lebanese village, characteristics of, 130
legitimation of decisions, 258, 265, 277
Lele of Kasai, 195
leopardskin chief, among Nuer, 265
Lévy-Bruhl, L., Evans-Pritchard's debt to, xv–xvi
Lewis, I. M., 189; explanations of absence of accusations, 170; Somali witches, 167
liability, limitations on liability, 84, 85, 93. *See also* strict liability
Lienhardt, G., 37, 166, 167, 175, 188
lightning, 13
Lindemann, *see* Cherwell
lineage: fertility threatens Zulu, 12f; Nupe, 20; South-eastern Bantu, 11; Yao, 30
Livingstone, D., rain-making, xvi–xix
Llan demography of, 109, 112, 117–18, 128–9, 159–60; dispersed habitat,

119, 127; farms in, 119, 128; kinship in, 119, 125–6; religion in, 124, 127–128, 131–2; social groupings in, 125–127
Llanfihangel, *see* Llan
Lovedu, sex of witches, 206
Lowie, R. H., primitive lack of interest in motive, 60
Lübeck, air raid on, 266
Lugbara, 25f; religion, 171
Lupton, Thomas, 258, 275–6, 278–9

Maasai, 188
Macha, Galla, 175
Mackenzie, W. J. M., 278; influence of Evans-Pritchard, on anthropology, xi, xii
magic, Evans-Pritchard on, 221
magical solutions, Ndembu, 32–3
Maine, Sir Henry, evolutionary development of law, 54, 56
malediction, and witchcraft, 204
Malinowski, B., reciprocity and individual rights, 56
Mandari, 163–4, 167; 'Eyers' among, 187; mobility among, 177; witches, 165–6
Marett lectures, 257; by Gluckman, M., 176, 188
Marett, R. R., tribute to, 1f
marriage: in Maaloth, 284; of Moroccan Jews, 317; and social control, 156
Marsabit District, 168
Marshall, E. M., 188
Marshall, Loma, 188
Marwick, M., 30f, 163–4, 170, 184, 186, 189, 194, 219
Marx, E., 251; summarized, xxi–xxii
Masai, *see* Maasai
Mayer, P., 186
mazenge demons (Kalanga): 228, 243–247, 249–50, 252; conception of, 246–248; invocation of, 232, 242–3, 249, 253; and moral rules, 243, 245; transmission of, 233–4
mediation, and women in ritual (Kalanga), 228, 233–5, 237, 238, 249, 250–1, 253–4
medicines, of Pedi ngaka, 222–54
Meek, C. K., Ibo collective liability, 88
men: overt conflict with women, 264; and golden mean, 22–3; as group, 265; social attitudes distinguished from women, 263; and women. divided interests of, 265
menstrual blood, 13
Middleton, J., 25f; Lugbara religion, 171
military organization, 290–1
Ministry of Aircraft Production, 266, 269
minutes: Cherwell's of 30 March, 1942, as incident in a social process, 262; Portal's of February 1942, 261; dates of crucial, 266; of football club, 264
misfortune: breach moral order, 17; and cattle, 172; causes of (Pedi), 201–203; explanations of, 163, 171; of Hapi, the milk waster, 174–5, 186; meaning of, 184; particularity of, 6–7; responsibility for, 172; why seen morally, 22; and witchcraft, 144–5, 152
Mitchell, C. M., 184–5
Mitchell, J. C., 29f, 194, 229, 230, 231, 252
mobility: among Boran, 177; among Dinka, 178; among Karimojong, among Mandari, 178; among Nandi, 177; among Nuer, 178; relation to accusations, 177; among Samburu, 178; among Somali, 178; among Turkana, 178
monastic settlements in Wales, 265
Monnig, H. O., 223
Moore, S. F.: criticism of Gluckman's analysis, 42 summarized, xx–xxi
moot, Kalanga, 240, 244
moral authority: in Lebanese village, 130–31; in Tripolitania, 133
moral community: definition of, 129; relationships in, 157; and youth group, 130
moral control, 155–6; conditions for, 134; and corporations, 132; and rank, 139; and social relationships,

moral control—*contd.*
and witchcraft, 142–6, 156–7; and youth groups, 134, 156–7. *See also* social control
moral crises: and conflicts of value, 33; defined, 2, 25; in group development (Tiv), 36; in kin groups, 10; among Lugbara, 26; outsiders' role in, 36–7; and sectional interests, 24f; solutions of (Ndembu), 32
moral obligations, as against legal obligations, 69
moral order, natural and social worlds, 17
morality: breach of, 229, 238–43; and the demons (Kalanga), 243, 247; and religious authority, 131–2; and responsibility (Kalanga), 228, 233, 250; and ritual, 4; rules of, 227; and social change, 121; and social control, 109, 130; in social relationships, 17; span of, 157, 123–4; and theory of witchcraft, 8; of witchcraft (Azande), 227; and youth group, 130
Morocco, Jews in, 294–5
mortality, factionization of, 133
mother's brother, among Bedouin, 135, 137
motivation, and performances, 197–8
motive, and legal responsibility, 60
Mpaayei, J. T. O., 188
Mpondo, 11f; village splits, 16; witchcraft, 20, 40
Muslims, Sunni, 133
myths, mathematical, 266

Nadel, S. F., 186; on Nupe witchcraft, 19–20
naming ceremony, among Boran, 173, 182
Nandi, 163, 164, 167; mobility among, 177; witches, 165–6
Nash, M., 195
Naval Staff, 260, 266, 267, 277; views of, on strategic air offensive, 262
Ndembu, 32f, 254
Nethone Hospital, 274
Newman, P. L., 319
Ngaka, see diviner
Nonconformity, in Wales, 131–2
norms, native of village, 263
north Wales village, 265
Nuer, 163, 185, 189, 285–7; mobility among, 178; role of leopardskin chief, 265; witches, 167
Nupe: ambivalence of talents, 22; witchcraft, 19–20
Nyakyusa: ambivalence of talents, 22; witchcraft, 20–1

occult: defined, 45; beliefs and disharmony, 18; forces in social life, 16
Oedipus, 44–5, 259
officials, and clients, 291, 294–9
Old Bailey, 273, 274
oracles (Azande), 227; and consensus of opinion, 152; Evans-Pritchard on, 146–50; hierarchy of, 146, 148; reliability of, 147–8; and selection, 149; types of, 146–7; use of, 141, 143–4, 148; verdicts of, 152–4
Orestes, 257
organization: military, 290–1; political (Bedouin), 288–90; political (Nuer), 285–7
outsiders, distinguished from strangers, 264
outsiders: role in moral crises, 37; among Tiv, 36
overriding systems, 277; consultant's choice of, 259; represented by jury, 275

particularistic, illuminating universalistic, 258
pastoralism, and incidence of accusations, 165–7
pastoralists, and townsmen, 184–5
'peace of the Boran', 173
peasants, W. Hazlitt on, 172
Pedi: court cases, 217; girl songsters, 218; labour migration, 212ff; leaders among, 211ff; witchcraft beliefs, 204
Pedrini case, 273, 274
performances, and motivation, 197–8
personal attributes, influence of, 260

Peters, E. L., 130, 132, 251, 253; on Azande oracles, 96; segmentary lineage models, 75–8, 97; summarized, xxiii–xxv
Pitt Rivers, J. H., 218
Pokot, 188
Polanyi, M., on stability and experiment, xiv–xvi
police, 290–1; Israel, 282, 317
political office, ritual of, 18f
politics: closed, 260; committee, 260; courts, 260; hierarchical, 260
polygyny, jealousy in, 10; Zulu, 11–12
Portal, Sir Charles, 261, 266, 268–70
Pospisil, Leo: multiplicity of legal systems, 58; wars and feuds, 71
Pound, Admiral Sir Dudley, 266, 268, 270
Pound, Roscoe: stages of legal evolution, 52; strict liability, 60
power, distribution of, 285–7, 288–9, 290–3
Prime Minister, 265–8, 270
private law: early stage of legal evolution, 57; Hoebel interpretation, 73
processes, 258; and static structuralism, 277
production, as encompassing system, 259
property: as cattle, 176; and witchcraft, 28
prosperity: communal and individual, 18f; cost of—Tiv, 34; at fellows' cost, 23
protective devices, and Islam, 169
psychiatrist, in law courts, 258, 259, 273
'public', xxvi; for decisions, xx; and violence, 301, 304, 307–8, 310–12
public law: definition of public, M. G. Smith, 58; late stage of legal evolution, 57; and private dispute, 74

quarrels, among Azande, 176

Radcliffe-Brown, A. R., 205, 301; on joking, 114, 136–9
rain-making, Livingstone on, xvi–xix
Ramsoy, Odd, 277, 280
rank: absence of, 131, 134; Azande, 139; and moral control, 139, 157; and religious authority, 131; South-eastern Bantu, 11; and social control, 131, 134, 140, 157; and witchcraft, 140
rate-fixer, 259, 275, 276
reason, in tribal life, 3
Rees, Alwyn D., 109–33, 136, 159, 160, 218
reliability, of oracles, 147–8
religion: in Llan, 124, 127–8; and morality, 131–2; and social control, 127, 131
Renault works, air raid on, 266
Rendile, 169, 187, 188
responsibility, 224; African—for offences, 6; attribution of, through social action, 258; collective, 116; criminal—in Britain, 43–4; diminished, 273; externalization of (Kalanga), 249, 250; for fellows, 3–4, 5, 8, 41f; Hart on, 43; of host (Kalanga), 250; individual, 227–8, 242; joint (Kalanga), 228, 234, 237, 250; jural (Kalanga), 234, 237; in Kalanga ritual, 228–54; for Lugbara illness, 27; mutual—exaggerated, 18; occasional and general, xxvi; ritual—of leaders, 18f; and social disturbance, 257, 77; tribal enquiry into, 42; undefined concept, 258; and youth groups, 117, 118, 120, 122. *See* collective responsibility
responsibility, individual, *see* individual responsibility
Richards, A. I., 23
risk-taking, 297, 299
ritual: cases (Kalanga), 238–43; domestic (Kalanga), 232–4, 245–51; handles changes, 17; offerings (Kalanga), 238, 243–5; roles in (Kalanga), 232–4, 237; symbolic events in (Kalanga), 246–50; venue (Kalanga), 235, 248, 250. *See* *mazenge*; sorcery accusation; spirit possession
role, 277

Roosevelt, F. D., 270
Rotary Club, and Polish United Workers' Party, compared, 258
rules, manipulation of, xxvi

Samburu, 163, 187, 188; mobility among, 178; witches, 167
sanctions, social and legal, 90, 91
Sansom, B. L., summarized, xxi
Sansom, C. D., xii
Sanusi, 265
Schaff, A., 277, 278, 280; quoted, 257
Schapera, I., xvi, 16, 25, 204, 207, 253, 254
science, application of, in wartime, 259
scientists: dangers of, in high places, 268; power of, 263; social relationships of, xvi; as strangers, 266, 275
seances, with witch-doctor, 146, 150–4
Seavey, W. A., Western legal tradition, 60
secondary elaboration, xiii–xiv
secular solutions, Ndembu, 32
seduction, 187; Pedi case, 217
self-help: Bedouin, 290; and collective liability, 86; and expanding disputes, 67; fighting and aggressiveness, 64, 65; Nuer, 287; as stage of legal evolution, 52–4; and strict liability, 67
separation: effects of (Ndembu), 33; justified by witchcraft, 16
Service, E. R., 188
sexes, relationship between, 124
sexual familiars, 13, 18; Mpondo, 29
Shack, W., 187
shamans, among Galla, 175
shrines, among Tallensi, 265
sin: cultural stereotypes of, 227, 251; and ritual (Kalanga), 233, 245, 248
Sinclair, Sir Archibald, 266, 267
Singleton, Mr Justice, 269
Singleton report, 270
sisters, in matrilineal systems, 29f
Smith, E. W., and Dale, A. M.: Ila fighting, 65; group enforcement, 81, 82
Smith, M. G.: definition of 'public', 58; non-corporate assemblage, 80
Snow, Sir Charles, 259, 260, 262, 263, 266, 268, 269, 279, 280
social change: and morality, 121; process of, 121; and youth groups, 121; and witchcraft, 154–5, 158
social control: and change, 158; and courtship, 156; and kinship, 126; and marriage, 156; and morality, 109, 130; and rank, 131 134, 140, 157; realms of, 127; and religion, 127, 131; in Tripolitania, 133. *See* moral control
social groupings: in Lebanese village, 130; in Llan, 125–7
social order, disturbance of, 277
social relationships: criteria of, 129; and moral control, 156–7; and witchcraft, 140–6, 152–3; responsibility for disturbance of, 257; scientists' reasoning about, xvi; witchcraft reasoning about, xvi
Social Science Research Council, 251
Sofer, C., 37f, 258, 271, 272, 280
Somali, 163, 169; absence of accusations, 170; mobility among, 178; witches, 167
songsters, Pedi, 218
sorcery: Azande, 8; 'oral', 204; theft of crops, 23; triad of (Chewa), 31
sorcery accusations, *see* accusations of sorcery
Sorel, G., 292
Sotho-Tswana, kinship and witchcraft, 205–6
Southern Rhodesia, 229, 251, 252
Southwold, M., 278
Soviet Union, 262
Spencer, P., 167, 178
spirit possession: described (Kalanga), 245–51; and domestic ritual (Kalanga), 228, 232, 235, 238–43, 243–6; explanations of, 233, 235, 249, 250, 253; women and (Kalanga), 233, 234–5, 246, 250
spirits: ancestral (Kalanga), 245–6, 248; cult of affliction (Kalanga), 245–

251; invocation (Kalanga), 228, 231–232, 235, 242, 243, 249–50; invocation (urban), 230, 243; kinds among Kalanga, 245
stability of beliefs, xiv–xvi
Stanley, Sir H., 189
static structuralism, and process contrasted, 277
stationary societies: ideology of, 17; Lugbara, 7
status, degradation of, 197ff, 218ff
Stengel, E., 311–12
stereotypes, of witches, 165
stock, see cattle
strangers: and blame, 265; defined, 264; distinguished from outsiders, 264; experts as, 270; inconsistency of, 265; psychiatrist as, 275; scientists in role of, 266;
strategic air offensive, 259; favoured by Air Staff, 266; and views of Naval and Air staffs, 262
strategic bombing, 260
strategy: in football, 263; *v.* tactics, in aerial warfare, 260
stratification, absence of, 128
strict liability, 42–3; Gluckman explanation of, 55, 60, 61–3; and the habit of using force, 64–6; and long-term relationships, 62; as stage of legal evolution, 52–3
struggle, to control audience, xxi
sub-system, 277; relation to overriding system, 259
suicide attempts, 308–12
suitor, *see* courtship
supporters' club, 264
Swazi, 11f
symbols, disputes as symbols of relationship, 97
system, encompassing, 258

tactics, in football club, 263
talents, ambivalence of: Lugbara, 27; Nupe and Nyakyunsa, 22–3; Tiv, 33
Tallensi, 170; divination among, 258; pre-natal destiny, 44; shrines among, 265
Tavistock Institute, 271
technology: increasing skill in, 40f; tribal, 3, 4, 21; validity of Azande, xvi
tempo of sociation, 210
tensions: inadequacy of theory of, 4; Marwick's theory of, 31; and witchcraft, 9
theories of: Douglas, 31–2; Evans-Pritchard, 6f; Horton on ritual, 45; of Marwick re tensions, 31; younger anthropologists, 15, 28
threats, 292, 296, 298
Tiamus, 167
Tiv, 33f, 179
Tizard, 260, 262, 263, 267–9; clash with Cherwell, 262; questions Cherwell's calculations, 266
Tonga, joking relationships, 135
towns, in Central Africa, 184
townsmen: accusations among, 184–5; and pastoralists compared, 184–5
Tripolitania, 133, 134
trivial: converted to cosmic, 257; world-shaking events diminished to, 257
Tswana, 253; ancestral wrath, 25, 203; splitting of wards, 16
Tuareg, 163
Turkana, 163; mobility among, 178; witches, 167
Turner, V. W., 32f, 187, 231, 252

uncertainty: and accusations, 194, 211; of Zulu wife's rank, 12
United States, 262
United Workers' Party of Poland, and Rotary Club, compared, 258
unity: highly valued, 16; Lugbara, 27; of Tiv agnates, 35; of village, 265
universalistic, illuminating particularistic, 258
urban, Africans and misfortune, 229–231, 252

values, and youth group, 123
Van Velsen, J., 46
vengeance—magic, Azande, 9

verdict, of community, 146; of oracles, 152–4
Vernant, M., 278
vicious feelings, activate witchcraft, 8
victim, in triad (Chewa), 31
village, 260; and chiefs of staff compared, 258, 265; as encompassing system, 259
village unity, 265
violence, 281–321; and child-rearing, 286–7, 292, 295, 300–1, 308–10; and courts, 290, 299; definitions of, 285–292; degrees of, 287; and dependence, 297, 301, 303–4, 306–7; against officials, 292, 295–9; and public, 301, 304, 307–8, 310–12; rationality of, 312–14; repetitive, 302–12; types of, 315

Wangala, 196, 219
war: as encompassing system, 259; state of, in 1942, 261
weapons, 287, 297
Weber, M., 277, 291
Webster and Frankland, 261, 278–280; conclusions on bombing offensive, 270
welfare assistance, Israel, 283–4, 307
well, blessing of, 183
Wenner Gren Foundation, 278
Werbner, R. P., 159; summarized, xxi
White, L., 1f
wickedness: exaggeration and minimization, 5; minimization in Britain, 40
Willoughby, W. C., 254
Wilson, M., 186, 188; on liability for homicide, 87; on Mpondo teacher, 40; on Mpondo witchcraft, 20; Nyakyusa self-help, 71, 72; on village splits, 16
Wilson, P. J., 253
witch beliefs, decline in, 164
witchcraft: and adultery, 143, 145; Azande beliefs, 140–1; autopsy (Azande), 155; and caste, 220; and 'censorship', 200–1; in Central Africa, 194, 195; colonial law of, 229–30, 252; and courts, 142, 193, 217; divination of, 207–10; in India, 195, 219; inheritance of (Azande), 8, 10, 141; and kinship, 205–7, 143, 144; Lugbara, 27; in Mexico, 195; and misfortune, 144–5, 152; and moral control, 142–6; morality of (Azande), 227; not simply tensions, 9; Nupe, 19–20; Pedi belief, 204; and rank, 140; and relations between sexes, 144, 155; and social change, 154–5, 158; and social relationships, 140–6, 152–3; and status degradation, 197–200; Tiv, 34f; in towns, 229; transmitted by females, 10; *Witchcraft, Oracles and Magic among the Azande*, 227, 251. *See also* sorcery accusations
'witchcraft communities', 139–40
witch-doctors: and consensus of opinion, 152; role of, 150–2; and seances, 146, 150–4. *See also* diviners
'witch hunt', 41
witches, Azande, 7; Boran, 167–8; Dinka, 166–7; female (Zulu), 14; Karimojong, 167; Mandari, 165–6; Nandi, 165–6; Nuer, 167; Samburu, 167; sex of, 205–6; Somali, 167; stereotypes of, 165; Turkana, 167
wives ambivalence of fertility (Zulu), 12f; Chinese and Indian, 13; mischiefmakers in agnation, 13f; rank among the South-eastern Bantu, 11f; strengthen and weaken group, 24; Zulu—nucleatic property, 28; Zulu rank uncertain, 12
women: and accusation (Zulu), 14; Azande—not accused by men, 9; conflict with men comes into open, 264; eligibility for cult (Kalanga), 233–4, 237, 246, 252; and golden mean, 22–3; in labour migration, (Kalanga), 236–7, 253; and men divided interests of, 265; Nupe, 19–20; responsibility (Kalanga), 228, 233, 249–50; rights and status of (Kalanga), 237, 249; as sisters, 29; social attitudes distinguished from

men, 263; symbolic space of (Kalanga), 246; in transactions (Kalanga), 233–5
Wootton, B., 43, 258, 273, 280

Xhosa, 11f

Yako, 164
Yao, 29f
Yibir, 167
youth groups (Welsh), 218; activities of, 110–13; and anonymity, 116–17; and community, 124–5; composition of, 110, 113–18, 127; and consensus of opinion, 117–18, 120; and courtship, 112, 114, 121–2; emblem of community, 115, 158; and joking, 116; and morality, 123–4, 130, 134; and outsiders, 112; pattern of behaviour of, 114, 116; and rank, 131, 134; representativeness of, 118; and responsibility, 115, 117, 120, 122; and social change, 121; and values, 123
youths, and adults, 112–15, 118—20

Zulu, 11f, 196; divination, 14f; exogamy and witchcraft, 206; witchcraft, 13f; wives' nucleate property, 28